Artifice & Indeterminacy

An
Anthology
of
New Poetics

Artifice & Indeterminacy

An Anthology of
New Poetics

Edited by
Christopher Beach

The University of Alabama Press
Tuscaloosa and London

1   2   3   4   5   6   7   8   9   0   ●   07   06   05   04   03   02   01   00   99   98

∞
The paper on which this book is printed meets the minimum requirements of American National Standard for Information Science-Permanence of Paper for Printed Library Materials, ANSI Z39.48-1984.

Library of Congress Cataloging-in-Publication Data

Artifice and indeterminacy : an anthology of new poetics / edited by
    Christopher Beach.
        p.   cm. — (Modern and contemporary poetics)
    Includes bibliographical references and index.
    ISBN 0–8173–0946–2 (cloth : alk. paper).
    ISBN 0–8173–0954–3 (paper : alk. paper)
    1. Poetics.   I. Beach, Christopher.   II. Series.
PN1055.A76   1998
808.1—dc21   98–21775

British Library Cataloguing-in-Publication data available

CONTENTS

Section 3: Institutions and Ideology

Section 4: Poetics and Gender

Preface

In 1960, Donald Allen prefaced his path-breaking anthology *The New American Poetry* with the sweeping assertion that the "new younger poets" of his collection shared "a total rejection of all those qualities typical of academic verse." In the changed context of the late 1990s, however, any such unqualified agenda of poetic and institutional identification would seem inappropriate and somewhat naive; we have seen the blurring of such clear distinctions as those between "academic" and "nonacademic" schools of poetry, between institutional structures and avant-garde communities, between insiders and outsiders. Books by poets of the avant-garde, until recently relegated to the margins of American literary publishing, have now been published by such presses as Harvard University Press, Princeton University Press, and Routledge. Members of this same avant-garde hold teaching positions at such institutions as the University of Pennsylvania, Temple University, Wayne State University, the University of California at San Diego, and State University of New York at Buffalo. Studies dealing entirely or in large part with the poetic avant-garde have been written by such prominent academic critics as Marjorie Perloff, George Hartley, Linda Reinfeld, Peter Quartermain, Alan Golding, and Maria Damon. And essays and articles on Language poetry and related avant-gardes, which until recently could only be found in specialized forums like *Temblor* and *Poetics Journal*, can now be read in mainstream academic journals (i.e., *American Literature, Contemporary Literature,* and *American Literary History*).

Yet despite the coming of age of the poetic avant-garde in the 1990s, it is by no means clear that the work of the avant-garde has been entirely co-opted by the academy; nor can we announce, with fashionable skepticism, that it has lost its radicalizing or subversive potential. While it may no longer be fruitful to generalize the situation of avant-garde poets as that of "outsiders" in determined opposition to the "ruling party" of official, mainstream, or academic poetry, it is nonetheless important to recognize what Alan Golding has called the "provisionally complicit resistance" of Language writing and other forms of avant-garde poetry and poetics to the dominant institutions of American literary, critical, and social practice. As a new generation of poets and readers encounters for the first time the language and ideas of Susan Howe, Charles Bernstein, Ron Silliman, Nathaniel Mackey, Rachel Blau DuPlessis, and others—whether on the Internet, in the classroom, or in the library or bookstore—there are increased possibilities for an intellectual cross-fertilization that challenges received disciplines and discourses. These poets have produced texts that can be read in dialogue with such disciplines as critical theory, cultural studies, feminism and gender studies, aesthetics, literary history, and media studies. Read within the context of the respective disciplines to which they make reference—say, Susan Howe's essay alongside traditional Dickinson scholarship, or David Antin's talk-poem alongside academic discussions of the avant-garde—these texts reveal their genuinely subversive power, their potential to engender new forms, new conceptions, and new discourses.

The proliferation of recent anthologies devoted to what has variously been called "experimental poetry," "avant-garde poetry," "postmodern poetry," "innovative poetry" or "outsider poetry" has brought to the attention of a wider readership the work of poets too long confined to a marginal status with respect to the literary world at large. Anthologies such as Eliot Weinberger's *American Poetry Since 1950: Innovators & Outsiders*, Paul Hoover's *Postmodern American Poetry*, Douglas Messerli's *From the Other Side of the Century: A New American Poetry 1960–1990*, Andrei Codrescu's *Up Late: American Poetry Since 1970*, Dennis Barone and Peter Ganick's *The Art of Practice: 45 Contemporary Poets*, Peter Gizzi and Connell McGrath's *Writing from the New Coast*, and Leonard Schwartz, Joseph Donahue, and Edward Foster's *Primary Trouble: An Anthology of Contemporary American Poetry* clearly demonstrate the wealth of poetries existing beyond the bounds of what Charles Bernstein has called the "official verse culture." This postmodern avant-garde is hardly the monolithic entity that some of its detractors have characterized it as being; instead, as both Hoover and Messerli make clear in the introductions to their anthologies, the poetry reflects a wide range of styles, approaches, and influences. Hoover identifies two major forms of postmodern poetic practice in Language poetry and performance poetry as well as important but less dominant forms of poetry based on "deep image" and aleatory procedures. Messerli divides the poetic avant-garde into four groupings or "gatherings": that descended from the Objectivist and post-Objectivist concern with culture, myth, politics, and history; that following the New York poets' concern with issues of self, group, urban landscape, and visual art; that emerging out of concerns with language, reader, and writing communities; and finally, that focusing on performance, dialogue, and the manipulation of voice. Clearly, if we expand the definition of the avant-garde beyond its frequent association with Language poetry to include other nonmainstream poetries such as performance poetry and multicultural poetry, we can also include in our list of anthologies the collections edited by Walter Lew (*Premonitions: The Kaya Anthology of New Asian North American Poetry*) and by Miguel Algarin and Bob Holman (*Aloud: Voices from the Nuyorian Poets Cafe*).

Yet despite the existence of such a range of anthologies devoted to collecting the *poetry* of these writers, there has been no comparably wide-ranging anthology of their *poetics*. Since the appearance of two collections of essays in the mid-1980s, *Writing/Talks*, edited by Bob Perelman, and *Code of Signals*, edited by Michael Palmer, there has been no general collection of poetics by experimental or avant-garde American poets. Perhaps the most important critical collection to appear in the past decade has been *The Politics of Poetic Form* (1990), edited by Charles Bernstein. But while Bernstein's anthology contains essays by a number of important practitioners of Language writing and related poetries, it focuses more particularly on issues relating to the intersection of poetic praxis and ideology and does not aim to provide a broader spectrum of the work being done in experimental or Language poetics.[1]

None of these collections attempts anything like the project of *Artifice and Indeterminacy*: that of bringing together the most significant previously uncollected essays by avant-gardist poets and critics. The anthology was put together according to a few simple parameters. First, it includes only material written after 1980, thus marking in convenient if somewhat arbitrary fashion what appears to have been an important watershed between the current generation of the avant-garde and the previous one, that most often identified, following Allen's designation, as the New American Poetry. Second, the anthology contains no material previously collected in anthologies. Third, it attempts to collect the strongest and most representative examples of postmodern avant-garde poetics, given the above restrictions and the limitations of space. While there has been some attempt to systematize the organization of the anthology by dividing it into sections, these thematic divisions were not themselves the motivating factor in choosing the essays to be included: in fact, in several cases a given essay speaks to two or more of the section headings. Finally, I decided to include not only essays in conventional format but works in other forms as well: Bernstein's essay-in-verse, Antin's talk-poem, and James Sherry's prose-poem/essay along with experimentally hybrid pieces by Lyn Hejinian, Rachel Blau DuPlessis, and Susan Howe. All of these works emphasize the nature of the project of contemporary avant-garde poetries: to break down formal boundaries between poetry and prose, criticism and creative writing, theory and practice.

The four sections into which the anthology is divided represent four sets of issues that relate to the practice of contemporary avant-garde poets. Section one brings together a group of essays concerned—in very different ways—with form, language, and the communicative potential of poetry. These essays reflect the central importance to poets of the contemporary avant-garde of problematizing traditional understandings of referentiality, poetic closure, voice, and lyric subjectivity. By examining changing practices of both writing and reading poetry, these essays suggest expanded possibilities for our relationship to the poetic text.

In section two, these expanded possibilities are articulated through a set of concerns that is less directly formal or linguistic: David Antin uses the narrative form of the talk-poem to explore the various implications of the term *avant-garde*, finding that the spirit of avant-gardism may be located more in shared patterns of experience than in historically specific movements or art works; Leslie Scalapino examines a range of instances of the "simulacral" translation of lived experience into poetry; Lyn Hejinian speculates on the way in which various forms of "description" relate more closely to the "strangeness" of dream logic than to conventional conceptions of realism; and John Taggart meditates on the fundamental presence of song, and in particular of the circular form of the fugue, in the poetry of Louis Zukofsky.

The essays in section three demonstrate the extent to which poetry and poetics can engage in a project of political critique or serve as an arena for exploring basic questions about political thought and action. The relationship of poetry, poetic communities and movements, and poetic institutions to larger political and ideological structures has been of vital concern to poets of the avant-garde ever since the publication of the journal $L=A=N=G=U=A=G=E$ in the late 1970s and early 1980s, and it continues to be a major focus of debate within the context of experimental poetry. The essays collected here explore a range of issues relating to ideology: from the poem as textual "economy," to the larger socioeconomic structures affecting poetic production, to the implications of ethnic and racial difference for the production and reception of poetry.

Finally, section four presents three essays that serve as very different models for a feminist or gender-inflected poetics. Whereas Allen's *New*

American Poetry contained only four women among its forty-four poets, the current avant-garde has moved beyond the male-dominated poetics of the postwar avant-garde to ask increasingly complex questions about the intersection of poetics and gender. The essays in this section look at women's writing in different historical contexts and with different methodological and thematic focuses: Rae Armantrout uses examples from contemporary women's poetry to examine the meaning of "clarity" within a feminist context; Rachel Blau DuPlessis explores the issues confronting any writer engaged with the project of radical experimental feminism; and Susan Howe examines the treatment of Emily Dickinson's nineteenth-century texts as an example of the misunderstanding and misappropriation by (male) scholars and textual editors of a woman poet who refused to conform to the rules of conventional verse.

Neither dismissive of the aesthetic value(s) of poetry nor afraid to articulate the ways in which aesthetic evaluation is complicated by the mediating influences of history, culture, class, gender, race, and academic status, the essays in this anthology celebrate the "artifice" of the poetic text while also accepting as a given the "indeterminacy" of its inception and reception. These essays demonstrate both the range and the brilliance that have characterized the best thinking about poetry over the past two decades; they demonstrate, too, that the field of poetics has itself undergone a significant change during that time, breaking with traditional generic boundaries and with conventional interpretive frameworks.

NOTES

1. Other collections of essays that have included material on avant-garde or experimental poetry are *The Line in Postmodern Poetry*, ed. Robert Frank and Henry Sayre (Urbana: University of Illinois Press, 1988), which, as its name implies, focuses on the formal unit of the line; *Postmodern Genres*, ed. Marjorie Perloff (Norman: University of Oklahoma Press, 1988), which foregrounds the question of genre and which includes forms other than poetry; *Contemporary Poetry Meets Contemporary Theory*, ed. Antony Easthope and John O. Thompson (Toronto: University of Toronto Press, 1991), which combines discussions of experimental poetry with readings of more mainstream British and American poets; and *The Poetics of Criticism*, ed. Juliana Spahr, Mark Wallace, Kristin Prevallet, and Pam Rehm (Buffalo: Leave Books, 1994), which consists primarily of shorter essays by younger poets.

Form

Syntax

Speech

1   *Artifice of Absorption*
Charles Bernstein

MEANING AND ARTIFICE

> Then where is truth but in the burning space between one letter and
> the next? Thus the book is first read outside its limits.
>
> —Edmond Jabès[1]

The reason it is difficult to talk about
the meaning of a poem—in a way that doesn't seem
frustratingly superficial or partial—is that by
designating a text a poem, one suggests that its
meanings are to be located in some "complex" beyond an accumulation of devices & subject matters.
A poetic *reading* can be given to any
piece of writing; a "poem" may be understood as
writing specifically designed to absorb, or inflate
with, proactive—rather that reactive—styles of
reading. "Artifice" is a measure of a poem's
intractability to being read as the sum of its
devices & subject matters. In this sense,
"artifice" is the contradiction of "realism," with
its insistence on presenting an unmediated
(immediate) experience of facts, either of the
"external" world of nature or the "internal" world
of the mind; for example, naturalistic
representation or phenomenological consciousness
mapping. Facts in poetry are primarily
factitious.

Veronica Forrest-Thomson, in *On Poetic Artifice*,
notes that artifice in a poem is primarily marked
by the quality of the poem's language that makes it
both continuous & discontinuous with the world of
experience:

Anti-realism need not imply, as certain French theorists might claim, a rejection of meaning. All that Artifice requires is that nonmeaningful levels be
taken into account, and that *meaning be used as a technical device* which makes it
impossible as well as wrong for critics to strand poems in the external
world.[2]

The artificiality of a poem may be more or less
foregrounded, but it is necessarily part of
the "poetic" reading of any document. If the artifice
is recessed, the resulting textual transparency
yields an apparent, if misleading, content.
Content never equals meaning. If the artifice is
foregrounded, there's a tendency to say that there
is no content or meaning, as if the poem were a
formal or decorative exercise concerned only with
representing its own mechanisms. But even when a
poem is read as a formal exercise, the dynamics &
contours of its formal proceedings may suggest, for
example, a metonymic model for imagining
experience. For this reason, consideration
of the formal dynamics of a poem does not necessarily
disregard its content; indeed it is an obvious
starting point insofar as it can initiate a
multilevel reading. But to complete the process
such formal apprehensions need to move to a
synthesis beyond technical cataloging, toward the
experiential phenomenon that is made by virtue of
the work's techniques. Such a synthesis
is almost impossible apart from the tautological
repetition of the poem, since all the formal
dynamics cannot begin to be charted: think only
of the undercurrent of anagrammatical
transformations,[3] the semantic contribution of
the visual representation of the text,[4] the
particular associations evoked by the phonic
configurations. These features are related to the
"nonsemantic" effects that Forrest-Thomson
describes as contributing toward the "total image-complex"
of the poem (but what might be better called its total
meaning complex, since *image* may suggest
an overly visual orientation):

The image-complex is the node where we can discover which of the multi-tude of thematic, semantic, rhythmical, and formal patterns is important and how it is to be related to the others. For the image-complex alone oper-ates on all levels of sound, rhythm, theme, and meaning and from it alone, therefore, can be derived a sense of the structure of any particular poem. . . . Critical reading must never try to impose meaning in the form of an exten-sion of meaning into the non-verbal world until the reader has determined by examining the non-meaningful levels just what amount of meaning is required by the poem's structure from each phrase, word, and letter. Only when this is done can the critic hope to reach a thematic synthesis which will make contact with the poem itself on its many levels and not with some abstract, or indeed concrete, entity created out of his own imagina-tion. The reader must . . . use his imagination . . . but he must use it to free himself from the fixed forms of thought which ordinary language imposes on our minds, not to deny the strangeness of poetry by inserting it in some non-poetic area: his own mind, the poet's mind, or any non-fictional situation. (16)

So there is always an unbridgeable lacuna between
any explication of a reading & any actual
reading. & it is the extent of these lacunas—
differing with each reader but not indeterminate—
that is a necessary measure of a poem's
meaning.

There is, however, something I find
problematic about Forrest-Thomson's account. It
seems to me she is wrong to designate the nonlexical,
or more accurately, extralexical
strata of the poem as "nonsemantic"; I would say
that such elements as line breaks, acoustic
patterns, syntax, etc., *are* meaningful rather than,
as she has it, that they *contribute* to the meaning
of the poem. For instance, there is no fixed
threshold at which noise becomes phonically
significant; the further back this threshold is
pushed, the greater the resonance at the cutting
edge. The semantic strata of a poem should not be
understood as only those elements to which a
relatively fixed connotative or denotative meaning
can be ascribed, for this would restrict meaning to
the exclusively recuperable elements of language—a

restriction that if literally applied would make meanings impossible. After all, meaning occurs only in a context of conscious & nonconscious, recuperable & unrecoverable, dynamics.

Moreover, the designation of the visual, acoustic, & syntactic elements of a poem as "meaningless," especially insofar as this is conceptualized as positive or liberating—& this is a common habit of much current critical discussion of syntactically nonstandard poetry—is symptomatic of a desire to evade responsibility for meaning's total, & totalizing, reach; as if meaning was a husk that could be shucked off or a burden that could be bucked. Meaning is not a use value *as opposed to* some other kind of value, but more like valuation itself; & even to refuse value is a value & a sort of exchange. <u>Meaning is nowhere bound to the orbit of purpose</u>, <u>intention</u>, or <u>utility</u>.

While this is a crucial distinction, its significance for Forrest-Thomson's view is not as great as it is in many more recent commentaries because her terminology is intended to foreground artifice as much as possible & for this reason she wishes to cede as little as possible to the conventional semantic arena—a decision that makes her book, if flawed in this respect, so powerfully informative in the first place.

Forrest-Thomson's account compares interestingly with Galvano della Volpe's "dialectical paraphrase" in his *Critique of Taste*, in which the ideological paraphrase is specifically contrasted with the way this ideological content is expressed in the work. This method, says della Volpe, "is in a position to avoid both formalism & fixation on context."[5]

The dialectic of della Volpe's "dialectical paraphrase" involves the weighing &

measuring of the poetic artifice of the work. "Do
not forget," says Wittgenstein in a passage quoted
by Forrest-Thomson, "that a poem, even
though it is composed in the language of
information, is not used in the language game of
giving information" (x). She adds that "form and
content are [not] identical, still less are they
fused . . . they must be different,
distinguishable in order that their relations may
be judged" (121).

The hermeneutic rejoinders of della Volpe &
Forrest-Thomson are primarily aimed at discouraging
an exclusive emphasis on the overt ideology or
content of a poem, though they might equally apply
to exclusively formal readings. A poem composed in
the language of artifice & device is not
necessarily without content. What does
one make as a content paraphrase of this stanza
from P. Inman's "Waver"?

it was only her curved say
  leaving till any more
i want
    to write noise
      a white
        out of betweens,
          think off-misted
            (piled holster)
          wouldn't say "fault."
      stills by size
    glass cattle
(denominations between her work)
      kints grasp
        off that
          cinder ink
            dreadlocks pollen
              seems to any on
            draws as pang
          waiting for a keyboard
        "so much depends

on starch"
   ute broils
     Keats with the wrong facts
      everything took place at all[6]

In a sense, the procedure of dialectical paraphrase
must be reversed in reading this poem. An attempt
must first be made to elucidate the "nonsemantic"
elements of the poem ("to write noise/a white/
out of betweens"), but the reading should not stop
there ("piled holster"), as it all too often might.
This first survey must be dialectically contrasted
with how the noted devices might have been
used to different ends, what type of overall
architecture is constructed by the particular
sequence of devices ("curved say"), what semantic
associations can be attributed to the specific
"nonsemantic" elements & which ones are relevant
in the particular context of the poem. That is,
the devices must be differentiated from the image
complex to which they contribute. When I say that
della Volpe's procedure must be reversed in reading
"Waver," I mean that because the formal dynamics of
the poem are the most overt, identifiable feature,
they have the weight of "content" in a more
traditional poem ("Keats with the wrong facts");
just as the content threatens to naturalize
(Forrest-Thomson's term) the artifice of a more
conventional poem in an undialectical reading ("'so
much depends/on starch'"), so here the form
threatens to negate the content in an undialectical
reading ("kints grasp"); for this reason, "Waver"
destabilizes the polarities of form & content,
undermining the dialectic's value for thinking
about (as opposed to deciphering) the poem
("wouldn't say 'fault'"). By fully semanticizing
the so-called nonsemantic features of language,
Inman creates a dialectic of the recuperable &
the unreclaimable, where what cannot be claimed is
nonetheless *most* manifest.

The obvious problem is that the poem said in any
other way is not the poem. This may account for
why writers revealing their intentions or
references ("close readings"), just like readers
inventorying devices, often say so little: why
a sober attempt to document or describe runs so
high a risk of falling flat. In contrast, why not
a criticism intoxicated with its own metaphoricity
or tropicality: one in which the limits of
positive criticism are made more audibly
artificial; in which the inadequacy of our
explanatory paradigms is neither ignored
nor regretted but brought into fruitful play.
Imagine, then, oscillating poles,
constructing not some better diadicism, but
congealing into a field of potentialities
that in turn collapses (transforms) into yet other
tropicalities. This would be the criticism of desire:
sowing not reaping.

Adapting Steve McCaffery's terms from "Writing as a
General Economy," the economy of reading suggested
here is not a utilitarian "restricted economy" of
accumulation (of contents, devices) but a "general
economy" of meanings as "nonutilizable" flow,
discharge, exchange, waste. An individual poem may
be understood as having a restricted or general
economy. Indeed, part of the meaning of a poem may
be its fight for accumulation; nonetheless, its
text will contain destabilizing elements—errors,
unconscious elements, contexts of (re)publication
& the like—that will erode any proposed
accumulation that does not allow for them.
McCaffery derives his idea of a general economy
from Bataille, whom he quotes:

> The general economy, in the first place, makes apparent that excesses of en-
> ergy are produced, and that by definition, these excesses cannot be utilized.
> The excessive energy can only be lost without the slightest aim, conse-
> quently without meaning.[7]

McCaffery continues:

> I want to make clear that I'm not proposing "general" as an alternative econ-
> omy to "restricted." One cannot replace the other because their relationship
> is not one of mutual exclusion. In most cases we will find general economy
> as a suppressed or ignored presence within the scene of writing that tends
> to emerge by way of rupture within the restricted [paragrams], putting
> into question the conceptual controls that produce a writing of use value
> with its privileging of meaning as a necessary production and evaluated des-
> tination.

These "nonutilizable" excesses are related to
Forrest-Thomson's "nonsemantic domains," while
clearly being a conceptually larger category. In
this context, I would again argue against ascribing
to meaning an exclusively utilitarian function.
Loss is as much a part of the semantic process as
discharge is a part of the biological process. Yet
the meaning of which I speak is not meaning as we
may "know" it, with a recuperable intention or
purpose. Such a restricted sense of meaning is
analogous to the restricted senses of knowledge as
stipulatively definable. But let's look at how
these words are used or can be used:
You know what I mean & you also mean
a lot more than you can say
& far more than you could ever intend,
stipulatively or no.
It is just my insistence
that poetry be understood as epistemological
inquiry; to cede meaning would be to undercut
the power of poetry to reconnect us
with modes of meaning given in language
but precluded by the hegemony of restricted
epistemological economies (an hegemony that moves
toward the negation of nondominant restricted
economies as much as repressing the asymptotic
horizon of the unrestricted economies). As
McCaffery puts it, "such features of general
economic operation do not destroy the order of
meaning, but complicate & unsettle its

constitution and operation." They destroy, that
is, not meaning but various utilitarian &
essentialist ideas about meaning. To this point
it must be added that to speak of the nonutilizable
strata of a poem or a verbal exchange is as
problematic as to speak of nonsemantic elements—
for what is designated as nonutilizable
& extralexical is both useful & desirable
while not being utilitarian & prescribable.

These comments are partly intended as caution
against thinking of formally active poems as
eschewing content or meaning—even in the face of
the difficulty of articulating just what this
meaning is. That is, the meaning is not absent or
deferred but self-embodied as the poem
in a way that is not transferable to another code
or rhetoric. At the same time, it is possible
to evoke various contours of meaning
by metaphorically considering the domains made real
by various formal configurations.

ABSORPTION AND IMPERMEABILITY

> If we studied societies from the outside, it would be tempting to distin-
> guish two contrasting types: those which practice cannibalism—that is
> which regard the absorption of certain individuals possessing dangerous
> powers as the only means of neutralizing these powers and even of turn-
> ing them to advantage—and those which, like our own society, adopt
> what might be called the practice of *anthropemy* (from the Greek *emein*, to
> vomit); faced with the same problem, the latter type of society has cho-
> sen the opposite solution, which consists in ejecting dangerous individu-
> als from the social body and keeping them temporarily or permanently
> in isolation, away from all contacts with their fellows, in establishments
> especially intended for this purpose. Most of the societies we call primi-
> tive would regard this custom with profound horror; it would make us,
> in their eyes, guilty of that same barbarity of which we are inclined to
> accuse them because of their symmetrically opposite behavior.
>   —Claude Lévi-Strauss, *Tristes Tropiques*

> The entire reality of the word is wholly absorbed in its function of being
> a sign.
>   —V. N. Voloshinov, *Marxism and the Philosophy of Language*

Ever wonder why one person can eat a meal of French toast and sausage, followed by a glass of milk, to little effect, while if you . . . Absorption problems.

—*Guide Amber à la Gastronomie*[8]

In thinking about how to respond
to a request to do a reading of one of my poems,
I've found myself
thinking about "absorption" & its obverses—
impermeability, imperviousness, ejection,
repellance—both as a compositional question
& as
a reading value.[9] The terms began to consume
my imagination, a pataphysical extravaganza
of accumulating works & fields absorbed
into this tropic zone without benefit
of underlying unity of perspective. There seemed no
limit to what
the absorption/antiabsorption nexus could
absorb.

Thinking of Canada, where I initially presented my
speculations, the political metaphor kept erupting:
Canada does not wish to be absorbed into the U.S.
cultural orbit any more than Quebec wishes to be
absorbed by Canada; but then Quebec feminists may not
want to be absorbed by a male-dominated "free" Quebec.
Identity seems to involve the refusal to be absorbed
in a larger identity, yet the identity formed as
a result of an antiabsorptive autonomism
threatens to absorb differential groupings
within it. It's as if the very desire not
to be absorbed creates a new threat
of absorption—down to the individual divided
against itself—its nonsocial "identity"
at odds with its social "selves."[10]

& then there are the biological senses
of absorption & excretion: the body's narration.
Steve McCaffery pointed out
that having an infant around

for the first time had had its effect:
I had been changing a half-dozen superabsorbent
diapers a day, ever in fear
that they would not be superabsorptive enough
& spillage would result. So this
is the answer to that
persistent & irritating question: Has having a child
affected your writing?

Moreover, the nature of absorption as a dynamic
of reading needs to be understood as a key element
in any ideologically conscious literary criticism.
This can be taken as the central polemic of
Jerome McGann's *Romantic Ideology*.[11] The
uncritical absorption of a poem of William
Wordsworth, for example, entails an absorption
of Romantic ideology that precludes an historically
informed reading of the poem. In order for a
sociohistorical reading to be possible, absorption
of the poem's own ideological imaginary must be
blocked; the refusal of absorption is a
prerequisite to understanding (in the literal sense
of standing *under* rather than inside). Indeed,
absorption may be a quality that characterizes
specifically Romantic works. This is suggested by
McGann when he discusses the "romantic" rationale
behind a persistent preference for a version of Keats's "La
Belle Dame sans Merci" that substitutes "Oh what
can ail thee, knight-at-arms" for the more
ambivalent or ironic "Ah what can ail thee,
wretched wight" (where *wight* means both brave &
base as well as being deliberately archaic).
"By 'romantic' here I mean simply that [the preferred]
text does not distance itself the way the [other]
text does. The former is a more self-absorbed and
self-absorbing text, whereas the latter is more
self-conscious and critical."[12]

Insofar as I make a distinction between the
absorptive & antiabsorptive, these terms
should not be understood as mutually exclusive,

morally coded, or even conceptually separable.
Absorption & antiabsorption are both present
in any method of reading or writing, although
one or the other may be more obtrusive or evasive.
They connote colorations more than dichotomies.

From a compositional point of view
the question is, What can a poem absorb?
Here, think
of a text as a spongy substance, absorbing
vocabulary, syntax, & reference. The idea
of a poem absorbing these elements is meant
to provide an alternative to more traditional
notions of causal narration or thematic
relevance as producing a unified work.
A poem can absorb contradictory logics,
multiple tonalities, polyrhythms. At the
same time, impermeable materials—or moments—
are crucial musical resources for a poem,
though not all impermeable materials will work
to create the desired *textural* space.
There are relative degrees
or valences of impermeability that can be angled
against one another to create
interlinear or interphrasal "gaps" that act
like intervals in musical composition. Pushing
further, impermeable elements may fuse together
dysraphicly to create a hyperabsorptive textual
gravity in which the different originary elements
are no longer isolable.[13] In this sense,
the absorbed & unabsorbed cleave,
since *cleave* means both to divide
& to hold together.

One criterion of whether the nonabsorbed
material in a poem "works" is
whether it furthers or hinders the absorption
of the reader in the writing. The
author may intend either or both.
Creating an absorptive text may or may
not be the object of a poem. But the dynamic

of absorption is
central to all reading & writing.

So we can speak of a bloated poem,
of a burst text, adding evaluative qualification:
well bloated or bloated but blundering; exquisitely
burst or dismally popped; elegantly engorged or
haplessly logorrheic.

In nineteenth-century North American writing,
the subject matter of absorption is prominent.
Poe is credited with inventing the three main
genres of absorptive fiction: the horror story,
science fiction, & the detective story; his
theoretical writings constantly confront issues
relating to absorption, for example the hypnotic
effect of his highly rhythmic poems. In Poe's
fiction, horror is a means not only of absorbing
the reader in the tale but also, explicitly,
obliterating the self-consciousness of the story's
characters, who commonly fall into states of
absolutely rapt presentness, or rapture, or terror,
or reverie.

Consider this poem of Dickinson:

> I would not paint—a picture—
> I'd rather be the One
> It's bright impossibility
> To dwell—delicious—on—
> And wonder how the fingers feel
> Whose rare—celestial—stir
> Provokes so sweet a Torment—
> Such sumptuous—Despair—
>
> I would not talk, like Cornets—
> I'd rather be the One
> Raised softly to the Ceilings—
> And out, and easy on—
> Through Villages of Ether
> Myself endued Balloon

By but a lip of Metal—
The pier to my Pontoon—

Nor would I be a Poet—
It's finer—own the Ear—
Enamored—impotent—content—
The License to revere,
A luxury so awful
What would the Dower be,
Had I the Art to stun
myself
With Bolts of Melody!¹⁴

On the surface, the highly disruptive punctuation
& obscure or elusive allusions create an
antiabsorptive formal effect, both jarring & off-
balancing. The capitalization & dashes
seem to insist on a jerky, or hesitant, reading,
cutting sharply against the grain of the singsong
prosody that is foregrounded in the depunctuated,
& widely circulated, bowdlerized version
of this poem. Yet the poem registers (& that's
the precise word for it) the need for *jolts*
against the conditions for absorption, a radically
antiabsorptive poetics meant to contrast sharply
with what Susan Howe has described as the
"polished, pious" work of, for example, Anne
Bradstreet, but by extension the bulk of American
verse published in Dickinson's time.¹⁵ The poem
enacts an "impossible" preference not to represent
the world or look at it as if it were a
representation—that is, something one can
look out *onto*—but to dwell *in*, *on*, be of.
Not to describe or incant but to be
the thing described, "endued"—endowed—"Balloon";
to be inside, lighter than, "things,"
inflated by them, so absolutely absorbed as to be
floating "Enamored—impotent—content"; for
such enrapturement leaves one impotent to affect
the world, since to be able to affect requires
that one is removed from; & this armless
connection not only leaves one content but also, & the

double sense is crucial to the metaphysics
of the poem, makes one content, thinged—bolts
one to the other side of the see/seen divide.
Yet to be able to be absorbed into this other side
requires jolts, an antiabsorptive disruption
of complacent pictorial "talk." So to "stun" is
to shock into one's senses, an ecstatic,
perhaps mystical, transport into what Howe calls
the "thrilling anonymity" of Dickinson's poetics.
Author disappears & by this act "licenses"
the "luxury" of a deeper absorption, by the reader,
in the poem than otherwise imaginable.

The idea of absorption is also linked
to reverie, especially as it has been articulated
in twentieth-century poetics from Proust through
surrealism. Reverie suggests that absorption
is the subject matter of the poem & that the reader
may become absorbed by such poems. However,
the process need not be symmetrical. Certain
surrealist works use reverie as an absorptive process
of creation without creating a text that makes this
absorption transparent.

While transparency is a central technique
of absorptive realisms (conjuring the thing seen
before our eyes, the page dissolved)
& absorptive irrealisms (conjuring the memory
or the dream), transparency is not the
equivalent of absorption; rather transparency is
but one technique for producing absorptive works.

Realism, using
transparency as its
major effect, has
often relied on absorption
as its theoretical
raison d'être. No one articulates
this more buoyantly than Ford
Madox Ford in his homage to
Flaubert, *The English Novel*:

*From the Earliest Days
to the Death of Joseph Conrad.*
In the course of this book, Ford makes
what is in effect a *summa
contra antiabsorptus:*

Inasmuch as an authentic rendering—a rendering made with extreme artistic skill—will give you more the sense of having been present at an event
than if you had actually been corporally present, whereas the reading of the
most skillful of literary forgeries will only leave you with the sense that
you have read a book the artistic rendering is the more valuable to you and
therefore the greater achievement. I once heard a couple of French marine
engineers agreeing that although they had traversed the Indian Ocean many
times and had several times passed through, or through the fringes of ty-
phoons, neither of them had ever been in one till they had read Conrad's
"Typhoon" . . .
   To produce that or similar effects is the ambition of the novel today . . .
   The fact is that with Elizabeth English became a supple and easily em-
ployable language and, making the discovery that words could be played
with as if they were oranges or gilt balls to be tossed half a dozen together
in the air, mankind rushed upon it as colts will dash into suddenly opened
rich and easy pastures. So it was, for the rich and cultured, much more a
matter of who could kick heels the higher and most flourish tail and mane
than any ambition of carrying burdens or drawing loads.
   In the end, however, what humanity needs is that burdens should be carried and provided that things get from place to place the name of the carter
or horse is of very secondary importance. If it is the fashion we will go
down to the meadow and watch the colts cavorting: but all the while we
are aware that the business of words as of colts or of the arts is to carry
things and we tire reasonably soon of watching horse-play! For if I say: "I
am hungry," the business of those words is to carry that information to
you, and if you read the "Iliad" it is that the art of that epic may make
Hecuba significant to you . . .
   The struggle—the aspiration—of the novelist down the ages has been to
evolve a water-tight convention for the frame-work of the novel. He as-
pires—and for centuries has aspired—so to construct his stories and so to
manage their surfaces that the carried away and rapt reader shall really
think himself to be in Brussels on the first of Waterloo days or in the
Grand Central Station waiting for the Knickerbocker Express to come in
from Boston though actually he may be sitting in a cane lounge on a beach
of Bermuda in December. This is not easy . . .
   It is for instance an obvious and unchanging fact that if an author in-
trudes his comments into the middle of his story he will endanger the illusion conveyed by that story—but a generation of readers may come along

who would prefer witnessing the capers of the author to being carried
away by stories and that generation of readers may coincide with a generation of writers tired of self-obliteration. So you may have a world of Oscar
Wildes or of Lylys. Or you might, again, have a world tired of the really
well constructed novel every word of which carries its story forward: then
you will have a movement toward diffuseness, backboneless sentences, di-
gressions, and inchoateness.[16]

These marvelous passages deserve fuller &
closer attention than I propose to give them.
In any case, they speak well for themselves.
But it is useful to understand that Ford's
antiaestheticism (he grew up in a household where
Swinburne was a frequent guest) is related to
the Vorticist pronouncements of his friend Ezra
Pound (direct treatment, no word that does not
contribute), to which, inevitably, I shall return.
Ford here makes the classic case for a transparent
language that in no way interferes with the
reader's absorption in the story being told; he
dismisses any form of opacity or self-consciousness
or formal play as hindering this readerly
absorption. It is striking that this position is
consonant with, rather than opposed to, powerful
currents within early modernism; he means by
his remarks to negatively target
Dickensian character-typing as much as literary
ornamentation, stilted "verse" diction
(the dominant form of magazine verse at the time),
& experimentation. While writing this
humorous & close-to-parodic study, Ford marshals
his arguments to support Conrad; but
it should be remembered that, for Ford, the
"Master" would always be James, & James
was not the master of transparency but of artifice.
(I hope I need not reiterate
that Conrad's writing consciously
employs artifice fully as much as Oscar Wilde's
& that readers are likely to be conscious of, &
to appreciate, the artifice of both writers.
Ford's study is indeed a brief
for the greater technical control required to

achieve the effects of Flaubertian artifice.)
In any case, what Ford fails to account for
in his giddy study is that impermeable textual
elements may actually contribute toward
absorptive effects, & that such textures
may be particularly vital at a time when readers
are skeptical of the transparency effect, whether
it is used to reveal unmediated inner states or
external narrative spaces.

By *absorption* I mean engrossing, engulfing
completely, engaging, arresting attention, reverie,
attention intensification, rhapsodic, spellbinding,
mesmerizing, hypnotic, total, riveting,
enthralling: belief, conviction, silence.

Impermeability suggests artifice, boredom,
exaggeration, attention scattering, distraction,
digression, interruptive, transgressive,
undecorous, anticonventional, unintegrated, fractured,
fragmented, fanciful, ornately stylized, rococo,
baroque, structural, mannered, ironic,
iconic, schtick, camp, diffuse, decorative,
repellent, inchoate, programmatic, didactic,
theatrical, background muzak, amusing: skepticism,
doubt, noise, resistance.

Absorptive & antiabsorptive
works both require artifice, but the former may hide
this while the latter may flaunt
it. & absorption may dissolve
into theater as these distinctions chimerically
shift & slide. Especially since,
as in much of my own work, antiabsorptive
techniques are used toward
absorptive ends; or, in satiric writing (it's a put-
on, get it?), absorptive means are used
toward antiabsorptive ends. It remains
an open question, & an unresolvable
one, what

will produce an absorptive poem & what will
produce a nonabsorptive one.

These
textual
dynamics
can
be
thought
about
in
relation
to
the
reader
&
to
the
structure
of
the
poem.

NOTES

1. *The Book of Questions: Yael, Elya, Aely*, trans. Rosmarie Waldrop (Middletown, Conn.: Wesleyan University Press, 1983), 7.

2. Veronica Forrest-Thomson, *On Poetic Artifice: A Theory of Twentieth Century Poetry* (New York: St. Martin's Press, 1978), 132; italics added. This remarkably precocious book carries Empson's criticism one step further than Empson was willing to go—into the realm of what Forrest-Thomson calls the "nonmeaningful" levels of language that she sees as the vital future for poetry. Her considerations of John Ashbery and Prynne are particularly valuable, as is her critique of the flaws inherent in "confessional" poetry—she speaks of the "suicide poets," from whom she is at great pains to exclude Sylvia Plath. At times, Forrest-Thomson's work is frustratingly claustrophobic; but its uncompromising, fierce, and passionate seriousness makes it an enormously moving experience to read. Forrest-Thomson, whose *Collected Poems* were published in 1990 by Allardyce, Barnett, died in 1975 at the age of twenty-seven, after receiving her Ph.D. from Cambridge.

3. Steve McCaffery discusses how anagrams drove Saussure to distraction near the end of his life when he was studying late Latin Saturnian verse: "Implicit in this research is the curiously nonphenomenal status of the paragram. [It is] an inevitable consequence of writing's alphabetic, combinatory, nature. Seen this way as emerging from the multiple ruptures that alphabetic components bring to virtuality, meaning becomes partly the production of a general economy, a persistent excess, non-intentionality and expenditure without reserve through writing's component letters. . . . The unavoidable presence of words within words contests the notion of writing as a creativity, proposing instead the notion of an indeterminate, extraintentional, differential production. The paragram should not be seen necessarily as a latent content or hidden intention, but as a sub-productive sliding and slipping of meaning between the forces and intensities distributed through the text's syntactic economy." "Writing as a General Economy," in *North of Intention* (New York: Roof Books, 1986), 201–21. The essay is also reprinted as chapter 12 of this anthology.

4. Johanna Drucker has been exploring this area in a systematic way. Her "Writing as the Visual Representation of Language" was presented at "New York Talk" on June 5, 1984. See "Dada and Futurist Typography: 1909–1925 and the Visual Representation of Language," Ph.D. diss., University of California, Berkeley, 1986.

5. Galvano della Volpe, *Critique of Taste*, trans. Michael Caesar (London: Verso, 1978), 193. Quoted by Jerome McGann in his conclusion to *The Romantic Ideology* (Chicago: University of Chicago Press, 1983).

6. "Waver," *Abacus* 18 (1986).

7. See n. 3.

8. Claude Lévi-Strauss, *Tristes Tropiques*, trans. John Weightman and Doreen Weightman (New York: Atheneum, 1984), 388; V. N. Voloshinov, *Marxism and the Philosophy of Language*, trans. Latislav Matejka and I. R. Titunik (New York: Seminar Press, 1973), 14; Claudio Amber, *Guide Amber à la Gastronomie* (Graisse, N.Y.: White Castle Press, 1950), unpaginated.

9. Michael Fried's *Absorption and Theatricality: Painting and the Beholder in the Age of Diderot* (Berkeley and Los Angeles: University of California Press, 1980) was my starting point for these considerations. I discuss issues related to absorption in "Film of Perception" (see especially the discussion of movies that begins the section) and "On Theatricality" in *Content's Dream: Essays 1975–1984* (Los Angeles: Sun & Moon Press, 1986).

10. Nick Piombino makes this distinction in "Writing, Identity, and Self," *Difficulties* 2.1 (1982).

11. See n. 5; I discuss this work more fully in "McGann Agonist," *Sulfur* 15 (1986).

12. McGann, *The Beauty of Inflections* (New York: Oxford University Press, 1985), 40.

13. "Dysraphism," a medical term, means congenital misseaming of embryonic parts. The root *raph* means seam, as in rhapsody—what is stitched together.

14. The text follows Thomas H. Johnson's edition of *The Poems of Emily Dickinson* (Cambridge: Belknap Press of Harvard University Press, 1955), no. 505, 2:387–88, although I have adopted two of the variants (*provoked* for *evoked*, *luxury* for *privilege*) and followed the apparent lineation of the manuscript, rather than Johnson's, in regard to the penultimate line. Think though of Stephen Sondheim's *A Sunday in the Park with George* as an opposite perspective on what it would be like to be in a painting: Sondheim has the figures in Seurat's *A Sunday Afternoon on the Island of La Grande Jatte* express a feeling of being hot and trapped as they stare down on carload after busload of museum patrons.

15. Susan Howe, "The Captivity and Restoration of Mrs. Mary Rowlandson," *Temblor* 2 (1985): 113–21; reprinted in *The Birth-Mark: Unsettling the Wilderness in American Literary History* (Middletown, Conn.: Wesleyan University Press, 1993). Howe presented this remarkable essay at the New Poetics Colloquium in Vancouver, where an early version of my own essay was also performed. Among a number of parallels with my work, Howe's theme of "captivity" is an allegory for absorption: the fear of, and attraction to, being absorbed by Indian culture and the taint—from the white man's perspective—of temporary, or partial, absorption in that culture.

16. Ford Madox Ford, *The English Novel: From the Earliest Days to the Death of Joseph Conrad* (Philadelphia: J. B. Lippincott, 1929), 62–63, 70–71, 86, 148–49. This work was especially prepared for Lippincott's "The One Hour Series." In his wonderfully digressive and ornately self-conscious preliminary remarks, Ford writes, "I should like to observe for the benefit of the Lay Reader, to whom I am addressing myself—for the Professional Critic will pay no attention to anything that I say, contenting himself with cutting me to pieces with whips of scorpions for having allowed my head to pop up at all—to the Lay Reader I should like to point out that what I am about to write is highly controversial and he should take none of it too much *au pied de la lettre*" (31).

2   Parataxis and Narrative:
The New Sentence in Theory and Practice
Bob Perelman

> "I'm new, said she, I don't think you'll find my card here. . . . I'm new, said the oval moon. . . . I'm new, said the quartz crystal. . . . I'm new, said the mist rising from the duck pond. . . . I'm new, says the great dynamo."
>
> —William Carlos Williams, *The Great American Novel*

DEFINITIONS

According to the old grammars, parataxis involves placing units together without connectives or subordination. "I came. I saw. I conquered." is paratactic;

> Of Man's First Disobedience, and the Fruit
> Of that Forbidden Tree, whose mortal taste
> Brought Death into the World, and all our woe,
> With loss of *Eden*, till one greater Man
> Restore us, and regain the blissful Seat,
> Sing Heav'nly Muse, that on the secret top
> Of *Oreb*, or of *Sinai*, didst inspire
> That Shepherd, who first taught the chosen Seed,
> In the Beginning how the Heav'ns and Earth
> Rose out of *Chaos*: or if *Sion* Hill
> Delight thee more, and *Siloa's* Brook that flow'd
> Fast by the Oracle of God; I thence
> Invoke thy aid to my advent'rous Song,
> That with no middle flight intends to soar
> Above th'*Aonian* Mount, while it pursues
> Things unattempted yet in Prose or Rhyme.

is hypotactic. Hypotaxis involves grammatical subordination, and one might think, making Milton paradigmatic, that grammatical subordination entails political and moral subordination as well. But thinking, which arrives, sees, conquers instantaneously, setting up empires in the blink of an eye, needs to be supplemented by reading, empirical, tor-

24

toiselike, always stuck in the provinces of a particular work, page, sentence. *Paradise Lost* may well counsel submission to authority, but its first sentence begins with disobedience and ends with Milton boasting.

In both Caesar's and Milton's world, rhetoric was a key human science, and parataxis was one move among many in a verbal environment where expectations were highly codified. Parataxis of a more thorough and disorienting kind than anything the old handbooks could cite is the dominant if seemingly random mode of our time. It is hard to imagine escaping from atomized subject areas, projects, and errands into longer stretches of subjectively full narrative—not to mention a whole life. As targets of the media we are inundated by intense bursts of narrative-effect: a few seconds of heart-jerk in a life insurance ad (the wife looks longingly at the dead husband's smiling picture as she and the kids sadly leave the now-empty house), blockbuster miniseries four nights long, the six-month approach of the apotheosis of *Jurassic Park* or whatever major venture comes next. These sweeping affective beginnings and endings that shower upon us become visible as tightly managed packages when set against the corporate background that produces them. Those who teach literature (half of my presumed readers here, along with poets) might hope that they deal with more permanent, meaningful narratives, but such local totalities seem more than ever a relative affair— one's Joyce is another's Morrison is another's Hegel. Think of the standard Modern Language Association juxtapositions: "Androgyny in Chaucer" at 9:00 in the Wales Room; followed at 10:30 by "Yeats and Real Estate." Such titles make for easy jokes; the punch line is always the strained relation between literature and the world.

These obsessive spasms of narrative are symptoms of just how divided the present is. Spheres are separate (science, the arts); within spheres, fields are separate (poetry, music, sculpture); each field itself is balkanized; or, to switch from a geopolitical to a financial metaphor, there are marketing niches. Even such choices in metaphor represent the parataxis that is ubiquitous in our sentences: spheres, fields, niches may be incommensurate shapes, but they are also densely interspersed. A map for poetry would contain Language writing, Chicano poetry, academic poetry, cowboy poetry, workshop poetry, *et cetera*—there would always be an *et cetera* at the end of this or any other list. For many poets, the notion of personal autonomy—voice—makes an enclave from such atomization, as do the themes of love, loss, death, landscape, and seasonal time. Such themes present images of totality within their niche. The kind of literary parataxis I will be discussing can be totalizing, too, but inasmuch as its broken surface is antinarrative it can seem to be a mere symptom of contemporary atomization. The tension between symptom and critique will be constant here.

THE NEW SENTENCE

My focus will be "the new sentence," a term that is descriptive of a writing procedure but is also, at times, a sign of literary-political prose-lytizing. While the theory behind the name is meant to politicize litera-ture, the name itself smacks of common marketing practices: "the new Dodge," "the new Coke," "the New Frontier," "the New Covenant"—almost any noun can serve. Such overlaps do not necessarily signal any permanent discredit, however. The new sentence is both a symptom of the age and a formal device that is highly motivated by literary-histori-cal concerns. It marks an attempt to move literature closer to daily life, which is certainly dominated by markets; at the same time, by equating the verse line and the prose sentence, it also marks the pursuit of a writ-ing "unattempted yet in Prose or Rhyme."

The term was coined by Ron Silliman. While it was not a theoretical fiat (Silliman was analyzing writing that he and others had been produc-ing), there was a sense in his discussion that the new sentence marked an advance in literary history.[1] Much more was at stake than a formal innovation: before introducing the new sentence, Silliman sketched the histories of linguistics, literary criticism, and poetry.[2] In fact, from a purely formal perspective, the new sentence was not a very drastic in-novation. A new sentence is more or less ordinary itself but gains its effect by being placed next to another sentence to which it has tangen-tial relevance: new sentences are not subordinated to a larger narra-tive frame nor are they thrown together at random. Parataxis is crucial: the autonomous meaning of a sentence is heightened, questioned, and changed by the degree of separation or connection that the reader per-ceives with regard to the surrounding sentences. This is on the imme-diate formal level. From a larger perspective, the new sentence arises out of an attempt to redefine genres; the tension between parataxis and nar-rative is basic. Among other things, Silliman wanted to escape the prob-lem of the novel, which for him was of a piece with the larger problem of capitalism:

> Freed from a recognition of the signifier and buffered from any response
> from an increasingly passive consumer, the supermarket novelist's language

has become fully subservient to a process that would lie outside syntax: plot. The dynamic implicit in the novel's rise toward the illusion of realism is this divorce, conducted in stages over the centuries, of the tale from the gravitational force of language. . . . This dream of an art with no medium, of a signified with no signifiers, is inscribed entirely within the commodity fetish.[3]

Accompanying this devaluation of the novel was an expansion of the definition of poetry. In "The Chinese Notebook," written at about the same time as the excerpt just quoted, Silliman insists that the series of Wittgensteinian prose meditations on poetry is itself poetry:

76. If I am correct that this is poetry, where is the family resemblance to, say, *The Prelude?* Crossing the Alps. . . .

156. What if I told you I did not really believe this to be a poem? What if I told you I did? . . .

179. How far will anything extend? Hire dancers dressed as security personnel to walk about an otherwise empty museum, then admit the public. Could this be poetry if I proposed it as such? . . .

220. When I return here to ideas previously stated, that's rhyme.[4]

"The Chinese Notebook" and the essays in *The New Sentence* were written in the seventies, when faith in the rebirth of modernist ambition and of the cultural centrality of poetry was easier to maintain than in the nineties. Today parataxis can seem symptomatic of, rather than oppositional to, late capitalism. And where fast cuts from all "walks of life" demonstrate the ubiquity and omniscience of AT&T, they are paratactic. This similarity between the new sentence and current media practice has been pounced on rather gleefully by critics of Language writing: "the stylistic gesture most characteristic of language writing is the nonsequitur. . . . It is the product of a generation raised in front of a television: an endless succession of depthless images and empty sounds, each cancelling the previous one. A non-sequitur implies a loss of memory, an erasing of history. 'Language' poetry as it is practiced by its strictest followers is identical to the speech of television's masterpiece, Ronald Reagan."[5] If attention deficit disorder (ADD) had been a current term when this attack was made, doubtless it would have been included in the attacker's arsenal. New sentence writing can in fact require more attention rather than less from its readers, but if that attention is not granted, then the results might make a reader feel as if she was suffering from ADD. The bluntness of such an attack demonstrates that the new sentence claims a fundamentally different cultural function for poetry. Clearly, the nature of the units and the ways they are juxtaposed need to be considered before useful judgments can be made.

Judgments are being made, however, and not just in local poetry wars. As one of the marks of the postmodern, parataxis has been yoked together with a host of cultural-literary terms in a basic controversy between parts and whole. On one side, there is narrative, totality, the subject, presence, depth, affect; and on the other, fragmentation, simulacra, schizophrenia, surface, pastiche, and, standing side by side with its allies (as it should, etymologically), parataxis. These literary, rhetorical, medical, philosophic, and topographic terms are not, as readers of critical theory know, neutral. Fredric Jameson, in "The Cultural Logic of Late Capitalism," identifies language writing not only with the new sentence but with depthlessness, Lacanian schizophrenia, the erasure of history, and the end of personal identity. Jameson's style, with its long periodic sentences, the clauses packed with qualification, seems far removed from such phenomena, but in the overall organization of its materials, his essay is itself paratactic: Andy Warhol's *Diamond Dust Shoes*, my poem "China," Michael Herr's *Dispatches*, the Bonaventura Hotel are among the units it yokes together. Jameson does not intend an easy moral denunciation of postmodernism—he almost celebrates it in places; but in discussing the parataxis in "China," his vocabulary registers significant alarm: he writes that when "the relationship [of signifiers to each other] breaks down, when the links of the signifying chain snap, then we have schizophrenia in the form of a rubble of distinct and unrelated signifiers."[6]

But we should examine this rubble more closely before Language writing is swept wholesale into the depthless phalanx of postmodernism. While it may suggest fragmentation and schizophrenia to Jameson and others, in my experience the new sentence had an import in the development of Language writing that was precisely the opposite. Later, I will discuss "China" briefly; for now, I will cite the first few lines:

We live on the third world from the sun. Number three.
Nobody tells us what to do.

The people who taught us to count were being very kind.

It's always time to leave.

If it rains, you either have your umbrella or you don't.

The wind blows your hat off.

The sun also rises.[7]

What from one perspective may look like a sign of radical disconnection may from another be a gesture of continuity. For some, there may be utter gulfs between these sentences; others, however, may find narrative within any one of them and narrative linkages between them (the number three and counting; telling us what to do and teaching us; rain, wind, and sun). In the context from which I was writing, each sentence of "China" seemed to me almost transgressively relaxed, prosy, novelistic.[8]

This was because, at the beginning of the Language movement, the primary writing techniques or genres involved a high degree of syntactic and verbal fracturing. This writing was irregularly accompanied by much less fractured theories. Some such as Silliman with conscious Marxist critiques connected commodity and referential fetishism; others with less fluency in theory felt intuitional sense of the liberatory— or at least literary—potential of nonnormative language. But given the cultural urgency felt by Marxists, lyricists, and syntactic guerrillas alike, the prevailing techniques and theories did not provide much possibility for direct statement.

For some Language writers, working in complete sentences was one way to bring practice and daily life closer together. Writing in fragments might have kept one safely uncontaminated by the larger narratives of power, but to write in sentences was to use a publicly legible unit. Sentences per se were not the answer, however, as they were also being written by other poets who had quite different political and aesthetic aims. The following is an excerpt from a fairly widely circulated poetry anthology:

Today I am envying the glorious Mexicans,
who are not afraid to sit by the highway
in the late afternoons, sipping tequila
and napping beneath their wide sombreros
beside the unambitious cactus. Today
I am envying the sweet chaparita who waits
for her lover's banjo in the drunken moonlight
and practices her fingers against the soft tortilla.
Today I am envying the green whiskers of God . . . [9]

The smug colonialism of this is offensive (like the old kitchen towels that say "Manana"); but its main formal feature is not uncommon in much mainstream poetry: the poetry sentence, laden with adjectives ("glorious," "unambitious," "drunken"), verbal moods a sign of emotion (the repeated "I am envying"), nouns chosen for piquancy ("cactus," "chaparita," "banjo"). The incantatory lyricism of the poetry sentence, where writer finds voice and depoliticized universe fitting together without struggle, is an ideal environment for aggrandized sensitivity and myopic or minimized social context.

The new sentence, on the other hand, is defiantly unpoetic. Its shifts break up attempts at the natural reading of universal, authentic statements; instead they encourage attention to the act of writing and to the writer's multiple and mediated positions within larger social frames. The following is a small excerpt from Silliman's book-length poem, *Ketjak*:

> Those curtains which I like above the kitchen sink. Imagined lives we posit in the bungalows, passing, counting, with another part of the mind, the phone poles. Stood there broke and rapidly becoming hungry, staring at the nickels and pennies in the bottom of the fountain. Dear Quine, sentences are not synonymous when they mean the same proposition. How the heel rises and ankle bends to carry the body from one stair to the next. This page is slower.[10]

Making the sentence the basic unit of composition separates the writer from three widely held positions. First, it is arbitrary, driving a wedge between any expressive identity of form and content. What Silliman is doing goes directly against the grain of the poetics of "Projective verse," in which Charles Olson gives primary place to Robert Creeley's statement "FORM IS NEVER MORE THAN AN EXTENSION OF CONTENT."[11] In Silliman's case, form is clearly primary. But, second, to avoid a self-expressive stance does not then throw the writer into the arms of a transindividual language. Foucault's statement may apply to some positions in Language writing but not to Silliman's: "The philosopher is aware . . . [that he] does not inhabit the whole of his language like a secret and perfectly fluent god. Next to himself, he discovers the existence of another language that also speaks and that he is unable to dominate, one that strives, fails, and falls, silent and that he cannot manipulate."[12] Generating one sentence after another is, on the contrary, a sign of confident manipulation. A third distinction: to use the sentence rather than the line as basic unit is to orient the writing toward ordinary language use. Although collage is basic to the new sentence, the elements that are juxtaposed are quite different from those used in Ted

Berrigan's *Sonnets*, where an emphatically artificial line not based on breath is the focal point:

XV

In Joe Brainard's collage its white arrow
He is not in it, the hungry dead doctor.
Of Marilyn Monroe, her white teeth white—
I am truly horribly upset because Marilyn
and ate King Kong popcorn," he wrote in his
of glass in Joe Brainard's collage
Doctor, but they say "I LOVE YOU"
and the sonnet is not dead.
takes the eyes away from the gray words,
Diary. The black heart beside the fifteen pieces
Monroe died, so I went to a matinee B-movie
washed by Joe's throbbing hands. "Today
What is in it is sixteen ripped pictures
does not point to William Carlos Williams.[13]

Number Fifteen is unique among Berrigan's eighty-three sonnets in that it can be "uncollaged" by reading the lines in the following order: 1, 14, 2, 13, 3, 12, etc. Still collage is the reigning principle here and not a mere baffle; it is crucial to the effect that lines end on hyphens and that capitals and quotation marks do not always make linear sense. But to display the materiality of language is not the goal: as is the case with much of Berrigan's writing, this is elegiac, and art is the ultimate consolation. Marilyn Monroe and William Carlos Williams have what eternal life they do because of Brainard's collage and Berrigan's art: "and the sonnet is not dead" is a cry of aesthetic resurrection. (Given Williams's disdain for sonnets, there's a touch of insurrection involved too.)[14]

Silliman makes no attempt to highlight the pathos (and humor) of a separation of art from life, or poetry from philosophy. Far from being fragments, his sentences derive from a coherent, wide-ranging political analysis. Contrary to Jameson's description of the new sentence, this writing seems to me self-critical, ambitiously contextualized, and narrative in a number of ways. In fact, Silliman's political analysis is quite similar to Jameson's; it is less nuanced, but to the extent that it factors in its own writing practice it is, in an essential dimension, wider. Many of the sentences are themselves brief narratives, but more important is the overall frame Silliman shares with Jameson: the Marxist master-narrative that sees commodification as a necessary stage through which history must pass. This master-narrative links what would otherwise be the very different levels of the sentences in the above excerpt from *Ketjak*: the domesticity of the kitchen with the spectacle of identical bungalows with the minute units of the pennies in the fountain with the small verbal differences between sentences that Quine ignores; the renter with the homeowner with the homeless person; housing policies with positivism with writing practices. Silliman's sense of the broken integers produced by capitalism is inseparable from his commitment to the emergence of a transformed, materialist society.[15] The issue of literary quality is less important than the egalitarian politics of these sentences. Very ordinary ones are allowed in: "Those curtains which I like above the kitchen sink."[16]

New sentences imply continuity and discontinuity simultaneously, an effect that becomes clearer when they are read over longer stretches. In the following juxtaposition—"Fountains of the financial district spout soft water in a hard wind. She was a unit in a bum space, she was a damaged child" (3)—we have switched subjects between the sentences: the child and the fountains need not be imagined in a single tableau. This effect of calling forth a new context after each period goes directly against the structural impatience that creates narrative. It's as if a film were cut into separate frames. But in a larger sense, girl and fountain are in the same social space. Throughout the book, Silliman insists on such connections as the one between the girl and the wider economic realities implied by the corporate fountains. The damage that has been done to her has to be read in a larger economic context.

But we don't focus on the girl: she is one facet of a complex situation; she is not singled out for novelistic treatment. There's a dimension of tact involved: she's not representative of the wrongs done to children, but she's not given the brush-off either.[17] The degree of attention Silliman accords her can be read as analogous to the way one recognizes individuals in a crowd (as well as perceptions in a crowded urban setting), giving each a finite but focused moment of attention. This can be favorably compared to the generalized responses of Eliot and Wordsworth to London: phobia in the case of Eliot—"I had not thought death had undone so many"[18]—and despairing scorn in the case of Wordsworth, for whom urbanization resulted in minds "reduced to an almost savage torpor."[19] Of course, to compare Silliman to Eliot and Wordsworth can seem ill-proportioned to some; but if we can lay aside absolutist ideas of literary quality, then Silliman's writing can be read as an exemplary guide to contemporary urban life. The absence of an explicit plot serves it well in this capacity.

In fact, it is interesting to see Jameson, in another context, write that "new readers can be electrified by exposure to *Tarr*, a book in which, as in few others, the sentence is reinvented with all the force of origins, as sculptural gesture and fiat in the void. Such reinvention, however, demands new reading habits, for which we are less and less prepared."[20] While this sounds like praise for something close to the new sentence (as well as a call for the new reading habits the new sentence implies),[21] we should remember that the sum of Lewis's electrifying sentences is the novel *Tarr*, a narrative that Jameson reads as, among other things, a "national allegory," with Kreisler as Germany, Soltyk as Poland, Anastasya as Russia, all against the background of World War I. In other words, he sees in Lewis's sentences a thoroughgoing homology between part and whole—even though in the same study he writes that "every serious practicing critic knows a secret which is less often publicly discussed, namely, that there exists no ready-made corridor between the sealed chamber of stylistic investigation and that equally unventilated space in which the object of study is reconstituted as narrative structure."[22] By refusing to constuct larger narrative wholes beyond the provisional connections made at the time of the reading (or to put it another way, by making the reader renarrativize), Silliman avoids the impasse Jameson mentions: with the new sentence there is no separation between style and plot, between reading at the level of the sentence and reading for narrative.

Silliman often attacks the homogeneity of large-scale narrative for drawing attention away from the materiality of the words of the page; the novel, to reiterate, is a primary target: "Details differ,/thus they mean"; "Narrative suppresses immediate attention": "That each line is created equal/is contranarrative."[23] Each new sentence is to reinvigorate verbal perception: where Jameson reads signifying chains snapping, Silliman reads the technicolor epics of false consciousness being swept away.[24] But alongside such denarrativization, I want to emphasize (though Silliman often does not) that possiblities of renarrativization are continually offered.

Even though his analysis omits it, one device that is crucial to his initial work with the new sentence is a highly developed structure of repetition. *Ketjak* is written in a series of expanding paragraphs where the sentences of one paragraph are repeated in order in subsequent paragraphs with additional sentences inserted between them, recontextualizing them. As the paragraphs double, the space between the reoccurrence of the sentences doubles and the context from which they reemerge grows thicker. In this, they have reminded some in the Language movement of characters in a novel.[25] But the narrative effect is more peculiar as the sentences keep reappearing juxtaposed against different sentences. For example: "Look at that room filled with fleshy babies, incubating. We ate them." In the next paragraph: "Look at that room filled with fleshy babies. A tall glass of tawny port. We ate them." Next paragraph: "Look at that room filled with fleshy babies, incubating. Points of transfer. A tall glass of tawny port. The shadows between the houses leave the earth cool and damp. A slick gaggle of ambassadors. We ate them." The new sentence questions anaphora, so that reference is not guaranteed to extend beyond sentence boundaries. Thus "We ate," not babies, not port, not ambassadors, but only "them." On the other hand, Silliman is clearly enjoying the juxtapositions on his verbal or virtual smorgasbord. In moments like these, he seems to be playing a kind of fort-da game with readers' expectations for continuity.

In a more recent book, *What*, Silliman does not use repetition devices, thus embodying a more "pure" degree of parataxis.[26] The results seem significantly different, though it will be hard to demonstrate the difference here, because a short excerpt will seem similar to the previous excerpts:

> The cash register makes a deeper tone
> if the Universal Product Code isn't picked up
> by the sensor. One after another,
> cars bounce in the pothole. . . .
>   "No on F,"
> "Stop dirty politics," giving no clue whatsoever
> what the issues might entail. (92–93)

These three sentences deal with the same content as before. Silliman is "narrating" the story of the decontextualized units of late capitalism: grocery store items, cars, bumper sticker slogans all passing through the grids of the service economy. But in the earlier work the repetition and recombination of sentences distanced, framed, questioned, and at times ironized their contents; here, with no chance for recontextualization, the act of writing each sentence repeatedly pits writer against world (and against the mass of prior sentences), building up pressure for validity and for novelty, which can seem to merge with the story of cultural commodification against which the writing directs itself: the "new" of the new sentence is poised here between symptom and critique. In other words, can "One after another,/cars bounce in the pothole" be read as a description of the sentences themselves?

To suggest this is seemingly to circle back to Jameson's vision of the ahistorical anomie of postmodern schizophrenic production. But simply to homologize the cars and the sentences, the pothole and the experiential vacuum created by multinational capitalism would be to ignore the oppositional stance implicit in the sentences as they simultaneously depict and critique their world.

This critique is personal: a primary element of each sentence is the fact of Silliman writing. This fact surfaces in the many references to the physical act of writing; but it also appears in the content: for instance, one can follow, in separated but sequential sentences, the story of Silliman's marriage and his grandmother's death. At such times, the writing seems autobiographical, even though the narrative is focused more on the tip of the pen than in the memory of the writer. Larger narrative frames, theoretically repressed by Silliman's use of parataxis, clearly return, even within a single sentence. Consider the following:

> I have flight (half-light). The audience
> for poetry not being "the masses" can be
> quite specific—you choose the poem
> or it chooses you (years later possibly
> you meet the author at a party, a little, bald
> bespectacled fellow, talking not art or politics
> but baseball and gossip, the edges of everything
> general and rounded) and your life is altered
> irreparably by that decision, you change majors,
> jobs, become passionate suddenly in ways
> opaque to your lover, and frightening:
> you didn't know poetry could be like that
> but it's what you'd wanted all along,
> so deeply in fact that you think for awhile
> it might be genetic or that you were "destined"
> as that poem seems also to have been destined
> for a particular life, and maybe you are
> and it was, if not in that sense in some other,
> the way it has for all the others been just likewise,
> each one choosing the poem, the poem choosing them,
> even the ones who seem to you (for who are you
> to judge?) completely muddied in what they do,
> in how they think, the ones who publish
> a single chapbook and get no response, no one
> coming to their readings and they
> going to fewer each year, writing less and
> one day they realize they haven't even thought
> of publishing in ages, the job is harder, the kids
> demand time, and yet almost as if at random

copies of that chapbook dot the crowded shelves
of small used bookstores, just waiting
to be chosen and to choose, loaded
as a minefield. I heard mindfield. (94–95)

The length of the second sentence strikes me as exemplary of the un-
resolved pressure for narrative that Silliman's practice of the new sentence creates. This excerpt is not purely paratactic, as these three sentences are somewhat anaphoric. "Mindfield" refers back to "minefield";
and the various anxieties over the success of careers, methods, and
schools that stir so disturbingly through the elephantine sentence can
be detected, in germ, in the pun of the first: have flight/half-light. Is
one, as a poet, really flying with Pegasus or is one simply a dimwit? But
these qualifications aside, the relatively complete commitment to parataxis in the later work also entails a commitment to Silliman's moral
authority as a writer, inasmuch as there is nothing else to motivate
the appearance of the next new sentence. The long sentence is anoma-
lous; nevertheless it demonstrates that the new sentence, by its freedom
from older social narratives, creates euphoria ("your life is altered . . .
you . . . become passionate") while at the same time producing pressure to get everything—including life stories—said before the period.

THE NEW SENTENCE AND THE NOVEL

I have been concerned here not to generalize: what I have written about
Silliman does not apply as accurately to other Language writers or, in
fact, to some of his own books. I will turn now to the work of Lyn
Hejinian. Her work is formally somewhat close to Silliman's, but it demonstrates that the new sentence can be used for quite different narrative
and political-rhetorical effects, and that a new-sentence novel need not
be an unthinkable genre. The following passage is from My Life:

> What were Caesar's battles but Caesar's prose. A name trimmed with col-
> ored ribbons. We "took" a trip as if that were part of the baggage we car-
> ried. In other words we "took our time." The experience of a great passion,
> a great love, would remove me, elevate me, enable me at last to be both spe-
> cial and ignorant of the other people around me, so that I would be free at
> last from the necessity of appealing to them, responding to them. That is,
> to be nearly useless but at rest. There were cut flowers in vases and ceramic
> bouquets, but in those days they did not keep any living houseplants. The
> old fragmentary texts, early Egyptian and Persian writings, say, or the works
> of Sappho, were intriguing and lovely, a mystery adhering to the lost lines.

At the time, the perpetual Latin of love kept things hidden. It was not his fate to be as famous as Segovia. Nonetheless, I wrote my name in every one of his books. Language is the history that gave me shape and hypochondria. And followed it with a date, as if by my name I took the book and by the date, historically, contextualized its contents, affixed to them a reading. And memory a wall. My grandmother had been a great beauty and she always won at cards. As for we who "love to be astonished," the ear is less active than the eye. The artichoke has done its best, armored, with scales, barbed, and hiding in its interior the soft hairs so aptly called the choke. . . . Of course, one continues to write, and thus to "be a writer," because one has not yet written that "ultimate" work. Exercise will do it. I insert a description: of agonizing spring morning freshness, when through the open window a smell of cold dust and buds of broken early grass, of schoolbooks and rotting apples, trails the distant sound of an airplane and a flock of crows. I thought that for a woman health and comfort must come after love. Any photographer will tell you the same. So I wouldn't wear boots in the snow, nor socks in the cold. Shufflers scuff. That sense of responsibility was merely the context of the search for a lover, or, rather, for a love. Let someone from the other lane in.[27]

Clearly, there is paratactic organization at work here, though recurrent attention to specific areas of memory makes the gaps between the sentences less didactic than is often the case with Silliman. The passage does, however, display a similar allegiance to the project of disrupting unities of poetic voice and narrative. A sentence containing only a bare metaphysical image ("And memory a wall"); a sentence of conventional reminiscence ("My grandmother . . . always won at cards"); a sentence mixing lyricism and aesthetics ("As for we . . . the ear is less active than the eye"): such a sequence foregrounds its artifice. The larger organization of the book does the same. In a gesture that is similar to many of Silliman's a priori procedural decisions, the first edition of My Life, written when Hejinian was thirty-seven, contains thirty-seven chapters of thirty-seven sentences each. The second edition, written eight years later, adds new chapters and inserts new sentences into earlier chapters to make forty-five chapters of forty-five sentences. So the sentence beginning "I insert a description" is a formal pun, since it is one of the new, second-edition sentences.

Nevertheless, the artificially inserted memory is emotional and lyrical. While not a traditional autobiography, My Life does not belie its title. Each chapter takes up—loosely, to be sure—a single year of Hejinian's life. I've quoted from the seventeenth chapter; once the frame of Hejinian at seventeen is placed around these sentences, quite a bit of the paratac-

tic effect recedes, and a particular meditative and at times almost novelistic cast emerges. An adolescent hero-worship that admires Caesar,
the father's library, "ultimate" masterpieces, is mixed with a budding
awareness of sexuality. These strands unite closely in the intriguing lost
lines of Sappho and the not-quite-decipherable "perpetual Latin of love."
These complex senses can attach to most of the sentences. "Let someone
from the other lane in," can be read as referring to a moment of traffic contemporaneous with the writer's present and thus as a paratactic
jump; but it also can be read as a metaphor for the expansion of the
literary-erotic sympathies that the passage as a whole continually glances
at. Sometimes an artichoke is just an artichoke, but it can also be an
image of emergent sexuality quite appropriate to adolescence, both unopened bud and armored Joan of Arc.

The intermittent past tense helps establish this quasi-narrative coherence: again, once the frame is suggested, a little can go a long way. But
throughout the book Hejinian also keeps the present moment of the
writing in the foreground. At times she keeps her younger self at a critical distance, as when the older writer comments caustically on the sev-
enteen-year-old's desire for a great passion: "That is, to be nearly useless
but at rest." But writing and prior experience are more often mixed.
From the twentieth chapter:

> What memory is not a "gripping" thought. Only fragments are accurate.
> Break it up into single words, change them to combination. So we go into
> the store shopping and get, after awhile, you know, contralto! Thinking
> about time in the book, it is really the time of your life. I was experiencing
> love, immensely relieved. It was, I know, an unparticular spirit of romance.
> She apologizes and seizes us in the grip of her inadequacies. Giving the
> back-up o.k. to the loaded semi. (55)

The first sentence is most easily read as present-time meditation; the
shopping sentence, on the other hand, seems pure reenactment (and is
about as close as Hejinian ever gets to Valley talk). In "It was, I know,
an unparticular spirit of romance," both times exist: "I know" and
most likely the allusion to Pound's *Spirit of Romance* belong to the time of
writing; but the feeling of being caught up by standard-issue feelings
belongs to Hejinian's twentieth year. The next sentence switches to the
third person and critiques the prior sentence: "[Since she now finds her
early romance boring,] She apologizes and seizes us in the grip of her
inadequacies." The goal is for writing and living to be continuous:
"Thinking about time in the book, it is really the time of your life." A
more comic presentation of the multiple acts of this writing—remem-

bering, reliving, and creating—occurs in the image of the loaded semi and the person standing behind supervising its backing up.

In a later book, *Oxota: A Short Russian Novel*, the relationship between the sentences and their narrative burden is complex in different ways.[28] As the title suggests, Hejinian does not seem fazed to approach the problematic genre, the novel. But the book is far from a conventional novel; it is hardly a record of Hejinian's time in what was then Leningrad: only the vaguest chronicle can be constructed from the almost 300 fourteen-line poems (referred to as "sonnets" on the back cover in a gesture toward the sonnets that make up Pushkin's *Evgeny Onegin*). But the opacity of external event does not lead back to the sense that language is a privileged entity. In this respect, *Oxota* is quite different from Silliman's writing. The root of Silliman's political aesthetics is faith in language as the site of an active community, not inheriting meanings but creating them through precise acts of reading and writing, most aptly exemplified in the lines: "The point at which you read each word (the/only point there is), two minds share a larger whole."[29] But *Oxota* does not display any larger wholes: the line is a provisional unit, always ending without a period. The construction of rudimentary interpretation and identity are predominant. Two minds share a two-sided conundrum:

Chapter Eighty-Nine

Misha should be a major character in the Russian novel
Sasha, too, and Nadia
You will start with the third chapter, Arkadii said, and
        the first sentence must be attributed to Emmanuel Kant
        as follows: everything happens so often, that speaking
        of it makes no sense
You will meet people accompanying their ghosts, said
        Alyosha, and speak with them
Kolya, Shura, Borik, Sveta, Tanya, Natasha, Igor, Vladik,
        Vanya, and the other Misha
Zina stood on a chair
Arkadii waved the ghosts aside
There must be a sentence which claims a chapter for itself
And a name at the vanishing point in a person's description
So that the days will seem not to have gone by—and in fact
        names are relationships with a remarkable economy while
        descriptions are profligate
But pleasure is a mental process too as well as the producer
        of an aesthetic object
It is not what I knew

Our Russian workers like to dig holes, Arkadii said, while
    Americans prefer machines that scoop
The coincidence of experiences occurring with experiences
    already had produced identity—but it spills (101)

Arkadii, or whoever pronounces the eighth line, seems to ask that "the
Russian novel" (i.e., *Oxota* itself, whose production is discussed in many
of the poems) contain something like the new sentence: "a sentence
which claims a chapter for itself."[30] But while *Oxota* is more or less paratactic from line to line, the lines themselves gesture toward a continuity
with their Russian surroundings in a spirit that is much different from
the new sentence.

Leningrad, a collaborative account of a prior trip to the Soviet Union
written by Hejinian, Silliman, Barrett Watten, and Michael Davidson, records a Russian saying to Silliman: "You speak as one who comes from
a land of objects, therefore it is easy for you to conceive of language as
an object, as objective, whereas we do not."[31] The generalization that
writers of the West do not see language as subjective seems odd in the
light of the widespread commitment in poetry to authenticities of the
self; nevertheless, this remark is suggestive in that the new sentence can
be seen as arising specifically from a culture of consumerism.[32] This
does not automatically mean, however, that the parataxis of Language
writing is automatically equivalent to shopping or channel surfing: to
repeat, parataxis can be used oppositionally. But *Oxota* demonstrates one
way parataxis operates in a context of scarcity. In the West, overloads of
objects, viewpoints, schools, channels, typefaces, marketing strategies
create pressure that can make the sequential coherence and drama of
the novel seem like Victorian coincidence. In the world of *Oxota*, on the
other hand, there is not enough of anything: chickens, paper, living
space are constantly being sought; connection itself becomes a luxury
and metaphorical extravaganzas fill the gaps between things: "Ostap
pointed toward a slab of frying spam and said, that organism is what
we call fruit" (47).

Rather than an exact instrument to create a utopian textual politics
as with Silliman, in *Oxota* language continually verges on the comic.
Each word is foreign, deliberately nonauthoritative:

Upstairs I met with Evgenii Ivanovich, who was translating
    the American metaphorist Raymond Chandler
A pale man with a tiny pad
He turned away and lifted its page

What does it mean, please, "The woman has rubber lips with
    no tread"
She's lost her grip on the truth
Or maybe what she says goes by him
We have no such metaphors, he said, but maybe I'll find one
Maybe something like, "The circle she made with her mouth
    was warped" (198)
   . . . .
In the Hermitage there was no coffee
Cunt of weakness! an American mumbled carefully, reading
    transliteration from a handy traveller's book
There was an original resemblance and the young painter
    slashed it
No coffee, no cold, no hole in this reality, Liuda said
We had descended—tea must be without feminism
It was a terrible thing—a great separation—this young
    painter's knife had a butterfly's wings
But it is our feminism to recall the village, Liuda said (193)

Comedy is not the main point, however. The mixed diction of "What
does it mean, please, 'The woman has rubber lips with no tread'" could
make for a punch line; but the passage goes beyond it to a provisionally
effective translation. Neither the classic (or "classic"—it hardly matters)
American language of Chandler nor the foreignness of the Russian's English is allowed a settled status. Rather, as the end of chapter 53 puts it:
"The excitation of the same experience by two grammars—it's not impossible" (63). Silliman's credo makes any one point of language absolute: "the only point there is"; here the words are a provisional place
of initial contact of different cultures and languages. Oxota seems poised
between the West's late capitalism and the peculiar status of Russia in
1990, where there is no settled social system: hence rhetoric and genre
are not fixed either.

Franco Moretti, among others, has shown how the novel was an element in the construction of the nation-state in the eighteenth and nineteenth centuries.[33] If one accepts this, then one can find in the rapid
exactitude of the new sentence a way of drawing useful maps in a post-
national (and postnovel) environment—at least, to the extent that the
new sentence is motivated by an ethic of activist prodding. Oxota demonstrates a way of reacting to a more uncertain situation. Some of the
characters in the book evoke prenovelistic images of village folktale motifs with great longing—"grannies," "great Siberian soup," etc.—but

these are not certainties that Hejinian hopes to recapture. "But it is our feminism to recall the village"—which way does that read? It is poised between a cosmopolitan Western feminism and a rural partiarchy, articulating an unstable territory where American English has no claim to authority; it is simply an interested onlooker.

DENARRATIVIZATION AND RENARRATIVIZATION

To care for the readings I have tried to sketch here requires a commitment to unities that are provisionally autonomous: poetry, Language writing, the work of individual Language writers. Such qualifications need to be set back into a more totalized context, however. It is of value, in other words, to set the new sentence beside postmodern architecture and television, as Jameson does. But any specific work using the new sentence will lose focus if it is not read with some attention to the original context, even though in the case of Language writing that context (poetry) is itself called into question.

Discontinuity or continuity in writing results from complex conditions of reading. Whitman's paratactic catalogs seemed bizarre and discontinuous to most of his contemporaries, yet for this century's readers they are more likely to suggest connection and a totalizing embrace of society. (One can see a doppelgänger of this embrace in the economically calculated shots in the ads I alluded to at the beginning: the airline pilot, the old couple, the stockbroker, the black construction worker, the waitress, and so on. There is often a patriotic subplot to these ads that also recalls Whitman.)[34] Novels, on the other hand, which would seemingly be connected narrative by definition, can register as paratactic in a number of ways. Camus's use of the *passé composé* in *The Stranger* is commonly pointed out to students of French as a mark of discontinuity: "What," asks *Cliffs Notes*, "does [Mersault's] habit of not relating events to one another tell us about his character?"[35] And the sentence-by-sentence writing in *Bouvard and Pecuchet*—as well as the plot as a whole— is comic precisely because there is no contact between items that are supposedly in immediate connection with one another. Bouvard and Pecuchet's pedantic steps toward understanding the world lead nowhere.

First, what is beauty?
For Schelling, it is the infinite expressing itself in the finite; for Reid, an occult quality; for Jouffroy, a fact incapable of analysis. . . .
And there exist several kinds of beauty: a beauty of science, geometry is beautiful; a beauty of behavior, it cannot be denied that the death of Socrates was beautiful. A beauty of the animal kingdom: the beauty of the dog con-

sists in its sense of smell. A pig could not be beautiful on account of its filthy habits; nor a snake, because it awakes in us ideas of baseness.

Flowers, butterflies, birds may be beautiful. In fact the first condition of beauty is unity in variety; that is the root of the matter.

"Yet," said Bouvard, "two cross-eyes are more varied than two ordinary ones and produce a less good effect, as a rule."

They entered upon the question of the sublime.[36]

Each sentence or phrase here is something of a "new sentence," though for a very different purpose than is the case with Silliman or Hejinian. The elementary completeness of each little pronouncement here is the result of authoritarian abbreviation. The ironic gaps that Flaubert wants us to read between each assertion reveal the lunatic abyss underlying the pedagogical narrative of organized knowledge. The lack of necessary connection is a cause for ultimate despair on Flaubert's part; for Hejinian and Silliman it creates an opening for the next new sentence.

I should remark here that the rhetorical tone of "China"—to my mind one of the salient features of the poem—is the opposite of the irony in *Bouvard and Pecuchet*: the poem touches on the matter-of-fact utopian feelings that early education can evoke.[37] The opening line—"We live on the third world from the sun. Number three. Nobody tells us what to do."—combines rudimentary astronomy with an assertion of complete independence, as if learning about the solar system in second grade marks a liberation from older narratives of fate. But despite the ingenuous tone of the poem, irony does appear in the assertions of collectivity. Nobody (from other planets or from heaven) tells us what to do: but that doesn't mean that "we" don't tell each other what to do. The same tension appears in a subsequent line such as "Everyone enjoyed the explosions." It means one thing if "everyone" refers to a rural village celebrating the new year with firecrackers; there is a solidarity, camaraderie. But if the context is the Vietnam War, the meaning changes: the explosions now are deadly, and "everyone" loses its communal character and embodies colonialist violence. Recall one of the etymological roots of parataxis: soldiers standing side by side. Paratactic composition can bring up this major conundrum of contemporary society: are we on the same side, or are we each in separate armies in the war of "all against all"?

Let me conclude by reiterating that Jameson and Silliman both make wide theoretical claims; both are trying to fight the random parataxis of commodification with a more committed, oppositional parataxis— the positing of structural similarities across categories. While Hejinian's use of parataxis coexists more amiably with narrative, her sentences are also committed to breaking up any smooth narrative plane. Denarrativization is a necessary part of construction in these wider paratactic arguments. But this process needs to be seen for the combined reading and writing practice that it is: renarrativization is also necessary. If we try to separate the results of these practices, we are left with fictions, metaphorical condensations: the purely autonomous, politically efficacious new sentence on the one hand, and the rubble of signifying chains on the other.

NOTES

1. While I will use Silliman's analysis in my initial discussion, I should point out that, in addition to group cohesiveness, there is also a parataxis of individuals within a group so that in some ways what Silliman writes is precisely what others do not. A debate between Silliman and Leslie Scalapino over narrative and gender was an overt sign of this. Silliman wrote that

    Progressive poets who identify as members of groups that have been the subject of history—many white male heterosexuals, for example— are apt to challenge all that is supposedly "natural" about the formation of their own subjectivity. That their writing today is apt to call into question . . . such conventions as narrative, persona and even reference can hardly be surprising. At the other end of the spectrum are poets who . . . have been [history's] objects. . . . These writers and readers—women, people of color, sexual minorities, the entire spectrum of the "marginal"—have a manifest political need to have their stories told. That their writing should often appear much more conventional, with the notable difference as to whom is the subject of these conventions, illuminates the relationship between form and audience.

    Scalapino took issue, writing that Silliman's use of "conventional" implied "inferiority," that his argument was "authoritarian." Rather than exploding persona, Silliman's "critique of the unified subject. . . . the concept of 'objectivity' constitutes a unified subject." She went on: "You have a Marxist narration. . . . You are defining innovation as the repository of white men who are supposedly free of connection. Even if they could be free of connection, why should they be? E.g., why would that be viewed as innovative? I'm defining narrative as 'constructing.' "
    The debate can be found in Poetics Journal 9 (1991): 51–68. Scalapino uses some of the phrases of this debate in "Orion." See The Return of

44   Bob Perelman

Painting, the Pearl, and Orion: A Trilogy (San Francisco: North Point Press, 1991), 151–54. Scalapino's approach to narrative is not paratactic—it owes more to the meditative style that Gertrude Stein developed in works such as The Geographical History of America; but a comparison of Scalapino's prose with new sentence writing would be very worthwhile.

2. Ron Silliman, "The New Sentence," in The New Sentence (New York: Roof Books, 1987), 63–93.

3. Ron Silliman, "Disappearance of the Word, Appearance of the World," in The New Sentence, 14.

4. Ron Silliman, "The Chinese Notebook," in The Age of Huts (New York: Roof Books, 1986), 50, 59, 62, 66.

5. Eliot Weinberger, "A Note on Montemora, America, and the World," Sulfur 20 (1987): 197.

6. Fredric Jameson, Postmodernism, or, the Cultural Logic of Late Capitalism (Durham: Duke University Press, 1991), 26.

7. Bob Perelman, The First World (Berkeley: This Press, 1981), 60.

8. George Hartley discusses "China" in Textual Politics and the Language Poets (Bloomington: Indiana University Press, 1989), 60.

9. Michael Blumenthal, "Today I Am Envying the Glorious Mexicans," in The Morrow Anthology of Younger American Poets, ed. Dave Smith and David Bottoms (New York: Quill, 1985), 95.

10. Ron Silliman, Ketjak (San Francisco: This Press, 1978), 17.

11. Charles Olson, "Projective Verse," in Selected Writings of Charles Olson, ed. Robert Creeley (New York: New Directions, 1966), 16. Olson's Creeley is echoing not just Valery, but Hegel. "The aesthetics of idealism grasps the work of art as a form/content unity. 'True works of art are such, precisely by the fact that their content and their form prove to be completely identical,' says Hegel." Peter Bürger, The Decline of Modernism, trans. Nicholas Walker (University Park: Pennsylvania State University Press, 1992), 20.

12. Michel Foucault, "Preface to Transgression," in Language, Counter-Memory, Practice: Selected Essays and Interviews, ed. Donald Bouchard, trans. Donald Bouchard and Sherry Simon (Ithaca: Cornell University Press, 1977), 41–42.

13. Ted Berrigan, The Sonnets (New York: Grove Press, 1964), 20.

14. Compare Robert Grenier's reenactment of Williams's "castigation of the sonnet" discussed in Perelman, The Marginalization of Poetry: Language Writing and Literary History (Princeton: Princeton University Press, 1996), 38–44.

15. The impulse to map the global condition can make the phrases of Jameson's own sentences somewhat analogous to Silliman's new sentences:

A roomful of people, indeed, solicit us in incompatible directions that we entertain all at once: one subject position assuring us of the remarkable new global elegance of its daily life and forms; another one marvelling at the spread of democracy, with all those new "voices" sounding out of hitherto silent parts of the globe or inaudible class strata (just wait a while, they will be here, to join their voices to the rest); other more querulous and "realistic" tongues reminding us of the incompetencies of late capitalism, with its delirious paper-money constructions rising out of sight, its Debt, the rapidity of the flight of factories matched only by the opening of new junk-food chains, the sheer immiseration of structural homelessness, let alone unemployment, and that well-known thing called urban "blight" or "decay" which the media wraps brightly up in drug melodramas and violence porn when it judges the theme perilously close to being threadbare. (Jameson, *Postmodernism*, 375–76)

This sentence was called to my attention by Jim English's review of *Postmodernism* in *Postmodern Culture* 1.3 (May 1991). Comparing them to new sentences, English describes Jameson's sentences as follows:

They are often . . . "impossible" in the sense that the two-hundred-word aphorism is impossible. A . . . refusal of any posture of poeticism or transcendence, coexists improbably with the bravura and self-involvement of Jameson's idiolect. Polemic is put into virtual abeyance by the tendency to stray across various and incompatible discursive fields, "picking up" bits of language here and there, celebrating the syntactic detour. And yet polemic . . . always reappears at the next rest stop, only to be lost again in the joyous (or is it tiresome?) intensity, the weirdly inappropriate euphoria, of another Jamesonian sentence.

16. Barrett Watten has compared the use of quotidian details in Williams and Silliman: for Williams "the inconsequential is dramatized as a single moment of truth that is also ironic." When Silliman describes a plastic fork from McDonald's, Watten sees the sentence as commenting "on larger social forms. Monopoly capitalism will produce many such forks, but there can be only one in the poem. . . . The only solution is for the poem to keep going." *Total Syntax* (Carbondale: Southern Illinois University Press, 1985), 109.

See also Jeffrey Nealon's discussion of Williams and Watten in *Double Reading: Postmodernism after Deconstruction* (Ithaca: Cornell University Press, 1993), 139.

17. Especially in subsequent expanded versions of the sentence: "She was a unit in a bum space, she was a damaged child, sitting in her rocker by

the window" (6, 7, 11, 18, etc.). I discuss these repetitions later in this essay.

18. T. S. Eliot, "The Waste Land," in *The Complete Poems and Plays* (New York: Harcourt Brace Jovanovich, 1971), 39.

19. "Preface to the Second Edition of *Lyrical Ballads*," in *William Wordsworth: Selected Poetry*, ed. Mark Van Doren (New York: Random House, 1950), 679. Also, see the description of London in book seven of *The Prelude*, especially lines 656–92.

20. Fredric Jameson, *Fables of Aggression: Wyndham Lewis, the Modernist as Fascist* (Berkeley and Los Angeles: University of California Press, 1979), 2. The Jamesonian "we" is an odd construction; he is exempting himself from the "we."

21. Jameson concludes "The Cultural Logic of Late Capitalism" with a similar gesture: "the new political art . . . will have to hold to the truth of postmodernism . . . the world space of multinational capital—at the same time at which it achieves a breakthrough to some as yet unimaginable new mode of representing this last" (54).

22. Jameson, *Fables*, 7.

23. Ron Silliman, *Demo to Ink* (Tucson: Chax Press, 1992), 131, 50, 107. (The title indicates a collection of six books from Silliman's ongoing series, *The Alphabet*; *Demo* is the first of the six.)

24. In "Disappearance of the Word," Silliman writes that commodified language becomes inseparable from entertainment spectacles: "the consumer of a mass market novel such as *Jaws* stares at a 'blank' page (the page also of the speed-reader) while a story appears to unfold miraculously of its own free will before his or her eyes" (*The New Sentence*, 13).

25. Schematically, the pattern of *Ketjak* looks like this, with each letter representing a sentence, and the uppercase letters representing a repeated sentence:

a.
A. b.
A. c. B. d.
A. e. C. f. B. g. D. h.

The opening pages of *Ketjak* do not quite conform to this scheme, though the bulk of the book does. Silliman's next book, *Tjanting* (Great Barrington, Mass.: Figures, 1981), uses a much more complex system involving Fibonacci numbers. See the Silliman issue of *Difficulties* for an interview, where Silliman compares this structure to class struggle. In the discussion in Barrett Watten's talk, "Russian Formalism and the Present," Watten and David Bromige speak of *Ketjak* as a novel. Watten says:

"Each sentence is a device . . . this is close to Shklovsky's characterization of Sterne. *Ketjak* is a typical novel in the tradition of *Tristram Shandy*." Bromige: "You find out more about each sentence as you go along, in the way that you find out more about a character." See *Hills* 6/7 (1980): 66.

26. Ron Silliman, *What* (Great Barrington, Mass.: The Figures, 1988).

27. Lyn Hejinian, *My Life*, 2d ed. (Los Angeles: Sun & Moon Press, 1987), 47–48.

28. Lyn Hejinian, *Oxota: A Short Russian Novel* (Great Barrington, Mass.: The Figures, 1991).

29. Silliman, *What*, 40.

30. For instance: "In the evenings particularly we made notes and took dictation in anticipation of writing a short Russian novel, something neither invented nor constructed but moving through that time as I experienced it unable to take part personally in the hunting" (12). *Oxota* is Russian for "hunt."

31. Michael Davidson, Lyn Hejinian, Ron Silliman, and Barrett Watten, *Leningrad* (San Francisco: Mercury House, 1991), 124.

32. For a very funny, and ultimately serious, acting out of the consequences of trying to live as an artist amid the West's sea of objects, see Steve Benson's performance-talk, "Views of Communist China," in *Hills* 6/7 (1980): 74–103.

33. See Franco Moretti, *The Way of the World: The Bildungsroman in European Culture* (London: Verso, 1987).

34. I owe this observation to Dana Phillips.

35. Quoted in Alice Kaplan, "The American Stranger," *South Atlantic Quarterly* (Winter 1992): 91.

36. Gustave Flaubert, *Bouvard and Pecuchet*, trans. T. W. Earp and G. W. Stoner (Westport, Conn.: Greenwood Press, 1954), 166–67.

37. I wrote the poem after looking, not at a book of photographs as Jameson writes, but at some sort of Chinese primer containing simple four-color pictures of "the world": family, kitchen, school, rivers, airports, and village festivals.

3   *Total Syntax:*
      The Work in the World
      Barrett Watten

The possibilities for statement in art are taken in quite different directions in the work of three contemporary poets: Clark Coolidge, Ron Silliman, and Steve Benson. Like the sculptor Robert Smithson, all three work toward a greater scale in art, and their solutions to the problems of scale reveal new developments in syntax.[1]

In *Nadja,* André Breton makes a curious statement, but one that indicates his own priorities: "As far as I am concerned, a mind's arrangement with regard to certain objects is even more important than its regard for certain arrangements of objects, these two kinds of arrangement controlling between them all forms of sensibility."[2] The "mind's arrangement with regard to certain objects" is certainly at the basis of syntax in the work of both Breton and Smithson. Breton's surrealist image fixes the flux of automatism in static images, simple objects. Later, an object can be incorporated directly into the poem, which is essentially an oneiric form, without any loss in translation. Nadja is one such oneiric object—a woman. Smithson's generative syntax begins with tropes that are refractions of a single object seen through the lens of an ironic observer. They prepare the ground for other objects on larger, more monumental scales—such as the Spiral Jetty.

In the work of Coolidge, Silliman, and Benson there is, without wishing to overdraw a comparison, a syntactic basis in a "regard for certain arrangements of objects." A relation *between* things, a situation with its *own* laws, is the point of departure. Any given "object" has an essential relation to other objects as well as a disposition to the observer. The observer, rather than being ironic, is responsible to the contingencies of any thing that might compel him or her. The situation as a whole must be taken in—linguistic, social, psychological—and is not just a projection of the observer. The syntax of the world is elusive, though what is seen in this syntax is different in the case of each writer.

Clark Coolidge must be given credit for realizing the possibilities of *extension* of a syntax of "arrangement," although a number of writers have preceded him in recognizing its possibilities for art. The mimicking of the painterly surface in the first generation of New York School poets (John Ashbery, Kenneth Koch, Frank O'Hara), as well as the performance values of experimentalists such as John Cage and Jackson Mac Low, are the two major influences, with Gertrude Stein and Williams's experimental prose in the shadowy past. Coolidge's extension of this possibility proceeded in a deliberate, step-by-step manner over the course of his work. Its contribution to the question of scale in art is due to its exploration of the psychological implications of "arrangement"—extending experimentalism where it may have reached a dead end in painterly surfaces or performance values.

Coolidge's first collection, *Space*, shows the influence of the painterly surface of the New York School poets, and it also shows the beginning of the path beyond. The book is divided into four sections, each a characteristic area of work. A number of works in the first section bear a close resemblance to the kind of cut-up, painterly lyricism of John Ashbery's *The Tennis Court Oath*, which uses a number of "exterior" procedures on found texts in a kind of "all-over" mimicry of the surfaces of abstract expressionism. The materials used are generally ironic and aestheticized at the same time; false scenarios, inappropriate remarks, and a skewed, unmotivated syntax reflect the mind at work, along with a continual hint of the philosophical relevance of the impossibility of statement. However aestheticized, the work was a significant breakthrough, as evidenced by the number of its immediate followers. A work by Coolidge that is relevant to this context is the second poem in the book, "The Image Furnace, Under Brine":

> "the good ease!," sighed slamming his pencil
>   vacuum of the light bulb drop, the sigh
>   sign vent of its
>   slat
>   way[3]

The gestures here are much like Ashbery's: "sighed slamming his pencil" betrays the anxiety of the fragmentary; "the sigh/sign vent of its/slat" seems to find a high irony in the problem of representing a mental state. But the emphasis of these anxious fragments is differently arranged than in Ashbery—there is a stronger, more propulsive pulse, an underlining of rhythmic play. This emphasis on the rhythmic, purely temporal dimension sets Coolidge off from the other imitators of *The Tennis Court Oath*. Coolidge sees Kerouac's "spontaneous bop prosody" in these cool surfaces, bringing to mind Coolidge's brief career as a jazz drummer. The temporal axis gives the go-ahead into a different aesthetic space, in much the same way that pure mental projection gave Smithson his permission. The materials and impulses can be given a kind of play—in the ironizing of meaning in Smithson, or in its basic mutability toward sound in Coolidge.

The jazz drummer is clearly visible in "Bontecou Chandelier":

jars   jars   jars   oil   staples   donuts
wire, at the wrist, the Hey
Crenulated.   Absolving.   Holiday Swells.
meant snake to draw   to slight slide to it
cuss snow car crust   (drainage, Albany)   rubble
can in sincerity   (lumps, jeers)
bent nose ends fires   (mattress, Iron)
      Jersey, Jersey (16)

If sound is leading Coolidge into the words, the sense is not far behind. The word stock of the above passage is consistently "American Industrial," a vocabulary of castoffs and slag heaps that might be typical of visual artists like Rauschenberg, Johns, and later, Smithson. The listing "jars jars jars" gives an immediately cultural component to the rhythmic drive—one could also have "cars cars cars" or "bars bars bars" and be giving a good picture of what actually follows, "Jersey, Jersey." The scenario in these works is quite different from the more abstract compositional plane of Ashbery—it is the practical, object-oriented, American cultural desert that Coolidge is trying to beat into life. The identification with Kerouac, in a form quite different from the spontaneous sketching of *Visions of Cody*, is still marked. A new value is being given to "calling up things by their names" in the willful drive of the sound. This syntax is certainly far from that asserted on the dust jacket, where "syntax . . . is simply removed."

Words in Coolidge are cultural facts, rhythmic and semantic imponderables. There are, in real time and space, whole landscapes of such imponderables; they stare one in the face with artifice and inertness, as in Las Vegas. No cultural nationalist, however, Coolidge is not tied down to any simplistic tagging of his materials. The America of his word stock is assumed, leaving open more universal questions as the ontology and psychology of such language. From the development of work in *Space* (which may not be chronological), Coolidge appears to be increasingly drawn to a scrutiny of words, to questions of their ultimate nature. The third section moves away from the more extended works, which still appear to be bounded by the single page frame of the conventional lyric, to constructions that deliberate over weights and balances of words in highly delimited arrangements. Words are not being given "object status" here; rather, they are being questioned in terms of their relations with other words. One such poem, quoted in full:

> ounce code orange
> a
>   the
>   ohm
> trilobite trilobites (68)

Coolidge discusses his motivation in this work in the following terms: "I couldn't stand the idea of one word. I don't think there is one word. . . . I was really trying to work with the words, look at the words, try to use all their qualities. There's no question of meaning, in the sense of explaining and understanding this poem. Hopefully, it's a unique object, not just an object. Language isn't just objects, it moves."[4]

The power of words is not in their status as objects but in their relation to each other. This concern, which runs deep in Coolidge's work, is also stated in an earlier interview: "That's like my idea about arrangement . . . an old alchemical notion that if you take objects, like the objects on this table, any objects, and arrange them in the correct order, that some incredible shift, or something, would happen. Something would be affected. Like the power is in the arrangement not in the objects."[5] It is the arrangement of words that unlocks their energies, drives the temporal event. But if words are like objects in an arrangement, there is still a question, for Coolidge, of particular qualities of these entities motivating their possible arrangements. His attention to words is to their differential status on a number of linguistic levels that qualify their use in combination:

> "ohm" is the unit of electrical resistance, a quality of metal, let's say, that requires a certain amount of juice to go through. In other words, this is a fuzzy, resistant word. . . . "trilobites": you know what a trilobite is, it's an early animal of the Paleozoic Age that was a crustacean divided into three lobes. As a word to me it's completely irreducible. What are you going to do with it? "A trilobite": it's like a clinker. ("Arrangement")

Here Coolidge looks into the word—it is not just a question of surface characteristics. The meditation on semantics is enacted in the way the words are placed on the page.

This meditation on semantics can be seen even in those works that use entities below the level of the word, in Coolidge's case morphemes such as "ed," "ing," "tion," and so on. The following is from the last page of "A D," the last work in *Space*:

erything
eral
stantly
ined
ards
cal
nize   (120)

These morphemes become words, motivated by their (vertical, sequential) arrangement to the same possibilities of statement. Each is a whole, and like "trilobites" they are irreducible "clinkers."

Possibly Coolidge's most famed investigation into the possibilities of arrangement is in a work published as a separate pamphlet, *Suite V.* The poems in this work are composed of two words per 8 1/2-by-11-inch page, placed at the top and bottom, with plenty of white space in between. All the words are four-lettered, and all have an *s* at the end. Some of these minimal pairs are: "taps / / buns," "keys / / ohms," "cans / / arms," and so on.[6] The amount of space between the words is significant—there is a palpable time-lag between them. The page is being used to specify an interval in time. The temporal gap here induces a certain energy between the words, similar to that of Pierre Reverdy's "light of the image" produced by the pairing of unrelated verbal images, though without particular attention to time. Coolidge has also explored this semantic potential energy gap in a work involving tape loops, in which two loops at different speeds are phased in and out with each other and the phase interaction is recorded. The words on the two tape loops can be heard as two separate words at their maximum temporal spread, or as a phrase of some kind when occurring close to each other in time. The question is when and under what conditions this phrase linkage will occur and what kind of energy will be produced. The phenomenology of syntax is being considered quite literally here, though it should be remembered that Coolidge is listening to the energy of the statement as a compositional possibility for his work.

This analytic interest in the potential energies of words in arrangements is equaled by an expressive impulse in Coolidge that reflects his reading of Kerouac. The opposite of the technical, this identification is cultural (New England) as well as stylistic ("spontaneous bop prosody"). Coolidge's contribution to *The World*'s "Autobiography" issue begins:

let's chug it up to Diamond . . . maybe or Calumet . . . Jesus, Calumet in the
dark? . . . or go climb the Geofort . . . naw, you crazy? we'll get snagged in
our basement coats . . . shit on the fucking around we gotta go . . . well,
Ray, you know, if we go, we'll end up with your a——s on fire . . . well
actually, . . . if you light . . . my ass . . . on fire . . . those guys in the project
put their lights'll always go on . . . let's go . . . maybe we can practice to shit
off the edge a thousand feet & then the beercans . . . Jesus Ray, remember
that time we were goin up in the dark & you got around above somewhere
somehow & pushed a huge fucking block loose & down past us? . . . saw the
blue sparks . . . Jesus, you really scared the shit out of us . . . Dave . . .
HA-HA! HA-HA![7]

The spontaneous verbalizing here has an adolescent character; names
and dates on granite in white paint are a similar graphemic response to
the New England mentality. The "mouthing off" in this piece seems to
be a linguistic "carrier frequency" that can go on indefinitely. In Kerouac
an echo of this kind of verbalizing produced a breakthrough in prose,
one that is very much on Coolidge's mind:

> I was thinking of those long, long sentences [in Kerouac] where he's doing
> what he calls sketching. He might literally be in front of the subject, or it
> might be in his mind. It might be a brick wall, or that incredible section
> of the food in the windows, or the cafeteria section in the beginning of
> Visions of Cody. Where it goes on for endless pages. It's this beautiful line, it's
> always changing. Things'll just pop up, and you can see that he didn't think
> of that. It just came, because he was following this line, what's next, what's
> next.[8]

As opposed to the possibilities of combination and recombination
Coolidge sees in arrangement, this mode of writing is not reducible to
components. Coolidge is interested here in the vectoral potentials of
work on a single scale—that of the writer in time. In this sense writing
is self-sufficient, a "pure product of America," adequate in itself.

In work that appeared after the publication of Space, Coolidge moves
away from the conventional page frame of the lyric poem into longer
forms. The Maintains builds a 100-page poem from language taken from
the dictionary (and possibly other sources). The breakthrough in this
work is Coolidge's use of an "equivalency principle" in the line that demands a larger form. The syntax of statement in the poem is not only
word-to-word (as in "jars   jars   jars") but line-to-line:

the canna seats
a shine-hard common

so-called boat tooth of like shape
from the rolls
on which hue a saturation is secured
as a candle about the mouth
mosquito cans stated limes
recorded off the bark or mummy
overhang to sing
a fine coal
or book list of good mass or omen
mustard simple
uses clot in another machines
pie star sliding
a perpetual vow[9]

There is a metalinguistic architecture, derived from the dictionary definition, behind every line. Each line could be a definition of the line previous, and they all might be understood as definitions of "word." A "shine-hard common" could be a definition of "canna seats," with the advantages of ambiguity ("seats" is a noun or a verb) and a synaesthetic image in "shine-hard seats." The play of language is built on the structure of the line. It is possible to see each line as commenting on the one above or as an independent arrangement. The poem continually argues this edge between self-sufficiency and connection. Individual words or phrases may stand out as entities, but they are motivated by their sequence. Language is being proposed as a relation between words— ironically or perhaps didactically, as the dictionary is the source of that language.

The structural concerns of The Maintains are developed in the course of Coolidge's next 100-page poem, Polaroid. The "nounal" emphasis of the line is undermined, first by the use of nonsubstantives and then by the breaking up of the line's accretive "equivalence principle." The last section of the poem is a kind of synthesis of these developments; a new line has been produced in the process, one that increases the ambiguities of syntax as it allows for greater rhythmic variation:

few part once and then one as around leaves close stays then
    some
of you few head so forth by whom why leave either to go
part and it leaves once you then some do you within stays
    behind
either few or just some once of either leaving miss it to
    close to it beside

the either one or it you part per whom via either one or
few do stay once it's close to you missing the whole either one[10]

The phrase structure of these lines could be bracketed in numerous
ways; "few do stay once it's close" could be, at least: (few do) (stay
once) (it's close); (few do stay) (once it's close); (few do stay once) (it's
close); and (few do) (stay once it's close). In addition, each word could
be given temporal autonomy, as in a list. The possibilities for variation
of stress in reading the work, given these multiple bracketings, are
enormous. Where the bracketing of the line in *The Maintains* is reinforced
by the dictionary definition, in *Polaroid* the bracketing is plural, reflecting
the multiple elliptical constructions of American English (a structure
much more complex than its dictionary). Here there is what Williams
called a "buckling" of syntax; words snap in and out of different combinations in a line. The rhythmic play is much more various than in the
simple reiterative structure of *The Maintains*.

In Coolidge's work after *Polaroid* words are not only used for their potential energies in possible arrangements but point simultaneously to
other contexts in the world or in the mind. This expansion of scale parallels a shift in technique from the lyric frame to long verse structures
in accretive lines to a mode that Coolidge has designated as "prosoid":
an extended, dense, lyric prose form that has past examples in Williams's
Kora in Hell, Stein's *The Making of Americans*, surrealist automatic texts, and,
more contemporary, Robert Creeley's *Presences*. One such work is "Smithsonian Depositions," based on Smithson's writings as well as on numerous other sources such as:

William Carlos Williams: The Selected Letters; Paterson
Jean-Luc Godard: Pierrot Mon Ami; Les Carabiniers
Alain Robbe-Grillet: Last Year at Marienbad
Salvador Dali: The Secret Life of Salvador Dali
Joseph Le Conte: Elements of Geology . . . [11]

as well as journals and newspaper clippings. Content is layered in the
work in a "geological" manner, inspired by the "language as matter"
formulation of Smithson's work. The text is evocative of the strata of the
linguistic bedrock, the reality of which is psychological (memory) as
well as cultural (historical time), while still maintaining Coolidge's basic writing values as "spontaneous bop prosodist."

Coolidge's breakthrough work in the "prosoid" form, *Quartz Hearts*, is
in fact a preparatory study for his still untitled "longwork." "It is in
every sense a hinge work," begun during writing of the last section of
Polaroid. The work is densely argued, involving a querying of the words

as they are being produced to make sentences. Statements exist as words
and in their "other," referential contexts:

He walked up and knocked at the front.
His shoe was the same color as the step.

The car had an open top that he never
looked out of as he drove straight
ahead. An iron mushroom.

Walking up close to the wall, I felt
the heat from above, and heard the
horn below the floor.

A black tree on a purple shoulder.
The sock hidden in the stump. Pliers
in a room beneath a wind across a valley.[12]

The balance of words within a sentence, again an arrangement, is as
much the subject matter here as what the sentences actually say. But possibly there really *were* "Pliers in a room beneath a wind across a valley."

There was a block on the door.
The handle turned out to be square.

Little women sending postcards from a
donut factory. They swim toward the
end of the land. An opening gradually
presents itself and arrives.

The work seems to be arguing inward, starting from simple, if ironic,
units of statement in language. There is a metalinguistic underpinning
that is being used to fabricate the context for the next statement, as in
"An opening gradually presents itself and arrives." Reference builds
structure into statement by virtue of a querying of its essential purposes.

Only sections of the "longwork" have been published as yet, so it is
difficult at this point to have an accurate sense of it as a whole. Initially
intended to go to 1,000 pages, Coolidge read the first 200 pages over
seven nights at Eighty Langton Street, San Francisco, in 1979.[13] It is generally understood to be based on a limited number of subject areas, such
as geology, the movies, the music of Ives, the writings of Beckett and
Creeley, and so on. These are the sources for language materials to be
used in the work. There are "topic" sections, in which one particular

subject is developed, and "transitional" sections, between subject areas. Medial spaces between areas of language are being "bred," much as in the "geological" interaction of materials in "Smithsonian Depositions," and the work undertakes a large-scale assimilation of related language (taken in at the point of writing, from more "daily" frames) in its development. The steady force of construction is in a constitutive voice, a kind of "verbalizing" carrier frequency generally located "in back of" the utterances of speech (or conventional lyric poetry), a foregrounding of the involuntary memory. The weight of the linguistic materials is balanced in multiple "buckling" prosoid lines. The work mimics an assertion of the self-evident world in a highly elaborate cross-referencing of multiple arrangements. Within the work there is a constant play of unusual "light of the image" between the variously juxtaposed arrangements of words. In this created world there are endlessly refracted interstices, shadows of words creating space for new words in the shadows. In real time and space, the voice in the work intends a present: "What moves can make space," as Coolidge said in writing of Larry Eigner. Physical space is being carved out of linguistic space by means of vectors through the combinatorial potentials of the American word stock. The work is presented as an unanalyzable, though completely refracted, whole.

There is, in this work, a definite monumentality. Unlike the Spiral Jetty, the monument is temporal, not spatial, but perhaps it does approach an "object status." Coolidge's gesture after reading the work— prior to any discussion—was simply to place its two volumes on the table between the writer and his audience: "Here it is." However, the work has not yet been named. From "Weathers," a section of the work:

> Slipping from, tell me, this is a star and that a fin. That bottle keeps its
> blink on its side red from horizon. He left it to sun in the hard, black is
> not black it's night. State of Cadmium set in stint. This is blurring not what
> could be said from a table to be a ledge. Where, losing firm, is the percola-
> tor or perimeter. Thus and so, parts of a limb on a walk, of a bird, myself
> or have I thought myself febrile.[14]

The writer appears to be out in the "welter of forms of these events," the events being writing first of all but mimicking a condition as all-encompassing as the weather. Journals kept of weather phenomena were the basis for this section, but observations of "daily life" and the weather are functionally close at the level of words. The need to repair the typewriter, the word "Cadmium," and a dark lowering cloud at 4

P.M. are equivalent terms of the work. A more strictly literary area of language is explored in another section:

> Caught an eryops. The sander says misericordia. Coronal of thicket plums. A stanchion of much aisle, even, though wooden. Blending stonelight with cornhusker's cellmate. Left themselves open to the announcement none of these people died on time. Though Huxley's faith in Iguanodon's bipedality was totally vindicated in 1878 when an entire troupe of iguanodonts emerged from a coal mine in Belgium, the fissure filled with Cretaceous marls. As the thought to tower an erect beast, an enigma remains itself a plural impasse.

"Eryops" is a word from Smithson, though it segues back to its geological home to meet "an entire troupe of iguanodonts." There are other such delimited zones of vocabulary ("misericordia," "cornhusker"), along with a running comment that is the compositional drive of the work: "an enigma remains itself a plural impasse."

Coolidge is not forthcoming on his techniques, but I imagine a writing scenario as follows: words or materials (open books, clippings) are on a table next to a typewriter. Some of these materials might be past pages of the work. The writing is a spontaneous invention starting from these "exterior" materials, and the argument of the work that develops is a projection of the interior voice onto exterior words within a specific temporal frame. This argument is both associative (words lead to arrangements in terms of linguistic affinity and memory traces of their prior use) and dissociative (sequence is used to disrupt habitual patterns of thought). The exterior vocabulary is the cue for both the association and the dissociation—it can lead into a new arrangement, or it can introduce a dissonance that disrupts an arrangement. The "light of the image" that is being given off by these arrangements is an object of meditation as the work progresses, although it is primarily sound, as rhythmic variation being driven by subliminal verbalizing, that is leading the writing from word to word.

The concerns of this work have much to do with surrealist automatism, though for Coolidge any such "pure psychic automatism" is coincident with words as objects—perhaps literally, in front of him on the writing table. The incorporation of purely literary information, such as the Huxley anecdote above, is evidence of this without any confirmation from the author. The vocabulary in the work is not limited to the word stock of surrealism, with its basically interior and organic scenarios, which often seem overly delimited by the past example of Lautréamont.

The surrealists excluded large sections of language as quotidian, and certainly words *as words* had no status for them. The sign is united with its object—there can be no dissociation at this level of language; once used in the writing process, a word or an image is used up. In Coolidge's work the sign is a multiple and possibly exterior reality, and words like "thus and so" have the status of substantives in the work. The relation to language is evaluative as opposed to convulsive—there is a "thinking with things as they exist" as much as any flux of the automatic image. Other aspects of the phenomenology of language than the irruption of the pleasure principle are primary—namely, the axis of memory and the associative contiguities of words. The word *iguanodon*, established in a brief narrative, may have a continuing life in the work, and it is given a value in contiguous strata (in "eryops" above). Any word in the text can become the enigma of the plural impasse; the act of writing is the continual querying of these impasses by words.

The status of involuntary memory is quite different in Coolidge than in surrealism. In surrealism, the involuntary memory is to some extent theoretical—it gives a value for the automatic image; but in actual practice the work is voluntary and literary—the language of automatism is bounded by fixed parameters of style. Surrealist automatic images often seem to be "exemplary" of the possibilities of automatism—there was no need for the investigation of the automatic impulse on a large (say, 1,000-page) scale. This fixity of the surrealist image is the principal defect in its claims for "pure psychic automatism," rendering the project only partially successful in terms of psychology. But in literary terms, the use of the automatic image as a philosopher's stone leads to its success—the more developed formulations of Breton's theoretical works and of *Nadja*.

In Coolidge, involuntary memory is taken on directly. The improvisatory mode of writing has access to the vectors of subjectivity precisely because its initial objects—words—are conceived of as exterior to the writer, to be taken on in the ongoing construction of the work. The scale of Coolidge's improvisatory mode is very large in terms of the language and states of mind it can reach; the position of the writer, however, is fixed—there is no travel to the Yucatan, even with mirrors. Writing is a daily task, and the temporal demands of the work are a part of its argument with existence. Language is no philosopher's stone for Coolidge—any theoretical extension of the project is blocked at the "point of production." Coolidge declines to make a metaphor of his work; the querying of language by language in time is the method.

The work is driven into its particulars by this refusal of metaphorical scale. Where Smithson proposes the scale of his work as a metaphor for art, Coolidge holds back from such structural metaphors. The question of overall form is therefore problematic. Where earlier works such as *The Maintains* and *Polaroid* coincide at least with temporal frames (they are each one year's writing), the time frame of the "longwork" is open-ended, and it is unclear what it would mean for it to end. Perhaps the only developing structural metaphor in Coolidge's work is that of the romantic subject, certainly an unwieldy figure to maintain.

But Coolidge's syntax is not to be understood only in its temporal sequence. There is a "spatial" syntax of the work as well. The writing continually foregrounds language as its primary reality in the uninterrupted refractions of the form. In the extended time frame of the work, a word at any moment must stand for the whole. Starting from these particulars, the work has a point-by-point structural basis in *metonymy*. In a standard example of metonymy "Moscow" stands for the system of government located there. One can say, "Go ahead, Moscow, I'm listening," but Coolidge would substitute the word *word* there instead: "Go ahead, *word*, I'm listening," in a device to be found everywhere in his work. The various linguistic levels—word, line, phrase, sentence, paragraph—are all structural metonyms for "language" and, ultimately, for "the writer in time." By means of this continual metonymy, the large-scale forms of Coolidge's work, and whatever metaphorical meaning they might have, are argued in the work at numerous levels of language.

For example, in the early lyrics the status of words as American imponderables is a metonym for the actual "state of the art." These atomized "associative contiguities" are inspired by similar values for individual words in Kerouac's sketching. The dictionary definition of *The Maintains* offers a metonym at another linguistic level; the definiendum is the "part" to the "whole" of the semantic component in language, which is ironically addressed. In the long line of *Polaroid*, the shifting brackets of phrase structure are a metonym for the "indeterminacy" of the whole. In *Quartz Hearts*, the sentence is a metonym for the act of writing, and the "prosoid" paragraph is a metonym for the time frame of the entire work. In the "longwork" the shifting line of the improvisation stands in a part/whole relation to the fixed position of the writer. In each of these works, in addition, the word-to-word argument is a metonym for structure at each point in time. "Iguanodon" is a partial assertion of the possibility of naming; when iguanodonts march out of the cave's mouth, they can only be ironic. Any such acts are never more than accidents of parts that interact with each other within the totalizing whole.

Smithson's work invokes a stopped, ironic time, to extend the scale of the work. For a similar reason, the time of the work in Coolidge wants never to end. Its "association by contiguity" is unrestricted; language can only be a metonym for the writer in time. The possibility of naming is inferred, but nothing other than that is actually named. This holding back gives a kind of timelessness to the writer's act in time—all energy of statement is potential. A deferred approach to the world motivates the expansion of scale. Coolidge's time frame approaches the literal, while the work stands apart.

The querying of the status of the "other" is a central motive in the work of Ron Silliman and Steve Benson. "A bus ride is better than most art"—a total syntax is not limited to art but extends into larger structures. The paradigm of art or the position of the writer establishes not a hierarchy of forms but one perspective among many. In order to call into question the "other" it is necessary to call into question both the self and the work.

The point of departure in Ron Silliman's work is an analogy between the structures of the text and of the world. Here structure is not an abstraction; it must show itself in concrete terms if it is to exist at all. All the possibilities of language are contiguous with all the structures of the world. The argument of such a poetics demands an exact attention to the values of scale in any representation.

How are structures of the world to be approached? According to The Chicago Manual of Style: "The semicolon is used to make a more important break in the sentence flow than that marked by a comma. Use the semicolon between the two parts of a compound sentence when they are not connected by a conjunction: The controversial portrait was removed from the entrance hall; in its place was hung a realistic landscape."[15]

Here there is a proposition in two parts: a description of a structure followed by an example of its use. In terms of art, the one motivates the other to make both the semicolon and the sentence perceptible in a way that they would not normally be. The temporal sequence of "controversial portrait" to "realistic landscape" is given a value in the sentence that is precise—accounting for appearances in a way that a single representation would not. The repesentation is no longer automatic, and the perception of its components is enhanced. This juxtaposition of descriptions with examples of structure is a tactic pursued throughout the course of Silliman's work. It is often unclear which is the description and which is the example—both are equally motivated. Scale is not as polarized in terms of a single trope as it is in Smithson and Coolidge but is multiple and ambiguous.

Silliman's works are investigations of a variable scale—as opposed to the more determinate though expanded scales of Smithson and Coolidge. In a note on Silliman's writing in L=A=N=G=U=A=G=E, I gave an account of this variable scale in terms of the mathematical concept of "fractals":

> An article in the April issue of *Scientific American* on mathematically generated music refers to "fractal curves," which show the same fluctuating patterns over time for any duration. Ten minutes of event would have the same ratio of peaks to troughs as ten years, but "the fractals that occur in nature—coastlines, rivers, trees, star clustering, clouds and so on—are so irregular that their self-similarity (scaling) must be treated statistically." In language self-similarity (statement) is irregular and constant while words can shift scale. Kid says, "You die!"—not having the same outcome as in the movies or in war. But the words in each case point an abstract finger to exert will. Imagination, thinking build on these facts of natural language: "The so-called idea of the word . . . is the so-called *word itself—the word*."[16]

The notion of a "self-similarity" of statement here is difficult and must be demonstrated to be understood. Silliman's early work *Mohawk* seems now to be such a demonstration—in it Silliman investigates the possibilities of a textually determined "self-similarity" of statement in a word stock limited to a fixed set of words, generally monosyllabic nouns, over a range of thirty pages. The work is both asymmetrical and precise in the range of variation possible; given the initial terms (words like *wet, loom, star, wicker, silt*), the constructed work is a determination of their potential—and limits—as structure. The individual words have a precise value as "units," with image and sound values in a kind of balance, that permits repetition and interaction up to an exact point. The relation between the values of the words and the completed statement is a paradigm of scale. It is at the scale of the entire work only that the "self-similarity" of this set of words is achieved.

In Silliman's book-length works, *Ketjak* and *Tjanting*, the sentence rather than the word is the unit of investigation into scale. Materials from the world at large are taken in and integrated into the ongoing construction; they are given an initial scale in the form of the sentence, but otherwise their origins are diverse. Descriptive writing, journal prose, overheard remarks, media hype, complicated puns, examples of language as language, fragments of ideology are all possible areas in the work. Each isolated sentence has a simultaneous value as both description and example of structure—and the argument of the work is the interanimation of this relation as it develops. Logical, narrative, or simply accretive orders build up and break down in complex displays. The scale of the work is an argument of the status of "other" as it can be determined by its possible representations in language. It would be only partial to follow any of the unitary syntaxes of statement (logical, narrative, or accretive)—rather, the "self-similarity" of statement must be established on a larger scale—tending toward more open limits, the scale of the world.

In *Ketjak*, written in 1974, there is a self-conscious structure of devices, most notably the "doubling" of paragraph units in the text.[17] There is at all points in the work a question of whether a sentence has occurred in the text before or is a new element; this provides a kind of continuous underlining of statement, very close to the motivation of description and example above. The work keeps opening up to admit more, but there is simultaneously a reiteration that is occurring parallel in time. The scale of the whole can only extend through the device of doubling up to a certain limit—the point at which it no longer can be perceived. This limit determines the length of the text.

In *Tjanting*, written from 1977 to 1980, there is a greater atomization of devices—sentences may come back, but they do so unexpectedly and in much more radically altered forms, like cryptic art messages in a bottle.[18] Rather than relying on a device as mechanical as the doubling in *Ketjak*, Silliman is ready to let the words themselves do the work—although there is a complicated system of counting underlying the text that is not readily apparent. The structural basis is more transparent, and for this reason the scale of "self-similarity" in *Tjanting* is increased.

Not this. Outward momentum presses down. Several tiny cuts on his upper lip. Watch waiters. Two Yankees, two out, too late. The beds in motel rooms are disproportionately large, high up off the floor. Small white plastic fork whose handle ends in the figure of "golden" arches. Self forcing to one it. The distinction between crayons & small cigars. Less croations are rested. Blue sweater forgotten on a red chair. Read into reading. Residue of watercress netted in sink's drain. Between slices, a hill of fog. Hands never completely dry. It would be with a new blue pen. Light wars. Not wanted is not not-wanted. Kitsums. Than what? Body remembers what brain forgets. This knot. Officer off-duty. Self given to one it. Sees bra strap thru blouse. Time laps catches sky. See's candies. Around town find roads. In the shade flowers fade. Gray cirrus roils deep. The even weave of freeways. Of about to under to—within to which of what—without into by of by. Patterns of wire in library windows. Wind bent the palm. In the distance red hills where the sun has yet to set. Flesh gathers in folds at the elbows as one grows older. As city darkens, lights appear. War replays pyrotechnics. (25)

The scale of the inconsequential is marked here. Silliman's insistence on the unheroic particulars is reminiscent of Williams's techniques in poems like "Proletarian Portrait"—where the "nonaesthetic" observed detail is the key to social insight, the opposite of the heroic aggrandizement of the social realism of the time. But in Williams this distance conveys a certain fatality—the inconsequential is dramatized as a single moment of truth that is also ironic, while in Silliman its use is in a much more radical, ongoing process of evaluation. For example, "Small white plastic fork whose handle ends in the figure of 'golden' arches" is a moment of truth that comments exactly on larger social forms. Monopoly capitalism will produce many such forks, but there can be only one in the poem, leaving aside the question of the other ten million. For Silliman, any such moment indicates a multiplicity of relations— the only solution for the poem is to keep going, to argue the work into a lived present that can take such multiplicity into account.

The motivation of this question of scale is not only formal; there is an ethical value being given to the particulars that are taken in. In the last paragraph of my note on Silliman's work I conclude: "Only someone who had thought intensely about the fate of other people's lives could have written *Ketjak*. . . . To imagine another life without power gives value to the fact. Identity is all that literary politics can produce. . . . Identity in Silliman's work is open-ended."

Identity as a literary project can be given a political value in the proletarian literature of the 1930s. The use of dissonance, disjunction in Williams's work of the period is partly its critique. But the identity involved in Williams's project is still that of a professional insisting on the facts (and the diagnosis and prognosis) of the case. There is no such professional distance in Silliman but rather a relation of complicity between the writer and the facts. The argument of the poem is equally a criticism of the subject—Silliman admits his limits into the system as one source of observed detail among many.

This has a formal dimension; a criticism of the adequacy of statement is a basis for continuity in the work. In *Tjanting* sentences are pared down from previous models, rather than being built up. There is a constant "writerly" revision, an inwardness somewhat opposed to the orally expressive outwardness of the earlier *Ketjak*. Statement is necessarily partial—it can at any point be linguistically undermined. The poem progresses from "not this" and "what then?" to "this knot," "knot this," "not so," and "what exactly?" Other kinds of sentences go through similar permutations—from material taken in, to puns, to "language as language"—making the scale of statement ambiguous. The poem writes its way into the world by making use of this necessary partiality. It is the precedence of the facts of writing and of the world over the erring subject that motivates the text. The subject is continually corrected. Silliman solves the ethical dilemma of heroic identity and professional distance by giving priority to the object of these methods—the world as it can be perceived.

A partiality of representation is analogous to facts of the world that more aestheticized writing cannot perceive—the facts of necessity, work, deferred impulses, limits. These are conditions in which anyone lives, and the question is their transformation. Where Williams ironized these facts, in Silliman's poem they are given a more straightforward representation, along with a skeptical account of aesthetic options, as in "As city darkens, lights appear." The syntax of the poem is a dialogue between the scales of these facts; the transformation of the poem is its admission to the scale of the world. The argument compels a recognition. There is a mutuality of oneself and others as seen through the text, which is structurally democratic.

Though written, the syntax of these works has permitted their reading in public places outside the environments of art—*Ketjak*, at the corner of Powell and Market Streets, San Francisco, in 1978, and *Tjanting*, at the Church Street Muni Metro Station, San Francisco, in 1983.

A point of departure in Steve Benson's work is the uneasiness of the speaker. The manner as opposed to the matter of what can be said is the object of his address. Beginning with a lyrical expansiveness derived from the poetry of the New York School, Benson submits such lyricism to devices of estrangement, introducing dissonances of scale that call the speaker into account. Where in the discursive work of O'Hara and Ashbery there is a large-scale architecture of the speaking subject, Benson shifts the foundations of that architecture, partly breaking it down. From "Non-Events," a poem of twenty-five stanzas of five lines each:

> So it's a good play, who cares about the style, it's the
>   *idea* that counts.
> And Frederick found no chance to speak. N buried on,

Wasn't I only just saying like in the case of Praslin
Interruption by Hussonet
Look we've heard this a million times. Forget it.

Not as though the words were hard to make out in groups
but really in a reasonable and open way
as though he were telling just what happened
to a friend who made sense, whom he could let know
the most personal telling things he had to say.

He never had any intention of getting married at all!
Who so irresponsibly started these rumors up?
The same way, this story's been going around he was born
    with a tail.
That's so ridiculous, not to say indecent and disgusting,
that I know I don't have to try to disprove it to you.[19]

The poem alters the time of expectation, constantly getting in its way
and setting the events adrift by undermining their narrative basis. Each
of these stanzas is strangely autonomous, although they are contained
within the range of a single voice. The stanzas represent a fragmentation
of that voice into several voices. There is almost a roomful of autonomous characters in the poem; each is given a chance to speak and expose the strengths and weaknesses of his temperament and mood.

Though played out in multiple voices in "Non-Events," this calling
the speaker into question is the basis of Benson's more unitary later
work "Narcissus," a prose poem of twenty-eight parts:

I hardly say anything, just sit there reading. They look out, wave their little
hands from the drear red and green light emptying the sky from sun. The
fear others will see what's different in me, hold me to it, eats my mind.

The road bends round about here and wanders to meadow. One of us may
be nobody. I stand myself. Nobody the same as you remember them, yet
you go on, as if good hands held you in mind till child-murderers pass.

Coming down here, shattering and beaming isolate flecks, the movie
freezes. Stand for myself, carefully cutting and joining. I write everything
out in my head on long walks.

A camel bashes the line of vision across a white shed. I adore you.[20]

A number of the sentences seem to come from a kind of middle
ground—they are both assertive and reactive at the same time. This

middle ground could be the space of a relationship between persons, but in the poem it is unclear whether there are two persons or one. There is a *you* in the poem—"One of us may be nobody"—but in the middle of the address it tends to disappear as the other and return to the self—"Nobody the same as you remember them, yet you go on." Making the *you* into language can be a device of estrangement: "A camel bashes the line of vision across a white shed. I adore you," or later, "Put more sand in my pocket, or die." Hearing the work, it is unclear whether the poet is addressing an other or himself. The poem seems to be straining at a "capillary tissue" between the speaker's language and the *you*. This medial arena is not assumed but argued in the terms of the work. The language of the speaker is looking at itself, and it is not sure what it sees. Intentionality of statement is made multiple and ambiguous by a constant reference to itself.

Benson's performance work is notable for its mixing of different levels of intentionality.[21] In "Views of Communist China," the narrative illusionism of the citizen, Mr. Chen, is acted out in a staged setting, followed by a tour of Benson's apartment, which has been relocated in the performance space. The presentation of the tour guide is acted out as a kind of ultraspeculative trivialism in real time, but it is first of all given a value in the shifted foundations of the illusionistic sets. Perhaps life in real time exists permanently on such shifted foundations for Benson. In another performance work, verbal improvisations are integrated into a reading of the poem "Echo," and the results are recorded on tape and played back, forming the basis for further improvisations. The argument of the work is being invented and undermined at the same time. In Benson's performance "Blindspots," the performer acts out a continually reflexive encounter with his language, trying to hear what it is saying and respond verbally at all points. The total self-involvement can only undermine its own authority; the other is rendered intact, but it is simultaneously the speaking subject that is the other. Benson's work casts the shadows of lyrical self-consciousness in Ashbery and O'Hara into the light of public discourse. The self-consciousness becomes virtually utilitarian as a result.

Benson's language is formed on the ambiguous edge between attack and retreat, which are being acted out in a role-playing manner. The structure of identity is being exploded in the form of a three-dimensional literary method in which the borders of personality, of self and nonself, are being argued as simultaneous and conflicting modes of expression. That this is being done in public locates the writer on a new and expanded scale.

1. As originally published in *Total Syntax* (Carbondale: Southern Illinois University Press, 1985), the essay began with a discussion of the work of sculptor Robert Smithson.

2. André Breton, *Nadja*, trans. Richard Howard (New York: Grove Press, 1960), 16.

3. Clark Coolidge, *Space* (New York: Harper and Row, 1970), 4.

4. Clark Coolidge, "Arrangement," in *Talking Poetics from Naropa Institute*, vol. 1; quoted in L=A=N=G=U=A=G=E 2.2 (1979).

5. Barrett Watten, "Conversation with Clark Coolidge," *This* 4 (1973).

6. Clark Coolidge, *Suite V* (New York: Adventures in Poetry, 1973).

7. Clark Coolidge, "Room for Three Guys," *World* 28 (1973): 10.

8. Barrett Watten, "Conversation with Clark Coolidge," in "A Symposium on Clark Coolidge," ed. Ron Silliman, *Stations* 5 (1978): 11–14.

9. Clark Coolidge, *The Maintains* (San Francisco: This Press, 1974), 20.

10. Clark Coolidge, *Polaroid* (New York and Bolinas, Calif.: Adventures in Poetry and Big Sky, 1975), 92.

11. Clark Coolidge, *Smithsonian Depositions & Subject to a Film* (New York: Vehicle Editions, 1980), 44.

12. Clark Coolidge, *Quartz Hearts* (San Francisco: This Press, 1978), 4–6.

13. Sections of the work have appeared in *This* 6 and 10, *United Artists* 6, and *Big Sky* 10.

14. Clark Coolidge, "Weathers," section 22, *United Artists* 6 (1979).

15. *The Chicago Manual of Style*, 12th ed. (Chicago: University of Chicago Press, 1976), 117.

16. Barrett Watten, "Mohawk and Ketjak," L=A=N=G=U=A=G=E 1.4 (1978).

17. Ron Silliman, *Ketjak* (San Francisco: This Press, 1978).

18. Ron Silliman, *Tjanting* (Great Barrington, Mass.: The Figures, 1981).

19. "Non-Events," in *As Is* (Great Barrington, Mass.: The Figures, 1978), 63–64.

20. Steve Benson, "Narcissus," in *Blindspots* (Cambridge: Whalecloth, 1981), 57–58.

21. For transcripts of some of these performances, see "Views of Communist China," in *Hills/Talks*, ed. Bob Perelman (published as *Hills* 6/7 [1980]), as well as "Blindspots" and "Echo" in *Blindspots*.

"*Skewed by Design*":
       From *Act* to *Speech Act* in Language Writing
       Michael Davidson

The gestural potential of language occupies a privileged position in modern poetry, but since World War II it has witnessed two distinct treatments. The first stems from expressivist aesthetics derived from Romanticism and the second from a range of linguistic theories that would include Russian formalism, speech act theory, and the dramatistic rhetoric of Kenneth Burke. Although both treatments share a common concern for the materiality of language—its physical presence on the page or in the voice—they differ widely on the ends that this materiality must serve. I would like to explore that difference, using *gesture* as an operative term for what poetry *is* as an aesthetic entity and what it *does* as a socially significant act.

In the painterly aesthetics of the late 1940s and early 1950s, the term *gesture* had a rich and varied application. At one level it referred to the painter's physical stroke on the canvas—the record of specific physical actions on a flat, two-dimensional surface. At another level, the uniqueness of that stroke embodied the painter's individual signature, the stylistic mark by which originality and authenticity could be measured. Harold Rosenberg's use of the phrase "action painting," his description of the canvas as an "arena in which to act," provided the major critical terms not only for abstract painting but for a wide range of cultural forms—from poetry and music to theater and happenings. To some extent, these terms gained a further philosophical valence through their implicit reference to existentialist ideals of engagement and commitment. By treating the canvas as an event *within* the world rather than a representation *of* it, the painter signaled levels of personal freedom in a world marked by increasingly alienating social institutions.

Poets of this generation appropriated many of these same physical metaphors (energy, action, gesture) in their quest for a poetics of unmediated statement. Charles Olson's emphasis on "breath," Robert Duncan's physiological and biological poetics, Michael McClure's "beast" language and Beat "bop" prosody are only some examples of a poetics for which muscular and physical response is valued over reflective or discursive moments. The most direct statement of this position is Olson's essay, "Human Universe," which argues that "habits of thought are the habits of action" and that art "does not seek to describe but to enact."[1] For Olson, Western thought has been dominated by a reflective metaphysics in which language has become "the act of thought about the instant" rather than "the act of the instant." Olson and other poets of his generation hoped to defeat such reflectiveness by restoring the physiology of the poet's breath, musculature, movement in the composition process.

If one wanted to discover a change between the New American Poetry of the 1950s and 1960s and that which it spawned in the 1970s and 1980s, one could usefully speak of the latter's revision of the term *gesture*, now used to describe the speech act rather than the act of speech. Whereas gesturality for the generation of Olson and Ginsberg implied single expressive moments, recorded spontaneously on the page and realized in oral performance, for writers of a more recent generation gesture refers to the interactive, social web in which language exists. This is particularly the case with Language writing that offers the most thorough critique of expressivism in postwar writing, even while it builds upon the earlier generation's stress on poetic materiality.

The form that this critique takes involves an emphasis on relationships between poem and reader for which speech act theory offers a set of useful descriptive tools. Without rehearsing well-known features of speech act theory, let me at least emphasize several aspects that pertain to our topic. Speech acts (or what Wittgenstein calls language games) define utterances in terms of their pragmatics, the relationships established between addressor and addressee. These relationships are rule-governed, bound by laws of appropriateness and acceptability. The ability of any recipient to respond to an utterance depends on the fulfillment of what John Searle calls "appropriateness" and J. L. Austin calls "felicity criteria."[2] The effectiveness of a command depends on there being someone to carry it out; a question assumes a respondent capable of answering. These positional relations in discourse situate individuals in relation not only to each other but to the ideological formations that every utterance assumes—and serves. Speech act theory, with few exceptions, has been silent on the ideological basis of pragmatics, but the poets with whom we are concerned have made this issue central to their poetics.[3]

By saying that recent writers foreground the pragmatics of speech acts, I do not mean that they invent new ones (one cannot single-handedly "invent" unique speech acts any more than one can invent a new language) or that they necessarily deform those that already exist. Rather,

Language writing seizes upon the framing operations that situate speakers within specific social discourse situations. When Lyn Hejinian repeats a series of quaint adages about women ("pretty is as pretty does") within her long autobiographical work, *My Life*, she underscores both the sexist implications of such remarks and the role that such truisms play in the production of a female subject. The same could be said for Bob Perelman's *Face Value*, which employs the rhetoric of enumeration and description to embody the ways that consumer society transforms individuals into products: "There is a store, it is an individual / like you, me, a body, corporate." Or consider the following passage from Ron Silliman's *Sunset Debris*, a thirty-page poem made up entirely of questions:

> Do you feel compelled to defend the position? Do you eat meat? Were those pelicans? Does it embarrass you? Will these clothes ever be the same again? Does the flow of traffic deceive you, taking on the texture of natural process? Is it straight yet? . . . Are you listening? Is everybody happy? How can you keep your stories straight? What are the limits of large? Who do you trust?[4]

By eliminating the interlocutor's response, Silliman also eliminates the dialogical aspect of interrogatives, injecting them with a level of threat and violence. In such work, foregrounding the linguistic medium coincides with a speculation about the social relations that this medium upholds. When questions have no function other than to interrogate, they begin to act *on* rather than *between* the individuals using them.

The speech act that most dramatically exemplifies language's ability to act on others is the performative.[5] Such utterances (promises, oaths, declarations, wagers) are characterized by their ability to put into motion what they announce. When a judge declares a couple husband and wife or when a ship's captain christens a ship, the utterance actually *performs* the declarative or contractual function. The appropriateness criterion for a performative pertains to legal sanction as much as to the fulfillment of a verbal contract: the person making the contract of marriage must be legally empowered to do so; the recipients of the performative must be in a position to receive it (i.e., they must not be already married).

Many poems rely on the expressive force of the performative—the ability to use language to alter consciousness or defamiliarize—but they do so by claiming ontological priority rather than by acknowledging the pragmatic frame in which the utterance occurs. When Charles Olson, in *The Maximus Poems*, asserts, "I compell / backwards I compell

Gloucester / to yield, to / change," he attempts to give performative status to what is otherwise a simple assertion: "I compell." It is an expressive moment of great power, but unlike a performative, its authority is vested in the speaker's will and not in any official sanction. In fact, one could say that Olson attempts to demolish a polis based on such sanction by one created out of individual, idiosyncratic utterances. Polis, as Olson says elsewhere in the poem, is "eyes," a community of citizens constituted by their ability to see and witness.[6]

When Barrett Watten employs a performative gesture in his poem, *Progress*, the effect of assertion is quite different:

> I hereby christen
> This destroyer the *Rosebud*
> As the ape shows its teeth,
> Alternately smacking her lips. . . .
>
> In expression of the abstract,
> Sound
> A reading must be
> Above ground in the light
> Of heartbeats in the dark. . . .
>
> As parked cars turn on engines
> Simultaneously.
> McNamara,
> Johnson, Westmoreland, Rusk.
> The names are no pun intended. . . .
>
> A present dispersing its edges,
> But I call them Bald Eagles
> For lust,
> lusty and silly
> Happy and holy men and girls. . . .[7]

Here, the performative is bracketed as an official act, linked to other forms of power. The ceremonial act of christening a ship is performed not so much by a person as by an institution whose darker purpose is deflected through patriotic rituals of naming. Watten italicizes the "I" who performs the act in order to emphasize its arbitrary status as subject-position—very different from Olson's ontologically grounded speaker. In Watten's example, the pronoun stands for the appropriate official (or, more likely, official's wife), but the "true" antecedent is a litany of Vietnam-era leaders ("McNamara, / Johnson, Westmoreland, Rusk") who are ultimately the actors behind each national speech act. Their names cannot be confused ("no pun intended") but stand as the final, real condition of all national naming rituals.

Watten has done more than imply a connection between pronoun and antecedent; he has linked them structurally by creating lines that, however discontinuous semantically, are nonetheless linked syntactically. Each line modifies the next so that one may read the entire passage as a long, highly subordinated, period. Watten's point seems to be that "progress," both poem and social ideal, is not based on purposive, sequential evolution but upon discrete acts, held together by a common infrastructure. When "progress" becomes synonymous with a war economy—the production of new destroyers as an index of national strength—it loses all associations with an Enlightenment narrative of growth and improvement and becomes metaphor for routinized production. The poem attempts to circumvent this form of production by creating an alternative, one that links logically disconnected elements (apes and destroyers, parked cars and Vietnam) by discovering structural homologies. The fact that the ship's name, *Rosebud*, is also that of Citizen Kane's sled adds an additional irony. Given William Randolph Hearst's (Kane's) famous remark about the relationship between war and news ("I'll supply the war; you supply the copy"), perhaps the ship has been more appropriately named than we know.[8]

This brief example suggests a challenge and a crisis for any materialist poetics. Unlike most political poetry of the last twenty years, Language writing bases its analysis of authority not on the author's particular politics but in the verbal means by which any statement claims its status as truth. Moreover, by foregrounding the abstract features of the speech act rather than the authenticity of its expressive moment, the poet acknowledges the contingency of utterances in social interchange. The incompletion of each element in the verbal sequence demands a reading that is not recuperative but critical.

There is some question, however, whether this critical function can be adequately performed by any reader. For the critique of expression in Language writing depends on its own felicity condition: that there be some interplay between poem and reception, that the expressive conduit between addressor and addressee be broken in order for the reader to be reinvented as active agent in meaning-production. If the terms for reading are already anticipated in the formal design of the poem, there is little room for the reader to interact with the actual pragmatics of literary discourse. Instead of being revealed as agents of ideological interests, speech acts become thematized as types of dramatic moments, no one of which has any more claim on our attention than another. The reader becomes a voyeur upon an artful attempt to seduce him/her into playing by the rules. Hence the felicity criterion upon which the poetic speech act is based becomes more of a horizon than a fact.

These qualifications aside, I feel that Language writing thinks through such questions, often incorporating them into the work itself. When Ron Silliman introduces his anthology of Language writing, In the American Tree, by using Bob Grenier's phrase, "I Hate Speech," he articulates the distance that he and others in that volume feel from the speech-based poetics of projectivism. At the same time, the violence of the phrase overdetermines its subject, pointing away from the direct object, "speech," back at the discursive act itself. Far from being merely an attack on speech in favor of some indeterminate écriture, "I hate speech" embodies its own problematic of presence by shouting louder than it needs.[9] The phrase refers "to" at the same time as it refers "by means of." Silliman has been aided, in this respect, by an earlier generation of poets who treated the poem as gesture—as an act addressed by the poet to an audience that has forgotten how to hear. It has been for Silliman's and Watten's generation to explore the relationship between the two parties.

NOTES

1. Charles Olson, "Human Universe," in Selected Writings of Charles Olson, ed. Robert Creeley (New York: New Directions, 1966), 54, 61.

2. John Searle, Speech Acts: An Essay in the Philosophy of Language (Cambridge: Cambridge University Press, 1969). J. L. Austin, How To Do Things With Words (Cambridge: Harvard University Press, 1977), 14–15. See also Mary Louise Pratt, Toward a Speech Act Theory of Literary Discourse (Bloomington: Indiana University Press, 1977), 79–99.

3. The exception to this rule is the work of Mary Louise Pratt (see n. 2), which offers an important critique not only of speech act theory but of Roman Jakobson's theories of "literariness" as a discrete area of verbal experience. One could say, also, that the work of Mikhail Bakhtin in its general emphasis on the social stratification of heteroglossia would be another useful vein. See his "Discourse in the Novel" in The Dialogic Imagination: Four Essays, ed. Michael Holquist (Austin: University of Texas Press, 1981), 259–422.

4. Ron Silliman, "Sunset Debris," in The Age of Huts (New York: Roof

Books, 1986), 14. Other works referred to in this paragraph include the following: Lyn Hejinian, *My Life* (Los Angeles: Sun & Moon Press, 1987); Bob Perelman, *Face Value* (New York: Roof Books, 1988).

5. See Austin, *How To Do Things*, 101–32.

6. Charles Olson, "Maximus to Gloucester, Letter 27 [withheld]," in *The Maximus Poems* (Berkeley and Los Angeles: University of California Press, 1983), 185.

7. Barrett Watten, *Progress* (New York: Segue, 1985), 111–12.

8. Watten has commented extensively on this passage in an interview in *Ottotole* 2 (Winter, 1986–87) in which he describes actual sources for several of the lines, including a private association for "Rosebud" linked to the name of an ape at the Oakland Zoo. In private conversation, the author has informed me that "Bald Eagles," in addition to the obvious reference to the American military, was a phrase used for child prostitutes in Saigon during the Vietnam War. I have chosen not to use Watten's commentary in forming my own reading in order to test what I take to be his larger pedagogical purpose—namely to provoke the reader into working with the materials of his poem toward new and perhaps unexpected interpretations. Unlike critics who might find in this decontextualizing strategy an argument for the liberation of neutral, free-floating signifiers, I would say that Watten has carefully delimited the ideological horizon of his lines so that meaning production ("progress") will occur within flexible boundaries.

9. Ron Silliman, "Language, Realism, Poetry," in *In the American Tree* (Orono, Maine: National Poetry Foundation, 1986), xv.

5   The Changing Face of Common Intercourse: Talk Poetry, Talk Show, and the Scene of Writing
Marjorie Perloff

> . . . the natural words in the natural order is the formula.
> —W. B. Yeats[1]

> . . . the natural object is always the adequate symbol.
> —Ezra Pound[2]

> "Natural": the very word should be struck from the language.
> —Charles Bernstein[3]

I

In his famous lecture "The Music of Poetry" (1942), T. S. Eliot declares:

> there is one law of nature more powerful than any [other] . . . the law that
> poetry must not stray too far from the ordinary everyday language which
> we use and hear. Whether poetry is accentual or syllabic, rhymed or rhyme-
> less, formal or free, it cannot afford to lose contact with the changing face
> of common intercourse.[4]

And a few pages later:

> So, while poetry attempts to convey something beyond what is conveyed in
> prose rhythms, it remains, all the same, *one person talking to another*. . . . Every
> revolution in poetry is apt to be, and sometimes to announce itself to be, a
> *return to common speech*. This is the revolution which Wordsworth announced
> in his prefaces, and he was right: but the same revolution had been carried
> out a century before by Oldham, Waller, Denham, and Dryden; and the
> same revolution was due again something over a century later. . . . No po-
> etry, of course, is ever exactly the same speech that the poet talks and
> hears: but it has to be in such a relation to the speech of his time that the
> listener or reader can say "that is how I should talk if I could talk poetry."
> (23–24; my italics)

Poetry as the simulation of natural speech: taken at face value, Eliot's
precept is, by his own account, in the straight line of Wordsworth; the
poet, according to the 1800 "Preface to the *Lyrical Ballads*," is first and

foremost "a man speaking to men."[5] Not that Eliot shares Wordsworth's faith in the language of "low and rustic life" as that which is most attuned to "the beautiful and permanent forms of nature." "It is not the business of the poet," he writes, "to talk like any class of society, but like himself—rather better, we hope, than any actual class."[6] "Common speech," in this context, means not the speech of the lower classes but that which is common to everyone, that is, natural or everyday speech as we perceive it in our daily lives.

The criterion of "natural speech" was, in any case, to become a cornerstone of high modernist poetics.[7] "I have tried," writes Yeats to his father in 1913, "to make my work convincing with a speech so natural and dramatic that the hearer would feel the presence of a man thinking and feeling."[8] In a similar vein, Pound insists, in a 1915 letter to Harriet Monroe, that the language of poetry "must be a fine language, departing in no way from speech save by a heightened intensity. There must be no book words, no periphrases, no inversions . . . nothing that you couldn't in some circumstance, in the stress of some emotion, actually say."[9] From here it is just a step to the conviction that the speech act itself has poetic potential. "Poetry," as David Antin was to put it in the early seventies, is "made by a man up on his feet, talking."[10]

The identification of poetry with manhood is a subject I shall take up later; for the moment, consider the curious emphasis, in modernist discourse, on the role of poetry as purgative—a kind of cold shower. "The norm for a poet's language," observes Eliot, "is the way his contemporaries talk,"[11] provided, of course, that such talk—the language of the tribe, as Eliot, following Mallarmé, puts it—is purified, cleansed, given a well-deserved lift, the social function of poetry being, in Eliot's words, no less than "to affect the speech and the sensibility of the whole nation" (OPP, 12). And Yeats describes his own process of self-modernization as an infusion of "cold light and tumbling clouds."[12]

Conversely, the declared enemy of modernism was said to be artifice, specifically the artifice of separating the word from the "natural object" to which it ostensibly refers. "We should write out our own thoughts," says Yeats in his autobiography, "in as nearly as possible the language we thought them in, as though in a letter to an intimate friend. We should not disguise them in any way" (Auto, 102, my italics). Hence Eliot is critical of Valéry because "the words set free by [him] may tend to form a separate language. But the further the idiom, vocabulary, and syntax of poetry depart from those of prose, the more artificial the language of poetry will become" (PV, xvi). For Eliot, artificial is a derogatory term because it implies that words can somehow be detached from things; as he puts it in his essay on Swinburne: "It is, in fact, the word that gives him the thrill, not the object. When you take to pieces any verse of Swinburne, you find always the object was not there—only the word."[13] And why would this be so bad? Because "Language in a healthy state presents the object, is so close to the object that the two are identified." Whereas in Swinburne: word and object "are identified . . . solely because the object has ceased to exist, because the meaning is merely the hallucination of meaning, because language, uprooted, has adapted itself to an independent life of atmospheric nourishment" (ESE, 327).

The fear that the word will no longer adhere to the object haunts the poetics of modernism; it is a fear already latent, for that matter, in Wordsworth's "Preface." "Low and rustic life was generally chosen," explains Wordsworth in a famous passage, "because such men hourly communicate with the best objects from which the best part of language is originally derived; and because, from their rank in society and the sameness and narrow circle of their intercourse, being less under the influence of social vanity, they convey their feelings and notions in simple and unelaborated language" (WWP, 869–70). From Coleridge on down, critics have insisted that this statement cannot be narrowly construed: in Coleridge's words in chapter 17 of the *Biographia Literaria*, "a rustic's language, purified from all provincialism and grossness, and so far reconstructed as to be made consistent with the rules of grammar (which are in essence no other than the laws of universal logic, applied to psychological materials) will not differ from the language of any other man of common-sense, however learned or refined he may be."[14] But from our perspective nearly two hundred years after the writing of the "Preface," the issue is less whether Wordsworth's language is that of the rustic or of Coleridge's broader category, the "man of common-sense," than that Wordsworth's preoccupation with "the language really spoken by men" can be seen as a kind of holding operation against the encroachments of an industrial mass society in which that language would undergo modes of mediation that would hardly involve communication "with the best objects from which the best part of language is originally derived." Indeed, a few pages further into the "Preface," Wordsworth refers somewhat bitterly to the "multitude of causes, unknown to former times, now acting with a combined force to blunt the discriminating powers of the mind. . . . The most effective of these causes are the great national events which are daily taking place, and the increasing accumulation of men in cities, where the uniformity of their occupations produces a craving for extraordinary incident, which the rapid communication of intelligence hourly gratifies" (WWP, 872).

The hourly gratification of a "craving" on the part of the masses "for extraordinary incident," a craving produced by the increasing "uniformity" of human occupation: here Wordsworth uncannily anticipates the problematic that now haunts some of our most original poetry. In Charles Bernstein's words in "Dysraphism":

Blinded by avenue and filled with
adjacency. Arch or arched at. So there becomes bottles,
hushed conductors, illustrated proclivities for puffed-
up benchmarks. Morose or comatose.[15]

A line like "Blinded by avenue and filled with / adjacency," for that matter, surely brings to mind Wordsworth's "The world is too much with us, late and soon, / Getting and spending we lay waste our powers." But what has happened to "the language really used by men"? To "the natural words in the natural order"? "In the room the women come and go / Talking of Michelangelo": there is a straightforward "normal" declarative sentence that anyone who has heard of Michelangelo can understand. Or again, "April is the cruellest month": a sentence that, if not quite plausible as a natural utterance, April conventionally being the month of spring rebirth, is certainly readily apprehended as a syntactic unit: subject nominative, copula, predicate nominative. But what sort of sentence is "Arch or arched at"? Is "Arch" a noun or a verb? If a verb, who is doing the arching? What does it mean to be "arched at"? And is the meaning of "Arch" the same as that of "arched"?

It may be that the fracture of language found in a poem like "Dysraphism" is merely perverse, the sort of willful and pretentious obscurantism Eliot warned about when he declared that poetry "cannot afford to lose contact with the changing face of common intercourse." Or is it possible that Eliot himself paid insufficient attention to the potential for *change* that "common intercourse" was inevitably undergoing? Despite the self-declared classicism of his later years,[16] there is no suggestion that Eliot ever abandoned his Romantic, indeed Rousseauistic faith in writing as the making present of a prior *natural* speech. In *Burnt Norton*, we read:

                    Words strain,
Crack and sometimes break, under the burden,
Under the tension, slip, slide, perish,
Decay with imprecision, will not stay in place,
Will not stay still.[17]

The implication is that ideally, if the poet were equal to his task, words could and should represent the realities behind them, realities, so Eliot would have it, that belong to both poet and reader. Precision, in this context, means accuracy of transcription: the poet conveys, more precisely than can his nonpoetic counterpart, the meanings inherent in a particular set of experiences. <u>Writing, by this argument, makes present what the poet wishes to say</u>.

In the early twentieth century it still seemed possible to act on this doctrine. When Yeats visited peasant cottages in Galway and Sligo, gathering folk material that might find its way into the fabric of his poetry, when Eliot used the overheard speech of his cleaning woman—what he called "pure Ellen Kellond"—as the basis for the Cockney monologue of Lil's malicious friend in "The Game of Chess," the working classes, whether rural or urban, still represented an exotic *other*, an other whose speech might be drawn into the poetic text in the interest of authenticity.[18] Thus when Eliot produced a poem that contained the speech of a malicious low-class female gossip,

> But if Albert makes off, it won't be for lack of telling.
> You ought to be ashamed, I said, to look so antique.
> (And her only thirty-one).
> I can't help it, she said, pulling a long face,
> It's them pills I took, to bring it off, she said.
> (She's had five already, and nearly died of young George.)
>
> (ECP, 42)

such early readers of *The Waste Land* as F. R. Leavis and F. O. Matthiessen were quick to proclaim Eliot's triumph in capturing the *actual rhythms* of pub talk in 1920s London. And we continue to marvel at the vivid "realism" and precision of the Lil section, the brilliant juxtaposition of mock mimetic, as in the passage above, with the biblical rhythms of "HURRY UP PLEASE IT'S TIME" and the plaintive "Good night ladies" of Ophelia.

"Every revolution in poetry is apt to be, and sometimes to announce itself to be, a return to common speech." Eliot's dictum applies neatly to the self-declared revolution of the *New American Poetry*, as Donald Allen called his famous anthology of 1960. The work in question, says Allen in his introduction, "has shown one common characteristic: a total rejection of all those qualities typical of academic verse"[19]—a reference, no doubt, to the traditional metrics, elaborate metaphor, and formal diction used by poets like Allen Tate, Howard Nemerov, or the early Robert

Lowell. Allen's *New American Poetry* was soon followed by Stephen Berg and Robert Mezey's *Naked Poetry: Recent American Poetry in Open Forms* (1969), in which the editors state in the introduction, "We began with the firm conviction that the strongest and most alive poetry in America had abandoned or at least broken the grip of traditional meters and had set out, once again, into 'the wilderness of unopened life.'"[20]

The creation of this new "wilderness," of what Robert Duncan called the "opening of the field," as that opening was conceived by such diverse groups as the Projectivists and Beats, the San Francisco poets and "Deep Image" school, is by now a familiar story,[21] but I want to approach it here from a rather different angle, my own hunch being that the very aggressiveness of the new demand for a free-verse and speech-based poetics testifies to a growing anxiety about the viability of the "natural style" in a world where nature is increasingly subject to the hitherto unimaginable operations of the various "quiet" revolutions of our time, especially that of the information revolution.

We might note, to begin with, that for the open-field poetics of the fifties, the speech base is no longer that of "common speech," as it was for Yeats and Eliot, and for Wordsworth before them, but the very personal utterance of the individual poet. Phrases like "finding one's voice" or "capturing the breath" now become prominent. In his famous manifesto "Projective Verse" (1950), Charles Olson sets himself apart from the "closed" or "print-bred" verse of modernism and proclaims that "Verse now, 1950, if it is to go ahead, if it is to be of *essential* use, must, I take it, catch up and put into itself certain laws and possibilities of the breath, of the breathing of the man who writes." And a few pages later he declares that the requisites for the poetic line are:

> the HEAD, by way of the EAR, to the SYLLABLE
> the HEART, by way of the BREATH, to the LINE

Further "breath allows *all* the speech-force of language back in (speech is the 'solid' of verse, is the secret of a poem's energy)."[22]

Poetic speech is the making present, via the breath, of internal energy—not "common speech," the purview of such giant agencies as the OWI (Office of War Information), where Olson worked during the Second World War, but *this* speech, *my* speech. If "FORM" (according to Olson's second rule, which he took over from Robert Creeley) "IS NEVER MORE THAN THE EXTENSION OF CONTENT," the implicit corollary is that content is never more than the extension of the true voice of feeling.

As such, sixties poetics is largely consistent in its call for natural speech, direct utterance, and the line as breath unit. "Each line of *Howl*," explains Allen Ginsberg in 1959, "is a single breath unit. . . . it's a natural consequence, my own heightened conversation."[23] And two years later, "the mind must be trained, i.e., let loose, freed—to deal with itself as it actually is, and not to impose on itself, or its poetic artifacts, an arbitrarily preconceived pattern. . . . The only poetic tradition is the Voice out of the burning bush. The rest is trash, & will be consumed."[24] The stress on speech as vision is carried even further by Gary Snyder: "Breath is the outer world coming into one's body. . . . Breath is spirit, 'inspiration.' . . . Yet the muse remains a woman. Poetry is voice, and according to Indian tradition, voice *vak* (vox) is a Goddess. . . . As Vak is wife to Brahma . . . so the voice, in everyone, is a mirror of his deepest self."[25]

The heroic stance of the male poet drawing inspiration from the female muse in the guise of goddess or Burning Bush constitutes what I take to be a kind of first-stage alert in the face of the accelerated social and political change that characterizes the sixties. To put it another way: in a society where, as Arthur Kroker and David Cook put it, "class has disappeared into mass and mass has dissolved into the new black hole of the 'blip,'"[26] the poet's first response (and this is just as true of the women poets of the period) is likely to be what we might call the by-pass mode, that is, the desire to establish a direct line between self and spirit. "A partial definition of organic poetry," observed Denise Levertov in 1965, "might be that it is a method of apperception . . . based on an intuition of an order, a form beyond forms. . . . How does one go about such a poetry? I think it's like this: first there must be an experience, a sequence or constellation of perceptions of sufficient interest, felt by the poet intensely enough to demand of him [sic] their equivalence in words: he is *brought to speech*."[27]

Brought to speech: this might be the epigraph—or perhaps the epitaph—of sixties poetry in America.[28] For by 1971 we find a poet like Robert Grenier writing: "Why imitate 'speech'? Various vehicle that American speech is in the different mouths of any of us, possessed of particular powers of colloquial usage, rhythmic pressure, etc., it is *only* such. *To me, all speeches say the same thing.* . . . I HATE SPEECH."[29] And a few years later, Charles Bernstein observes that "There is no natural look or sound to a poem. Every element is intended, chosen. That is what makes a thing a poem" (CD, 49).

II

Why is the natural now regarded with such suspicion? The reasons are many and complex, but we might begin by considering the role of the "common man" (or, increasingly, the "common woman") at our historical moment. "Think like a wise man," said Yeats, "but express ourselves like the common people." But how do the common people, as distinct from others, express themselves in our late twentieth-century mass culture? As far as the media are concerned—and this is where most of us come into contact with representations of the people—class difference as determinant of language use has become insignificant. True, soap operas and sitcoms now pay lip service to ethnic and racial diversity by including, say, a bit of the stereotypical ghettospeak of young blacks (e.g., Drusilla on CBS's *The Young and the Restless*), but such variations only serve to emphasize the television norm, which is that "real" people (as opposed to actors playing fictional roles), people like Dan Rather or Connie Chung or Barbara Walters or Tom Brokaw, slight differences in accent notwithstanding, use the same language, an up-to-date Standard American English with reassuringly uniform vocabulary, syntax, idiom, and even inflection. Reassuring, in that viewers from Maine to Hawaii must be able to understand what is said on the CBS *Evening News* or on the *Today Show*.

No longer, in any case, is the hypothetical "common man" a presence to be memorably apprehended in the Scottish highlands like Wordsworth's Solitary Reaper or down at the village pub like Yeats's Old Tom, nor is the poet's contact with the exotic "common man" any longer likely to be the relationship with one's servants, as in the case of Eliot's Albert and Lil or, for that matter, Williams's Elsie, with "her great / ungainly hips and flopping breasts / addressed to cheap jewelry / and rich young men with fine eyes." Indeed, what Eliot called "the ordinary everyday language which we use and hear" has now entered an arena where "natural talk," filtered through the electronic media, packaged and processed, becomes the TV "talk show," *talk show* being an apt name for the transformation of speech into spectacle.

Poststructuralist theory (in this case most notably Derrida's "Writing before the Letter" in *Of Grammatology*) has of course been much preoccupied with this problem. Thanks to Derrida's elaborate dismantling of Western logocentrism, we now know—or do we?—that writing is by no means the natural representation of a prior speech, that indeed writing cannot be confined "to a secondary and instrumental function" as "translator of a full speech that was fully *present* (to itself, to its unsignified, to the other)."[30] But in accepting as axiomatic Derrida's argument *contra* the priority of speech, we sometimes forget that this argument too has its historical dimension. Surely, that is to say, it is not coincidence that the poststructuralist attack on "natural speech" as the embodiment of presence has come at a time when the available channels of speech communication have been so thoroughly mediated. As Michel de Certeau puts it in an essay called "The Jabbering of Social Life" (1980):

> Never has history talked so much or shown so much. Never, indeed, have the gods' ministers *made them speak* so continuously, in such detail and so injunctively as the producers of revelations and rules do today *in the name* of topicality. Our orthodoxy is made up of narrations of "what's going on." . . . From morning till evening, unceasingly, streets and buildings are haunted by narratives. They articulate our existences by teaching us what they should be. They "cover the event," i.e., they *make* our legends. . . . Seized from the moment of awakening by the radio (the voice is the law), the listener walks all day through a forest of narrativities, journalistic, advertising and televised. . . . Our society has become a *narrated* society in a three-fold sense: it is defined by *narratives* (the fables of our advertising and information), by *quotations* of them, and by their interminable *recitation*.[31]

Narratives, quotations, recitations: the contemporary speech overload can hardly help but have an impact on "the changing face of common intercourse." Consider—and this point brings me finally to my chapter title—the modus operandi of a television show first aired in 1968 and still running strong: namely, the Donahue show. Phil Donahue now has quite a few competitors like Oprah Winfrey or Geraldo, but their programs are predictable variations of the model, the talk-show formula being almost identical whether the interviewer is male or female, black or white, East Coast or West Coast, and so on.

What sort of authentic speech do we hear and see expressed on *Donahue*? From Monday to Friday, five days a week, for a full hour, Phil Donahue, the all-American clean-cut average guy, performs what looks like a high-wire act as he leaps around the studio, recording the comments of his audience members on the topic of the day. Topics are almost always and reassuringly "everyday" and amenable to "normal speech"— for example, premarital and extramarital sex, masturbation, impotence, incest, rape, the rights of gay fathers and mothers, artificial insemination, surrogate motherhood, in-laws, day care, two-career couples, older man–younger woman marriages and the converse, alcoholism, drug abuse, AIDS education in the public shools—the list is all but endless. For each of these topics, Phil Donahue brings in a set of guest "experts"—experts falling into two categories: those who have "been there" and those who analyze "having been there."

Thus, in a "daring" program on incest, the "expert" (this actually happened!) is likely to be a woman whose father, a prison warden, forced her to commit incest with him. The father is also on the show, as is the pitiful mother. These three principals are sure to be flanked by two "real" experts—in this case, two psychiatrists or therapists who have written about incest and who, as is invariably the case on talk shows, hold so-called opposite points of view on the issue. Or if the topic is drug abuse, the panelists are bound to include former abusers as well as, once again, the proverbial therapists. Significantly, no one seems to exist who is *currently* on drugs just as no one on the incest panel is currently having sexual relations with his or her child. The reason for this omission is simple: the media mechanism cannot permit the disruption that might take place if Donahue really permitted the natural words to occur in the natural order. Suppose, for example, that a few drunks were brought off the street and placed on the Donahue stage, and suppose they promptly fell asleep or asked for a drink or started singing dirty songs or threw empty bottles at members of the audience. Suppose, for that matter, that the talk-show guests just sat there and stared at the interviewer. How, in such a case, could the time frame contain its requisite plenitude?

"Every return in poetry," says Eliot, "is apt to be, and sometimes to announce itself to be, a return to common speech." Now let's look more closely at what "common speech" sounds like over the TV channel. To give a specific example: on Friday, 1 April 1988, the Donahue topic was "couples who consider their marriage to be over but continue to live together." The author of a book on this subject was present as were three couples who were still living together, presumably "for the sake of the children," even though their practice was to invite their respective boyfriends or girlfriends over whenever they liked. As is usual on *Donahue*, a mock debate was in session, certain viewers expressing the opinion that such a sham marriage "is a big cop-out," others maintaining that, on the contrary, "In this day and age you don't have to lie about the way you really feel." One wife on the podium expressed the sentiment that "This way I still have both my guys near me . . . but I only sleep with one of them." This statement, like many other "outrageous" remarks, produced gales of laughter and applause from the audience. Evidently, audience members were amazed and delighted, if also a shade embarrassed, to see that a woman rather like themselves in appearance could have her cake and eat it too!

Along the way, the men and women who spoke both in favor of and against the living arrangement in question would begin with the clause "I think . . . " or "I believe . . . " or "It seems to me that. . . . " The constant reference to "I," coupled with a close-up shot of the speaker, would seem to suggest that the Death of the Subject, proclaimed in our more sophisticated intellectual circles, is vastly exaggerated. Here, acting as the home viewers' surrogates (7 to 7.5 million home viewers per day watch *Donahue*), are people of all ages, both sexes, different races, and from all walks of life (with the proviso that they have applied to be guests on *Donahue* and have been screened as being "appropriate"), who have strong opinions about personal feelings.[32] Phil himself, moreover, seems to express strong feelings, speaking, as he does, from his location in the audience, not on the podium, taking phone calls, scoffing at what X says, and baiting Y.

But if one listens carefully, these seemingly contradictory opinions are conveyed in a curiously consistent vocabulary. On *Donahue*, the seven virtues have been reduced to three: caring, compassionate, and candid. Given this three-c attitudinal profile as well as a big retrospective R for regret ("I now regret that I ever did such a thing!"), one can be forgiven—indeed admired—for almost anything. The gray-haired man on the screen actually committed incest with the unattractive young woman who is his daughter. But he now *regrets* it and, besides, she has managed to develop into a compassionate and caring young woman—a woman candid enough to tell all about her ordeal in a new best seller.

All these bits—or should we say bytes?—of common speech, funneled into Phil's eagerly waiting microphone, are perhaps best understood as what Jean Baudrillard had called *simulacra*—"models of a real without origin or reality: a hyperreal."[33] For if, so Baudrillard argues, "one agrees to define communication as an exchange, as a reciprocal space of a speech and a response, and thus of a *responsibility*," then television is (or the media in general are), by definition, that which "always prevents response"[34]—prevents it not because, as traditional Marxism would have it, our mass media are controlled by the consciousness industries of late capitalism, but because the media are themselves "the *effectors* of ideology" (RM, 128). Indeed, once it is understood that "ideology does not exist in some place apart, as the discourse of the dominant class *before* it is channeled through the media," it follows that "all vague impulses to democratize content, subvert it, restore the 'transparency of the code,' control the information process, contrive a reversibility of circuits, or take power over media are hopeless—unless the monopoly of speech is broken; and one cannot break the monopoly of speech if one's goal is simply to distribute it equally to everyone" (RM, 128–29).

It is precisely the "undifferentiation" of the audience that governs talk-show talk. The masses, as Steve McCaffery observes, become a "nebulous asocial abstraction, serialized into atomistic simulacrities (the 'privatism' of the family television receiving identical content as millions of other homes, *simulates* individuality)." Media narrative thus "absorbs communication as a model into its circuits."[35] We can, to take a concrete example, learn that Jim X "has chosen virginity" as a way of life; we even learn that Jim is a first-year medical student at Harvard; but our response to his situation is entirely constructed; there is no reciprocity between ourselves and the simulated "problem." Indeed, the next day more or less the same studio audience will respond just as favorably (or unfavorably) to John Y who is a sex addict. "Have a nice day," says Phil (or Oprah or Geraldo) at the end of the hour, smiling into the camera. But are "we" having a nice day? And who is to know whether we are or not?

The hyperreality of "the natural words in the natural order" is especially remarkable in the TV segments that cover national political campaigns. Consider, for example, the special broadcast in August 1987 in which the then-seven Democratic candidates were given the opportunity to make brief video segments about themselves and their families. Invariably, each segment opens with the smiling candidate, each in his neutral blue suit, flanked by wife, children, and a pet or two, against the backdrop of a "normal," "nice," but nondescript house. Invariably, the sun is shining and there are likely to be autumn leaves (but not too many!) underfoot. The candidate identifies family members by name and provides a "telling" detail here and there: for instance, "This is Johnny. He just passed his driving test." And then, dues to family values having been paid, the camera quickly removes the family and cuts to a close-up of the candidate's face.

The comment on the teenager's passing of the driving test is one that interests me, being the perfect synecdoche of the "language really used by men" as it appears on television. The candidate cannot tell "us"—the nameless and faceless—that his son is an athlete for that might offend those whose sons are *not* athletes or those who have no sons. But he can't say that his son is a bookish introvert either. He can't describe what kind of school the boy goes to without potential offense to someone out there. He can't describe the fights his son has with his daughter. Or his speeding ticket. Or his experimenting with speed. Indeed, the more we think about it, the more we realize that the candidate cannot say anything more specific about his son than that he is now legally driving a car. This is the level of abstraction to which the dream of a common language descends. Actual speech, no longer the exchange of "a man speaking to men," is emptied of all particularity of reference. The "real," as Steve McCaffery puts it, "is no longer the referent but the model absorbed" (NI, 41).

III

What does all this have to do with the writing of poetry? The logical answer to this question is that poets are precisely those who, faced with the abstraction and emptying out of the mediaspeak I have been describing, strive to "reaffirm," in Louis Simpson's words, "the primacy of feeling," the conviction that "poetry is not a game played with words . . . it is in earnest." Indeed, "We need to speak again about common life . . . about offices and the people who work in them. About factories and the people who live in mean streets. . . . If we cannot bring these into poetry then something is missing—the life most people know."[36]

Simpson's view of the poet as sensitive other, giving voice to the "primacy of feeling," carries on what I have called the holding operation of the fifties and sixties, the poetic demand, if no longer for common speech, at least for *authentic speech*. To be a poet at midcentury was to "find one's own voice," to "bring to speech," as Denise Levertov put it, one's own experience. "Almost the whole problem of writing poetry," said Robert Lowell in 1961, "is to bring it back to what you really find."[37]

In Lowell's own case, this produced the remarkable poems of *Life Studies* and *For the Union Dead*, in which the simulation of voice—of a man actually speaking—is marked by what the poet himself was to call "the grace of accuracy":

"I won't go with you. I want to stay with Grandpa!"
That's how I threw cold water
on my Mother and Father's
watery martini pipe dreams at Sunday dinner.
                    ("My Last Afternoon with Uncle Devereux Winslow")

All night the crib creaks;
home from the healthy country to the sick city,
my daughter in fever
flounders in her chicken-colored sleeping bag.
"Sorry," she mumbles like her dim-bulb father,
        "sorry."

                                        ("During Fever")

Nothing! No oil
for the eye, nothing to pour
on those waters or flames.
I am tired. Everyone's tired of my turmoil.

("Eye and Tooth")[38]

The "natural look" of these lines is, of course, cunningly contrived: the casual juxtaposition of "cold water" and "watery martini pipe dreams" introducing the central life-death theme of "My Last Afternoon," the ironic transference of the poet's anxiety to his baby daughter's "chicken-colored sleeping bag," the subtle water-fire tension and off-rhyme ("oil," "turmoil") of "Eye and Tooth," and so on. What seemed—and still seems—so memorable about these poems is the conjunction of careful artistry (the network of resonant images and metonymies) and an admirable candor—the willingness of the poet to write about his own "real" pain and to characterize himself self-deprecatingly as the baby's "dim-bulb father," to admit that "Everyone's tired of my turmoil."[39]

But the demands made on the "authentic" self were extremely difficult to sustain, even for a poet like Lowell, whose outsider status (a blueblood "Mayflower screwball" turned "fire-breathing C.O."—jailbird and mental patient) was a guarantee of an identity as representative as it was singular. Even in the case of such special selfhood, however, the tension between the "unique" consciousness and the increasingly indifferent external world could hardly be expressed without falling into the not entirely unrelated inflections of Donahue talk, with its similar accountings of coming "home . . . to the sick city" or the "martini pipe dreams" of one's relatives. "At their best," says Charles Altieri of Lowell's Notebook sonnets, "the poems include the reader in Lowell's charmed circle of those who, because of their despair, have developed the power to appreciate the limited joys and moments of shared feeling or clear insight that are all one can have."[40]

By the early seventies, such "moments of shared feeling" had too often shrunk into the wry anecdotalism of John Berryman's Love and Fame:

Oh! I had my gyp prepare that tea.
But she wasn't hungry or thirsty, she wanted to talk.
She had not met an American before,
to talk with; much less an American poet.

I told her honestly I wasn't much of one yet but probably
    would be.

She preferred Racine to Shakespeare; I said I'd fix that
& read her the King's cadenzas in *All's Well*
about that jerk Bertram's father.[41]

This reminiscence of Berryman's Oxford exploits fulfills with a vengeance Eliot's criteria for a poetry that "must not stray too far from the ordinary everyday language which we use and hear." The exclamatory "Oh," the words italicized so as to simulate the girl's speech inflections, the "I said . . . she said" account, and the reference to the unattractive hero of *All's Well That Ends Well* as "that jerk Bertram"—these are designed to create intimacy, informality, immediate presence. The problem—a problem Eliot tried to solve, at least in his earlier poetry, by attributing his "natural speech" to Prufrock or Lil or the Lady in *The Game of Chess*—was how to make one's own self a representative self, how to make what happens to that self matter, at a moment when the media were manufacturing and packaging "selves" by the hundreds and presenting them for our inspection. When, in the poem cited above, Berryman informs us that his girl's father is "an expert on sleep: praised, pioneered by Aldous Huxley. He lives by counselling in London," we are not far away from the mode of the *New Yorker* profile, for example, "A prominent London psychiatrist whose mentor was Aldous Huxley, Jane Doe's father is an expert on sleep disorders."

At his best, in *The Dream Songs* and *Sonnets*, Berryman is of course much more subtle and more interesting than this, but *Love and Fame* testifies to the increasing difficulties of placing the "self" in the "world" at a time when "sensitivity," "authenticity," and "being in touch with one's feelings" have been co-opted by the voices and faces on the video screen. "Were you very upset when you found out?" asks Geraldo of the man whose wife has just told the CBS audience that she has been a prostitute for years. "At first I was real upset," the man replies with a little smile, "but now I'm glad she has a job that she finds satisfying." "Upset," "glad," "satisfying"—what, one wonders, do these adjectives really mean given the context? And how does this talk-show exchange of feelings-designators affect the "finding" of one's "poetic voice"?

Asked by an interviewer whether he is trying to create a "language of revelation," Philip Levine replied: "I don't know if I'm trying to create a language. I've never really thought about that. In a curious way, I'm not much interested in language. In my ideal poem, no words are noticed. You look through them into a vision of . . . just see the people, the place."[42] Language, for the poetry that persists in its demand for authenticity, seems to be something of a distraction, interfering as it does with the direct communication between poet and reader; perhaps poetry can dispense with it altogether and go for the unmediated image. The resulting "transparency" is likely to look like this:

To Cipriano, in the Wind

Where did your words go,
Cipriano, spoken to me 38 years
ago in the back of Peerless Cleaners,
where raised on a little wooden platform
you bowed to the hissing press
and under the glaring bulb the scars
across your shoulders—"a gift
of my country"—gleamed like an old wood.
"*Dignidad*," you said into my boy's
wide eyes, "without is no riches."
And Ferrente, the dapper Sicilian
coatmaker, laughed. What could
a pants presser know of dignity?
That was the winter of '41, it
would take my brother off to war,
where you had come from, it would
bring great snowfalls, graying
in the streets, and the news of death
racing through the halls of my school.[43]

To say that the language of a poem like "To Cipriano" is "transparent," that the words are to be "looked through," is not, of course, quite accurate. We see *through* such language not because it is really "natural"—no one, after all, actually addresses a pants presser with the phrase, "Where did your words go, / Cipriano"—but because the "natural look" has been carefully manufactured by a phraseology that ensures a desired response on our part. "That was the winter of '41, it / would take my brother off to war"—oh yes, we know what that was all about. Indeed, Levine's celebrated *honesty*, the authenticity of his "spare" and "taut" idiom,[44] has to do less with what Yeats called "the presence of a man, thinking and feeling," than with the representations of such presence one meets in the world of *them*—the world of the politicians and media people the sensitive poet supposedly distrusts.[45] Cipriano, the pants presser, and Ferrente, "the dapper Sicilian / coatmaker," are true sentimental sitcom figures, even as the poet's "sensitive" memories of World War II have the inflections of a miniseries like *The Winds of War*. But then why should it be otherwise, the "common speech," as Levine receives it, always already bearing the imprint of the media circuits through which it is processed? As we read "To Cipriano," we can easily visualize the screen version, beginning with the shot of the teenage boy shyly chatting with the old pants presser "in the back of Peerless [get the irony?] Cleaners," and then cutting to scenes of Bataan, the Allied troops liberating the Sicily from which Cipriano came, and so on.

"Where did your words go, / Cipriano[?]" asks the poet, a rhetorical question if ever there was one, because he knows exactly not only where crusty old "Cipriano's" words went but who put them in his mouth. Such poems—and they are legion—testify to the mounting pressure on the "authentic speech" model to be as graphic as possible, to make sure that "the scars / across your shoulders" illuminated by the "glaring bulb" are seen, even as we are to hear the "hissing press" punctuating such remarks as Cipriano's "*Dignidad . . .* without is no riches." Imperceptibly, the norms have become those of the teleculture that "poetry" supposedly scorns. At the same time, the more radical poetries of the past few decades, whatever their particular differences, have come to reconcieve the "opening of the field," not as an entrance into *authenticity* but, on the contrary, as a turn toward *artifice*, toward poetry as making or praxis rather than poetry as impassioned speech, as self-expression.

"Artifice," says Charles Bernstein in the long verse essay *Artifice of Absorption*, "is a measure of a poem's / intractability to being read as the sum of its / devices & subject matters."[46] And further:

To be absorbed in one's own immediate language practices
& specialized lingo
is to be confronted with the foreignness
& unabsorbability of this plethora of
other "available" material;
the ideological strategy of mass entertainment,
from bestsellers to TV to "common voice" poetry
is to contradict this everpresent "other" reality through
insulation into a fabricated "lowest" common
denominator that, among its many guises, goes under
the Romantic formula "irreducible human values." (*AA*, 40)

The "plethora of *other* 'available' material" may prompt withdrawal into a world of one's own, where "natural" speech and authentic feeling still reign supreme. But once it is recognized that "the Romantic formula 'irreducible human values'" is itself "fabricated," withdrawal tends to give way to the urge to come to terms with the "unabsorbability" of other discourses.

The "artifice of absorption" takes, of course, many different forms, from, say, the gestural and playfully parodic lyric of John Ashbery, to the concrete or sound-text poem, to the *Oulipo* (rule-generated) work, to collage-text and performance,[47] and to the "antisyntactical" and "antireferential" lyric that goes by the name of Language poetry. All these are difficult poetries, difficult at least if one's norm is the "direct speech, direct feeling" model dominant in the sixties and early seventies. Confronted for the first time by the poetry of, say, Michael Palmer or Lyn Hejinian or Steve McCaffery, the reader is likely to lose patience—for instance with this:

A cut of light
            or a cutting
grows of a whole night composed
of day as well
the day the crystal's axes in a swarm drill
preciseness bristles of an emptiness sure
caught to tongue and left to lip
imitant blur
a night caught in such angles lit

                    (Clark Coolidge, *The Crystal Text*)[48]

"A cut of light": the first line looks reassuringly Romantic, but here what purports to be a sudden stab of insight is, so to speak, *denaturalized* by the proffered alternative: "A cut of light / or a cutting / [that] grows of a whole night." If the "cut" is more properly a plant cutting that takes a whole night to grow and if, further, the night is "composed / of day as well," the poem is describing, quite impersonally, how ideas, lodged deep within the mind, come to the surface of consciousness. Coolidge's structure is so tightly woven that we cannot extricate familiar syntactic units: "swarm," for example, may be a noun, indicating the place where the "crystal's axes" "drill." Or again, it may be an adjective signifying a particular kind of drill, a group drill within which preciseness bristles. To read this passage is to make connections, not via mimetic syntax, but via sound location: *cut, light, night, lit; crystal, drill bristles; left to lip, lit,* and so forth. As such, constellations of meaning do begin to emerge: the poem opposes sharpness of focus ("A cut of light," "the crystal's axes," "preciseness bristles," "angles lit") to the "emptiness sure," the "imitant blur" of being inexpressive, "caught to tongue" (tongue-tied), "left to lip." It takes, evidently, a "whole night," a "night composed / of day as well," which is to say perpetually, to get beyond that emptiness. But in the end we cannot be sure whether the "angles lit" illuminate the night or, conversely, whether they continue to be obstructed by the "night caught" in their beam. It is this sort of syntactic indeterminacy that prompted the perplexed graduate student from Yugoslavia to ask, in my poetry seminar at Stanford, "Why can't they write like Kafka?"

IV

Why *can't* they write like Kafka? Why is Kafka's extraordinary lucidity, the natural speech and "normal" syntax that paradoxically convey the densest and most ambiguous meanings, no longer a viable model? There is no easy answer to these questions, but we might begin with the notion that whereas Kafka positioned himself vis-à-vis the discourses of law, of justice, of business, and of the bourgeois respectability and normalcy that characterized the Prague of his time and place, our own contact with these discourses tends to be always already mediated by a third voice, the voice of the media. Consequently, the poetic attempt to hold on to some measure of a unique and natural voice—what Charles Bernstein calls, with reference to Olson, "the phallacy of the heroic stance"[49]—with its masculinist allegory of language as the stride of a man and its idealization of voice as the locus of authority—is increasingly giving way to a poetry that, as Bernstein says of Ron Silliman, "emphasizes its medium as being constructed, rule governed, everywhere circumscribed by grammar & syntax, chosen vocabulary: designed, manipulated, picked, programmed, organized, & so an artifice, artifact—monadic, solipsistic, homemade, manufactured, mechanized, formulaic, willfull" (CD, 40–41). This catalog is purposely bombastic so as to emphasize what has become an article of faith for Language poetry: "Every phrase I write, every juxtaposition I make, is a manifestation of using a full-blown language: full of possibilities of meaning & impossibilities of meaning" (CD, 46). And again, "there are no thoughts except through language, we are everywhere seeing through it, limited to it but not by it" (CD, 49).

This is a long way from Levine's "In my ideal poem no words are noticed." The emphasis on the word rather than on the object behind it or the vision beyond it has had startling consequences. For one thing, the Image, conceived by modernist poetics as the "primary pigment" (Pound), the "objective correlative" (Eliot), the "vector" (Olson), begins to lose its authority as the poetic signature par excellence. For another, and this is my concern here, the new emphasis on the poetic medium as *constructed* and *rule-governed* calls into question the primacy of natural speech, spontaneous rhythms, and what Eliot called "common intercourse."

The case of Robert Creeley is instructive in this shift. Many readers who admired the Creeley of the fifties—a Creeley, so it seemed, still squarely in the Williams mode—became increasingly uneasy when Creeley published *Pieces* (1969) and *A Day Book* (1972). Thus M. L. Rosenthal, in what was to become a rather notorious review of the latter for *Parnassus*, complained that "there are too many passages . . . done either in telegraphese or in a comma-spiked, anti-idiomatic style that befuddles one's memory of the English tongue." For "few effects are as satisfying as the assimilation of natural speech into a powerful and melodic poem." Comparing Creeley's "The Edge" ("Place it, / make the space / of it") to its parent text, Williams's "Love Song" ("I lie here thinking of you"), Rosenthal remarks on Williams's "rich," "full-bodied," and "active imagery," imagery that "the Creeley poem echoes . . . but makes . . . almost static and reduces the emotion to an abstraction. Without Williams' phrasing—'yellow,' 'stain of love,' 'upon the world,' 'selvage'— it would have neither vigor nor concrete reference."[50]

But perhaps "natural speech," "active imagery," "vigor," and "concrete reference" are not what the Creeley of *Pieces* is after. Consider the opening section of "Again":

One more day gone,
done, found in
the form of days.

It began, it
ended—was
forward, backward,

slow, fast a
sun shone, clouds,
high in the air I was

for awhile with others,
then came down
on the ground again.

No moon. A room in
a hotel—to begin
again.[51]

There is no use trying to read such a poem as a confessional lyric ("Here's what happened to me and how it made me feel"). Creeley's is less a form of witnessing than of paragram, which is to say, following Leon S. Roudiez, that "its organization of words (and their denotations), grammar, and syntax is challenged by the infinite possibilities provided by letters or phonemes combining to form networks of signification not accessible through conventional reading habits" (quoted in NI, 63). "The percolation of the word through the paragram," says Steve McCaffery, "contaminates the notion of an ideal, unitary meaning and thereby counters the supposition that words can 'fix' or stabilize in closure" (NI, 63).

"One more day gone, / done, found in / the form of days": there's a sentence you are sure never to hear on *Donahue*, a sentence whose "content" is not extractable from its form. The "One," to begin with, is embedded in both "gone" and "done" on either side of the first line break so that we can virtually *see* the "day" erode before our eyes. But what is "done" is also "found"—the *o* and *n* reappear together with the *d* of *day* to call up the "form of days" once more; indeed, the paragram of "form—of" enacts the cycle of the title "Again." Line 4—"It began, it"—is another version of this circular process, but the reassurance of cyclicity finds itself challenged by the equally prominent dialectic of "forward, backward, / slow, fast . . . high . . . down." In this context, "No moon. A room in" is almost a palindrome, a "room" being what one has when there is "No moon." Yet the "room in / a hotel" is a transit station, a preparation (note the rhyme of "ground" in line 12 with "found" in line 2) "to begin again." Indeed, the line endings in the final tercet make up a three-step unit—"in," "begin," "again"—in being the quality that stubbornly inheres in Creeley's "beginning again and again."

"The paragram," writes McCaffery, is "that aspect of language which *escapes* all discourse" (NI, 64). Discourse of the sort we meet in lines like "And Ferrente, the dapper Sicilian / coatmaker, laughed. What could / a pants presser know of dignity?" Given the overproduction of such instrumental discourses in late-twentieth-century America, with its glut of junk mail, advertising brochures, beepers, bumper stickers, answering-machine messages, and especially its increasing video coercion (on cross-country flights, it is now customary to show the preview of the film-to-be-shown with the sound on in the entire cabin, and this is only the beginning!), poetry (at least in the industrially advanced countries, the situation in, say, Eastern Europe or Latin America being very different) is coming to see its role as the production of what we might call an alternate language system. Hence the name, pretentious but essentially accurate, Language poetry—a label that, like all group labels, names of -isms, and so on, will probably have a limited life span as the designation of a specific poetic school, even as it will, paradoxically, become more significant as we begin to see "Language poetry" as part of a larger movement that began in the sixties. Let me conclude with two examples:

Consider certain emotions such as falling asleep,   I said,

(especially when one is standing on one's feet), as being similar
to fear, or anger, or fainting.   I do.   I feel sleep
in me is induced by blood forced into veins
of my brain.   I can't focus.   My tongue is numb
and so large it is like the long tongue of a calf or
the tongue of a goat or of a sheep.   What's more, I bleat.
Yes. In private, in bed, at night, with my head
turned sideways on the pillow. No wonder I say that I love to sleep.
                                                    (Leslie Scalapino)[52]

Posit gaze level diminish lamp and asleep(selv)cannot see

   MoheganToForceImmanenceShotStepSeeShowerFiftyTree

   UpConcatenationLessonLittleAKantianEmpiricalMaoris

   HumTemporal-spatioLostAreLifeAbstractSoRemotePossess

   ReddenBorderViewHaloPastApparitionOpenMostNotion is

blue glare (essence) cow bed leg extinct draw scribe   sideup
even blue (A) ash-tree fleece comfort (B) draw scribe   upside
                                                    (Susan Howe)[53]

Both these extracts come from long poetic sequences of the 1980s; both were written by women loosely associated with the Language movement. Their concerns are otherwise quite different. Leslie Scalapino's *hmmmm*, whose opening poem is the eight-line lyric above, is framed as a series of anecdotes of the "So I said and then he said and she said" variety, alternating with short explanatory poems like "I know I am sick . . . when all I can eat is something sweet" (LS, 5). In many of the twenty-eight poems in the sequence, the title doubles as the first line, as it does in "Consider certain emotions," so as to initiate a discourse that seems to simulate ordinary speech, with its short phrases, irregular rhythms, and gratuitous repetitions. "I can't focus. My tongue is numb"—these are the sort of locutions a guest on the *Donahue* show might easily use in explaining a particular disorder or state of mind.

But Scalapino uses this confessional model only to turn it inside out. "Satisfied this morning because I saw myself / (for the first time) in the mirror," the narrator tells us in "Seeing the Scenery" (LS, 16) but then adds, with a deflationary twist, that she sees herself "in the mirror as a mountain." In "Consider certain emotions," "falling asleep" is compared to "emotions" like "fear, or anger, or fainting." The third noun is at least plausible: fainting is a physical event like sleeping. But how can sleeping be an emotion like fear or anger? The poem presents itself as a logical argument, but the "reasonable" explanation proffered turns out to be absurd, and besides reason quickly gives way to the simple assertion, "I do." As the anatomy of "sleep" continues, the explanations become more and more farfetched, culminating in "What's more, I bleat. / Yes. In private, in bed, at night, with my head / turned sideways on the pillow." In this context, the "No wonder" conclusion is no conclusion at all; the reader has been given no explanation for why the poet says, "I love to sleep."

Scalapino's choppy, ungainly antilyric thus plays parodically both on the conventions of the traditional "longing for sleep" poem (e.g., Sydney's sonnet "To Sleep") and on the conventions of modern expository discourse with its drive to provide rational explanations. The refusal to name the personae of hmmmm (they appear as "I" or "one" or "you"; as "the man," "the young man," "he," and "she") or to specify the poems' referents, together with the extensive use of white space and oddly placed punctuation (sometimes three or four spaces intervene between the last letter of a word and the comma or period that follows it), produces a bleak atmosphere of noncognition. Who are these people and what is happening to them? Edith Jarolim has pointed out that Scalapino's poetry is "cinematic or 'videomatic' in its extensive use of the quick pan and cut techniques of the nonnarrative, avant garde film or the rock video: a poem or sequence will scan an event or image and then move quickly to 'shoot' it from another linguistic angle."[54] Thus the opening shot of "falling asleep" quickly pans to "standing on one's feet" at the same time as the tense shifts from past to present and "I" gives way to "one." Such decentering of the subject foregrounds the artifice of the verbal process: this is patently not "natural speech" as we might hear it on *Donahue*.

Susan Howe's *Articulation of Sound Forms in Time*, from which the second passage above is taken, draws its materials not, as in Scalapino's case, from everyday life and observation but from historical and literary documents, from archives and letters. The story of the Reverend Hope Atherton—who, having been separated from the Hatfield militia he was accompanying on an Indian raid in 1676, surrendered himself to the Indians only to have them reject him in fear, thinking him "the Englishman's God"—becomes the subject of the poet's meditation on power and marginality and, by implication, on the marginality of the woman poet (Howe plays variations on the name *Hope*, which is, of course, usually a woman's name) in America.

In one sense, then, Howe's is a more "referential" text than Scalapino's, but its actual "articulation of sound forms" is, if anything, even more fragmented. The poem welds together a series of harsh-sounding nouns and verbs, all filler (function words, conjunctions, prepositions) being cast out, so as to produce the chantlike rhythm of

ReddenBorderViewHaloPastApparitionOpenMostNotion *is*

where the italicized copula is startling in its disruption of the line's curious drumbeat. First-person reference is conspicuously deleted, the narrative voice being that of the chronicle, but a chronicle in shards or fragments, as if retrieved from a fire or flood and collaged together with other particles. In this context, words often point in two directions: in line 1, for example, it is not clear whether the "gaze" or the "lamp" is said to diminish; again, the person "asleep" may be Atherton or the Mohegans or we as readers whose "selv" is also a reduced particle. In line 2, the coalescence of words referring to the Mohegan raid startlingly culminates in the words "FiftyTree," where we expect to hear "Fifty-three," the "tree" pointing ahead to the "ash-tree" in the final line, even as the "shower" oddly turns into a "fleece."

The next four lines seem to describe Atherton's experience with the Mohegans but each of the words annexed in the linear chain without a space between them (e.g., "ToForceImmanence") is charged with a variety of meanings. We can only say that the stanza refers to the terrible conflict brought on by the "SoRemotePossess" of the colonialist settlers and their priest. Indeed, "SoRemotePossess" works to "ReddenBorderView"—greed, we might say, leads to bloodshed. The final couplet conveys a catalog of jumbled impressions, most probably the impressions of Atherton on his journey back to "civilization," whose "sideup" finally reveals itself to be "upside" as "(A)" yields to "(B)." But then again, these two isolated words—*sideup* and *upside*—also refer to the "scribe" who "draws" the picture for us—a scribe whose "articulation" of "sound forms" changes in the time-course of the poem.

"Posit gaze level diminish lamp and asleep(selv)cannot see": Howe's intricate network of p's, l's, and s's of near-rhymes ("level"/"(selv)," "sleep"/"see") and consonantal echoes ("lamp"/"asleep"), binding together words whose grammatical position is generally ambiguous (e.g., "gaze" "level"), produces a dense "writerly" texture ("draw scribe sideup . . . upside") that makes no attempt to simulate speech patterns, whether the Reverend Atherton's or the poet's own. Consciously or unconsciously, the poem's artifice may be a reaction to the mediaspeak that forms its environment. For imagine a segment of *Donahue* in which the Reverend Atherton is trying to explain his motivations at the time of the skirmish with the Mohegans. "If you ask me, Reverend," says the man in the double-knit suit, "you had no business joining an army in the first place. You're supposed to be a man of God." "I disagree," says the lady in red across the way. "I think it was a very caring and compassionate thing to do."

Both parties, no doubt, are right. Just as both of them are wrong. Poetry, in any case, has moved elsewhere.

NOTES

1. W. B. Yeats, *Letters on Poetry from W. B. Yeats to Dorothy Wellesley* (London: Oxford University Press, 1964), 56. Hereafter abbreviated as *LDW*.

2. Ezra Pound, "A Retrospect," in *Literary Essays of Ezra Pound*, ed. and intro. T. S. Eliot (New York: New Directions, 1954), 5. Hereafter abbreviated as *LE*.

3. Charles Bernstein, "Stray Straws and Straw Men," in *Content's Dream: Essays 1975–1984* (Los Angeles: Sun & Moon Press, 1986), 40. Hereafter abbreviated as *CD*.

4. T. S. Eliot, *On Poetry and Poets* (New York: Noonday Press, 1961), 21. Hereafter abbreviated as *OPP*.

5. William Wordsworth, "Preface to the *Lyrical Ballads*, with Pastoral and Other Poems" (1802), in *The Poems*, ed. John Hayden, vol. 1 (New Haven: Yale University Press, 1977), 877. Hereafter abbreviated as *WWP*.

6. T. S. Eliot, *The Use of Poetry and the Use of Criticism, Studies in the Relation of Criticism to Poetry in England* (1933; reprint, Cambridge: Harvard University Press, 1964), 63. Hereafter abbreviated as *UPUC*. Wordsworth's emphasis on rustic life, says Eliot, has to do with the particular social conditions of his time, when rural life was increasingly destroyed by rapid indus-

trialization: "It is Wordsworth's social interest that inspires his own novelty of form in verse, and backs up his explicit remarks upon poetic diction" (65).

7. I purposely say poetics, not poetry: in practice, of course, "natural speech" was itself a carefully crafted simulation, especially for Yeats whose syntactic and verbal artifices are legendary. But what interests me is that, with notable exceptions like Gertrude Stein and Hart Crane, the major Anglo-American modernists regarded the speech model as normative. Indeed, the "artifice" of Crane's style was held against him in his own day; only in the later twentieth century has this style come in for revaluation and we are now witnessing a Crane influence, for instance in the style of Charles Bernstein. On the artifices of Stein's poetry (again now exerting a strong influence on the poetry of Lyn Hejinian, Rae Armantrout, Bruce Andrews, and others), see my *Poetic License: Essays on Modernist and Postmodernist Lyric* (Evanston: Northwestern University Press, 1990), 145–59.

8. *The Letters of W. B. Yeats*, ed. Allan Wade (London: Ropert Hart-Davis, 1954), 583. Unlike Eliot, Yeats took seriously Wordsworth's concern for the "common man." A few years before his death, he told Dorothy Wordsworth that the correct formula for poetry was to "think like a wise man, yet express our selves like the common people" (*LDW,* 58).

9. Ezra Pound, *Selected Letters, 1907–1941,* ed. D. D. Paige (New York: New Directions, 1971), 48–49. Cf. Pound's review of Robert Frost's *North of Boston,* in *LE,* 384: "Mr. Frost has dared to write, and for the most part with success, in the natural speech of New England; in natural spoken speech."

10. David Antin, "Modernism and Postmodernism: Approaching the Present in American Poetry," *Boundary* 2 1.1 (1972): 131.

11. Eliot, "Introduction," in *Paul Valéry: The Art of Poetry* (New York: Vintage, 1961), xvii. Hereafter abbreviated as *PV.*

12. W. B. Yeats, *Autobiographies* (London: Macmillan, 1966), 48. Hereafter abbreviated as *Auto.*

13. T. S. Eliot, *Selected Essays* (London: Faber and Faber, 1953), 326. Hereafter abbreviated as *ESE.*

14. Samuel Taylor Coleridge, *Biographia Literaria,* ed. James Engell and W. Jackson Bate (Princeton: Princeton University Press, 1983), 52. On the large question of Wordsworth and "rustic language," see Engell and Bate's "Editors' Introduction," civ–cxiv; Karl Kroeber, "William Wordsworth," in *The English Romantic Poets: A Review of Research,* 4th ed., ed. Frank Jordan (New York: Modern Language Association of America, 1985), 329–39.

    It is interesting that Eliot cites "a remarkable letter of Wordsworth's in 1801 which he wrote to Charles James Fox [a "fashionable politician"] in sending him a copy of the *Ballads*." In this letter Wordsworth speaks of the "spreading of manufactures," the "heavy taxes upon postage," the "workhouses, houses of industry, and the invention of soup shops," as well as the "increasing disproportion between the price of labour and that of the necessities of life" as eroding "the bonds of domestic feeling among the poor." Eliot concludes that Wordsworth's predilection for humble life as poetic subject is thus motivated by social concern (UPUC, 64–65).

15. Charles Bernstein, *The Sophist* (Los Angeles: Sun & Moon Press, 1987), 44. Hereafter abbreviated as *S*.

16. Eliot's strongest position statement on the subject was the declaration in the preface to *For Lancelot Andrewes* (London: Faber and Faber, 1928) that he was "classicist in literature, royalist in politics, and anglo-catholic in religion" (ix).

17. T. S. Eliot, *Collected Poems, 1909–1962* (New York: Harcourt Brace and World, 1970). Hereafter abbreviated as ECP.

18. T. S. Eliot, *The Waste Land: A Facsimile and Transcript of the Original Drafts including the Annotations of Ezra Pound*, ed. Valerie Eliot (London: Faber and Faber, 1971), 127.

19. Donald Allen, ed., *The New American Poetry* (New York: Grove Press, 1960), xi.

20. Stephen Berg and Robert Mezey, eds., *Naked Poetry: Recent American Poetry in Open Forms* (Indianapolis: Bobbs-Merrill, 1969), xi.

21. The two best treatments of the "opening of the field," the first primarily theoretical and the second primarily historical, are Charles Altieri's *Enlarging the Temple: New Directions in American Poetry during the 1960s* (Lewisburg, Pa.: Bucknell University Press, 1979) and James E. B. Breslin's *From Modern to Contemporary: American Poetry, 1945–1965* (Chicago: University of Chicago Press, 1984).

    As in the case of high modernism (see n. 7 above), I don't want to claim that in practice Black Mountain poets and Projectivists adhered to a speech-based poetics; certainly Robert Duncan himself did not, his verbal patterns being closer to the late Romantics and pre-Raphaelites than to Eliot or Pound. What allies Duncan to the "natural speech" advocates, however, is his refusal of meter, traditional stanzaic structure, and what the New Critics called "key design" or "integral" metaphoric structure—a refusal on the grounds that such poetic features are too contrived, that they inhibit natural inspiration.

22. Charles Olson, "Projective Verse," in *Human Universe and Other Essays*, ed. Donald Allen (New York: Grove Press, 1967), 51–56.

23. Allen Ginsberg, "Notes for *Howl and Other Poems*" (1959), in *The Poetics of the New American Poetry*, ed. Donald Allen and Warren Tallman (New York: Grove Press, 1973), 319. Hereafter abbreviated as *PNAP*.

24. Allen Ginsberg, "When the Mode of the Music Changes the Walls of the City Shake" (1961), in *Esthetics Contemporary*, ed. Richard Kostelanetz (Buffalo: Prometheus Books, 1978), 335.

25. Gary Snyder, "Poetry and the Primitive: Notes on Poetry as an Ecological Survival Technique" (1967), in *PNAP*, 401–02.

26. Arthur Kroker and David Cook, *The Postmodern Scene: Excremental Culture and Hyper-Aesthetics* (New York: St. Martin's Press, 1986), 269.

27. Denise Levertov, "Some Notes on Organic Form," in *The Poet in the World* (New York: New Directions, 1973), 7–8.

28. I am referring to the dominant poetic mode of the sixties. There were, of course, notable exceptions. To give just one example, consider the opening of John Ashbery's "Clepsydra," which appears in *Rivers and Mountains* (1966; reprint, New York: Ecco Press, 1977), 27:

    > Hasn't the sky? Returned from moving the other
    > Authority recently dropped, wrested as much of
    > That severe sunshine as you need now on the way
    > You go.

    This is hardly a representation of "one person talking to another." Indeed, the relative neglect of Ashbery's poetry until the late seventies, when he published *Self-Portrait in a Convex Mirror*, may well have something to do with this poet's extreme artifice—an artifice that became acceptable only in the past decade or so. *The Double Dream of Spring* (1970) and *Three Poems* (1972) were written against the grain of sixties "authenticity."

29. Robert Grenier, "On Speech," in *In the American Tree*, ed. Ron Silliman (Orono, Maine: National Poetry Foundation, 1986), 496.

30. Jacques Derrida, *Of Grammatology*, trans. Gayatri Spivak (Baltimore: Johns Hopkins University Press, 1985), 8.

31. Michel de Certeau, "The Jabbering of Social Life," in *On Signs*, ed. Marshal Blonsky (Baltimore: Johns Hopkins University Press, 1985), 151–52.

32. See Donal Carbaugh, *Talking American: Cultural Discourses on "Donahue"* (Norwood, N.J.: Ablex Publishing Co., 1988), 3. According to Carbaugh, the show "airs in more than 200 markets, including Alaska, Hawaii, and Puerto Rico," and has won several awards including Emmys for "best show," "best host," and "outstanding achievement for a creative technical craft."

33. Jean Baudrillard, *Simulations*, trans. Paul Foss et al. (New York: Semiotext(e), 1983), 2. Hereafter abbreviated as Sim.

34. Jean Baudrillard, "Return for the Media" (1972), in *For a Critique of the Political Economy of the Sign*, trans. Charles Levin (Saint Louis: Telos Press,

1981), 169; reprinted in *Video Culture: A Critical Investigation* (Rochester, N.Y.: Gibbs M. Smith and Peregrine Smith Books, 1987), 129. Hereafter abbreviated as RM.

35. Steve McCaffery, *North of Intention: Critical Writings 1973–1986* (New York: Roof Books, 1986), 40–41. Hereafter abbreviated as NI.

36. Louis Simpson, "The Character of the Poet," in *What Is a Poet? Essays from the Eleventh Alabama Symposium on English and American Literature*, ed. Hank Lazer (Tuscaloosa: University of Alabama Press, 1987), 266.

37. Robert Lowell, "An Interview with Frederick Seidel" (1961), in *Collected Poems*, ed. Robert Giroux (New York: Farrar, Straus and Giroux, 1987), 266.

38. Robert Lowell, *Life Studies* (New York: Farrar, Straus and Giroux, 1959), 59, 79; idem, *For the Union Dead* (New York: Farrar, Straus and Giroux, 1964), 19. The phrase "the grace of accuracy" comes from "Epilogue," in idem, *Day by Day* (New York: Farrar, Straus and Giroux, 1977), 127.

39. I discuss the art of Lowell's "confessionalism" in *The Poetic Art of Robert Lowell* (Ithaca: Cornell University Press, 1973), esp. in chap. 3.

40. Altieri, *Enlarging the Temple*, 72.

41. John Berryman, "Tea," in *Love and Fame* (New York: Farrar, Straus and Giroux, 1970), 50.

42. Philip Levine, *Don't Ask* (Ann Arbor: University of Michigan Press, 1981), 101; hereafter abbreviated as DA.

43. Philip Levine, *One for the Rose* (New York: Atheneum, 1981), 60–61; reprinted in DA.

44. For a typical view, see Robert S. Miola, "Philip Levine," in *Contemporary Poets*, 4th ed., ed. James Vinson and D. L. Kirkpatrick (New York: St. Martin's Press, 1985), 496–97.

45. In the interviews that make up *Don't Ask*, Levine repeatedly attacks the government. For example: "We now exist in the kind of world that Orwell was predicting, and that simple insistence upon accurate language has become a political act. Nothing is more obvious than what our politicians are doing to our language, so that if poets insist on the truth, or on an accurate rendition . . . this is a political act" (DA, 13).
    Here is the "them" versus "us" posture that characterizes Levine's commentary on the Constitution, the Defense Department, and so on— a posture contradicted, however, by the language of his own poems.

46. Charles Bernstein, *Artifice of Absorption* (Philadelphia: Paper Air, 1987); reprinted in *A Poetics* (Cambridge: Harvard University Press, 1992), hereafter abbreviated as AA.

47. It should be noted that the very self-consciousness of the label "talk poetry," as David Antin uses it, or of an "oral poetics," as in the case of

Jerome Rothenberg, is understood as simulation. Antin's written versions of taped improvisations, for example, call attention to the equivocal status of performance and force us to consider the speech/writing relationship. See, on this point, Henry M. Sayre's excellent discussion in *The Object of Performance* (Chicago: University of Chicago Press, 1989), 174–210, as well as my *Poetics of Indeterminacy: Rimbaud to Cage* (Princeton: Princeton University Press, 1991), 288–339, and *Dance of the Intellect: Studies in the Poetry of the Pound Tradition* (Cambridge: Cambridge University Press, 1985), 192–96.

48. Clark Coolidge, *The Crystal Text* (Great Barrington, Mass.: The Figures, 1986), 33.

49. Charles Bernstein, "Undone Business," in CD, 332.

50. M. L. Rosenthal, "Problems of Robert Creeley," *Parnassus: Poetry in Review* 2 (Fall–Winter 1973): 211–12.

51. Robert Creeley, *The Collected Poems of Robert Creeley* (Berkeley and Los Angeles: University of California Press, 1982), 423.

52. Leslie Scalapino, *Considering how exaggerated the music is* (San Francisco: North Point Press, 1982), 3. Hereafter abbreviated as LS.

53. Susan Howe, *Articulation of Sound Forms in Time* (New York: Awede, 1987), unpaginated.

54. Edith Jarolim, "No Satisfaction: The Poetry of Leslie Scalapino," *North Dakota Quarterly* 55.4 (1987): 268–69.

Pattern

Experience

Song

6   what it means to be avant-garde
David Antin

in april of 1981 i was invited to a conference on the avant-garde that
was to be held in iowa city and i was a little surprised   for all i knew iowa
was a state of complacent farmers who raised hogs and corn and had a university
whose art and writing programs generated equally bland products   at the
same time most of the art world seemed to be returning to somewhat less bland but
equally predictable painted products   so it seemed like a strange time and
place for a conference on the avant-garde   it was news to me that the
university of iowa housed an extensive dada archive and under the shelter of some
odd department or other   also harbored a group of experimental video artists
and tolerated   a loosely connected artist performance group   so the art
historians who managed the dada archive invited a number of other art historians
and critics   roz krauss ed fry and a few others   to talk about the early
20th century avant-garde   along with the three richards   kostelanetz
schechner and higgins and jerry rothenberg and me   to give some kind of
reading of the contemporary situation

when i got to the campus a tornado was threatening   thunder
and lightning were storming outside while richard kostelanetz was defining the
avant-garde from the stage of a crowded hall   but the tornado missed
us   the next day was sunny   little ducks were walking around the
campus and richard schechner was lamenting a decline from the traditions of the
heroic avant-garde sixties and prophesying our entry into a terrible and dull new
time

because i knew there was going to be a kind of
transition between the readings that i knew we were going to have
here and the kind of talking i do   i thought i would surprise
everybody by   bringing a couple of clippings from newspapers
and reading from them along with my talking   and i decided
this improvisatorily   in the manner of my talking   as i
came upon them   fortuitously   on the plane coming from
san diego
i'm something of a newspaper buff   and setting off

this day in an airplane heading east toward iowa city   over
denver   with a copy of the san diego union   something
   made me want to read this copley newspaper   which like
many local newspapers   once you get past the first few
   pages   is filled with stories of surprising and unlikely
things   to which i have an attraction   as i have an
attraction to a newspapers organization   an attraction shared
by many artists   possibly because of its fractured collage-like
   structure   and as we flew out over the rising mountains
immediately to the east of san diego i was struck by the title of a
one column story

COLOR THE ISLES SOFT PINK

   christo   the story continued   the artist who gave the
world the VALLEY CURTAIN in the colorado rockies and the
RUNNING FENCE in california   now wants to color the
   islands of biscayne bay pink   the controversial artist unveiled
his newest project tuesday
                          how curious this language sounds when
you read it out loud
                          he plans to cover ten uninhabited islands in the
bay which separates miami from miami beach with   silky
   soft   pink   polypropylene fabric   because the
islands are not entirely uninhabited   if one considers all the
   world's inhabitants   something more gets said   the
effect the artist said   would be of a series of glowing water
   lilies   an homage to claude monets water lily paintings
                                                           like
any artist christo said   i will have my water lilies
                                                        he said the
project would be entitled

SURROUNDED ISLANDS PROJECT FOR BISCAYNE BAY
GREATER MIAMI

   it would cost from eight hundred thousand to one million
   dollars   and the money would come from the sale of the
   drawings and collages of the project   so its an ecological
project   of a sort   except for the polypropylene   the
work was commissioned by the

and planned for june 4 to june 26 1982 in miami   the festival
also features new plays by arthur miller edward albee and tennessee
   williams
               theres something about reading newspapers thats like
throwing the i ching

               now christo also said   and this is what i was
coming to   that he had consulted with the environmentalists
   and government agencies on this project and he had run into no
   objections   though he had not yet secured the required
permits
               our new department of the interior must have proved fairly easy

               according to christo helicopters would drop the fabric
   onto the islands over a ten mile stretch of bay from downtown
miami to sunny isles   then a crew of four hundred would pull
the pink cocoon into place all at once   and his water lilies would
   then remain in place for two weeks before coming down
                                                  it would
   be enchanting   not imposing or menacing but intimate and
lyrical the artist promised
                              this sounds like my old collage poetry
again   but i want to consider this from the point of view of
questions concerning the avant-garde
                              now i'm not proposing christo
   as an avant-garde artist   but if this art is avant-garde its not
   very challenging   to the chamber of commerce of greater
miami   because the chamber is perfectly cheerful about it
      and somebody is running interference for it with the rest of
the people of miami   probably lots of people   though
   mainly jeanne claude   and the work will get done   i
have no doubt   and i have no doubt that it will be juxtaposed
   with other avant-garde works by arthur miller tennessee williams
and edward albee

               about the same time or shortly after i came upon
another article that raised similar questions for me   it was one
   of those days when i was absolutely starved for news and wherever i
looked i found it   and this article read

what it means to be avant-garde III

ACTOR KEEPS HIS HEAD BUT KILLER DOESNT

every actor wants to be a movie star says joe spinell and everybody
    else wants to be in the movies including the usherettes   this
is in a section called THE ARTS   spinell is a new york born
character actor who decided that one way to become a star was to
        write and produce your own film   which he did and he put
himself in the lead   the film he wrote is called MANIAC and is
about a psychotic killer who murders and mutilates beautiful
women
            spinell gives a learned account of the plot structure   its
based on modern day killers who had problems with their mothers
        the style   here he turns to film history   through the
killers eyes   is taken from the peter lorre movie M
                                                                well maybe
    lorre is not the auteur   but thats all right we're close   but
unlike the lorre classic   according to the writer in the san
    diego union   MANIAC has such an abundance of blood that it
is difficult to get distributed by home box office or any of the other
regular distributors   in fact the los angeles times in a sudden
    access of morality has refused to take ads for the film because the
    victim gets his revenge on the maniac by tearing his head off full
    camera

                    why did spinell use so much violence?   to compete
says the forty year old actor   we had to come up with something
    new   now is joe spinell in the avant-garde   making it
    new?   its maybe not clear   because joe spinell will tell
you   "look dont tell me about violence and blood because then
i have to talk about ABC and CBS   for twenty-two years theyve
been bringing us the vietnamese war"
                                political morality enters
here   this is a moral form of the avant-garde   but he takes
    this no further   just says i'm making movies for people to
enjoy   "if you want art go to a museum   people give me
money to make a movie to make money   thats why we're
called an industry   the movie industry   the industry is in
    trouble and television is partly to blame   people are
inundated by tv and their brains are numb"
                                moralizing educational
and avant-garde roles are all preempted by movie maker joe

spinell   there appears to be no place to go here between lyrical
    intimate commercial avant-garde artist christo and avant-garde
    didactic moralist commercial shocker joe spinell

                and i was thinking about this while i was flying toward
    iowa and thinking about how everyone was going to be trying to
    locate the avant-garde   and about how almost everyone was
    going to agree that it would involve either shocking or making it
    new   and that i was supposed to be talking about this
    too   and i realized i was going to be confused   because
    practically every role classically attributed to the avant-garde has
    been preempted by something else   and i reflected that i
    myself have never really had a clear image of what it was to be
    avant-garde   though ive been thrust into the role often
        enough to know what it feels like to be avant-garde

                a friend of mine had written a book marjorie perloff had
    written a book dealing with american poetry as a kind of french
    connection   as opposed to the english connection which is
    conventionally supposed for it in the schools   now i personally
    think there are many roots to contemporary american poetry
            certainly my poetry and the poetry i admire   but i also
    know what writing a book means   in a book you have to
    organize your ideas pretty much one thing at a time   if its
    an important thing and you want to really get it done   and
    this is a book   designed to challenge what i have always thought
    of as the anglophiliac model of american poetry that is so dominant
    in those literary strongholds east of the mississippi   or the
        connecticut river   north of the monongahela   that are
    so strongly devoted to an anglican passion   that they give the
    impression of some kind of outpost in a novel by huxley or evelyn
        waugh   where the people are sitting around on a veranda
    sipping their gin slings in the shade of the local textile factory or
    integrated circuit fabricating plant   dreaming of playing polo or
        cricket or rugby in the greener older playing fields at eton or
        harrow   which they may never have seen   being often
        second generation eastern european jews from brooklyn or
        queens   or lithuanians from indiana or lutherans from
        wisconsin   and somehow there they are gathered on the
    veranda in new haven or manhattan in memory of the british
        empire   of which they are among the last supports   and

several columns of which this book is probably intended to take
away
            or maybe more precisely this book is only bringing the news to
those outposts that the british empire has long since passed
      away   and that the messages from england would no longer
be coming and had not been coming for a long time   and that
there was a french connection as there is a russian connection and a
      spanish connection   and for many a chinese connection or
japanese connection   there are lots of connections in this
world   but in a book you have to do one thing at a time
            the world may not happen one thing   at a time but in a
book you have to tell one thing at a time
                                                            and my friend was invited
to washington to be part of a discourse with some of these english
      emigres and refugees   among whom were numbered harold
bloom and john hollander and richard howard   who are
      certainly distinguished members of the refugee community

                        now marjorie was giving a talk based on the last chapter
of her most recent book   *the poetics of indeterminacy*   the
last chapter of which happens to deal with john cage and with me
and whatever differences there may be between cage and me
            and these are considerable   we were both obliterated by
the righteous wrath of harold bloom   who had hardly heard
      more than our names   when he denounced the proceedings as
ridiculous and us as nonpoets and stormed off the stage   i was
      told about this performance of blooms and thought it was
wonderful and forgot about it   but it was not long afterward
      that i was invited out to the very same place to do a talk
performance on the folger librarys little shakespearean stage
            and it happened that when i came to do the performance i had
something serious in mind   because a friend of mine had died
      two or three days before   after a sudden and unexpected
hospitalization from which we had all hoped she would come out
alive   and i wanted to make my piece a kind of homage
            a meditation and speculation on the nature of her life and
death

                        so in the course of things i told her story   or what
      i knew of it   and i tried to consider the nature of the fit

between the life we lead and the death we get   and what i
  wanted to think about was whether there was such a fit and if there
was   what kind it was   and i did the best i could under
the circumstances   of being there   then   which is
my image of what an artist does and is   somebody who does
  the best he can   under the circumstances   without
worrying about making it new or shocking   because the best
  you can do depends upon what you have to do and where
        and if you have to invent something new to do the work at
hand you will   but not if you have a ready-made that will
work and is close at hand and you want to get on with the rest of
  the business
                then youll pick up the tool thats there   a tool
that somebody else has made   that will work   and youll
lean on it and feel grateful when its good to you   for somebody
  elses work   and youll think of him as a friend who would
  borrow as freely from you if he thought of it or needed to
        because there is a community of artists   who dont
recognize copyrights and patents   or shouldnt   except
under unusual circumstances   who send each other tools in the
mail or exchange them in conversation in a bar
                                though i had a
couple of friends from whom i got a lot of things in the mail
        who got very nervous about exchanging things with each
other because they had ileana sonnabend looking over their
  shoulders   and one of them got so distressed because he had
  ileana looking over his shoulder forbidding him to collaborate with
the other friend   that when he wrote the text for the others
installation performance he never put his name on it   but this
is an unusual situation   and i only mention it because of that

        and i was there in washington doing the best i
  could   borrowing when i could and inventing when i had
to   and the audience was tolerant and reasonable   and
listened to me doing the best i could   and when i was
  through there was a small gathering of people who came up to talk
with me   because when you talk to people they naturally want
to talk to you   because theyve had some of you presented to
them   and a discourse has been initiated or suggested   at
  least in my kind of poetry   which is intended to open a

discourse and not close it   a discourse that can go on with or
without me once ive contributed to it   and the first question
   that anybody asked me as we were standing around the punch
bowl was what do you think of harold bloom?

                                        i said i'm sorry
          i dont think of harold bloom   they said but could you
think of harold bloom?   i said i could think of harold
bloom   i could think of harold bloom if i wanted to   you
want me to? all right   i'll try   they said what does harold
bloom have against you?   i said   its not personal
       they said   but he seemed so angry   he thinks i'm
trying to kill him   its an emigre condition i said   you
imagine people are threatening you from outside   and
everything outside seems terribly threatening   i dont blame
  him for being angry   if i thought somebody was trying to
kill me i might be angry at them   i'm not trying to kill harold
bloom
          they said   then really why was he so angry?

                                                  well i said i
   think he's suffering from a case of mistaken identity

                                             they said whats
that?
          i said   first he thinks he's part of a great tradition
       he's not   second he thinks he's a critic of poetry he's
not   and then he thinks he knows what the world of poetry
consists of   but he doesnt

                             they said what do you mean by
that?   and i said look   years ago   the first time i
ever heard of harold bloom   he came to my attention by
   accident   somebody i knew   an editor for an east coast
publishing house   who now works for the national
  endowment   said to me   you have to read this its
extraordinary   it was a work on william blake   it was
not extraordinary   it was what you would expect from an
   academic literary critic with a taste for romanticism   a more
or less plausible account of blake as a complex and ironic poet that
might have pleased any new critic   except that blake wasnt a
  catholic or anglican or even a presbyterian   but some kind of
funny   homemade   secular   religionist   whose
gospel tended to make most of the new critics laugh   both

because it was funny and because they had a strong taste for
institutional orthodoxy
                              but from harold bloom you dont get a sense
that theres anything funny about casting allegorical epics with a set
of entities that have names like orc and urthona and oothoon in
   places or states with names like golgonooza or ulro   which
blake comments on through a set of quirky drawings that make him
   one of the first and most peculiar concrete poets to work in
english
              but from harold bloom you dont get any sense at all only an
explanation   so i didnt think he was extraordinary at all but
   rather ordinary   and like most academic critics rather
useless   until he extended himself beyond romantic
poetry   or appeared to   and offered what he called a
   theory of poetry
                              now its not really a theory   because its not
at all testable and has no explanatory power   it is in fact only
a suggestion described as a theory   about the way poets who
   are not yet poets   come to be poets through the poetry of the
poets   that have preceded them   which as a suggestion is
not in itself extraordinary   but in the way bloom works this
out   which is fairly extraordinary   as a struggle of the
sons with the ghosts of their poetical   fathers   from
   whom they have learned what they want their poetry to be
   and whose poetical powers they want to acquire and consider
their own
              now what is extraordinary is not blooms seedy
   freudianism   the oedipal struggle between fathers and
   sons   which has continued to be fashionable in academic
literary circles far longer than its nineteenth-century imagery would
suggest   but the object of the struggle   a poetical style
or perhaps a poetical content   in any case a poetical
product   that bloom sees as a kind of commodity over which
   there is a copyright dispute
                              this is quite extraordinary and very
   funny   especially since as far as bloom is concerned there are
very few of these poetical products and they appear to have been
   disputed for centuries   since each father had a father with
   whom he must in turn have disputed the rights   so poor john
ashbery must have wallace stevens for a father who   you may

not believe this   will have whitman for his father who will
have emerson as his   as emily dickinson will also   and
pound may have browning who will have shelley who will have
wordsworth who will have milton who will have spenser who will
found the line   the abraham of post-enlightenment poetry
                                                            but
what is this product and what use could it possibly be in any time if
it remained the same over all that time three drastically different
centuries
            but for bloom time and culture count for nearly
nothing   cabalists and calvinists english lords   brooklyn
journalists hartford insurance executives and new york art
critics   as poets confront nothing but death and the crises of
the personal ego   so the whole line of blooms contending
"strong poets" turns out to be only the textbook version of english
romanticism   suitably trivialized and egotized by bloom and
called the tradition   now i have very little interest in what
anybody would call a tradition and no interest in anything you
could call a canon   but i can see the service bloom has
rendered graduate students of english literature   he has reduced
for them the great number of poets to a handful of "strong"
ones   who turn out to be the most familiar ones of the
textbooks   and set his students to work finding their poet
fathers   for which task he has equipped them with a mongrel
array of greek and hebrew technical terms   useful i suppose
mainly to console them for their lack of ability to read in any other
language than english   while for the rest of the general
educated public   if they read him   he has created the
consolatory sense of the increasing belatedness and progressively
more attenuated virtues of each successive generation of poets from
blake and wordsworth to the present   encouraging this reader
or nonreader to take comfort from his ignorance of the dozens of
contemporary poets working in his language   that it would
most probably not have been worth his trouble to make their
acquaintance at all
                        and thats what i told this man in
washington   or something to that effect   and what i
realized as i said it then   and realize as i say it now   there
is something of an idea of the avant-garde in harold bloom
        however inverted   and even he seems more at home with it
than i am   a notion of first comers whose achievements were

new and blocked the way to further achievements along the same
path   an idea of patented inventions   each one acting as
a roadblock   and the tradition as a series of bitterly fought
retreats till the last "strong" poet finds himself like kafkas rodent or
a beckett character backed into the last corner of the room   its a
funny view of a tradition   having it back you into a
corner   and comically a little like clement greenbergs version of
modernist painting   in which the brilliant achievement of
one artist closes an avenue to the next   but actually rather
more like the architecture of florence   where genius has
choked up the traffic and wont let you renovate the streets

            but at least the tradition of art history is based on a
serious cultural ideology   on the preeminence and power of
the nineteenth-century industrial state that traced the marvel of its
own spiritual development in a history that began with an ingenious
geography
            for as michel de certeau has pointed out in his great
book on "the writing of history"   all history begins with
    geography   first you mark out the place where it all
happened   and this   demarcation of the historical place
creates along its boundaries the nonhistorical place   where
nothing has happened in any developmental way   and there is
no history   only anthropology   because there are only the
customs and traditions and rituals that maintain   the primitive
traditional?   self   because history is the allegorical epic
of the development of the civilized citizen self

            so art history has been worked out as a fantastical
progress   from the fertile crescent to egypt   in a few
skips across the mediterranean to greece over the adriatic to
    italy   across the alps to culminate in paris   or perhaps
london or berlin   from ur to the eiffel tower   or if you
choose literature   from nimrod to arnold bennett or thomas
mann   which in the interests of a purely illusory sanity is
foreshortened in the schools and taught as the tradition of painting
from giotto to picasso which is no less maniacal   only less
intelligible   because it reduces hegels outrageous but
understandable pilgrimage from slavery to the freedom of the
german state to an intellectual rubble or pile of bric-a-brac
    which is a junk heap not a tradition   and to which the only

adequate response may be nietzsches comment that german
culture and education   for this read european institutionalized
culture is no culture at all   only a deeply entrenched
barbarism   but of course in the united states institutionalized
culture is not a deeply entrenched barbarism   it is only a sickly
barbarism   barely clinging to the saddle
                                                                    so when it
speaks   or groans   which is perhaps more appropriate
for harold bloom   of its tradition   it is not speaking from
    any particular institutional authority   just a provincial place
in new haven   which is why i do not normally think of harold
bloom and his tradition except as an entertainment and as somebody
    asks me in the present   because all that unites us in this
country is the present   and the difficulty of recognizing it and
    occupying it   which is why its so easy to slip into prophesy
and the emptiness of the future   that is so easy to occupy
because of its emptiness   that we will fill up so quickly with a
cargo of memories and attendant dreams

                            so just a moment ago richard schechner was trying to
tell us about the present state of the avant-garde   and gave us a
    cautionary account of how everything in theater and performance
now was a decline from the revolutionary great old days   how
even the best of the new artists are merely indulging in degraded
versions of the great techniques of the revolutionary predecessors
    instead of carrying on and developing the tradition   while
even the best of the old are no longer capable of going on in their
avant-garde way   but are at best repeating themselves
    and then he cautioned us that the loss of this tradition of the
sixties would cost us dearly   as the new fascism of the reagan
    government was almost upon us and we would once again need
revolutionary artists to lead a new resistance

                            and i marveled to hear this nostalgic account of the great
    past   and cautionary account of the terrible future
accompanying so trivial a grip on the present   in the mouth of
an avowed member of what for the lack of a better term we could
    call the sixties avant-garde   but maybe thats the problem
with the notion of the avant-garde   that it turns itself from a
    discourse into a tradition   whose members worry about its
    decline in a threatening future   and maybe thats why i'm such

a poor avant-gardist   because i'm mainly concerned with the
present   which if i can find it might let me know what to
do   and as for the future   it will find us all by itself
        whether we look backwards or forwards it will be there at the
top of the stairs   meanwhile i want to occupy the present

        and what is it at this moment in the united states
a rocketing inflation that no particular politician can make anything
        other than a rash claim to understand   a rising
unemployment that anyone can understand and underestimate as
        they understand   because as the number of people who lose
their employment increases   so the number of people who are
no longer eligible for unemployment compensation who become
        demoralized and no longer appear at the unemployment offices
        looking for employment or the help they can no longer
receive   increases as well   and these people disappear
        from the numbers of the unemployed as they cease to be counted
        among the job hunting poor   who as they are no longer
counted dont count and become some kind of indefinitely numerous
        ghosts   who no longer live in our affluent or struggling
        economy   but trouble it mysteriously nonetheless
                                        and if for a
        long time i didnt know what it meant to be haunted i begin to
know it now   in the present even as i read the newspapers or
walk down the street looking for it   and i pick up my
hometown paper   the san diego union and read about the grant
        hotel

                now the grant hotel used to be the only tall building in
san diego   it wasnt very tall   it was about ten stories
        tall   but for a long time it was the tallest building in sleepy
san diego   there are a lot of taller ones now   but for a
        certain kind of businessman clientele its had a kind of nostalgia and
        chic and was considered good for christmas and new years parties
and the like   though in the last couple of years it had gotten a
        bit rundown and a new ownership had just taken it over and was
planning to spruce it up
                        and whether in line with this or not
        the other day they were testing the hydraulic lift for the
outside fire escape   the mechanism failed and the falling fire
escape killed an eighty-five year old man named angel aquinero and

what it means to be avant-garde 121

his seventy-five year old friend sam marino who happened to be
walking by   and narrowly missed two twenty-two year olds
who scampered out of the way
                                        and while i find the whole story
interesting   i find it curious that the name of one of the fast
    twenty-two year olds was jack kemp   the same name as the
      distinguished supply side legislator who had been a fleet footed
    quarterback behind one of the worst offensive lines for the buffalo
      bills   where he had distinguished himself also for getting the
    hell out of the way in a hurry   and i imagine if the policies
      he has advocated result in a collapse he will once again be
    distinguished for getting the hell out of the way in a hurry   or
    a lot quicker than any elderly retired cook

                          and i asked myself as i was reading the paper   how
      come this fire escape being tested right in the middle of the day
    on broadway fell on two street smart old men just like that
          didnt they have any ropes or some sort of barrier and signs
    warning people away   no says the newspaper article
          there were no ropes or barriers or signs because theres no
    ordinance requiring them for testing the hydraulic lift of a fire
      escape   well i suppose not   perhaps theyd never had
    trouble before   but then had they had much experience
    testing it   had they ever tested it before   did they test it
      regularly   once a year maybe or just suddenly now
          because they were renovating and a city agency had just
    noticed them and required the test   but there was nothing
    about this in the paper either   still the paper mentioned two
    men in street clothing shouting people away
                                              now i have an image
      of angel aquinero eighty-five years old his hearing not so terribly
      good any more   concentrating on talking to his friend and
      listening to him while walking by   and when they shout at
    him he has things on his mind   more important than anything
        two punk kids could be calling out waving rudely at him and
      samuel marino   and he's got a life to live angel   its his
      street   and the people of the street recognize this by calling
      him the mayor the mayor of broadway   and i would think
          that the mayor of broadway deserves more consideration when he's
      walking down his own street   than to be yelled at and have a

fire escape fall on his head   but the hotel feels justified
        because it was operating within ordinances that didnt
recognize the dignity due the mayor

                                        and as i continued leafing
through the newspaper looking for the present   i came on
some letters relating to the problems of the tradition in the columns
        of dear abby   two letters   while i was sitting in the
plane thinking about the problems of the avant-garde   that
from two utterly distinct perspectives raised the problems posed by
        the present to the tradition

                                one letter could have been written by
        harold bloom

                "dear abby"   it went   "i am planning to
        marry this summer   my parents are divorced and my mother
is remarried   i have my heart set on having a traditional church
        wedding   who should give me away?   my father or my
stepfather?   both consider me their daughter and i love them
        both equally   my mother says the one who pays for the
wedding should have the right to give me away   probably my
stepfather   this is giving me an ulcer   ive even considered
eloping so i wouldnt have to make a choice   but i really do
        want a church wedding   i have a twenty-one year old
brother who could walk me down the aisle but he says he'd rather
        be an usher

                        please tell me what to do   i dont want to hurt any
feelings on my wedding day"

                but there is a second letter from a totally different point
        of view   and if the first one is harold bloom   the
second is a little more like me   this letter is from a second wife
who writes to console a writer of a previous day who had
complained of the problems of being a second wife

                "dont despair   i'm also a number two   the
man i married was previously married to a delightful woman
named sue   for years my mother-in-law called me sue
        my name is joan   she even gave me gifts on sues
birthday   she loved sue and she loves me too   now i'm
divorced and my ex is presently going with a lady named jean

i understand that my former mother-in-law is now calling jean
joan
joan"

so you can see why for me   joan   the
tradition will resolve itself in the present   and all you have to
do is find it   but if you dont it will find you   often quite
rapidly and without warning   but in any case my feeling is
that it will come as it came to me one day recently

not long ago i moved my mother to san diego from
brooklyn where she had lived for many years   now its a long
distance from brooklyn to san diego   and the life thats lived
here is as different as the climate   and i would never have
moved her but her life was falling apart   or at least she felt that
it was   she was getting older   she was seventy-eight or
seventy-nine   and the neighborhood that she'd been living in
for the last twenty years   ocean parkway   had been
running down and was now inhabited by strangers   who she
felt were menacing and strange   and she was finding it
progressively more difficult to manage her daily affairs   putting
her checks in the bank and taking care of the gas bill and the
telephone and the rent   so i moved her to an apartment in
pacific beach near the bay   and i cant really manage her affairs
very well   but even i can manage them better than she can

and i arranged to move her things from brooklyn and
flew out to get her   and i installed her in this sunny little
apartment on la playa in a small complex of apartments managed by
a very helpful and authoritarian ex-military man who looked out
for her and took her shopping when he could and called me when he
couldnt   and all seemed to be going fairly well
                                                    till she began
to have problems with the telephone company and san diego gas and
electric   with whom she quarreled over the bills even when i
arranged to pay them   and with the bank   that she was
convinced was defrauding her of her interest   so that she went
there every day to make sure it was recorded   and fought with
the tellers when they wouldnt satisfy her   and it got so that
the tellers would go to great lengths not to have to deal with
her   because from their point of view she would fly into

inexplicable rages over matters they didnt understand   and the
sight of a little white haired lady in a small brimmed orange cloche
hat coming through the doors of their bank would strike terror into
their hearts   and the more attentive of them catching sight of
her coming through the doors clutching her ancient purse to her
  chest and holding a bundle of bankbooks in her hand would beat
it quickly to the john or the coffee machine for a much needed
break
          and the manager would eventually call me and i would have to
drive down with her to straighten things out while they listened
          sympathetically and i tried to explain to her what they had
quite correctly done   which only made her angrier because
they appeared to be talking to me instead of to her   "and its
my money" she said

          but all this was manageable until she started to quarrel
with her apartment manager or until she started to suspect
  him   as she suspected everyone else   of stealing from
her   her money her bankbooks her toothbrush her needles and
  thread   and finally her ice cube trays

          at this point i moved her out into an apartment
  hotel   a resident hotel for elderly men and women where they
  got their meals cooked and served to them their rooms cleaned and
beds made   and lived with other men and women whose
  capabilities were not much greater than their own   which she
might have enjoyed   except that she was losing her grip on the
present so that it didnt mean much to her   and she complained
of it for reasons that seemed odd when she explained them
to me
          they were prejudiced against her because she was jewish
          because she was from scranton   and she wanted to go
back to where her people were   in new york   and it was
useless for me to explain to her that nearly thirty percent of the
people that lived in her hotel   were jewish   that i'd
heard them speaking yiddish and i'd heard her speaking with
them   and that her good friend with whom i'd seen her sitting
much of the time was italian   but she spoke yiddish too
          better than my mother who was really a native speaker of
english with a pennsylvania accent   who had never really
learned to speak a fluent yiddish at all

but what good would it do   all she wanted to do
was go home to the scranton of seventy years ago or the new york
of thirty or forty or fifty years ago   so i reminded her that
all of her remaining relatives were living in miami now and maybe
she would like to visit them   but that worried her because her
sister bessie would be nearly ninety now and sarah must be over
eighty-five   and sylvia   well sylvia

but i had an idea   i would call her brother irving
who was younger than she was   he was taking care of sylvia
and living in florida not far from her other sisters   she could
visit with him and get a chance to see sarah and bessie before they
died   and sylvia too   and the idea of being with her
family again her sisters and brother appealed to her because it was
her only idea of home   so i said that i would call irving
because i thought she could manage a plane trip if i put her on the
plane at one end and her brother picked her up at the other
        and i was about to do this   when i got a phone call
picked up the receiver and heard a hoarse voice that sounded like a
member of the mafia or an italian bookie   that i recognized
as my uncle irving saying "hello david"

now i hadnt heard that voice for years   but this
gentle heavy man spoke with the voice of a heavy   there may
be something about a persons life that brings one into the world as a
heavy   maybe running a candy store surrounded by bookies
and detectives he had come to sound like one of them
        developing over the years that kind of cracked and breathy
pharyngeal growl that i immediately recognized as my uncle

"hello irving" i said with a confidence that surprised me
but not him   though i had not spoken to him for nearly
twenty years
        and he said "listen sonny   i know youre taking
care of your momma"   i said "well she's all right   she's
not bad" i said   "she's in a hotel and she's not too happy
because she's not surrounded with family   but she's
comfortable"
        he said "look i know your momma is a difficult
person   she's never been very happy and i know youre doing

your best for her   but she's had a very hard life   and i
   think it would do her good to come down here and visit with her
family"   i said thats a wonderful idea how should we arrange
   it   and he says   "look she takes the plane to fort
lauderdale   i come in and pick her up right away and she'll live
   the life of reilly"

                "the life of reilly"   i hadnt heard that expression in
years   since i was a kid and william bendix played it on the
radio in the nineteen forties   and my uncle irving was
promising my mother a rerun in the nineteen eighties
                                                he said "yeah
she'll lead the life of reilly   its beautiful here   we'll take
   her all around she'll see the seashore   she'll see all the
children and grandchildren the beautiful houses they live in
        she'll live like a queen"

                i said "it sounds good   but why dont you call her
and talk to her too   itll do her good to hear your voice and give
   her confidence   she may be a little nervous about such a long
trip"

                "sure sonny i understand   but maybe you should
   give her my number too in case i cant reach her right away
        ive got kind of irregular hours   i'm working as a night
watchman   and sometimes i'm not in"

                "sure i said   ok irving"   but i knew she'd
never be able to make the call   though i coached her on how
to do it from the pay phone in the hall   by dialing the operator
   and billing the call to me   because i knew that she'd lose her
confidence or forget altogether   but i said sure and a week
went by   two weeks   three weeks   no irving
        and i couldnt figure out why irving hadnt called in all that
time
        so i asked my mother did you try to call irving   and this
was a very difficult if not entirely pointless thing to do
        because having a conversation with my mother about some
specific act or event that either did or did not occur in the recent
past was difficult   because of the way she loses hold of the

present about as soon as it goes past   and pointless because
what she says is so unreliable as she tries to cover up her losses
        but i tried to find out whether irving had called her   or
more improbably   whether she had called him   and she
    tried to remember   or more precisely to answer   so we
both tried and became exhausted with our effort

                    she felt spent with the immense effort of struggling with
an uncooperative long distance operator who refused to put her
    through   with a signal that didnt lead to a familiar voice at the
    other side   and ended in tears   for weeks she had been
trying to get irving she had called again and again   she was
exhausted with all of the trying she was describing   and still
    there was no irving and now she was close to tears because
something might be wrong

                    and while i didnt really believe this i decided to
    call   so i dialed him in the morning and nobody
    answered   i tried again in the afternoon and that night and
    the next morning   and i remember thinking it was
strange   because i knew that his wife fanny stayed home much
of the time looking after my aunt sylvia who had become something
of an invalid and spent all of her days on the couch looking at
    whatever was on television   so i thought it was strange and
kept on trying   and one day several weeks later i dialed the
    number and somebody picks up the phone and its a womans
    voice   and i say "hello   can i speak with irving"
        and a womans voice becomes hard and cold and says "is this
    some kind of joke"   and i say "no no   fanny is that
    you?"   she says   "david?   is that you"   i said
        yes   and she said "irving died"   "what happened?" i
said
        she said   "remember he called you?"   "yes"
        "well that night he went to work at his watchmans job
        he went out to get a cup of coffee during his break and a car
came around the corner and hit him and he got killed"

                    now i hadnt counted on the presence of fort lauderdale
or miami   or my uncle   who had appeared on the
    telephone and then disappeared   nothing within the horizon

of my discourse could have prepared me for that moment with my
aunt fanny   who had just lost the husband she'd lived with for
over forty years and was now on the telephone

                               and it seems to be
that if you cant respond to that youre not in the avant-garde

7   Pattern—and the "Simulacral"
Leslie Scalapino

The way things are seen in a time is that period of time and is the composition of that time. The way things are seen is unique in any moment, as a new formation of events, objects, and cultural abstraction.

> The composition is the thing seen by every one living in the living they are doing, they are composing of the composition that at the time they are living is the composition of the time in which they are living. It is that that makes living a thing they are doing. Nothing else is different, of that almost any one can be certain. The time when and the time of and the time in that composition is the natural phenomenon of that composition.[1]

Gertrude Stein's conception of a continuous present is when everything is unique, beginning again and again and again. *A* does not equal *A*, in terms of Stein's view of the continuous present. This leads to lists, which lead to romanticism in which everything is the same and therefore different.

> Romanticism is then when everything being alike everything is naturally simply different, and romanticism. (520)

Romanticism is not a confusion but an extrication. Culture is a transformative composite separate from individuals. The quality in the creation of expression in the composition has to do with the unique entity, being in balance and moving as it ceases to be identical with itself. This has to do with apprehending what occurs now—with it being *always* now, which constitutes being in a state of turmoil:

> There must be time that is distributed and equilibrated. This is the thing that is at present the most troubling and if there is the time that is at present the most troublesome the time-sense that is at present the most troubling is the thing that makes the present the most troubling. (522–23)

The present is the loci (i.e., multiple) of change. The travel book as a genre is a stylized mode having its own laws and pattern, which is realistic with present-time events and people: Hemingway, in *Green Hills of Africa*, creates a new form while using the travel book format describing an actual hunting expedition that lasted for a month.[2] It is not fiction; there is no beginning, middle, or end as such. There are potentially an infinite number of animals and events as the condition of writing.

Therefore his pattern is a list of places, objects, animals, and actions. Reading is somehow the means of their actual occurrence.

Style is cultural abstraction—i.e., that period—how relationships with people take place (how they're seen) in a period. They become visible by being simplified—by indicating this is occurring—as the canned scenario.

The narrator does not write while hunting, only reads. Therefore action is "doing something you are ignorant about." So killing is everything being the same and therefore different, the trigger of the gun being "like the last turn of the key opening a sardine can." A unique connection is the vulcanized rubber faintly transparent looking (as if miming) rhino discovered in death. As the relation between life and writing:

The rhino was in high grass, somewhere in there behind some bushes. As we went forward we heard a deep, moaning sort of groan. Droopy looked around at me and grinned. The noise came again, ending this time like a blood-choked sigh. Droopy was laughing. "Faro," he whispered and put his hand palm open on the side of his head in the gesture that means to go to sleep. Then in a jerky-flighted, sharp-beaked little flock we saw the tick birds rise and fly away. We knew where he was and, as we went slowly forward, parting the high grass, we saw him. He was on his side, dead. (78)

In *Green Hills of Africa*, the pattern of experience and the account (expressed as being the mode of "genre") are not parallel, which makes this text similar to the dissimulation and simulacra of artists of the postmodern period.

In Michael McClure's work, the concentration is on the individual unit—something being seen to be unlike anything else.[3] Oneself is the "simulacra": identity is defined in his poems in terms of other entities (we are "DARK FLESH MUSIC / LAYING OUT A SHAPE," we are "INSTRUMENTS / THAT / PLAY / ourselves," etc.). Therefore the author or the sense of self and the investigation of its desire is the pattern, which is neither present time nor the past. It is potentially infinite in form and number, as points of intuitional apprehension.

Cultural abstractions such as the love image in Jean Harlow or the perfect chill slot of space of Wall Street (in "Cold Saturday Mad Sonnet") are qualitative transformations as expressions of this instant of time. In the following passage from "La Plus Blanche," the juncture of connection is "How," and the new utterly wild formation is something referred to as "grace."

> you return love. Love returned for admiration! Strangeness
>   is returned by you for desire. How. Where
>   but in the depth of Jean Harlow is such strangeness
> made into grace? (*Selected Poems*, 15)

Some of McClure's poems are "genre" in the sense of being formal as sonnets, odes, or ballads but actually as unique, special, not the same as anything else. Therefore the new formations can't be replicated, as are images of Pop Art or as would be commercial images. The units of connection in the "Hummingbird Ode" are the "black lily of space," the "sweetness of the pain," and "the beautiful shabby colors / and the damp spots where the eyes were" of the dead hummingbird:

> WHAT'S
> ON YOUR SIDE OF THE VEIL?
> DID YOU DIP YOUR BEAK
>   in the vast black lily
> of space? Does the sweetness
>   of the pain go on forever? (*Selected Poems*, 18)

Dark Brown, for example, is writing as a self-analyzing surface that is vision. One is lost in the "simulacra" means "that the belief of something is necessary to its beauty." As in a Busby Berkeley follies, change or movement is by virtue of the intrinsic qualities of something: "The flow of energy through a system acts to organize that system."

In Ron Silliman's *Paradise* the unit of change occurs on the level of the sentence, many such changes occurring in each paragraph.[4] A series or list of simple sentences creates simple states of being, requiring that consciousness exist only in the moment of each sentence, that is, in an infinite series of succeeding moments. That experience actually occurs in the lovely light "clear" writing. An overt simplification or abstraction of a view of character, either reader's or writer's, is imposed to create these states of being, which may be the expression of a period or an inward state:

> In romance, sexual desire is freed from a relation to power. The real bandit queen of India, Madame Gandhi. Puffball clouds in a blue sky. Simple sentences, again and again. The old sisters walk to the store together, slowly,

one wearing bright slippers. Our lives are like this, quiet on a Sunday. Sink full of cups. (14–15)

Reading as imposing syntax is creating reality as imposition on or formation of one's thoughts and actions:

> This was and now you are constituted in the process of being words, your thought actualizing through the imposition of this syntax. Resistance alone is real (coming distractions). Cross against the light. Leave work to write a poem and not mention the dragonfly. (40–41)

New formations as words, fantasies, sounds, occur potentially infinitely. The "directorial intelligence" is seen to be either author or context or the one as the other. Therefore our being replications or something being replicated takes place "visibly" as an action.

So the process of cultural abstraction itself is the model or mechanism for the pattern. Reading imposing a reality on us is therefore the "response card referred to as the action." Deciphering oneself entails what one is; the concept of that entails the action of what the text is. We mime the simulacra, "syntax mimes space," in order to get at the real.

A variation on the notion of apprehending the inherent nature of a being, object, or event as motion is suggested by the Busby Berkeley follies or a dance concentrating on one point or juncture repeated but never the same, which cannot remain identical with itself.

In the example of a centralized pattern, the Busby Berkeley follies with skits or vignettes without necessarily a beginning, middle, or end: the pattern is submitted to the control of an overriding authority but with the notion that the finely tuned unit would avoid the distortion of the whole. Using the notion of the pattern being the inherent nature of something as movement, the model of such writing while possibly using a "format" ("genre"), would be tuned to change occurring on every level. As suggested by a model from physics, the individual person, general context of nature, social behavior, and specific event are undergoing change in one moment. The same scene will not be repeated. "The same pattern of things is not necessarily repeated at all levels; and secondly, we are not even supposing that the general pattern of levels that has been so widely found in nature thus far must necessarily continue without limit."[5]

A variation and extension of aspects of the discussion suggested here may be seen in Cindy Sherman's work.[6] Her early photographs refer to scenes or atmosphere from thirties or forties movies: an example of a projection or aping of a genre or mode fixed in time—but taken seriously in its establishing its own version or reality—therefore that which duplicates can't be easily duplicated.

Her work to date is a series of replicas—the subject is always Cindy Sherman herself; yet they are not self-portraits. The photographs become increasingly unrecognizable as to their subject. One photograph, for example, is a masculine figure, wet gravel on its face, seemingly having died recently, but on closer observation showing sores indicating the beginnings of decomposition; another figure is a blonde-wigged woman propped on her elbows on pebbles with her mouth open showing a bright red liquid bloodlike interior. The use of costumes, overtly staged and stagey scenes, produces a potentially infinite series of new characters.

Therefore the question as to the identity of the author and of oneself is apparently the subject—that conception itself being an expression or "analysis" of postmodernist sensibility, that is, the photographs overtly expressed as cultural abstraction or the critical conceptualization of the present art scene.

The following passage as an example of this critical conceptualization is from an essay by Rosalind Krauss, titled "A Note on Photography and the Simulacral":

> That Sherman is both subject and object of these images is important to their conceptual coherence. For the play of stereotype in her work is a revelation of the artist herself as stereotypical. It functions as a refusal to understand the artist as a source of originality, a fount of subjective response, a condition of critical distance from a world which it confronts but of which it is not a part. . . . If Sherman were photographing a model who was not herself, then her work would be a continuation of this notion of the artist as a consciousness that knows the world by judging it. In that case we would simply say that Sherman was constructing a critical parody of the forms of mass culture. With this collapse of difference, this radical implosion, one finds oneself entering the world of the simulacrum. . . . If the simulacrum resembles anything, it is the idea of nonresemblance. Thus a labyrinth is erected, a hall of mirrors, within which no independent perspective can be established from which to make distinctions—because all of reality has now internalized those distinctions.[7]

The criticism as description, using Krauss's essay as an example, is the process of creating convention—the description of ourselves as culture. Sherman's work is the convention and the revelation of that; as such, the focus is the mystery of the convention that is nonresemblance itself, that is, originality or subjectivity.

Examples of Sherman as unrecognizable subject: a photograph of a large figure with a long red artificial sensual tongue in the foreground behind which are ant-size humans; a shot of a head with a pig's snout, blood-like smears on the snout and cheek, the figure lying on a dark background. Another photograph shows a sweat-covered or moist figure unrecognizable as to gender, crouching, clutching, or sorting through pebbles, looking up at the camera with a wild expression showing a mouth of rotting teeth. The costume dramas in the collection, coming at the end of the series, cause the sequence of photographs to seem to fly apart.

Charles Bernstein's *The Sophist* presents a multiplicity and potentially endless proliferation of voices and characters.[8] In terms of the use of genre: the poem "Fear and Trespass" is an example of being entirely inside some other voice. The details of the circumstance of the couple in this piece are never given; but the circumstance is conveyed in a deliberately bathetic language of Harlequin romance or soap opera. Bathos and turgid vocabulary are as valid as any other information. There is no introspective or conscious voice that would have a different or outside perspective; in that sense the form of the writing goes beyond or outside the confines of the convention of a "poem" and is someone else's "book." The piece is language as a jostling whipped-up surface—its motion is entirely in that, in terms of it being the whipped-up singular perspective. So it is not simply satire.

Other examples of the use of "genre"—which are therefore unlike the model: "The Only Utopia Is in a Now" uses a voice or perspective reminiscent of eighteenth-century genre describing people's attitutudes and behavior and criticizing their manners and morals. The authorial voice criticizes the inhabitants of this imaginary utopia by assimilating their constucts of emotion and antiemotion:

> You see, emotion doesn't express itself only in words we already know. But people here who talk about emotion don't really want to experience it. They only want simulations of it in patterns of words they've already heard.

Other examples of "genre" are ostensible imitation of some other writer, as in "From Lines of Swinburne," in which the poem speaks of itself as a voice—maintaining that singular perspective—as aping itself, being a play on itself. The writing is different from either the old model or the present conception of a poem.

Poems may in *The Sophist* actually be plays, as in the piece titled "Entitlement," in which named characters speaking to each other—things being like something else—simply make statements of those resemblances, rather than having dramatic situations or action. The statements of resemblances are an aping of actions.

In "The Last Puritan," a hypothetical character is projected as "anything merely seen or heard." A single poem or prose piece may have multiple voices or perspectives. The voice in a piece may seem to be the author's, or there may be a variety of characters, or simply voices interweaving ideology, information, commentary on the writing, or contradiction of previously declared opinions or assertions. The text uses words that aren't real or are hybrids or deliberately misspelled; its language also consists of blank spaces, slang, nonsense sounds, capitalization of parts of words; the text introduces as one character a Mr. Bernstein who turns out not to be the author; it introduces someone else's book, *The Odyssey*, misquoting it. Word and object are expressions or formal projections of each other.

Bernstein comments in reference to the proliferation of perspectives or detail: "There is never annul / ment, only abridgement." Nothing is left out of the writing; so it goes past the confines of a "book." Distortion of the individual unit by the whole is part of the writing's acknowledged mode; comparable to Peter Schjeldahl's notion, in his introduction to Sherman's work, of "Presence" as emerging in the costume dramas with the photographer finally being there as only herself the actress.

The order of *The Sophist* is carefully composed to create "a single but layered structure." The book does not have a beginning, middle, and end as would occur in the unfolding of a drama or story. As in the play "Entitlement," which consists of statements of resemblances, there is no progression of development of a plot. The poem, "the order of a room," is a series of statements or types of order:

> a geometric order
> a cosmetic order
> a temporal order
> public order

Some of the ways of seeing the structure or order of the "book" are "hypostatization of space, the relations detemporalized," "idea of explaining the visible world by postulated invisible world," distance, arrangement of letters on the page, blanks that could be filled in thereby changing the order, abbreviations, and so forth. In terms of a geometric model, the notion is of the "book" being detemporalized and spatial.

Aping doing imitations (as in the Swinburne poem) is an example of incorporating a sense of relativity in terms of time.

The book is the "single but layered structure"—the notion of "a body that seemed genuinely music"—given more as the *idea* of music than the actual formal rendition and sound of that music. In other words, the latter occurs as the abstract configuration of the idea.

Similar to aspects of Stein's view of composition or Hemingway's cultural abstraction in *Hills*, yet seeing experience differently from them (for example, all times operating at the same time, a different sort of cultural analysis), Bernstein's work projects a symphonic structure that would reflect multiple changes occurring in the present instant. Such a projected work need not be seen as a dissipated version of modernism nor as leading to confusion but rather as actively engaging reality as Maya.

Bernstein's sense of the "idea" as being the shape and reverberation, a formal configuration of the "book," is a variation and contrast to the characteristics of Alice Notley's *Margaret & Dusty*.[9] The internal workings of her "book," in its process as if using itself up or being the same as its material, are the actual rendition and sound of that music.

A manifestation of postmodernism: the proliferation of the particular, which has to do with recognizing social definitions ("The composition is the thing seen by every one living in the living they are doing") as not intrinsic to reality or oneself.

Margaret & Dusty is composed of discrete poems, which are an interwoven pattern of voices and characters. Real individuals sometimes mentioned or addressed by name enter the conversation; people are quoted and designated by name as in "Bob & Simon's Waltz"; unnamed multiple voices interweave snatches of conversation; imaginary characters address each other as in the piece "Postcards"; a poem may be entirely a monologue by some other character as in "At the End-Of-School Party"; or the author carries on conversations with invisible presences, reading aloud from a book or newspaper or responding off-the-cuff to TV or movies as part of the conversation.

Parts of poems are designated as songs. The songs are formal variations and projections of the particular poem in which they're found.

The authorial voice in a chatty, daffy duration of a sort of "Macho Daisy Duck" (a poem in which she titles her own voice) becomes apparent as a social surface, or a constructed personality.

The subject of one's "life" is discussed in terms of the conventional conception of the separation of autobiography from the "book." This subject also relates to actual life and death—that is, the separation of life

from "book" is narrowed or erased—by the fact of the author dealing
with the occurrence of an actual death, thus going past the confines of
the book. Social construction and private experience of reality are seen
as the same, mirrored in each other:

> I learned two things from the play last night,
> God is Love, & when you're dead you're dead.
> Look at this picture, that was his look that when
> he looked at you like that you felt terrific.
> I'll never get to see him again.
> What's it like out?

The creation of the voices in *Margaret & Dusty* apes projections what
we think "life" is or what we think ourselves are. People are mimicked
to be seen as social configurations and also as "talk," the conversations
in the book that are the abstraction the only existence of the person.
That is, the poem or projections of the person are the news or conversations:

> Gloria Steinem will speak at length on abortion.
> Can I have 35¢ for baseball cards?
> I just want to be in my life!
> Where are you?
> In my life!
> I am a black lace fan.
> I need the paper & the many little mineral waters.
> Unacceptable to Winfield & Jackson.

Stock maxims, understood in the poem as socially derived sentiment,
occur as overtly imposed or mimicked voices—therefore the reader
comes to a view of sentiment, and to an accuracy in experience of a
sentiment, which is different from the stereotype.

As in Cindy Sherman's use of costume, the seeing of oneself as social
forms a kind of hyped Presence, causes oneself to open up and fly apart.

> All things belie me, I think, but I
> look at them though. Well boys, at
> least you're not dead, right? What's
> the date today? Until something. What?
> Of the lady of the whitening blow.
> I'm ashamed to keep on babbling
> as if I've always been oneself,
> diamond flow through. Humble
> flannel skeleton. Grin, laugh unbecoming
> Living at the bottom of the water may

have been obvious all the time. But
I forget. What's my plot? Hand
of a child, paw of an animal.

The sense of time in this book is a phase of intense emotion. The
process of the "book" is that of using itself up; the conversation of all
those people in the writing becomes the only stuff there is:

what would you think then? But I
wouldn't do that. Light surrounded oranges
towels clouds. You don't think you're my you.
Not here not you. You still think you're he. she.
Because I wouldn't "you" you, would I? I only
"you" some other he. she. I
who writes poems. When she writes them,
it's different . . .

The author in the "book" is just that person, which is simply and
purely the created other characters, such as Margaret and Dusty.

NOTES

1. Gertrude Stein, "Composition as Explanation," in *Selected Writings of Gertrude Stein* (New York: Random House, 1962), 516.

2. Ernest Hemingway, *Green Hills of Africa* (New York: Scribner's, 1935).

3. See Michael McClure, *Selected Poems* (New York: New Directions, 1986), and *Hymns to St. Geryon & Dark Brown* (San Francisco: Grey Fox Press, 1980).

4. Ron Silliman, *Paradise* (Providence: Burning Deck, 1985).

5. David Bohm, *Causality & Chance in Modern Physics* (Philadelphia: University of Pennsylvania Press, 1971).

6. Cindy Sherman, *Cindy Sherman* (New York: Pantheon Books, 1984).

7. Rosalind Krauss, "A Note on Photography and the Simulacral," *October* 31 (Winter 1984): 49–68.

8. Charles Bernstein, *The Sophist* (Los Angeles: Sun & Moon Press, 1987).

9. Alice Notley, *Margaret & Dusty* (Saint Paul: Coffee House Press, 1985).

8   *Strangeness*
Lyn Hejinian

> I stand in awe of my body, this matter to which I am bound has
> become so strange to me. . . . Talk of mysteries!—Think of our life in
> nature—daily to be shown matter, to come into contact with it—
> rocks, trees, wind on our cheeks! the *solid* earth! the *actual* world! the
> *common sense! Contact! Contact! Who* are we? *Where* are we?
> —Thoreau, *Ktaadn and the Maine Woods* (1848)

JULY 10, 1988

Because there is a relationship between the mind and the body, there
are inevitable experiences of instability and therefore of loss and discontinuity.

Loss of scale accompanied by experiences of precision.

JULY 11, 1988

Scale and precision do not contribute to a theory of description but
rather to a poetics of description, which I'm here basing on examples
of its exercise on two strange terrains, the terrain of dreams and the
terrain of what was in the seventeenth and eighteenth centuries *terra in-
cognita*, hence the terrain of exploration.

By description I don't mean after-the-fact realism, with its emphasis
on the world described (the objects of description), nor do I want to
focus on an organizing subjectivity (that of the perceiver-describer);
nor, finally, am I securing the term to a theory of language.

I propose description as a method of invention and of composition.
Description, in my sense of the term, is phenomenal rather than epiphe-
nomenal, original, with a marked tendency toward effecting isolation
and displacement, that is, toward objectifying all that's described and
making it strange.

Description should not be confused with definition; it is not definitive but transformative. Description, in the examples here, is a particular and complicated process of thinking, highly intentional while at the

140

same time ideally simultaneous with and equivalent to perception (and thus open to the arbitrariness, unpredictability, and inadvertence of what appears). Or one might say that it is at once improvisational and purposive. It is motivated thus by simultaneous but different logics, oscillating inferentially between induction and deduction.

Although my argument is based on examples of nonartistic description—dream reports and explorers' journals—description is obviously a problem of writing. Vocabulary and grammar are themselves an intense examination of the world and of our perceptual relations within the experience of it. One may agree with Ludwig Binswanger's aphoristic comment, "To dream means: I don't know what's happening to me," but its description is intended as a means of finding out.

Description then is apprehension.

AUGUST 4, 1988

The term *apprehension* is meant to account both for some motivating anxiety and for what *Webster's Dictionary* calls "the act or power of perceiving or comprehending"; apprehension, then, is expectant knowledge.

Both anxiety and a sense of anticipation or expectation excited by particles occur in dreams, or as dreams.

Descriptions of dreams, or dream reports, have increasingly come to interest me specifically as writing problems. The very writing down of a dream seems to be the act of discovering it (one "remembers" more and more as one writes until one wonders if it's the writing itself that "dreams") but it is also and problematically the act of interpreting it.

The dream of description challenges the appropriateness of selection, since peripheral items may turn out to be central after all, and because details may have been lost in the instability of the dream terrain or in one's own forgetfulness. In this case, dreams present reportage problems, not unlike the reportage problems that are an issue in explorers' journals (Captain Cook's, for example) or in writings like those of William Cobbett (*Rural Rides*) and in Gilbert White's Selborne journals. There is a disconcerting similarity between records of dreams and records made by the explorers—the same apparent objectivity, the same attempt to be accurate about details and to be equally accurate about every detail (presumably because one doesn't know which details are the important ones, either in Tahiti or in the dream).

The dream description also presents problems of framing. It questions the relationship between subject and object, because the "I" of a dream is often either unassimilated or diversely identifiable, so to speak reversible, wavering between selves called Me and Not-me.

"I," the dreamer, is not of necessity identical to the "I" of waking life. When, for example, I write of a dream, "I am in the locker room in a prison and use a key to unlock handcuffs so that three of us escape," who am "I"? Did it really feel (in the dream) that I was there in the way that it would if I was there?

In dreams, the opposition between objectivity and subjectivity is a false one. In fact, the dream's independence from binarisms like form-content, male-female, now-then, here-there, large-small, social-solitary, etc., is characteristic and makes polarity irrelevant or obsolete. Instead deliberate and complex disintegration, dispersal, and elaboration occur, in some instances with terrifying effect.

> My health was menaced. Terror came. For days on end I fell asleep and, when I woke, the dark dreams continued. I was ripe for death. My debility led me along a route of dangers, to the world's edge, to Cimmeria, the country of black fog and whirlwinds. I was forced to travel, to ward off the apparitions assembled in my brain.[1]

AUGUST 8, 1988

> Dream of September 28, 1987: A dress, or a woman wearing blue or black. She is a mannequin or a living woman. The figure fullface or maybe in silhouette. A view then or afterwards of a saddle-stitch stapler and a book nearby.

> Dream of January 31, 1987: K has written a novel—it is a large old oak desk. The top drawer is out of the desk; I think K is holding it. The bottom drawer is on the floor in front of C. B and C and K and I are discussing his novel. K explains that the first chapter sounds as if it had been written by someone who was "going nuts, which it was." This is a problem—he doesn't want it to sound like that. He is worried, too, that nothing happens in the novel. I say, "Going nuts is something." K and B break the drawer apart. "I could have an auction," says K. "I had to spend the whole first chapter naming things, but the readers could find out what they are when people bid for them."
>
> "Someone might bid for a dog," I say. This is very funny and everyone laughs. I'm pleased to have made a joke, but actually I'm only repeating what I thought I heard one of them say. It occurs to me that you really need a studio if you are a novelist, because novelists have to build things. All of this dream is occurring in a room, which is maybe a small backstage area. The light is "natural," but dim, more white than yellow—I'm not thinking about it, I don't notice that I notice, but I do notice the dust and

some black and white decor, maybe just panels, maybe just white ones and not black ones.

Now we are examining the end of the novel. Another drawer. It is falling apart too—the back is separating from the drawer, so there are gaps between the sides. I think to myself that it won't hold water. C is talking about the chapter. B is at the back of the desk, hammering a nail into its side.

Dream of November 2, 1986: I am taking part in a project to measure the planetary system. Other people are involved, including a tall thin man and a woman with enormous breasts. In the project to measure the planetary system each participant slips into place between other participants to form a sphere. We are like sections of a citrus fruit. Once in place, hanging upside down, we form a sphere and ride around pressed against each other for twenty-four hours. I am afraid of being smothered by the woman's enormous breasts. We pull out of the sphere and all talk about coming up with a better design for measuring the planetary system.

Among the things one notices about these dreams, keeping in mind that they are presented here as writing problems, not as psychological events, is that nonetheless persistent figuring occurs in them; the descriptions, like the dreams, proceed by virtue of various calculations and determinations. The dream of planetary measuring is exemplary of this, because it is *about* figuring and about the metaphoric processes that result. What appears to be a search for the right word is more often and more accurately a search for the right object, itself as unstable as the word and located in an unstable terrain. The figuring that occurs in moving through the mobility of the dream, and the literal refiguring of figures in the dream, take place also in the course of writing. For me, in this sense, the process of writing, like the process of dreaming, is a primary thinking process. Thinking explores, rather than records, prior knowledge or an expression of it.

AUGUST 9, 1988

It would be inaccurate and inappropriate, even ludicrous, to characterize the dream as an example of self-expression. I'm not even sure one can regard it precisely as an act of introspection, though it is impossible to think of dreams as myopic in this respect. But if dreams are not introspective, properly speaking, they nonetheless exhibit some of the effects of introspection on our experience of experience—which, at least in my case, often occurs as writing.

My use of the term *introspection,* and my sense of the introspective method and its effect on experience and ultimately their emergence in poetics, are indebted to William James's philosophy of consciousness and thereby of language. But it is Gertrude Stein who extended James's philosophy into literary practice, a practice foregrounding the consciousness of consciousness and its linguistic character. In essence, Stein proposes the act of writing as the organization and location of consciousness in legible units and not just of consciousness but of the consciousness of consciousness, the perceiving of perception. As she says in "Poetry and Grammar," "One of the things that is a very interesting thing to know is how you are feeling inside you to the words that are coming out to be outside of you."[2] What I am here calling the consciousness of consciousness, or the perceiving of perception, is the proper function of introspection.

The introspective method has certain consequences. James argues that consciousness can best be described as a stream—he speaks at length of the "stream of thought" and the "stream of consciousness"—but introspecting the contents of the stream, and, more precisely, a particular item floating along it, arrests the item, detaches and isolates it.

> As we take . . . a general view of the wonderful stream of our consciousness, what strikes us first is [the] different pace of its parts. Like a bird's life, it seems to be made of an alternation of flights and perchings. . . . The resting-places are usually occupied by sensorial imaginations of some sort, whose peculiarity is that they can be held before the mind for an indefinite time and contemplated without changing; the places of flight are filled with thoughts of relations, static or dynamic, that for the most part obtain between the matters contemplated in the periods of comparative rest. Let us call the resting-places the "substantive parts," and the places of flight the "transitive parts," of the stream of thought. . . . Let anyone try to cut a thought across in the middle and get a look at its section, and he will see how difficult the introspective observation of the transitive tracts is. . . . As a snowflake crystal caught in the warm hand is no longer a crystal but a drop, so, instead of catching the feeling of relation moving to its term, we find we have caught some substantive thing, usually the last word we were pronouncing, statically taken, and with its function, tendency, and particular meaning in the sentence quite evaporated. The attempt at introspective analysis in these cases is in fact like seizing a spinning top to catch its motion, or trying to turn up the gas quickly enough to see how the darkness looks.[3]

If one looks at my dream of September 28, 1987, one sees a sequence of substantives lacking their transitives. And this is true in several senses. There is a kind of oscillation, even reversibility, between the dress and the woman, which seem to be metonyms for each other, existing spatially (which is to say substantively) but atemporally (intransitively). The dress and the woman may stand for each other, but they are not synonymous nor even overlapping. The objectified figure, even if perhaps a live woman, is static, while the dreamer-observer, from whom "I" have been stripped or withdrawn, sees her or it from several vantage points: "fullface or in silhouette." The female figure is then replaced by a stapler and a book nearby.

"I," the dreamer-observer, experience no self-consciousness. I exist as if absorbed into an audience, or as if no one at all. But the female figure is me. I know this because of the familiar blue or black clothes. The saddle-stitch stapler I recognize as the particular heavy antique one that I used in putting together the Tuumba Press books. Now I have loaned it more or less permanently to someone who publishes a magazine. It is emblematic of certain things I've done and know how to do— make books, for example, both by writing them and by printing and publishing them—and of certain attitudes I have regarding literary communities.

The woman appears first in the dream, and the other three things are elements in a description of her. The dress, stapler, and book are three metonymic entries in a description. I recognize these various elements as me; however, they are entirely displaced—we are shifted apart from each other, indeed there are numerous removes, in a complex of dispossession. "To the psychologist," says James,

> the minds he studies are *objects*, in a world of other objects. Even when he introspectively analyzes his own mind, and tells what he finds there, he talks about it in an objective way. He says, for instance, that under certain circumstances the color gray appears to him green. . . . This implies that he compares two objects, a real color seen under certain conditions, and a mental perception which he believes to represent it, and that he declares the relation between them to be of a certain kind. In making this critical judgment, the psychologist stands as much outside of the perception which he criticizes as he does of the color. Both are his objects.[4]

AUGUST 10, 1988

Introspection has writing as its exemplar, as a radical method with disintegrating and dispersive effects.

The dream about measuring the planetary system may be an attempt to counter this, but "we pull out" in the end.

The elements in the September dream are atemporal, only spatial, though remarkably without the sense of continuity that is provided by landscape. They are like props, picked up by perception and then put back. They don't do anything, in a temporal sense.

On the other hand, the person, the so-called I, in the dream of planetary measurement is notably caught in a temporal figure, one that occasions a kind of spatial disintegration—first "I" am afraid of being smothered, and then I ("we") break the figure apart in order to regain some sense of integrity.

The disjuncture or discontinuity between the spatial existence and the temporal existence of a person ruptures the connection between body and the mind—it is a paradigm for all models and experiences of discontinuity, that fountain of postmodernity and anxiety. And it is the noncoherence of dreams, or of the objects in dreams, that is exactly what makes us suspect them of being unreal. It is thus that our dreams pose an epistemological problem to philosophy.

> Objects of sense, even when they occur in dreams, are the most indubitably real objects known to us. What, then, makes us call them unreal in dreams? Merely the unusual nature of their connections with other objects of sense. . . . It is only the failure of our dreams to form a consistent whole, either with each other or with waking life, that makes us condemn them.[5]

This is true only until our examination of the "real" is such that its components too are dispossessed of their obviousness and necessity. They are, at least in my experience, not so much decontextualized as arrested, until the entire universe of context seems to implode into them, abandoning the observer. It is the dreamer, the observer, the writer who is dispossessed. This is equally true when the object of inquiry is the self. As Theodor Adorno puts it:

> Absolute subjectivity is also subjectless. The self lives solely through transformation into otherness; as the secure residue of the subject which cuts itself off from everything alien it becomes the blind residue of the world. . . .
> Pure subjectivity, being of necessity estranged from itself as well and having become a thing, assumes the dimensions of objectivity which expresses itself through its own estrangement. The boundary between what is human and the world of things becomes blurred.[6]

This is one of the principal strategies of poetry, although perhaps *strategies* is not an accurate term in all cases—inquiry to such a degree is sometimes the motivation of poetry and sometimes furthermore the effect of poetry.

If one posits descriptive language and, in a broader sense, poetic language as a language of inquiry, with analogies to the scientific methods of the explorers, then I anticipate that the principal trope will be the metonym, what Roman Jakobson calls "association by contiguity." The metonym operates with several simultaneous but not necessarily congruent logics, oscillating inferentially between induction and deduction, depending on whether the part represents the whole (reasoning from the particular to the general) or whether the whole is being used to represent the part (reasoning from the general to the particular). Or again an object may be replaced by another adjacent, the cause by the effect or the effect by the cause, spatial relations may replace temporal ones or vice versa, an action may replace the actor or vice versa, and so forth. Metonymy moves attention from thing to thing; its principle is combination rather than selection. Compared to metaphor, which depends on code, metonym preserves context, foregrounds interrelationship. And again in comparison to metaphor, which is based on similarity and in which meanings are conserved and transferred from one thing to something said to be like it, the metonymic world is unstable. While metonymy maintains the intactness and discreteness of particulars, its paratactic perspective gives it multiple vanishing points. Deduction, induction, extrapolation, and juxtaposition are used to make connections, and even "a connection once created becomes an object in its own right."[7] Jakobson quotes Pasternak: "Each detail can be replaced by another. . . . Any one of them, chosen at random, will serve to bear witness to the transposed condition by which the whole of reality has been seized."

Metonymic thinking moves more rapidly and less predictably than metaphors permit—but the metonym is not metaphor's opposite. Metonymy moves restlessly, through an associative network in which the associations are compressed rather than elaborated.

Metonymy is intervalic, incremental—which is to say, measured.

A metonym is a condensation of its context.

But because even the connections between things may become things in themselves, and because any object may be rendered into its separate component parts which then become things in themselves, metonymy, even while it condenses thought processes, may at the same time serve as a generative and even a dispersive force.

AUGUST 18, 1988

Comparing apples to oranges is metonymic.

AUGUST 19, 1988

With respect to dream descriptions, psychological interpretation focuses primarily on identification and symbolism (metaphor), but a literary interpretation depends on the metonym (displacement and synecdochic condensation).

In my dream of K's novel, the novel is not a metaphor, and neither is the desk. They enter the dream as metonyms. The word *novel* (in the sense of new) means K, whose job includes writing for a company *news*-paper. Also I know that K has used lines from newspapers in some of the poems he has recently shown me. But *novel* means me, too. I've tried to make use of lines from newspapers in imitation of K, but I can't seem to get anywhere with it. And then there is the news itself, of course, or rather my despair over the efficacy (or inefficacy) of poetry in the course of events—the imperviousness of the world to such improvements as might be suggested by artistic work and artistic thought.

The dream is about writers and writing. The desk is writing—the place of production is substituted for the thing produced—agency replaces effect. In the dream we are improving the news; it is not irrelevant that several of us are working together to do so.

The phrase *going nuts* is initially metaphorical—the head looks like a nut, or it is hard on the outside and soft on the inside, or hangs on the neck, like a nut. But the plural is interesting; when one suffers from insanity one is transformed into a figure with several heads—one develops or suddenly has a fragmentary or multiple sense of self. The phrase here captures, albeit somewhat humorously, my own experience of extended introspection, undertaken until the self is utterly unfamiliar and threatens to disperse into separate and apparently foreign parts. When I say in the dream that "going nuts is something," I think I mean that introspection is a real activity, and a worthwhile one—a possible basis for writing.

Perhaps the dream arrived at the word *auction* by association with *ac-*

tion, not quite a homonym. K is saying that auctions are stronger than words. The dog that someone might bid for and the water that won't be held by the drawer actually belong together—the reference is to another group of poems, abandoned long ago, in a manuscript called "Water and Dogs," by which I meant the sublime and the ridiculous, or realities on vast and on quotidian scales. Nothing seems more timeless than water to me and nothing more daily than dogs. The dailiness of the dog is like the dailiness of news. My obvious worry is that the fragility of the poem can't contain information on the scale of water. We are apparently trying to patch it up.

AUGUST 21, 1988

The metonym, as I understand it, is a cognitive entity, with immediate ties to the logics of perception. To the extent that it is descriptive, or at the service of description, as is true in my own work, it also has a relationship to empiricism. That is, to the extent that metonymy conserves perception of the world of objects, conserves their quiddity, their particular precisions, it is a "scientific" description.

What I am thinking about to justify saying such a thing are particularly the writings of the explorers and of the natural historians who accompanied them in order to examine and describe what they encountered. In this connection, one of Jakobson's observations on the literary use of metonymy (in his study of the cognitive uses of metonymy and metaphor based on work with aphasics) is interesting: "The primacy of the metaphoric process in the literary schools of Romanticism and Symbolism has been repeatedly acknowledged, but it is still insufficiently realized that it is the predominance of metonymy which underlies and actually predetermines the so-called Realist trend."[8]

AUGUST 23, 1988

In order to understand the metonym as a cognitive, perceptual, logical unit, one has to go back, I think, to Sir Francis Bacon and the history of his influence, eventually on literary language but originally on scientific language. The project he called "The Great Instauration," of which only two parts were completed, the *Advancement of Learning* (1605) and the *Novum Organum* (1620), was to be a description of all knowledge, with an elaboration of the methods for obtaining it, in which writing figured prominently and essentially.

After having collected and prepared an abundance and store of natural history, and of the experience required for the operations of the understanding of philosophy, still the understanding is as incapable of acting on such materials of itself, with the aid of memory alone, as any person would be of retaining and achieving, by memory, the computation of an almanac. Yet meditation has hitherto [been] more [employed in] discovery than writing, and no experiments have been committed to paper. We cannot, however, approve of any mode of discovery without writing, and when that comes into more general use, we may have further hopes.[9]

Bacon goes on to speak of the "multitude and host" of particular objects, "lying so widely dispersed," which must be organized "in living tables of discovery" so as to be readily available as "the subject of investigation." And then, on the basis of "what we term literate experience," philosophers (scientists) may "invent a different form of induction from that hitherto in use. . . . We must not then add wings, but rather lead and ballast to the understanding, to prevent its jumping or flying."

In essence, Bacon set in motion a reformation of learning, demanding that scientific attitudes be purged of established systems and prior opinions. Instead the observer should experience direct and sensuous contact with the concrete and material world, in all its diversity and permutations, and unmediated by preconceptions. Bacon and his subsequent followers were convinced that the components of the natural world are "eloquent of their own history." Nature itself is a book.

The concept of nature as a book appears as early as Plotinus, who compares the stars to letters inscribed in the sky, constantly forming writing as they move. It recurs in literature from the Middle Ages on, and it played a significant role in the literary and art critical writings of the American transcendentalists. Barbara Stafford, in her study of illustrated travel accounts, *Voyage into Substance*, quotes the geologist John Whitehurst, who in his *Original State and Formation of the Earth* (1778) wrote of a particular geological formation that its history "is faithfully recorded in the book of nature, and in language and characters equally intelligible to all nations."[10] This belief in the universality and equal intelligibility of the language of nature is important.

During the eighteenth century there was a great deal of speculation about the origin of languages, and diverse projects were undertaken in the hope of discovering a universal language in past or present cultures analogous to that which seemed to occur in nature. Leibniz, while in England in 1673, set out to discover what he called "the real character" (what semioticians would call a sign) "which would be the best instrument of the human mind, and extremely assist both the reason and the memory, and the invention of things."[11] Eighteenth-century scientists and philosophers of science sought to determine and define the basics of such a language. In many ways this effort simply continued efforts proposed by Bacon in the *Advancement of Learning* to develop a philosophical grammar capable of examining the analogy between words and things. Interest in a universal language grew out of Bacon's insistence that knowledge should be communicated in what he called aphorisms. Writing in "aphorisms," which concentrate content, seemed to be identical with the inductive method of acquiring and inquiring sciences. It was basic to the "plain" style that Baconians advocated for delivering information taken directly from and in sight of particulars.

In their speculation about the origins of language, and under the impact of writings by travelers and explorers in Egypt, some theorists turned their attention to hieroglyphs. In 1741, William Warburton, in the second book of his *The Divine Legations of Moses Demonstrated*, argued that hieroglyphs were not secret symbols written by priests but rather public communication, universal, condensed, efficient, and "original." He sought to demonstrate that they were based on forms found in nature so as to convey information directly to the eyes.

> Warburton stresses the unmetaphoric, unsymbolic nature of the . . . hieroglyph: [it is, he says, a] "plain and simple imitation of the figure of the thing intended to be represented, which is directly contrary to the very nature of the symbol, which is the representation of one thing by the Figure of another. . . . " Further, Warburton indicates that this simple hieroglyph functioned metonymically, not metaphorically . . . by putting the principal part of the thing for the whole. . . . He implies that the return to metonymy, to the concrete fragment of nature, . . . is a return to tangible simplicity, to the convention-free.[12]

If the individual hieroglyph presents a single fragment of natural reality, a "paragraph" or collection of them could only be organized paratactically. Parataxis is significant both of the way information is gathered by explorers and of the way things seem to accumulate in nature. Composition by juxtaposition presents observed phenomena without merging them, preserving their discrete particularity while attempting too to present the matrix of proximities.

AUGUST 25, 1988

Bacon's model for the practice and description of the New Science had an enormous effect on a period when the world was opening into a field of inquiry and in which no hierarchy of inquirers had been established. Men, although not women, of letters were as "scientific" as anyone else and could and did travel to previously unknown regions as reporters of all that they saw. Thus a whole literature of description developed and with it a theory (or, actually, multiplicity of theories) of language, some of it the parent of linguistics and some of it the parent of poetics.

About twenty years after the publication of Bacon's *Novum Organum*, the Royal Society was established in England on Baconian principles, first as a forum for the discussion of new scientific discoveries and later, as the organization grew into a financial institution as well as an intellectual one, as a principal resource for funds for experiments and voyages of discovery and exploration, with the purpose of accumulating large stocks of data.

Bishop Thomas Sprat's *The History of the Royal-Society of London, for the Improving of Natural Knowledge* (1667) was its first history, written to defend the society from critics who felt that its scientific work was unholy. The volume is both a polemic and an anthology of the goals and achievements of the Royal Society's members and protégés.

> They have been . . . most rigorous in putting in execution . . . a constant
> Resolution, to reject all the amplifications, digressions, and swellings of
> style: to return back to the primitive purity, and shortness, when men
> deliver'd so many things, almost in an equal number of words. They have
> exacted from all their members, a close, naked, natural way of speaking;
> positive expressions; clear senses; a native easiness: bringing all things as
> near the Mathematical plainness, as they can: and preferring the language of
> Artizans, Countrymen, and Merchants, before that, of Wits or Scholars.[13]

Sprat insisted that the incorporation of new scientific data into poetry would make the data comprehensible to everyone, because poetry could thus take advantage of the universal character of scientific language. He attacks the "trick of *Metaphors*," which impose their deceptive beauty, obscuring information and limiting learning. Linguistic descriptive tasks are, rather, identical with scientific observational ones.

According to seventeenth- and eighteenth-century philosophers of science, there is a specifically scientific way of seeing that looks at, not over, the object of inquiry. Thus prospect, view, scene, and panorama are essentially unscientific—and the extent to which a metaphor is scenic is further ground for disqualifying it from realistic description.

Description narrates nature but principally by exhibiting its particulars. To the extent that metaphors can be said to give things names that properly belong to other things, they were held to be inconsistent with a respect for particularity. Ultimately, conditions are incomprehensible without the use of analytical conceptual structures, but an initial, essential recognition of difference—of strangeness—develops only with attention to single objects, while others are temporarily held in abeyance. The popularity of the explorers' writings was partially due to the narrative tension that was established between perceptual immediacy and a deferral of complete comprehension.

AUGUST 28, 1988

The explorers were in many respects required to be literary men. Information about what they saw, and what they knew about natural and new realities as a result of having seen them, could only be transmitted through descriptions and through the drawings and paintings made by the artists who often accompanied them on their voyages. The explorers' methods of discovery involved a nonmetaphoric examination of particulars, and this became a significant aesthetic element in their writings. Explorers and scientists sought to discover the tangibility and singular distinctness of the world's exuberant details and individualities without spiriting them away from each other. One important result was that the particular, under the pressure of persistent and independent seeing, emerged in the "low" genre of the travel narrative to give back the intensities normally associated with traditional "high" genres and the "elevated" emotions provoked by the heroic and the Sublime. The "literature of fact," intended for the instruction of the public, developing in response to the demand for verifiable truth enunciated by philosophers and scientists, revitalized literature just when it seemed to have become trivialized with "too much art and too little matter."

AUGUST 30, 1988

When the term realism is applied to poetry, it is apt to upset our sense of reality. But it is exactly the strangeness that results from a description of the world given in the terms "there it is," "there it is," "there it is" that restores realness to things in the world and separates things from ideology. That, at least, is what Bacon argued and what the practicing and theorizing empiricists believed, though argument over the adequacy or inadequacy of such a description, and of the knowledge we acquire from such a description, has propelled Western philosophy ever since—through Hume, Kant, Hegel, Russell, Wittgenstein, to the present. The ontological and epistemological problem of our knowledge of experience is, to my mind, inseparable from the problem of description.

An evolving poetics of description is simultaneously and synonymously a poetics of scrutiny. It is description that raises scrutiny to consciousness, and in arguing for this I am proposing a poetry of consciousness, which is by its very nature a medium of strangeness.

NOTES

1. Arthur Rimbaud, *A Season in Hell*, trans. Enid Peschel (Oxford: Oxford University Press, 1973).

2. Gertrude Stein, *Lectures in America* (New York: Random House, 1935), 209.

3. William James, *The Principles of Psychology* (Cambridge: Harvard University Press, 1981), 236–37.

4. Ibid., 183–84.

5. Bertrand Russell, *Our Knowledge of the External World as a Field for Scientific Knowledge in Philosophy* (London: G. Allen and Unwin 1926), 85, 95.

6. Theodor Adorno, *Prisms* (Cambridge: Harvard University Press, 1983), 262.

7. Roman Jakobson, *Language in Literature* (Cambridge: Harvard University Press, 1987), 312.

8. Ibid., 111.

9. Francis Bacon, *Advancement of Learning, Novum Organum, New Atlantis* (Chicago: University of Chicago Press, 1952).

10. Barbara Stafford, *Voyage into Substance: Art, Science, Nature, and the Illustrated Travel Account, 1760–1840* (Cambridge: Harvard University Press, 1984), 285.

11. Quoted in ibid., 310.

12. Ibid., 311.

13. Thomas Sprat, *The History of the Royal-Society of London, for the Improving of Natural Knowledge* (London, 1667), 113.

9 Come Shadow Come and Pick This Shadow Up
John Taggart

We return to texts because something cannot be forgotten or because something has, indeed, been forgotten. Both are involved in my return to Louis Zukofsky's "Songs of Degrees." Certainly, having thought and written about this series as key to the entire circle of Zukofsky's work, I have not been able to forget it. Nevertheless, having read Lisa Faranda's *"Between Your House and Mine": The Letters of Lorine Niedecker to Cid Corman*, I am reminded that Zukofsky read and commented upon the first two of the songs in the course of a National Educational Television film made in 1966.[1] I had seen the film but had somehow forgotten about it. I wish, then, to return to the first two poems in the "Degrees" series and to a comment made by Zukofsky in the film that the effect of these poems is "something like a prayer."

It will be useful to consider the following terms as indicated by the title for the series: *song, degrees,* and *valentine.* I will define these terms as they occur in book 12 of Zukofsky's long poem "A" and in his critical study *Bottom: On Shakespeare.* I concentrate on their occurrence in these works because of their central importance for Zukofsky and for their chronological placement. Book 12 is the hinge or pivot of "A" and is in many ways the single most important of the poem's twenty-four books. According to a chronology drawn up by the poet's wife, Celia Zukofsky, the first two poems of the series were begun and completed in 1953. Book 12 was completed in 1951; *Bottom,* while not completed until 1960, had been begun in 1947. Both these works are of an importance and of a placement to have a bearing on the first two songs of the series.

In "a final note" to the Origin Press edition of "A" 1–12 (1959), William Carlos Williams remarks on his own initial bafflement with Zukofsky's poetry, which would not read right according to his imagist expectations. One reason for this was Zukofsky's relation to music, in particular to the contrapuntal music of Bach. Williams: "It wasn't simple. . . . It was never a simple song as it was, for instance, in my case."[2] Zukofsky's never simple song can be defined in relation to Bach, the letters of whose name spell out the "theme" of book 12, and in particular to the contrapuntal principle and process called fugue. It is no accident that, immediately following the statement of the named theme on the second page of book 12, there should appear a reference to Bach's *Art of the Fugue* and to the composer's characterization of this principle and process as the behavior of reasonable men in an orderly discussion. Earlier, in book 6, Zukofsky asks what will serve as the presiding question for the entire composition of this long poem "of a life / —and a time":

> Can
> The design
> Of the fugue
> Be transferred
> To poetry?

(Zukofsky's recently published correspondence with Pound makes it clear he was aware of fugue "in the matter of musical approximation" no later than 1931.) Taking this as the presiding question for *"A"* as a whole and reducing Bach's contrapuntal music to an art of fugue, we can place Zukofsky's understanding and practice of song in an equation with fugue.

A few pages after the statement of the B-A-C-H theme and the reference to fugue, and after asking whether Bach didn't sometimes think like the Chinese, it's claimed that "the important thing" is what the composer of the *Guerre-Lieder* says. This is Arnold Schoenberg, whose statements with regard to fugue may be taken as definitions accurate with respect to musical composition and sympathetic with Zukofsky's understanding of his own practice as a poet. In *Fundamentals of Musical Composition*, Schoenberg states that a fugue is a composition with "maximum self-sufficiency of content."[3] The more such sufficiency is manifest "in the form of unity of material, the more all the shapes stem from one basic idea . . . from a single theme." And, as he states in an essay on Bach in *Style and Idea*, "one should not expect that new themes occur in . . . fugues, but that there is a basic combination which is the source of all combinations."[4] What these statements confirm is that, while individual fugues may attain individual forms, fugue itself is not a form. Rather, it is a process of continual expansion or growth, the many from the one, based on the principle of imitation. In *"A"*-12 the one theme or basic combination is stated through the letters of Bach's name, which unite such distinct but persistently entwined subjects for Zukofsky as Baruch Spinoza, Aristotle, his wife Celia, and Paracelsus, the last that "strange Renaissance personality so amply endowed with genius" whose original surname was von Hohenheim.

The statements of the theme in both the beginning and the close of book 12 are further and specifically focused upon the poet's wife, the object of his love:

(beginning)

> Blest
> Ardent good
> Celia, speak simply, rarely scarce, seldom—
> Happy, immeasurable love
>   heart or head's greater part unhurt and happy,
>   things that bear harmony
>   certain in concord with reason.

(close)

> Blest
> Ardent
> Celia
>   unhurt and
> Happy.

The "same" theme is given even greater distribution and focus in *Bottom*. Expressed as Shakespeare's theme, which is found to the nth variation throughout the entirety of the plays and poems, it is nonetheless Zukofsky's, his "Shakespeare theme": *love sees*. If the presiding technical question is whether the design of the fugue can be transferred to poetry, the presiding critical question is whether anything will be seen through the attempted transference. Admittedly, the two questions are but different aspects of the same question.

The transference can come about only by analogy. Zukofsky's poetry will have to be an "imagined music." The syllables, to quote from a statement concerning *Pericles* in *Bottom*, "are brought together like notes."[5] The analogous motion for the process of fugue, this bringing together, is conceived as a weaving in both *"A"* and *Bottom*. Thus in the poem the figure of the weaver is picked up from the *Phaedo*: "Weaving, instead of unweaving, / A fiddle—Or Penelope's web." Thus Zukofsky's very "persona" in writing his critical study on Shakespeare is none other than Nick Bottom of *A Midsummer Night's Dream*, a weaver and, according to Thisby, "eke most love Jew, / As true as truest horse." And thus it should come as no surprise to discover that, complementing Schoenberg's statements, one of the preeminent musicologists of the first half of our century and author of "a humane and readable analysis" of the *Art of the Fugue*, Donald Francis Tovey, should define fugue simply as "a texture."[6]

For when we look for the root of this new term, what we find is the Latin *textura,* "a weaving."

Modeled by way of analogy with Bach's fugue composition, Zukofsky's song proceeds as a weaving of words and their syllables on the single theme of *love sees.* To quote from *Bottom:* "Up, down, outwards—for even inversions and exact repetitions move on—are the melodic statement and hence the words' sense: or after syllables have been heard before in contiguity, they may also be augmented or diminished, or brought to crowd answer on subject in a great fugue." To quote from book 12:

> We begin early
> And go on with a theme
> Hanging and draping
> The same texture.

The technical and critical question, again, is whether the transference can be done and, if so, whether it can be done with sufficient skill so that the song/text woven on this single theme not only will provide a guiding principle and process for the working out of the poet's composition but will also result in something to be seen. Judging from his comment about prayer and, earlier in the NET film, about how the two songs show what could be done with twelve words (cf. Anton Webern on Bach's *Art of the Fugue:* "what else could this work be but the answer to . . . 'what can I do with these few notes?'"), Zukofsky was well aware of the question.[7]

It will be recalled from Schoenberg's statements that, as there is unity of material, the shapes stem from one basic idea or single theme. Shapes are the earliest indications of form. They appear as such in the opening lines of book 12 when, following the most primary of motivations— "*deep need*"—and made singular, shape, they are given as the first products of composition.

> So goes: first, *shape*
> The creation—
> A mist from the earth,
> The whole face of the ground. . . .

It is shape—in coordination with the other firsts of glyph, dance, and body cited in Zukofsky's demographic of composition—that orders the poem's rhythm and style. And while shape as a first apprehension of form may order the "intermediate" working out of rhythm and style, it may also be understood as a result of that working. This leads us to the consideration of what particular shape, if any, results from the composition of poems conceived as songs defined by the weaving principle and process of fugue.

We are helped in this by the painter Paul Klee, who was himself something of a musician and who is mentioned with regard to form toward the end of book 12. Klee's Bauhaus lectures contain valuable insights about the composition process.[8] In one of them he takes up the peripheral movement of color or the "canon of color totality." A canon is a condensation or concentration of fugue. As a term it derives from *fuga per canonem*, or fugue according to the strict rule. Webern, a student of Schoenberg and a composer partial to canons, provides a further definition: "a piece of music in which several voices sing the same thing, only at different times; often what is sung occurs in a different order." One of the orders is called mirror canon, a type of fugue that occurs in Bach's *Art of the Fugue* and with which Zukofsky was familiar. As he wrote in a letter to Lorine Niedecker (January 28, 1937) with respect to *"A"*-8, "I've let the intensity with which I've felt the material determine its order & the *effect* or *suggestion* is something like a mirror fugue in this section."

To connect this with the characteristic motion of fugue—weaving— it could be said that in canon the texture results from the weaving of the same kind of threads or the same thread. The effect of a mirror fugue or canon may be achieved when the "points" of syllables weave words into lines that define a plane. The effect is felt when, within that plane, the syllables and words reflect one another. In terms of music history, the form or shape that prefigures canon is the round. The visual shape we associate with such music is precisely what we find demonstrated in Klee's lecture, that is, a *circle* of color.

These observations are of interest because they suggest how what is essentially vertical, the song/text/poem, may be composed by means of a weaving and result in the effect of a circle that may also be "reflective." As Wilfrid Mellers writes in *Bach and the Dance of God*, a study that would have pleased Zukofsky for its linkage of Bach and Spinoza, "yet at the same time this existent passion is *objectified* since the canon is in mirror inversion" (my italics).[9]

Besides the constant oscillation of Zukofsky's theme and its combinatorial subjects throughout all of *"A"* and *Bottom*, there are several references to circles in book 12. I would cite two variations. The first fuses language from Spinoza's *Ethics* to make up the opening three lines, which are then joined by what I take to be three of a more personal invention.

Since no one cares about anything he does not love
And love is pleasure that dwells on its cause
He who loves keeps what he loves:
An image inwreathed with many things
That may flourish, that draws cause
To light up.

In the second example the same variation of the circle, the condition of being inwreathed, is joined with language that had been used earlier in the book to describe Bach's renewal of the arabesque.

For all inwreathed
This imagined music
Traces the particular line
Of lines meeting
  by chance or design

These variations remind us of the critical question attendant to the poet's theme. It is a question that has its own insistent variations. Will love see? How will it see? What will it see?

The answer is that love will see by dwelling on its cause (potentially anything, but particularly the four subjects, with a special emphasis upon Celia). It will see by virtue of the image that has been made not so much as an imagist picture poem but as that which is held, kept and reflected, in the inwreathing circle of the woven "line of lines" traced by the imaginary music of the poet's song.

What will be seen can only be what has caused the poet's attention to be attracted to what is outside the poem and to what is within its composition—that is, what the poet loves. According to Zukofsky's poetics, this is sincerity, the care for detail, attention to the particulars of the outside world and to those within composition. Williams's bafflement is hardly surprising. The image matters for Zukofsky, who has written perceptively of Pound and Williams both in his critical essays and in the later songs of the "Degrees" series, but it is an image grounded in a shape primarily determined by a musical principle and process. It is primarily an acoustic or cadential image. Zukofsky's song = fugue, the shape of whose weaving motion is a circle that, mirrorlike, would hold or keep what is loved.

Zukofsky's song, which is also text and poem, can be placed in an equation with fugue because words in his composition are treated like notes. This can be done, too, because the shape that is produced as effect or suggestion is, analogically, the same shape produced by fugue. The writing of song so understood moves toward a visual end. While related to imagist poetics, this is still distinct from Pound and Williams. For it does not *begin* as a visual report. The motivation behind Zukofsky's circular end and beginning, the creation of a musical or acoustic/cadential image, is to light up what is loved, to illuminate and to reveal the beloved as substantially as an object held in the mirror of that image. We must hear in order to see. We must hear and see in order to love.

In considering the second of the title terms, *degrees*, we can follow the alphabetic order of Zukofsky's theme, starting with Bach and with the term's use in music. Here degrees indicate the position of a note with reference to a scale and are sometimes called scale-steps. Degrees in music locate the position of a note or tone with reference to a predetermined range or space. Degrees locate notes with reference to the total space of a scale (from the Italian for ladder) and with reference to the internal spaces—the intervals—within its totality.

Applied to poetry, this usage refers to the tones of individual words or syllables and to the intervals of their exact or recognizably "near" recurrence. It is a reference Zukofsky seems to have had in mind when, writing in *Bottom*, he mentions "the tones of the syllables . . . the relations of their intervals" and the previously cited "up, down, outwards" description of how words may be composed like notes in a fugue. Or, expanding on Spinoza's conception of bodily motions in a later talk, "About The Gas Age" (1970), how they twine as stems around one another, "and the intervals at which they twine are of interest only mutually—considered 'perfect' or 'short of perfect' as the case may be." The degrees are the tonal points in themselves and in combination with others in the twining or weaving motion of the words' syllables and their intervals of recurrence.

Having mentioned Spinoza, whose *Ethics* is organized according to the geometric method, we should not forget that in geometry and trigonometry degrees are defined as parts of a whole, which is considered as the circumference of a circle.

There is another "B" usage of degrees, this one from part one of *Bottom*: "love, the seed of the writing . . . moves all the leaves of his book to sound different degrees of 'Love's mind' or its relative failures of judgment." This statement about the one thing said by all Shakespeare's works develops from Helena's speech at the end of act 1, scene 1, in *A Midsummer Night's Dream*:

Things base and vile, holding no quantity,
Love can transpose to form and dignity:
Love looks not with the eyes, but with the mind,

And therefore is wing'd Cupid painted blind;
Nor hath Love's mind of any judgement taste:
Wings, and no eyes, figure unheedy haste.

The order of Zukofsky's statement makes degrees equivalent with failures. Love's mind fails because it is not in proper alignment with the eyes, with what attention to particulars through them can inform those who would look with something more than "unheedy haste." These degrees are differences of relative failure based on the wrong relation of love, eyes, and mind. Like all differences, they distinguish themselves one from the other and at the same time point or "relate" toward a common reference, the right relation negatively defined in this case, that is, love : reason : : eyes : mind. Or: "love needs no tongue of reason if love and the eyes are 1—an identity." It is then that love sees.

Nothing, however, will be seen unless differences, degrees, are acknowledged. It is the differences that identify the reference or theme. Commenting on "Julia's Wild," his set of variations done as a "dark valentine" on the line "Come shadow, come, and take this shadow up" from *The Two Gentlemen of Verona*, Zukofsky notes that they ring "a difference." It is the acknowledgment of difference that offers evidence that eyes have looked without haste, with sincerity, and it is by means of ("through") such an acknowledgment that an image of the beloved object may be constructed.

Of the possible "A" uses of degrees, I wish to consider one from book 12 and another from Aristotle, one of the four subjects of the book's basic combination. From book 12:

What is the worth of their
Expounding the Torah:
All a man's actions
Should make him a Torah—
So to light up
Whether he moves or is still.
Given a share, the body
Comports the soul.
It sees its reflection
Only when it bends to it.
It is not the same
Asking a friend,
The world is its place.
It joins mouth and heart,
The place and its presence
Where each creature sings its song,

It is ruled and acts
First note to fourth,
Because of its holiness
Its song seems not holy at all,
As in the "Section of Praise"
Uniting the degrees:
As it is, created—
And—ashes and ear—
Do you hear yourself,
You must stop.

The passage is quoted at length for its demonstration of Zukofsky's way of working. Nearly all the lines derive from Hasidic sayings. My speculation is that they derive specifically from those collected in Martin Buber's *Ten Rungs: Hasidic Sayings*, and I will use Buber's titles in the following list.[10] It is a list of the lines from this passage identified by number and their Hasidic sources.

"To Say Torah and Be Torah" (1–4, 6)
"Body and Soul" (7–8)
"In Water" (9–10)
"He Is Your Psalm" (11–12, 22)
"The Beginning of Teaching" (13)
"The Mouth and the Heart" (14–15)
"All the Melodies" (16, 21)
"Hiding and Revelation" (17)
"Great Holiness" (19–20)
"Two Pockets" (23–24)
"On the Day of Destruction" (23–24)
"How to Say Torah" (25–26)

Nearly all the lines can be derived directly from the Hasidic sayings. It has not been unusual since at least *The Waste Land* footnotes for a poem to have many and diverse sources. The extent to which Zukofsky has borrowed from the sayings, however, is remarkable. Because single words and phrases have been lifted from several different sayings and recombined in a compact unit of lines, it is not obvious there has been anything borrowed at all.

A reader might assume that all these lines have something to do with Rabbi Leib, the name printed with a full colon immediately before them. But that is not the case. What Zukofsky has done is to separate the words and phrases from their original contexts to provide himself with a vocabulary for composition. So separated, they can be rewoven into a new song. What we have in this passage is the fully composed stage.

What we have in "A" 22–23, in comparison, is the separated-out material that has been deliberately left at an earlier stage as an offering of material—"a raft of stuff"—for others to compose, mix down, into their own songs. Zukofsky's originality is as a weaver, an unweaver, and a reweaver.

"Degrees" does not appear as such in the Hasidic sayings. What we find in "He Is Your Psalm" instead is: "the prayer a man says, that prayer, of itself, is God. It is not as if you were asking something of a friend. Your friend is different from you and your words are different. It is not so in prayer, for prayer unites the principles." And from "The Unity of Qualities": "emanating from God are ten qualities . . . seen with the true inner eye, they all form one simple unity. It is the task of man to make them appear a unity to the true outer eye, as well."

Zukofsky has translated Buber's principles and qualities into degrees. He has further translated them out of their religious context into one having to do with music, "where each creature sings its song." What were sayings concerned with religious experience become a vocabulary, a collection of "notes" newly released for composition. What is retained is the recognition, however radically translated, of the need for bringing the degrees into unity. It is through the unity brought about by the poet's weaving that "my song with an old voice is whole."

"Degrees" in Aristotle is a relative term of classification for analysis and argument. In book one of the *Posterior Analytics* its underlying reference is given in relation to more or less. "See if the terms cannot be compared as more or less, as is the case with a clear sound and a clear argument."[11] They occur more significantly in the *Nicomachean Ethics*, where Aristotle opposes the Platonic position that pleasure is indeterminate because it admits of degrees. In opposition, Aristotle reminds us that a thing admits of degrees in two ways, abstractly and concretely. When a thing has oneness and simplicity (i.e., unity), it doesn't admit of degrees in the abstract. To quote from Aquinas's commentary on this part of the *Ethics*, "but it can be predicated according to more and less of such a form, as is evident in the case of light which is an undivided and simple form." The conclusion drawn from this is double: (1) light itself is not predicated according to more and less; (2) a body, however, is classified as more or less luminous as it partakes of light more or less perfectly.

To this should be added a later development in Aristotle's argument that pleasures, which in themselves admit of degrees by reason of their admixture, can be both determinate and good. One of the cited pleasures is that which results from musical harmony and which Aristotle extends to health as a harmony in human nature. Harmony, the simultaneous sounding of notes, is a synonym for wholeness, but one that is known in hearing a whole (complex) sound through more or less related individual sounds. Aristotle's use of "degrees" as a relative term of classification takes us back once again to music. What should be remembered is that in harmony we hear the one through the many. We can be aware of the one through the many; we can be aware of the whole—be made whole, returned to health—by unification of the degrees.

I will combine the last two subjects of Zukofsky's theme, "C" and "H," Celia and Paracelsus. Celia is the seen object that initially causes song, and she is the final object, the face of which is contained, lit up, reflected, and revealed as the image in the mirror surface or plane suggested by the woven circle of the poet's composition. There are other subjects in the theme, and Zukofsky has written in response to many others, if only as "episodes," outside it. Even a cursory review of the canon of this work, however, must recognize the persistence of his attention over the years to this one subject, Celia, "our genius" and "our tutelary spirit." Something of the poet's own understanding of the causation involved is described in book 12:

So the instrument of knowledge
Plays only when the beloved's head
Turns from Passing to Being
So learns by degrees.

Granted the basis of these lines in the *Phaedo,* what's learned by the poet is that his instrument, the mind or imagination, has nothing to play without a seen object. What we learn is that there are two objects. The first is the thing seen, in this case Celia; the second is the image, also Celia but reseen, a by-product of composition that is experienced as an object.

This second object is necessary because the act of attention—sincerity, consciousness itself—makes for an increasing awareness of degrees, relative differences of more and less. Composition follows upon this awareness of differences—as an internal partitioning of the object itself and between subject and object—to unify the degrees, which are encountered as parts or aspects of the object and as measures of distance between the object and the desire of the poet's mind, to unify the degrees and to restore the object to harmony and wholeness. This is, at the same time, repeated on the level of language whereby words are more and more apprehended in their difference and are then resolved as a whole, complete song. There is, of course, the expectation that the poet's relation with the object, his love for her, is also restored.

This is the process of objectification that, with sincerity, is the other major term of Zukofsky's poetics. Celia is the initial cause, the seen object, but it is the poet's song as a composition that creates the reconstitution of the object, unification of the degrees, after the emergence of those degrees in the analytic multiplicity of consciousness.

The shape of Zukofsky's song is a circle. It takes that shape because of the fuguelike weaving of words and because of the poet's desire to hold and to light up the loved object. This is an image, a face, which, while never possibly complete in any literal sense, nevertheless suggests wholeness or the substantial (i.e., an object) as a result of the poet's care in observing the details/facets of the initial object and in attending to the details of composition. The second object is effect, an effect of the circle.

Many of the circles in book 12 derive from Paracelsus.

> Sane, vain and mad enough
> To call himself Paracelsus:
> In each (of Three Worlds) an urge to exceed
> And none wants to act with measure,
> To the end that balance be
> And no crooked thing,
> That nothing exceed the circle.
> Rests before the mirror
> Where its image rests. The image
> Is not sole object of knowledge. Nor is man
> Whose knowledge comes from outside him—
> The mirrored image he is.

These lines conflate and recompose the following statements that are to be found in the Bollingen 1951 edition of Paracelsus's *Selected Writings*: (1) "thus man is like the image of the four elements in a mirror; if the four elements fall apart, man is destroyed. If that which faces the mirror is at rest, then the image in the mirror is at rest"; (2) "everything that man accomplishes . . . must have its right proportion; it must follow its own line and remain within its circle to the end that a balance is preserved, that there be no crooked thing, that nothing exceed the circle."[12]

If something exceeds the circle, then the song's composition has been faulty. If the composition is faulty, then the mirror—if it can be made at all—reflects improperly, and the image of the loved object is distorted. The degrees will have to remain without unity. If the image is distorted, if the degrees have not been made harmonious, then there can be no rest (a term Zukofsky uses as equivalent to objectification). If there is no rest, there is no love.

I have emphasized the poet's love for the seen object. What should not be lost sight of is that, through sincerity and objectification, the poet seeks to make himself worthy of love in return. To exceed the circle is a double calamity. The poet enters composition with more than a casual interest. More is at stake than the production of a competent cultural artifact. Given such interest, the drive for completion becomes a serious matter. This is so much so that Zukofsky is faced with another critical question, one that is a consequence of the presiding question regarding the transference of fugue design to poetry. This is implicit in a later circle passage from book 12: "Once the circle is closed / It becomes very small / And very great."

We arrive at the appropriate critical question as we pay attention to the work. That is, the work proposes its own most appropriate and most exigent critical questions. The presiding one for Zukofsky may concern transference, yet that question leads to another of equal importance. This is not so much how there can be both a closed and an open circle but rather how—once the circle is closed—there can continue to be growth within its closure.

Playing these uses of degrees through Zukofsky's theme results in a complex but not inharmonious definition. Words and their syllables are treated like notes to compose a song the shape of which is a circle and the function of which is to hold the constructed image of the loved object so that it is reflected without distortion and lit up in the resolution of difference. The song's function is also to do this so that the maker of that rest-giving objectlike image is himself made worthy of being loved. Or, to quote from another poem from *Some Time* (1956), the collection in which the "Degrees" series first appeared, "So that even / A lover exists." [13]

Both the first two songs of the series are dated and carry the subtitle "with a valentine." This gives the impression that they are somehow accessories to actual, physical objects. Zukofsky's reference in the NET film to the second of the songs—"It's a valentine"—makes clear, though, that he considered the poems to be valentines in themselves. [14] We can follow his example in taking this term, after *song* and *degrees*, under consideration. We know that a valentine is a person chosen by another as a lover or special friend. We know that it is also a folded paper or card or letter, usually heart shaped, with verses "of an amorous or sentimental nature" sent on Saint Valentine's Day. What may be less familiar is that, as a verb, "valentine" means to greet with song, to sing.

"Julia's Wild," from *Bottom*, has already been mentioned in the consideration of degrees. What lends further interest to this set of finely realized variations on Shakespeare's line is that it is described by Zukofsky as a valentine. Yet when we read it we find nothing of an "amorous or sentimental" nature.

> Come shadow, come, and take this shadow up,
> Come shadow shadow, come and take this up,
> Come, shadow, come, and take this shadow up,
> Come, come shadow, and take this shadow up,
> Come, come and shadow, take this shadow up,
> Come, up, come shadow and take this shadow,
> And up, come, take shadow, come this shadow,
> And up, come, come shadow, take this shadow,
> And come shadow, come up, take this shadow,
> Come up, come shadow this, and take shadow,
> Up, shadow this, come and take shadow, come
> Shadow this, take and come up shadow, come
> Take and come, shadow, come up, shadow this,
> Up, come and take shadow, come this shadow,
> Come up, take shadow, and come this shadow,
> Come and take shadow, come up this shadow,
> Shadow, shadow come, come and take this up,
> Come, shadow, take, and come this shadow, up,
> Come shadow, come, and take this shadow up,
> Come shadow, come, and take this shadow up.

Although "Julia's Wild" is included in Mary Ellen Solt's *Concrete Poetry* anthology, it properly belongs to the class of song and not the more literal object-compositions of either a Baude Cordier or an Emmett Williams.[15] To quote again from Zukofsky's 1937 letter to Lorine Niedecker: "fugues in words don't really exist, because all the words go in one order—give one melodic line & can only suggest others between the lines going on at the same time."

What makes this poem a valentine is the suggestion of its technique. Certainly, the sentiment of Shakespeare's line can be understood as "love," if a darker and unsentimental version, and that should not be forgotten. Yet if it is not forgotten, it is because of the conscious and conscientious technique of Zukofsky, his care in weaving, unweaving, and reweaving all the degrees of this line. As he writes in a note in *A*

Test of Poetry (1948), "A poem is an emotional object defined not by the beliefs it deals with, but by its *technique* and the *poetic conviction* or *mastery* with which these beliefs are expressed."[16] Unless all the words of the line—which is like a scale—all their combinations and their intervals, unless all the possibilities of the line are weighed and measured, there is no loved object and there is no "love object," no valentine. Both exist, and the poet with them, because of technique.

Shortly after the opening of book 12 there appears a "more literal" valentine. Within its outlined heart we read:

Paul ♥ Louis
from
nice best best
friend of Louis

And under the outlined heart we read:

> Valentine's day because
> there are no hearts. There
> will be a heart because
> we will send you a letter
> that was from me to
> divide it in half.

Valentine's Day exists not to commemorate but to create. As the beloved may be said not to be, not able to turn from passing to being, until transformed by the lover's sincerity and objectification, there are no hearts—and no love—until they are made, composed and created. What is created is unification, from hearts to heart. We, Paul and his father, send you, Celia, "a letter," the valentine, in order that all three are unified and unfolded as one. The division allows for sharing and for a coming together. The valentine, variation on the circle, is closed, and the love of the family is made whole. All of this has taken place within the composition of a long poem of "a letter." It is the composition, its technique, that is the valentine.

It may be objected that if this is the case, then the shape of Zukofsky's canon is not so much a circle as it is one all-inclusive valentine. Given the dimensions of the canon—which in addition to the poetry includes a novel, a play, and a translation of Catullus—this claim will have to seem preposterous. There is simply too much of it for any one shape to apply to all its instances. Two factors, though, rule in its favor. One is Zukofsky's well-known belief that a poet writes one poem, one "continuing song," all his or her life. The other is the constant presence of highly conscious and conscientious technique. To quote Zukofsky quoting Wallace Stevens: "to every faithful poet the faithful poem is an act of conscience." This act is manifest in technique. It is also manifest in our reading: "an instant certainty of the words of the poem bringing at least two persons and then maybe many persons, even peoples together." Technique begins in the faithful care for detail, degrees of difference, outside and within the poem. It ends with the harmonious unification of all the degrees. There is a further bringing together in our reading the instant certainty of the words.

The world of Zukofsky *is* round. It is given a particular treatment or variation of roundness, the valentine, because of its author's weaving technique, which transcends the genres so that he could describe *Bottom* as prose and a long poem at the same time, and because of his theme: *love sees.* His technique and his theme—consciousness and conscience—are one. We, as his readers, are brought together with him and perhaps with others in reading his continuing song. It is in this way that the valentine-circle, while closed, can grow and become great.

In turning to the first two of the "Degrees" poems, I wish to return to Zukofsky's comment that their effect is something like a prayer. It is tempting, in making this return, to try to locate specific sources, other texts used for the weaving of these texts. Zukofsky's way of working renders such a temptation difficult and even misleading. As has been seen in considering the terms of the title, most of this material can be expected to come from those subjects within the basic combination of his ever present theme. I think most of Zukofsky's material does come from these sources, but more as a grid of resonating individual words and phrases—the way we remember Bach and Shakespeare—than as a group of discrete texts that will read the rewoven text for us. Locating sources has value only as it calls our attention to the skill of the poet's weaving, as it calls our attention to how objectification has been brought about.

That said, I would cite two sources in particular for these poems. One is somewhat outside the basic combination, Plato's *Alcibiades Major* dialogue, while the other is very much from within it, a "reduced score" of passages from Shakespeare's *Pericles* as put together by Zukofsky in *Bottom.* In the dialogue Socrates defines "taking proper care" as "improving" and, in passing, mentions the art of weaving.[17] Later, considering the dictum "know thyself," he asks Alcibiades if this would not then mean the eye should look at that in which it would see itself. Alcibiades concurs and identifies the objects in which we see ourselves as "mirrors and the like." Socrates suggests there is something of a mirror in our own eyes and, Alcibiades concurring, goes on to ask if he has observed that "the face of the person looking into the eye of another is reflected as in a mirror." Later in their exchange they agree that "he who is ignorant" will fall into error and that it is the obligation of those who would not be ignorant—who would know themselves and their own good—to look in the "bright and divine" mirror. Finally, Alcibiades having agreed to follow Socrates as a disciple, Plato has his teacher respond: "O that is rare! My love breeds another love."

In the *Pericles* reduction, the first passage is taken from the prologue as delivered by the "auntient" poet Gower, whose task is "to sing a Song that old was sung / . . . What now ensues, to the judgement of your eye, / I giue my cause, who best can justifie." Nothing could be more "conscious" than a poet quoting another poet's historic poet-character whose role is to produce a capitalized Song. We cannot help but be reminded of Zukofsky's conception of the poem as song, itself equated with the weaving principle and process of fugue. It is, further, an old song that the poet's son identifies in this pocket score of the play that appears as part of their own dialogue in the "Definition" section of *Bottom* as Shakespeare's *definition of love*. Gower's old song is his author's definition of love, which happens also to be that of the son's father, *his valentine*. The next passage, the single line "To glad your eare, and please your eyes," recalls the poet's musical sense of the image in order that the object of his love be illuminated and revealed. What follows, from Pericles' description of the princess "blithe and full of face," is an extolling of her beauty as "the book of praises."

It is because "thine eye" presumed to reach that book, reading Shakespeare's "reach" as both to create and to possess utterly, that "the whole heape" must collapse. I understand the heap as the lovers, their world, and, by extension, the song itself. The next passage is noteworthy for the "myrrour/errour" rhyme. It is followed by a longer passage that develops a figure for vice as the wandering wind that spreads itself by blowing dust in the eyes of others. And yet the end of its action is "bought thus deare": "The breath is gone, and the sore eyes see cleare: To stop the Ayre would hurt them." Vice or error is overreaching presumption that would obscure the sight of others. This cannot be maintained, and the eyes of those who have been hurt in the blowing eventually see clearly, if only as a consequence of what they have undergone.

What provides solace, as it provides clarity, is the Ayre or song itself. I skip two passages to come to a longer one in which the passions are defined as those pleasures to be shunned by the eyes and the end result of which is a "life by care." We may skip other passages to come to the final two: Pericles' blessing on the birth of Marina ("Now the Gods throw their best eyes vpon 't") and Gower's line from act 4 ("Your eares vnto your eyes Ile reconcile"). Hence we end with a blessing, which may have a bearing on the poet's attitude toward his own son and only child within the family circle, and with a line that once again recalls Zukofsky's desire that the image of the beloved be musical and so "lit up."

I have glossed portions of the dialogue and commented in somewhat greater detail on the play reductions as reflections of their prominence in the poet's resonating grid. The dialogue is suggestive. From it, for example, we learn to identify the mirror as existing within the eyes of another. The reduced play is more than that. It feeds directly into the poet's thought, in particular the need for an interweave of hearing and seeing. At the risk of seeming to reiterate the grid, squaring the circle, I will cite a note from Spinoza's *Ethics*, quoted in *Bottom*, as usefully qualifying crucial terms for our reading of the poems.

> Unhealthy states of mind and misfortunes owe their origin for the most part to excessive love for a thing that is liable to many variations, and of which we may never seize the mastery. For no one is anxious or cares about anything that he does not love, nor do injuries, suspicions, enmities arise from anything else than love towards a thing of which no one is truly master.[18]

The terms given qualification are "error" and "care." The error, generally ignorance in Plato and the specific crime of incest in Shakespeare, is excessive love, one expression of which is care, as in overreaching, "blinding" care.

All the twelve words of the poems can be found, with one exception, in the dialogue and play. Laid out as a scale or tone row in the order of their appearance in the first poem, they look like this:

hear   her   clear   mirror   care   his   error   in   her   is   clear

Care, significantly, is repeated to give a total of twelve words. The one word that cannot be found in either source, *hear*, I take to be the poet's variation on Gower's reconciliation of ears unto eyes, a variation that is in keeping with his own constant concern for an image that illuminates through musically grounded composition.

What follows is the third stanza and center of the second poem.

Hear her
Clear Mirror
Care his error
In her care
Is clear

This stanza is a chiasmus in itself and for the poem as a whole. At the intersecting center of this center is "Care his error." The function of this line may be understood, analogously, as an operation in geometry. The line functions in the stanza and in the larger poem as a mirror by means of which the reflection in a plane of symmetry may be held. This is an operation that can be performed only in the imagination or "by an optical trick such as the use of a mirror." The trick (technique) of Zukofsky is a composition of words that produces an effect like that of a mirror reflection. It is an effect that is further enhanced by our understanding of the Platonic sense of the mirror as existing within another's eyes.

The stanza and poem may be said to engender an effect like the reflection on a plane of symmetry, a mirror, by the use not of exact imitation (same words, same sequence, only reversed) but by lines and syllables. That is, while the central plane line of the center stanza stands alone, lines 2 and 4 reflect one another, as do lines 1 and 5. Whatever the poem "says," its form would have everything seen and heard through the centermost plane of his error of care or excessive love. His error is the immediate motivation for the poem's composition, which seeks to restore what has been obscured by his presumption—face and eyes of the beloved—to a bright clarity. And the poet himself is redeemed in this restoration. If, formally, we do not understand (hear) the function of the mirror in the poem, we can't expect to understand (see) its cause (content).

It is a critical nicety taught to students that the first-person pronoun in poems is to be identified only with circumspection. The lyrical "I" is a construction not to be mindlessly equated with the historical personality of the poet. The circular consistency of Zukofsky's canon, however, allows us to put this convention "under erasure." There is only one "peeress" of Zukofsky's song, and we know her to be his wife, Celia. She is the "her" of the poem, and the poet is the "his." His error is Zukofsky's error. We do not violate propriety if we imagine the motivating circumstance of the poem as involving an embrace. For it is only in such an intimate "space" that the eyes of one can serve as mirror for another. What has happened is that he has been too grasping in his care and so blinded Celia *and* himself. The poem is an attempt to restore clarity, "clear care," to them both.

There are two stanzas before and after the central stanza. In the first of those coming before, the poet addresses himself with what might be called a self-apostrophe that her care, which is none other than his error, be heard and acknowledged. It is she, Celia and her eyes, who is referred to by the parenthetical clear mirror. The clearing up of his error lies in her care and in her clear eyes. The second of these stanzas reweaves "the same idea" with two more lines and with different punctuation.

Hear her
(Clear mirror)
Care.
His error.
In her care—
Is clear.
Hear, her
Clear
Mirror,
Care
His error.
In her,
Care
Is clear

In this reweaving we are made acutely aware, on an almost microtonal level of differences, of the degrees of the poem as a composition of words with their intervals of recurrence and as a composition of the relationship between the lover and the beloved.

The two "after" stanzas further break down the combination of words, the same twelve words, and so heighten our awareness of the degrees. The first of these two, having no punctuation, forces us to speak each word, "hearing" its own individual melody before going on to the next. Wilfrid Mellers has written of Bach's music that the density of its texture is "inseparable from the fact that each line, while making sense as an independent melody, contains harmonic implications that suggest or even create polyphony and tonal movement existing in time." What Zukofsky has done in this stanza, and what is borne out by his own reading in the NET film, is in effect to "sing" the entire row in slow motion. It is as though a fabric is being held up to the light so that the precise nature of the material, its individual parts and their combination, can be better appreciated. It is as though the fabric has been unraveled to threads that are held under a microscope where they appear as enlarged cross sections of shining microfilaments.

One by one we must sound the degrees or tones of the row. It is a sounding that quickens our sense of their individual differences—differences emphasized by the closeness of their sounds—and that quickens, in turn, our sense of their resolution or unification. The harmonic implications should be apparent. His error is redeemed only in her care, in her eyes. Her care is clear only if he perceives his error in her eyes. The tonal movement is toward clarity, resolution, to a cadenced closure of "is clear."

The final stanza adds ornamentation (arabesque) to the poem's slow movement. It does so by the addition of punctuation.

Hear
Her
Clear
Mirror
Care
His
Error in
Her
Care
Is clear

Hear
Her
Clear,
Mirror,
Care
His
Error in
Her—
Care
Is
Clear

These stanzas enact what we have learned from the consideration of song and degrees. They are exceptional in their fineness of realization. They reflect extreme technical skill that inextricably involves an extreme trust that the degrees of language and of consciousness itself, *all* the degrees of difference, can be resolved to harmony not only for the two pairs of eyes directly involved but also for ourselves whose eyes and ears are called upon to judge and to validate this valentine.

Rarely has so much been attempted with so little. In our time it has its truest parallel not in literature but in the few notes and intense "rests" of Webern. It is their extreme concision that, as Schoenberg wrote of Webern's *Six Bagatelles,* is their eloquent advocate, but it is a concision that also stands in need of advocacy. As readers who may benefit from the example of Zukofsky's skill and from his definition of love, we may satisfy this need by reconsidering the second poem in terms of those critical questions that the work proposes.

Those questions were whether fugue design could be transferred to poetry and whether, if it can, anything will be truly seen as a result. There is the further question of whether, if a circle can be made and thus "closed," there can continue to be growth. These questions can be combined with what we have found in the dialogue and play. A fugue is a process of continual growth, the many from the one, based on the principle of imitation. The identifying motion of this process is a weaving of words. The words of the second poem *do* compose such a motion, if only because they are always the same words, though differently lined and punctuated, and because their individual sounds are all so close one to the other. They *closely* approximate a chromatic scale.

Listening as we read, particularly to the last two stanzas, what we have to hear is a continuous half-step weaving with a single thread. Recurring, reflecting again and again as sounds that are almost but never quite the same sounds, these same twelve words give the effect of a circle and a rather tight one at that. Within this circle, its centermost plane suggested by the syllable-points combined to make a line, the further effect of a mirror is suggested. What the chiastic organization of the poem holds is the plane of a mirror, her eyes, which hold "Care his error." What is held as well within that plane is the solution of her care. That is, her care resides in the clarity of her eyes, themselves a mirror for the poet who must permit them to exist as such, to see, in his embrace. His image has existence only in hers.

The sincerity of the second poem is severely internal. The world of the lover and the beloved is restricted to the intimate space of their embrace. The attention to detail is focused on the weave of the same twelve words, which always must be experienced as the same, but yet different. By restricting himself to such a row, the poet forces our own reading attention to focus closely on the degrees of difference between individual words and each word's same, but still always different, recurrence. Our eyes and ears can agree in judging the poet's sincerity to be of high order because his severe restriction must result in a like severity of exposure of his technique. T. S. Eliot: the great poets show us how *bare* poetry can be.

Objectification proceeds from sincerity as an effect. If the technique of composition has been sufficiently conscious and conscientious, then it will produce rest. The reader will feel no desire for further information, further words. As there always will be further information and words, this is where the *art* of poetry enters in. This finite number of words, the same twelve words, has been so composed that we desire no more and no more of their combinations. We feel as though we know the poem's emotion as substantially as an empirical object. As Zukofsky writes in *Bottom*, "a song when heard has that sense of the *substantial* rather like the seeing of the eye."

To repeat, there are two sorts of objects. One is the poem as a composition of words; the other is the image suggested by that composition. In the second song, the two are one. The composition, modeled on fugue principle and process, suggests a mirror—per Mellers with regard to Bach's objectification through a canon in mirror inversion. There is a mirror directly referred to in the text, the clear mirror of her eyes in which his error is held and clarified (clear and "cleared up"). The poem's mirror composition, as a whole structure, promotes rest insofar as it does not exceed its circle, that is, doesn't use words not present in the original row. The poem's mirror image promotes rest insofar as, going back to Paracelsus, that which faces the mirror—both poet and ourselves—is at rest.

While the image of the poem may be said to be complex, it is clear: his error is reflected in her eyes, whose clarity resolves him back to light and sight, his own rest, so that both exist in the loving interaction of a "seeing" embrace. Pulled in by its close weaving of degrees, pulled in and held, this is what we see in the image, mirror, of the poem. We are given rest, and the circle, while undeniably closed, has also grown greater. For what we see through the hearing of Zukofsky's song is none other than his *definition of love*, which, mirrorlike, also has been made to hold within itself, to hold as a bringing together, ourselves, its closely engaged readers.

Prayer is not a subject in Zukofsky's basic combination, nor is it prevalent in those that are. For example, Spinoza, in a letter to William Van Blyenbergh not quoted by the poet, writes: "I do not deny that prayers are very useful to us" and "for those who are not prepossessed by prejudices and childish superstition, it is the sole means of attaining to the highest degree of blessedness." So far as I know, these are the only prayer statements to be found in Spinoza. Going over the canon, we find only scattered references. There are several incidental ones in the Henry Adams essay (1929), and in 80 Flowers (1978) there appear the "prayer-plant eyes" of the zinnia. Also, there are occasional references in connection with his father's death in "A"-12, and Celia reported in a 1978 interview that the poet's parents had a rabbi or biblical student attempt to teach him to say his prayers in Hebrew and to read the Hebrew prayer book, "but that didn't last very long either." In one of his prose pieces, Ferdinand (1942), we read what could be a self-portrait: "This friend had nevertheless steeped himself in English and American scholarship to a degree emulating the devotion of his parents to their religion about which he never thought."[19] In general, Zukofsky's attitude would seem to be that of a line from his novel Little (1968): "fortunately a brief prayer."

The exception to this is what we have found in the Hasidic subtexts of book 12. "He Is Your Psalm" and "The Unity of the Qualities" identify prayer with unification of the principles or qualities (degrees) and state that "the task of man" is to make them appear as a unity to the true "outer" eye. This, I think, is Zukofsky's understanding of prayer as he uses it in the NET film. Factored into his poetics, prayer is the condition of unity or objectification. Its function is, through the object effect of the image, to bring rest. If a poem has something like the effect of prayer, then what it has, or suggests, is such unity. If a poem gives us a sense of this effect, if we are so affected through its technique of composition rather than its ostensive subject matter or its author's beliefs, then it is an effective valentine and an effective prayer. If the more typical usage of prayer as entreaty has any application, it would be the working assumption or trust that a composition of words can bring such an effect into effect for others and for the poet. Unless this can be done, we must live our lives in a state of unrelieved need, a "life by care" that can never be given rest, however momentary.

The correlation, too, of Zukofsky's explanation in his letter to Lorine Niedecker ("the effect or suggestion is something like a mirror fugue") with his NET film comment on the "Degrees" poems ("and the effect . . . it's something like a prayer"), a correlation spanning nearly thirty years, is striking in its exactness. Prayer, in effect, is fugue, the characteristic shape of which is a circle (or, modified, a valentine), the embodiment of completeness or unity that affects us as an object and thus promotes rest. Zukofsky has not been "born again" outside his experience as a weaver in composition. He has, though, introduced another term into the circle of his terms. Not surprisingly, any consideration of one must end up as a reflection of all the others.

As something of a test for what I would claim to be Zukofsky's understanding of prayer, we can put it up against what has been claimed for another poet, Wallace Stevens. While Zukofsky's original masters were Pound and Williams, it is Stevens with whom he came to feel he had the most in common. As he states in his 1971 talk on Stevens, a talk that entwines the career of the speaker around his subject, "reading him . . . I felt that my own writing . . . was closer to his than to that of any of my contemporaries in the last half century of life we shared together."[20]

In her critical biography of Stevens, *The Early Years, 1879–1923*, Joan Richardson connects Stevens with his contemporary Mina Loy and their predecessor Emily Dickinson.[21] The language of her rationale immediately, if not completely, reminds us of Zukofsky, a further connection of which Richardson herself would appear to be unaware. That is, the poets of her connection "wrested continuing possibility from the threat of conclusion" by forcing attention on the particular, by expanding instants of being, and by investing "any and every object" with the quality of sacredness. All of this, she tells us, is involved with the sounds of their words. Further: "each of their poems . . . was and is a prayer, a celebration exquisitely attenuating the lived moments." A few pages later, she links seeing each poem as a prayer with seeing each one as a "sacrament of praise." This she takes to mean that, for Stevens, the poem functions to celebrate "each moment of consciousness it instances." It does no harm if Richardson's claims are conflated and recomposed into one proposition: what identifies a poem as a prayer is the attenuation of consciousness.

It is not difficult to read the "Degrees" poems according to the Richardson proposition. In fact, "exquisitely attenuating" seems a peculiarly apposite phrase for these poems and for much else in Zukofsky. To attenuate is to make thin. But it is difficult to imagine how poems of such complexity could keep that complexity and be made thinner still. A quick glance attests to this. But reading Zukofsky is not a glancing matter. The fourth stanza of the second poem forced us to speak each of the same twelve words in order that each is heard in its own melody and in its larger collective harmonic implications for the entire row. The point of this slow-movement stanza is to accentuate, hold up to the light, and thus heighten our sense of the degrees. Without such a sense or consciousness, there is little if any corresponding sense of (or need for) unification of the degrees, of objectification and rest. The fourth stanza is not the final stanza, nor is it the central mirror or plane of the poem.

Difference is ultimately of more interest than sameness. Even as there is no difficulty in reading Zukofsky according to the Richardson proposition, the different motivations of these poets in conceiving the poem as a prayer, which in itself is something of an overstatement, should be noted. If Richardson's depiction of Stevens's motivation is accepted, the poem, with its emphasis upon sound and particulars, is that which seeks to forestall closure. In the terminology of Stevens's poetics, reality and imagination have been released for yet another meditation (i.e., a poem) concerning their relation and possible coordination to make a green poetry qua poetry. So long as poetry remains possible—and unrealized, an always open horizon—individual poems may continue to be written.

Zukofsky, however, is motivated by a deep need to close the circle. And he reads Stevens according to that need. Thus the statement, in his talk, about how the instant certainty of the words of a poem may bring people together is preceded by a quotation from Stevens's "Lack of Repose": "A few sounds of meaning, a momentary end / To the complication, is good, is a good." The difference between the two poets comes down to a distinction of Aristotelian more and less. For Stevens such a momentary end is *a* good; for Zukofsky it is *the* good.

It is also the source for critical questions and for whatever distinction the work may possess as the response to those questions. Zukofsky's consciousness is not merely a technician's self-consciousness about his work considered as a job. While both poets, in the company of Dickinson and others, may conceive the poem as a prayer or as having the effect of prayer, Zukofsky's own motivating desire is that the circle not be exceeded *and* that there be growth within it. The latter can be accomplished in more than one way, but all of them involve the active engagement of the reader. In these ways, whether as the reflective mirror of the second poem or as the "Precomposed" raft of stuff of "A" 22–23, ears and eyes are reconciled so that *love sees*. In that seeing, the poet's cause—his need to correct his error and to manifest his love, bringing rest to the beloved and to his readers—may be justified. In the figure of an embrace, as many as recognize the need for unification, having recognized the degrees of difference, may be brought together by the poet's composition of words, but in such a way that they can see and can be seen clearly.

Allow me to let Zukofsky speak for myself. In his preface to *An "Objectivists" Anthology* (1932) and in between a phalanx of quotations from Pound that rivals my own from him, he notes, "but a critic-poet-analyst is interested in growing degrees of intelligence."[22] It should be evident why this is so. Beyond sources, definitions, and critical questions—all of which, as they are proposed by the work, are to be taken seriously—there must be a growing awareness of the degrees, the degrees of the poem's language and of our experience in the world outside the poem, if we are to be alive or conscious at all.

The poetry of Louis Zukofsky is an incitement to such growth. As there is a growing awareness in reading it, so also is there an awareness that, for all its circular perfection, the word's own possibility for growth within its circle depends, as the justification of its cause depends, upon our own ears and eyes. Recently, literary criticism has been preoccupied with the recognition that texts are not passive creations for passive consumption. In this recognition poets are viewed as products of intertextuality, their lives lived in a context of texts (or library of Babylon). There is, in response, no denying the uneasiness that anyone may feel—trapped, grasped utterly—in reading Zukofsky. First there is bafflement with his musical conception of the image and his extreme concision, then there is incredulity and a proportionate discomfort with the realization of just how absolute his reflective symmetry is. There is the feeling, finally, of being trapped in a circle, all the "sides" of which mirror all the others.

We will remain trapped in this poetry so long as we do not read it with an attention that approximates the care of its composition. Perhaps such reading is necessary for all art of power, no less for Zukofsky than for Bach and Shakespeare. This is how, in fact, Zukofsky has read his own sources and so achieved an originality of weaving (and liberation from a predicative intertextuality). Eliot came to feel, reversing himself, that poets were sufficiently freed from Milton's reputation to approach the study of his work without danger. Zukofsky still enjoys no certain reputation, and I feel no need to reverse myself. Poetry of power is never approached without danger. What I have grown to learn in my return is that, for there to be a way out, a liberation, the circle of Zukofsky's poetry must be entered as a dwelling. In Spinoza's definition, we must dwell upon it as love dwells upon its cause. Otherwise, our attention is glancing, unheedy haste, and we remain haunted by a shadow that has not been properly picked up.

NOTES

1. Lisa Faranda, "Between Your House and Mine": The Letters of Lorine Niedecker to Cid Corman, 1960 to 1970 (Durham: Duke University Press, 1986).

2. Louis Zukofsky, "A" 1–12 (Ashland, Mass.: Origin Press, 1959).

3. Arnold Schoenberg, *Fundamentals of Musical Composition*, ed. Gerald Strang and Leonard Stein (London: Faber and Faber, 1967).

4. Arnold Schoenberg, *Style and Idea: Selected Writings*, ed. Leonard Stein (New York: St. Martin's Press, 1975).

5. Louis Zukofsky, *Bottom: On Shakespeare, with Music to "Pericles" by Celia Zukofsky*, 2 vols. (Austin, Tex.: Ark Press, 1963).

6. Donald Francis Tovey, *The Forms of Music* (Cleveland: Meridian Books, 1956).

7. Anton Webern, *The Path to the New Music*, ed. Willi Reich, trans. Leo Black (London: Universal Edition, 1963).

8. In Paul Klee, *The Thinking Eye*, ed. Jürg Spiller (New York: Wittenborn, 1961).

9. Wilfred Mellers, *Bach and the Dance of God* (New York: Oxford University Press, 1981).

10. Martin Buber, *Ten Rungs: Hasidic Sayings* (New York: Shocken Books, 1978).

11. *The Basic Works of Aristotle*, ed. Richard McKeon (New York: Random House, 1941).

12. Paracelsus, *Selected Writings*, ed. Jolande Jacobi, trans. Norbert Guterman (New York: Pantheon Books, 1958).

13. Louis Zukofsky, *All: The Collected Short Poems* (New York: Norton, 1971).

14. Louis Zukofsky, interview and reading on National Educational Television, WDNT, August 19, 1966.

15. Mary Ellen Solt, *Concrete Poetry: A World View* (Bloomington: Indiana University Press, 1970).

16. Louis Zukofsky, *A Test of Poetry* (Brooklyn: Objectivist Press, 1948).

17. Plato, *Dialogues*, 2 vols., trans. B. Jowett (New York: Random House, 1937).

18. Spinoza, *Selections*, ed. John Wild (New York: Scribner's, 1930).

19. Louis Zukofsky, *Ferdinand, including IT WAS* (London: Jonathan Cape, 1968). Reprinted in *Collected Fiction* (Elmwood Park, Ill.: Dalkey Archive Press, 1989).

20. "For Wallace Stevens," in *Prepositions: The Collected Essays of Louis Zukofsky* (Berkeley and Los Angeles: University of California Press, 1981).

21. Joan Richardson, *Wallace Stevens: A Biography: The Early Years, 1879–1923* (New York: William Morrow, 1986).

22. Louis Zukofsky, ed., *An "Objectivists" Anthology* (Le Beausset, Var, France: To Publishers, 1932).

Institutions
and
Ideology

10   The Boundaries of Poetry
James Sherry

> Such linkages constitut(e) the social networks within which individual subjectivities and collective structures are mutually and continuously shaped.
>
> —Louis Montrose, "Professing the Renaissance"

9. The leaders in the science of chaotic systems describe their discipline's relational structure as having a "sensitive dependence on initial conditions." What does this language closely resemble? The least change may vastly vary the functioning of what we know as the system.

As the boundaries of the state are breached, the boundaries of the poem, the line, the word, the text are extended beyond any individual tongue to all discourse, even nonhuman discourse. We no longer speak and write English without reference to the community of human tongues and translations of world-concepts into our national languages.

Dialectical formation and destruction takes place at every level in the poem as a political agenda, committeed by the parasites of preconception. Do we rest in English because we speak it? Do we conform to a prosody in order to be able to express ourselves? Yet we cannot reinvent all of language and poetry every time we write. There are aspects of the poem that can be redefined and aspects that are borrowed.

Appropriation in art and the use of modes of discourse not native to the writer in poetry pass through the border of the disciplines of the arts as if they had no mass. And yet they are visible everywhere in the interaction between the reader/viewer and the work. Rauschenberg painting on an image of Rembrandt exposes the assumption that the limits of art are individual expression. Or as Paul Blackburn said, "to write poetry is not a personal achievement."

When I write certain poetries, I accept the illusion of authorship in order to write. All discourse and discourse itself must be understood as mutually dependent on other discourses.

When I write in a genre other than poetry, I link to the notion of literary invention as well as literary convention. Not only is authorship questioned but property as well. When Baudelaire writes poetry in a prose format, the attachment of poetry to verse is severed. The way Silliman leaves a space between sentences throws the onus and attention of the writing from the writer to the reader. In these ways the boundaries of poetic form and discourse become permeable and a society is established composed of language, discourse, grammar, and vocabulary.

The poetry of borders—line, meter, or "free-verse" prosody that simply redefines the borders—within the striated space created by the state mirrors its bureaucracy as the structure of the atom mirrors the social structure. Alternative strategies such as I have just described are now being established as a primary poetics and interpolated into the canon. What changes will be wrought on this new day.

Anapests, "poetic" emotions, and cabinet bureaus furnish a cultural/political domicile populated by self-congratulatory bureaucrats. Modernism produced an alternative structure that recognized the limits of traditional prosody. Where modernism failed was in its description of the essentially social nature of language with aestheticized nature-oriented prosody. Modernism put political content in the poem where it was canonized and co-opted.

New writing like the nonlinear mathematics establishes a notation that is sensitive to the initial conditions of language, making real events in real systems accessible to its forms, not just triggers of preconstituted emotional states. The empirical reality assumed to lie behind each mode of discourse means that each theory is only knowable through its discourse. The nature of its existence depends on an adjective.

For example, in the post-Mallarmean field poetry, space is defined on the page in heterogeneous smooth space. Bruce Andrews's "elusive continent" where "hinges / ride / lava" bodes ill for the linear metrics of the Greeks and English. Length and stress are both mutated and redefined in an open area where language mobilizes a network of meaning using the open space as a kind of time divided by the unquantified movement of the eye and breath while reading—an anabasis.

This utopia tantalizes the reader. It idealizes a society where there is no pull between what we want and what we have to do, no conflict between the citizen and the legislator. It postulates an unalienated alternative. It may do so as a critique of contemporary society or it may do so as a sincere proposal, but to date it can only do so as the art of one person or a collaboration among a few.

Few artists or writers were able to comprehend that structure, by the fact of repetition, implied society. Yet a continuous appeal goes out to all minorities, disenfranchised, terrorists, sublanguage groups: "This is your poetry. Join the network to discover new ways of making meaning. Do not fixate on poem, voice, other striated and arbitrary meaning formulations. We offer a processual, unbounded methodology that can be applied to any language and can include all languages."

Like the Ayatollah's public version of Islam, poetry demands complete adherence to a redefined world, not one reformed or amended to be co-opted. (Of course I am not supporting Khomeini's absurd position regarding Rushdie. There are, however, difficult changes required if we wish to be thorough about what our ideas imply and we must closely question our motives. If we believe what we have said about new art, we must implement these changes ourselves or have those changes sweep us away. So far, however, all revolutionary discourse has not been powerful enough to sustain a retort from either the quotidian or from the arrow of time. The failures of socialism attest to that. But there are other avenues and alliances.)

Like the mathematics of chaos, art shows a world composed primarily of complex systems. Even the simplest of these do not have simple dynamic properties or remain unconnected to each other. On the other hand, art influenced by nuclear ideology relies on an abstraction, a hothouse where the author, subject, and prosody depend on manufactured fertilizer.

Avoiding facility in art to define a thing is easy. To define an interaction, a polity, is difficult, because all differences should be taken into account. The way things seem to work is that certain differences are enfranchised while others, because of their language, go unheard, languish. "Slow and rapid are not quantitative degrees of movement, but two types of qualified motion" (Deleuze and Guattari). Quality/qualification revives in order to define connection. Good and bad are adjectives, not greater and lesser amount of goodness.

Art resides in an objective zone of fluctuation contiguous to reality. Sensitive and sensible evaluations pose more problems than they solve. Even problematics is only one mode. And the heterogeneous open field is itself bounded by definitions of states of being experimental or avantgarde, a hangover from the state binge.

In contrast state (nuclear) poetry organizes around axioms of prosody, metrics defined by categories, state art around the quadrilateral, perspective, the technology of hand work, and the laws of image. This is the rigor against which one tests oneself, not by seeing how far away from it one can go, but without going back at all. What Webern described in *The Path to the New Music* as "not returning to the keynote."

The concept of time as well as the concept of space has been pluralized by postmodern art. Pierre Boulez distinguishes between two types of time in music: striated time broken up by measures that can be regular or irregular, but is always "assignable," and smooth time in which the partition "can be effected by the will."

Two types of space align the current conflict. One is measured by wave peaks and troughs and the other is measured by the movement of the water across the surface of each wave. The latter describes the problematic, pure movement of the next phase within which totalization has meaning and totipotent cells move freely across its inclined surface, clearing it of opposition, barriers, and division, which is the chief weapon of the state.

The national-state hierarchy is being systematically destroyed by these incursions to which the axiom-addicted scientists of the state reply with the threat of *One World or None*. Even they seek a unification as individuals that the state does not allow their thought, and if they don't get it, they offer the nuclear threat of a child in a playpen.

What Islamic intrusions represent at this stage in the dialectic is the tribe created by the disaffected of state authority defined as Western culture. Movement for its own sake. What Rushdie himself calls "a mere three or four generations removed from their nomadic past, when they were as rootless as the dunes, or rather rooted in the knowledge that journeying itself was home."

"Whereas the migrant can do without the journey altogether, it's no more than a necessary evil; the point is to arrive." To beat the sand into building blocks of cities with streets and avenues at right angles, positions for every man, woman, and child, through which the white tornado cleans, sweeping up every nonaligned particle.

11 The Political Economy of Poetry

Ron Silliman

Poems both are and are not commodities.[1] It is the very partialness of this determination that makes possible much of the confusion among poets, particularly on the left, as to the nature of their participation in (including, perhaps, opposition to) commodity capitalism through the process of making art. Any commodity is necessarily an object and has a physical existence, even if this aspect is no more than the vibrating vocal chords of a sound poet. But not all objects are commodities. That which exists in nature and has a use, such as water, is a good—the hiker comes to the stream and drinks. Only that which is *produced* for its utility achieves the status of product (the water is piped to a metropolitan reservoir and filtered). Of products, only those that are *made for exchange* (and specifically exchange for money) become commodities (Perrier).

The writer who composes a work and reveals it to no one, keeping it instead confined to her notebook, nonetheless has created a product that possesses real use value (part of which may be in the writing process) for its lone consumer. Likewise, two poets trading photocopies of their latest works are exchanging products. And even to the extent that a small press edition of a book of poems may have a certain portion of its run set aside for the author in lieu of royalties, and that many of those copies will be given away, it also will suffer a divided identity.

Yet books and texts do not exist at quite the same level, nor are they produced by exactly the same people. Further muddying the situation is the subsidization, however minimal, in most of the English-speaking nations of both writers and publications by the state. To what degree can we use the term *commodity* to describe a book sold in a store when its publisher has no hope of recouping original costs, and when these losses will be at least partly absorbed by a third party? Is its commodification nothing more than a strategy for maximum circulation, so that the volume might achieve a greater product-function? Should government patronage be seen as a metaconsumption, in which what is purchased is not textual, but simply the existence of poets and poetry as an ornament to the national culture?

Perhaps, but more important to the equation is the simple presence of consumption, for the role it plays, however dimly perceived by individual authors, in motivating the productions of texts for exchange. It was just this that Laura Riding discovered in her 1926 essay "T. E. Hulme, the New Barbarism, & Gertrude Stein," when she complained of "the forced professionalization of poetry."[2] The poet who writes with the idea of having her poems published, of having them collected into books and distributed through stores and direct mail purchases (which may at this point be the larger sector of the market), has inescapably been drawn into the creation of commodities.

The book, a commodity, radically alters the composition and potential size of an audience. Yet, although literary theory since the time of the New Critics has done much to elaborate the possible meanings in a given text, it has remained essentially silent about the relations of the social features of any actual, particular audience in the creation of such meanings. This absence banishes any serious consideration of the ideological component, which is reduced instead to a question of the politics of the writer or those of individual characters (an example would be Terry Eagleton's discussion of George Eliot in Criticism and Ideology).[3]

The role of the reader in the determination of a poem's ideological content is neither abstract nor beyond the scope of feasible examination. The question is contextual, not textual. As early as 1929, V. N. Voloshinov wrote:

> The actual reality of language-speech is not the abstract system of linguistic forms, not the isolated monologic utterance, and not the psychophysiological act of its implementation, but the social event of verbal interaction implemented in an utterance or utterances.
>
> Thus, verbal interaction is the basic reality of language. . . . A book, i.e., a verbal performance in print, is also an element of verbal communication. It is something discussable in actual, real-life dialogue, but aside from that, it is calculated for active perception, involving attentive reading and inner responsiveness, and for organized, printed reaction . . . (book reviews, critical surveys, defining influence on subsequent books, and so on). Moreover, a verbal performance of this kind also inevitably orients itself with respect to previous performances in the same sphere, both those by the same author and those by other authors. It inevitably takes its point of departure from some particular state of affairs. . . . Thus the printed verbal performance engages, as it were, in ideological colloquy of large scale: it responds to something, objects to something, affirms something, anticipates possible responses and objections, seeks support, and so on.
>
> Any utterance, no matter how weighty and complete in and of itself, is only a moment in the continuous process of verbal communication. But that continuous verbal communication is, in turn, itself only a moment in the continuous, all-

inclusive, generative process of a given social collective. . . . *Verbal communication can never be understood and explained outside of this connection with a concrete situation.*[4]

Contrast Voloshinov's perspective with that of New Critics René Wellek and Austin Warren: "the real problem must be conceived as a structure of norms, realized only partially in the experience of its many readers." Their argument in *Theory of Literature* (1949) is a thorough assault on all contextual approaches:

> What is the "real" poem; where should we look for it; how does it exist . . . ?
>
> One of the most common and oldest answers is the view that a poem is an "artefact," an object of the same nature as a piece of sculpture or a painting. Thus the work of art is considered identical with the black lines of ink on white paper or parchment or, if we think of a Babylonian poem, with the grooves in the brick. Obviously this answer is quite unsatisfactory. There is, first of all, the huge oral "literature." There are poems or stories which have never been fixed in writing and still continue to exist. Thus the lines in black ink are merely a method of recording a poem which must be conceived as existing elsewhere. If we destroy the writing or even all copies of a printed book we still may not destroy the poem. . . . Besides, not every printing is considered by us, the readers, a correct printing of a poem. The very fact that we are able to correct printer's errors in a text which we might not have read before or, in some rare cases, restore the genuine meaning of the text shows that we do not consider the printed lines as the genuine poem. Thus we have shown that the poem (or any literary work of art) can exist outside its printed version and that the printed artefact contains many elements which we all must consider as not included in the genuine poem.[5]

While the Saussurean bias against writing as anything more than a shadow of speech is evident enough in this classic passage, more telling (at least for its impact on subsequent literary theory) is the demand of a single aspect of the work that can be elevated to the status of *genuine*. In the cause of textual analysis, Wellek and Warren succeeded in delegitimating the fuller study of literature as a total social process.

This is not to be confused with the dialectical method of moving from the concrete to the abstract, from the printed poem to its social context, in order to identify principles and structures with which to return to concrete practice. Wellek and Warren's idealization of the text is a complete rupture, achieved by a stylistic sleight of hand (writing is only a record of speech, yet oral work is only literature in quotes, severing the text from any material finality). This dematerialization conspires to make "possible the continuity of literary tradition" and "increase the unity . . . of works of art" by banishing investigations of difference at other levels.

The career of William Carlos Williams demonstrates the real consequences of those aspects of literary production and consumption that New Criticism would dismiss. Many young poets today feel that his finest work is to be found in *Spring & All* and the other books composed between 1920 and 1932. Yet several of the "New American" poets of the 1950s are on record as having been primarily influenced by Williams's 1944 collection *The Wedge*. This means that young writers perceive the stamp of Williams's example, teaching, and prestige on the work of their immediate predecessors as having a value other than that presumed by those somewhat older poets. A poet who bears that mark heavily, such as Lew Welch, is apt to become marginalized by the process.

Spring & All was not available in the 1950s, though the poems in it were included (in an altered order) in *The Collected Earlier Poems*. To be certain, the texts themselves did not change, but their inaccessibility blocked communication, and by the time Harvey Brown's Frontier Press brought them back to a possible public, the audience itself had been transformed: in addition to their having experienced a greatly expanded educational system in the 1960s, a war in Vietnam that had already gone sour, and the familiarity with psychedelics, the new readers of *Spring & All* had often already assimilated the work of Olson, O'Hara, Creeley, and others.

An even clearer example of the literary (and therefore social) difference of different editions can be found in Jim Carroll's *Basketball Diaries*, a teenage memoir of sex, drugs, and rock-and-roll that over fifteen years went through piecemeal appearances in little poetry magazines, a slick small press edition, and finally emerged as a mass market paperback— reviewed and even excerpted in the nation's *sports* pages. At one end of this spectrum is a group of readers who found in Carroll a natural, even primitive, tough-lyric prose style, embodying many of the principles held by writers associated with the Saint Mark's Church in New York and articulated most forcefully by Ted Berrigan. At the other end is a group of readers who probably have never heard of Ted Berrigan and for whom the considerations of style, without which the *Diaries* would never have been printed, are utterly beside the point.

Even in cases, such as live performance, where the author is present, different audiences will receive and interpret a given work differently. In a talk given at San Francisco's 80 Langton Street, Robert Glück offers this example:

> At several Movement readings I was interested to see members of the audience come up afterwards and say where the writer had got it right (yes, that's my life) and where the writer had got it wrong. I want to contrast this with the audience that admires writing as if it were a piece of Georgian silver, goods to be consumed. Of course this depends on an identification with a community, a shared ideology. For example, I read a story at a gay reading about being "queer-bashed." The audience responded throughout with shouts of encouragement and acknowledgement. Afterwards people told me I got it right. I read the same story to an appreciative and polite university audience, and afterwards people told me they admired my transitions. To a certain extent, my story registered only in terms of form.[6]

Although Glück foregrounds here the role of context, he implicitly reproduces the Wellek-Warren presumption of "correctness," merely substituting a preferred definition (one that avoids addressing the political question of what is accomplished by correctness: the delegitimization of something, and by fiat, not argument). His characterization of an "audience that admires writing as if it were a piece of Georgian silver" is in fact incorrect, because he omits the fact that the second group's response is conditioned by their identification with Glück *as a writer* (and/or as an intellectual *because* he writes). What is shared is not the experience of homophobic violence but the problems of a craft.

What can be communicated through any literary production depends on which codes are shared with its audience. The potential contents of the text are only actualized according to their reception, which depends on the social composition of the receivers. The work of Clark Coolidge, for example, might seem opaque and forbidding at a gay reading, for the same reason that a Japanese speaker cannot communicate with an Italian: no codes are shared from which to translate from word to meaning. There may be several people at a gay reading who are as interested as Coolidge in geology, bebop, Salvador Dali, weather, and even the same kinds of writing problems, but these concerns are not what bring people to such an event.

The social composition of its audience is the primary context of any writing. Context determines (and is determined by) the motives of the readers as well as their experience, their history, that is, their particular set of possible codes. Context determines the actual, real-life consumption of the literary product, without which communication of a message (formal, substantive, ideological) cannot occur. It tells us very little to know only that one group was a "gay reading" and the other a "university audience." A school with a large English department and a creative writing major is entirely different from a school focusing on science and agriculture. A reading to a graduate-level class in rhetoric is not the same as another to the general student body.

It is here, at the question of context, a place that does not even exist within the system of Wellek and Warren, that both Riding and Glück complain in their very different ways of the "forced professionalization" of poetry. We can see here also that the "continuity of literary tradition" and the "unity . . . of works of art" is not a partial truth but a calculated fabrication that expresses, more clearly than its authors could have known, the ideology of late capitalism. Their "us, the readers," able to determine a "correct printing of a poem" and capable of restoring "the genuine meaning of the text," is not just any reader, but a particular one, unnamed, with a particular education and occupation. Glück's argument (although it fails to distinguish between the worker's concern for the quality and manufacture of her product and the attitude of a collector of Georgian silver) is an improvement to the degree that his naming of a "best reader" at least acknowledges the existence of other audiences.

The New Critics, however, were not solely responsible for the illusion of a "continuity of literary tradition" made possible by the banishment of other readers. Their task was to give this mirage a cloak of critical respectability. Wellek and Warren's comments, it should be noted, came during the long four-and-one-half-decade period (1911–1955) when the number of book titles published in the United States per year remained relatively static at under 12,000, in spite of the emergence of large corporate publishing firms, while membership in the Modern Language Association (MLA) rose from 1,047 to 8,453.[7] In short, the rise of a professional caste of "specialized" or, more accurately, bureaucratized readers occurred precisely at the moment when a new set of dynamics, characterized by such concepts as market position, penetration, and share, began to reorganize the distribution of what had for a long time been a fixed output. Thus corporate collaboration with the leadership of this new caste at least appeared to offer commanding control over the future of the market itself.

It was, more than anything else, the affluence of the United States after the Second World War that kept this "promise" from being met. New offset printing technology lowered the cost of book production, permitting the large publishers to further segment their markets and realize profits from an increased diversity of titles, while simultaneously enabling a dramatic expansion in the number of small, independent producers. Similarly, post-Sputnik higher education brought new masses into what had previously been the terrain of a more homogeneous, class-determined few. Membership in the MLA (itself much more diversified) was to peak in 1971 at 31,356, while the number of book titles published per year in 1980 exceeded 40,000.[8] Finally, beginning with the creation of the Literature Panel of the National Endowment for the Arts in 1966, state subsidies for poets and the publication of poetry became active forces in the decentralization of literature. The rise of the "New American" poetries and their successors, as well as that of writing coming out of the women's movement and from ethnic and sexual minority communities, can be viewed as a consequence of these social and technological transformations, each of which, in turn, is grounded in economic circumstance.

Yet, even with subsidies, there is not enough capital in the entire poetry industry to directly support poets and publishers. This partly determines who will be poets and at what period of their lives poets are more apt to be active and publish. More important, however, this means that nearly all poets will turn elsewhere to make a living. Thus poets as a group have a wide range of jobs. This in turn means both that poets see work (and the politics of the workplace) in a nonuniform manner and from a variety of perspectives and that they are less likely to perceive poetry as work (at least in the sense of the politics that would extend from that perception). It also partly explains why so much of the discussion of the politics of literature has been fixated on the lone aspect of content.

"Professional" poets include individuals who come from the entire spectrum of economic classes. The actual number of those who might accurately be described as bourgeois is small, and it is speculative to suggest that it exceeds the 2 percent figure that holds for the general U.S. population. The neobeatnik/neodada/street poet scene that manifests itself in every major urban center, on the other hand, might be characterized by the lumpen orientation of many of its participants. But the vast majority of poets fall in between. While many are traditionally working class and while there may be a somewhat higher concentration of classically defined petty bourgeois than in the general American economy, a significant concentration of poets falls into a category that the late Nicos Poulantzas called the New Petty Bourgeoisie:

> This is also where the current devaluation of educational certificates and attainments is most important, given the significance that these have on the labour market and for the promotion chances of these agents. It can be seen in the currently massive occupation of subaltern posts by agents whose edu-

cational qualifications led them to have different aspirations. In actual fact, this is the fraction into which young people holding devalued university degrees gravitate on a massive scale. It leads to the various forms of disguised unemployment that ravages this fraction: various forms of illegal work, vacation work, temporary and auxiliary work. These affect all those fractions with an objectively proletarian polarization, but are particularly pronounced in this case.[9]

Poets, for obvious reasons, tend to look at "disguised unemployment" as time to write, which partly explains their gravitation to part-time service sector jobs, such as clerking in bookstores or proofreading for publishers and law firms. Poulantzas also notes that "It now seems, however, as if the last few years have seen the development, in the majority of capitalist countries, of an actual mental labour reserve army, over and above any cyclical phenomena."[10]

Poulantzas, however, has a very restricted class model, considering mental work and service sector employment to be unproductive and therefore excluded from the working class as such (although conceding the "objectively proletarian polarization"). Still, the description, especially with regard to underutilized education and partial employment, is a close fit to the lives of many American poets under forty.

Erik Olin Wright, one of Poulantzas's most vigorous critics, uses a more complex model in which this same group is categorized as working class yet with a strong degree of contradiction as to class allegiance. Noting that more than 30 percent of economically active Americans had, by 1969, come into the "unproductive mental" labor sector, Wright notes that "The contradictory locations around the boundary of the working class represent positions which do have a real interest in socialism, yet simultaneously gain certain real privileges directly from capitalist relations of production."[11]

Situated within these complex and sometimes contradictory economic relations, the social organization of contemporary poetry occurs in two primary structures: the *network* and the *scene*. The scene is specific to a place. A network, by definition, is transgeographic. Neither mode ever exists in a pure form. Networks typically involve scene subgroupings, while many scenes (although not all) build toward network formations. Individuals may, and often do, belong to more than one of these informal organizations at a time. Both types are essentially fluid and fragile. As the Black Mountain poets and others have demonstrated, it is possible for literary tendencies to move through both models at different stages in their development.

Critical to the distinction between these structures are the methods of communication available to their members. A sociology of poetry, noting, for example, that a reading series requires far less start-up capital than either a book or magazine, or that the face-to-face interactions that take place in such settings seldom demand the initiative needed to begin a serious, long-distance correspondence with a stranger, would correlate such implications with the class backgrounds and orientations of both writers and readers, real and potential alike. Yet, if such a sociology is not to fall prey to technological determinism, it must ask not simply which methods of interaction are in use but, more important, to what end. Because capital, of which there is so little in poetry, is necessary for the elements of network formation, competition exists between networks and scenes. Underneath lie a hidden assumption of the hierarchical ordering of these groups and the idea that one can be the dominant or hegemonic formation according to some definition, at least for a period of time. Definitions vary, but major components include monetary rewards, prestige (often called influence), and the capacity to have one's work permanently in print and being taught.

Here the role of trade publishing and its allies is completely clear. Trade presses may produce less than 4 percent of all poetry titles, but in an anthology such as The American Poetry Anthology they represent 54 percent of all books used as sources for the collection.[12] University presses contributed another 31 percent. Nearly half of the remaining small press books come from Ecco Press, the editor's own imprint.

Trade publishing is the metanetwork of American poetry. It is the contemporary manifestation of the academic network for which Wellek and Warren argued more than thirty years ago, and university employment remains a primary social feature. But, because this is the network that is aligned with capital, it can and does incorporate poets from other groups on a token basis. While this serves to give them much broader distribution, they in turn legitimate the metanetwork, masking to some degree its very network structure.

This alliance with capital yields another major advantage: the relative efficiency of trade distribution virtually guarantees its predominance on college course reading lists, which is the largest single market for books of poetry, with 2,500 colleges and 200 writing programs in North America.

So long as capital, in the form of corporate publishers, can substantially determine the distribution of poetry in its major market, and so long as Daniel Halpern can call a collection of their network The American Poetry Anthology without challenge, this type of hegemony is not apt to be broken. The competition between other networks and scenes amounts to little more than jockeying for the token slots in the metanetwork.

But this is neither the only mode of hegemony nor necessarily the most important. Here the question is not whether a poet will be read in five or fifty or five hundred years, but whether that poet can and will be read by individuals *able and willing to act* on their increased understanding of the world as a result of the communication. A poetics for which the ultimate motive is nothing more than the maintenance of its own social position within a status quo reaches such an audience only insofar as it fosters no action whatsoever. The inclusion of blacks and feminists in the Halpern anthology functions precisely to keep the readers of those poets from questioning the presence of the white male college teachers who dominate the book.

What a consciously oppositional writer such as Robert Glück fails to consider when he dismisses one of his audiences in favor of the other is that their social composition is not identical. Any definition of response needs to be tailored accordingly. In part, this problem may reflect Glück's own overlapping membership in each community. It is, however, a major characteristic of the social codes of just those formations most often apt to attend a college reading not to know or speak their own name. In labeling that audience as consumers, Glück forgets that consumption *for further production* is a moment of production itself— it *is* action. It is through the question of transitions, for example, that the "seamlessness" (i.e., the "natural" or "inevitable" quality) of perceived reality, including that of the "continuity of literary tradition," might be revealed as the affect of a partisan ideological construct. A construct, in fact, which might also yield, as parallel states of "the inevitable," the social omnipotence of capital and the relative superiority of bourgeois (as distinct from economic) democracy as a method for governance in an imperfect world.

Still, just identifying Glück's university audience as a coalition of writers, teachers, and specialized readers falls short of connecting them to the larger social orders of which they are a strategic fragment. This self-invisibility has parallels throughout contemporary life. It has only been through the struggle of nonwhites, of women, and of gays that the white male heterosexual has come into recognition of his own, pervasive presence. In poetry, there continues to be a radical break between those networks and scenes that are organized by and around the codes of oppressed peoples and those other "purely aesthetic" schools. In fact, the aesthetics of those latter schools is a direct result of ideological struggle, both between networks and scenes and within them. It is characteristic of the class situation of those schools that this struggle is carried on in *other (aesthetic) terms.*

Poetry in America reflects struggle carried out, unfortunately, in an unorganized and often individualistic manner. This struggle is as much one between audiences as it is between poets (or, to be precise, it is one between social formations, including, but never limited to, economic classes, from which audiences are composed around individual authors). It is class war—and more—conducted through the normal social mechanisms of verse. The primary ideological message of poetry lies not in its explicit content, political though that may be, but in the *attitude toward reception* it demands of the reader. It is this "attitude toward information" that is carried forward by the recipient. It is this attitude that forms the basis for a response to other information, not necessarily literary, in the text. And, beyond the poem, in the world.

NOTES

1. This essay was originally given as a talk at the San Francisco Socialist School run by the Democratic Socialists of America; it was first published in L=A=N=G=U=A=G=E 4 (1981) and *Open Letter* 5.1 (1982).

2. Laura Riding [= Jackson], *Contemporaries and Snobs* (London: Cape, 1928), 123–99.

3. Terry Eagleton, *Criticism and Ideology* (New York: Verso, 1978), 110–24.

4. V. N. Voloshinov, *Marxism and the Philosophy of Language*, trans. Latislav Matejka and I. R. Titunik (New York: Seminar Press, 1973), 94–95.

5. René Wellek and Austin Warren, *Theory of Literature* (New York: Harcourt Brace, 1949), 142–43.

6. Robert Glück, "Caricature" (unpublished manuscript), 21.

7. J. Kendrick Noble, Jr., "Books," in *Who Owns the Media*, ed. Benjamin Compaine (New York: Harmony, 1979), 257; "Conventions and Membership," *PMLA* 99.3 (1984): 456.

8. The 1996 total was 140,000.

9. Nicos Poulantzas, *Classes in Contemporary Capitalism*, trans. David Fernbach (New York: Verso, 1978), 323.

10. Ibid., 311.

11. Erik Olin Wright, *Class, Crisis, and the State* (New York: Verso, 1979), 108–09.

12. Daniel Halpern, ed., *The American Poetry Anthology* (New York: Avon, 1975).

12   *Writing as a General Economy*
Steve McCaffery

I've chosen to approach writing and the written text as an economy rather than a structure. The latter tends to promote essence as relational, which has the clear advantage of avoiding all closed notions of the poem as "a well-wrought urn" but suffers from a presupposed stasis, a bracketed immobility among the parts under observation and specification. As an alternative to structure, economy is concerned with the distribution and circulation of the numerous forces and intensities that saturate a text. A textual economy would concern itself not with the order of forms and sites but with the order-disorder of circulations and distributions. A writing by way of economy will consequently tend to loosen the hold of structure and mark its limits in economy's own movement.

Specifically, I want to focus on writing as a general economy and start by presenting Georges Bataille's concise definition of it:

> The general economy, in the first place, makes apparent that excesses of energy are produced, and that by definition, these excesses cannot be utilized. The excessive energy can only be lost without the slightest aim, consequently without meaning.

The application of this definition extends far beyond scriptive practice and would include all nonutilitarian activities of excess, unavoidable waste, and nonproductive consumption in which one might specify orgasm,[1] sacrifice, meditation, the Last Supper,[2] and dreams.[3] It would connect too with the theories in Roland Barthes's later writings regarding a certain hedonism in reading and a shift in emphasis from a utilitarian understanding (including a readerly production of meaning) toward a pleasure or *jouissance* of texts.[4] Apart from a brief look at potlatch, however, I will limit the discussion to writing and approach the subject from two directions. The first will be descriptive and will try to indicate the unavoidable presence of general economic operations as an aspect of language's fundamental constitution. In a second part I will consider general economy as a model for writing, hinting toward an extremely tentative "poetics of the general" that might serve a praxis of challenge to conceptual dominants of traditional writing such as transmission theory of communication, the continuous subject, the valorization of representational and referential procedures, etc. and try to show how a strategy of the general economy can help loosen the philosophical hold that utility, as an unquestionable value, has maintained historically over the notion of writing.

We will oppose this economy to restricted economy the operation of which is based upon valorized notions of restraint, conservation, investment, profit, accumulation, and cautious proceduralities in risk taking. Both these economies need to be distinguished from political economy, which articulates the bourgeois theory of production, and from Rousseau's use of the term "general economy" in his *Discourse on Political Economy* of 1758 in which *general* and *political* are bracketed together and contrasted with *private* and *particular* economies, i.e., the economies of an individual household or family. I want to make clear that I'm not proposing "general" as an alternative economy to "restricted." One cannot replace the other because their relationship is not one of mutual exclusion. In most cases we will find general economy as a suppressed or ignored presence within the scene of writing that tends to emerge by way of rupture within the restricted, putting into question the conceptual controls that produce a writing of use value with its privileging of meaning as a necessary production and evaluated destination. Often we will detect a rupture made and instantly appropriated by the restrictive. The meaningless, for example, will be ascribed a meaning; loss will be rendered profitable by its being assigned a value. In effect, what will be dealt with is a complex interaction of two constrastive but not exclusive economies within the single operation of writing. Restricted economy, which is the economy of Capital, Reason, Philosophy, and History, will always strive to govern writing, to force its appearance through an order of constraints. The general economy would forfeit this government, conserve nothing, and, while not prohibiting meaning's appearance, would only sanction its profitless emergence in a general expenditure; hence, it would be entirely indifferent to results and concerned only with self-dispersal. A general economy can never be countervaluational nor offer an alternative "value" to Value, for it is precisely the operation of value that it explicitly disavows. It follows also that the general economy can never offer a full critique of value but only risk its loss, accompany it to its limit, and in the slide of value and meaning throw both into question. It will engender neither uses nor exchanges but eruptions without purpose within structures of restraint as that economy which shatters the accumulation of meaning.

To turn to the promised descriptive project and look at the presence of general economy in language's fundamental constitution: speech and writing "originate" as material substances in the act of incising graphic marks upon a substance, in the physical act of gesticulating (sign language for instance), and in the expulsion of certain sounds through the buccal cavity. In all three cases there is an uncontestable graphic, phonic, or gestural materiality that is a necessary condition of, yet insubsumable to, the ideality of meaning. A profit, in this way, shows itself to be predicated upon a loss, for the physical act of speaking or writing must withdraw so that what has been said or written can appear meaningful.[5] Meaning this way is staged as the telos and destination of the dematerialization of writing. The sound and rhythmic components of language can never be reduced to the operation of language per se. Hjelmslev is one of several contemporary linguists who distinguish language as a system from its material support in sound and ink. The phonē (i.e., any objective speech sound considered as a physical event regardless of how it fits into a pattern of meaning) is just such a threshold. As its material support, sound and ink are separable from the signifying process, but at the same time the process is unsupportable without it. In light of this one could consider language's materiality as meaning's heterological object, as that area inevitably involved within the semantic apparatus that meaning casts out and rejects. Language fractures at this radical point of support, severing the system per se from a plurality of speech and writing effects. It is because of this general economy of materiality that writing can function as an entirely referential project, pointing out beyond itself to an adequated zone of nonlinguistic "reality." When writing situates in a reference to a field of objects it relates to something other than itself, becoming projective and a carrier of meaning. So writing's initially general economy is immediately recuperated as a restrictive operation by which writing does not lose a world of objects but appropriates and retains this in itself as a homogenized territory of meaning, ideality, and sign.

As well as this expenditure of materiality from language, the field of objects must also dematerialize, drawing away into nomination and denotation (the targets for deixis) in order to be present *inside* language as a referent. Two instantly appropriated general economies, then, are immediately invested back into ideation. Under this restrictive action language never presents itself as a breached system involving two intersecting economies of both waste and retention. The language of instrumental reference will always repress this breach and downplay the constitutional presence of a material exhaustion.

I want to consider metaphor as a second example of a general economic operation. Clearly metaphor is not a simple designation but a substitutional device that carries a noun or nominal phrase (as a virtual designator) elsewhere *toward* another term. I am stressing the word *toward* because the problematics of the transit inform the very nature of the figure. We will examine this point shortly. Metaphor, in fact, attacks the notion of absolute meaning. At least one aspect of the metaphoric operation involves the institution of an identity between dissimilar things, an annexation of *otherness* and the suppression of difference, and if this aspect constituted the entire action of metaphoricity, then it would stand as a unilateral operation of equivalence that *prima facia* would sanction exchange. But this reduction of difference to identity is never an absolute moment in metaphor; there is always another constitution that threatens presence, an operation of metaphor not as trope but as locus for the contestation of difference. In effect, there is always the threat of substitution going astray in the substitutional passage, of the movement elsewhere toward the appropriation of the otherness collapsing and actually engendering a heterogeneity. Curiously enough it was Hobbes in *Leviathan* (1651) who first sensed the errant nature of metaphor. There Hobbes confined the figure to the realm of sedition. Approaching metaphor's more political and philosophical implications, he noted the radical ambivalence of metaphor, its striation of both truth and falsehood that commits it to general economy. Metaphor is seditious precisely because it loses that which it purports to retain, replacing the unequivocal relation of the word to truth with skew, breach, and uncertainty. In a simple metaphor such as "the talons of the law," there is a loss of clear, incontestable reference to bird and a similar loss of abstraction in the term "law." Rather than effecting an indisputable substitution (which would presuppose the transcendental principle of equivalence that institutes the exchangist economy), the semantic mechanism is rendered nomadic; meaning wanders from one term to another and any relationship through substitution and equivalence can only be asserted within the framing and staging of a certain loss.

We would examine further this constitutional ambivalence with a consideration of metaphor's binary *other* in the great structuralist drama—metonymy—and argue that metaphor, as a substitutional figure, requires a necessary passage through metonymy (its other term). Any purported resemblance between two terms (such as metaphor necessitates) must be predicated upon a contiguous scene, a prefigurational, prerhetorical placement of terms in a scene allowing the spatiocognitive assertion of resemblance. Now this is a metonymic predication. Jakobson, of course, in the footsteps of both Freud and Saussure, established metaphor (the axis of selection) and metonymy (the axis of combination) as a coupled opposition that subsequently became the diametrical matrix of all structuralism. But metaphor shows itself to be much more than a discrete figure; indeed it reveals itself to be radically contaminated by metonymy, unavoidably ambivalent in its functional relationship to both substitution and equivalence. Terms such as "mother tongue," "table leg," and "watch face" seem structured on this contaminated sense, an indecision between metaphor and metonymy, marking a hesitation between substitution and contiguity.

We can see metaphor as a figure of economy rather than structure, predicated upon a certain scarcity (i.e., the lack of a univocal designator of an object or target term) that distributes its indeterminacies among the significatory scenes it helps to establish, offering displacement as a *potential* disposition but fixing a residual potentiality between the two terms. What seems incontrovertible in this "improper" displacement of metaphor is the loss of both heterogeneity and identity. The move toward the annexation of the difference occurs as much because two things are *not* the same as because of any similarity between them. The movement to resemblance effects an escape of difference, yet there is always an irreducible, unmasterable remnant in the figure that is neither resemblance nor difference but the indeterminacy of both. Metaphor then, would inhabit the two domains of exchange and residue as well as being inscriptional of both profit and loss.

THE PARAGRAM

A text is paragrammatic, writes Leon S. Roudiez, "in the sense that its organization of words (and their denotations), grammar, and syntax is challenged by the infinite possibilities provided by letters or phonemes combining to form networks of significance not accessible through conventional reading habits."[6]

The percolation of language through the paragram contaminates the notion of an ideal, unitary meaning and thereby counters the supposition that words can "fix" or stabilize in closure. Paragrammatic wordplay manufactures a crisis within semantic economy, for while engendering meanings, the paragram also turns unitary meaning against itself. If we understand meaning in its classical adequation to truth and knowledge, then paragrammaticized meaning becomes a secretion, an escape or expenditure from semantic's ideal structure into the disseminatory material of the signifier.

The paragrammatic path is one determined by the local indications of a word's own spatiophonic connotations that produce a centrifuge in which the verbal center is itself scattered. Paragrams are the flow-producing agents in a text's syntactic economy inscribing themselves among that other economy in which the notion of word (as a fixed, double articulation of signifier/signified) upholds the functional distributions of a presentation. The paragram, moreover, is a fundamental disposition in all combinatory systems of writing and contributes to phoneticism's transphenomenal character. Paragrams (including anagrams) are what Nicholas Abraham terms *figures of antisemantics*;[7] they constitute that aspect of language which *escapes* all discourse and which commits writing unavoidably to a general economy and to the transphenomenal paradox of *an unpresentability that serves as a necessary condition of writing's capacity to present*. All of this suggests a constitutional nonpresence in meaning itself.

Ferdinand de Saussure's most controversial and least understood work is his extensive research into late Latin Saturnian verse. Saussure compiled 139 notebooks on paragrammatic and anagrammatic embeds in Saturnian verse, Homer, Virgil, Seneca, Horace, Angelo Politian, and the Vedic Hymns. What Saussure found in all these works was the persistence of a recurrent group of phonemes that combined to form echoes of important words. In the *De Rerum Natura* of Lucretius, for instance, Saussure detected extended and multiple anagrams of the name APHRODITE. Implicit in this research is the curiously nonphenomenal status of the paragram. For while assignable to a certain order of production, value, and meaning, the paragram did not derive necessarily from an intentionality or conscious rhetoricity and seemed an inevitable consequence of writing's alphabetic, combinatory nature. Seen this way as emerging from the multiple ruptures that alphabetic components bring to virtuality, meaning becomes partly the production of a general economy, a persistent excess, nonintentionality, and expenditure without reserve through writing's component letters. Through a very specific project, Saussure seemingly hit upon the vertiginous nature of textuality, seeing in this paragrammatic persistence an inevitable indeterminacy within all writing.

This unavoidable presence of words within words contests the notion of writing as a creativity, proposing instead the notion of an indeterminate, extraintentional, differential production. The paragram should not be seen necessarily as a latent content or hidden intention but as a sub-productive sliding and slipping of meaning between the forces and intensities distributed through the text's syntactic economy. Paragrams ensure that there will always be a superfluity of signifiers and a degree of waste and unrecuperability of meaning. Understood as a transphenomenal element of language, not an intention of the subject, paragrams open up a general economy on the level of signs and meanings.

Saussure himself remained puzzled by his discoveries. In 1908 he wrote to Léopold Gautier that "I make no secret of the fact that I myself am perplexed—about the most important point: that is, how one should judge the reality or phantasmagoria of the whole question."[8] In other words, does this persistence of anagrams indicate a conscious creation or could it be simply a retrospective "creation" evoked and projected by a reader? Saussure's dilemma on this point is symptomatic of a need to attach a value to transphenomenality and thereby evade the issues of a general economy. For if we admit that the paragram can be both fortuitous and intentional, a conscious creation and a transphenomenal infraproduction, then we must further admit to the infinite resourcefulness of language itself to produce aimlessly and fulfill in effect all the features Bataille assigns to a general economy: unmasterable excess, inevitable expenditure, and a thoroughly nonproductive outlay.

Such features of general economic operation as I've outlined do not destroy the order of meaning but complicate and unsettle its constitution and operation. They should destroy, through their presentation of constitutive contaminants (loss in presence, metonymy in metaphor, etc.) any essentialist notions of meaning and the operation of a subject within such unicities. Perhaps too, through the reader's own macrostructural applications of general economy, we might be warned of the sociopolitical implications of a yoking-of-passage, elusiveness, and decentralizing tendencies to the projects of self-interest, law, and truth.

At this point, however, I want to move on to the second part I promised and consider general economy's application as a speculative model of writing in which the sociopolitical and phenomenological implications, outlined and hinted at, might enter into a sign practice. I will begin with Hegel, whom Derrida describes as the first philosopher of the Book. Hegel offers a prima facia inspiring theory on the nature of transgression and the task he describes as "the labour of the negative" that involves "looking death in the face" as a confrontation with the meaningless. In The Phenomenology Hegel writes of this "labour" as the mind's basic work of theoretical appropriation: "The life of the mind is not one that shuns death, and keeps clear of destruction; it endures death and in death maintains its being. . . . It is this mighty power . . . only by looking the negative in the face, and dwelling with it. This dwelling beside it is the magic power that converts the negative into being."

One would initially suppose Hegel sympathetic to the general economy. Closer scrutiny of the whole section, however, exposes Hegel to severe critique, and The Phenomenology of the Mind has not escaped the attention of Kojève, Bataille, or Derrida. The section I want to dwell on is the section dealing with the independence/dependence of self-consciousness, where Hegel presents his famous and highly contentious master-slave dialectic that constitutes a keystone in his thinking on the nature of servitude and the subordination of one self to another. This dialectic is immense in its repercussions and, among other things, is vital to an understanding of Hegelian semiology and is still a lasting critique on Roman Jakobson and transmission theory of communication.[9]

Hegel posits two modes of consciousness: the master, a pure self-consciousness whose existence is in and for itself and is a thoroughly independent mode; and the slave, whose essence is to exist for another. In the dialectic of the master-slave, the master is self-conscious of his command of the slave (who is himself a consciousness defined by his dependence on the performance of work for the master). Hegel draws from this relation the conclusion that the self-consciousness of the master is not a pure mode but one defined by—and dependent upon—the slave's own dependence on him. The master hence is subordinated to the worker's servitude, while the slave in his turn enjoys the privilege of being his master's truth.

On close scrutiny, Hegel's dialectic of mastery shows itself to be precisely, though not obviously, a dialectic of prohibition and an example of restricted economic practice. Crucial in Hegel's argument is the inviolable, irreducible status of self-consciousness itself. Transgression and the negative in the Hegelian system do not risk the loss of subject. In the relation, subject and object, master and slave, mutually determine each other but do so across the partition that the preservation of self-consciousness (as a conserved category) erects and maintains. It is this prohibition—against the forfeit of self-consciousness and thereby a risking of the subject's own loss—that allows Hegelianism its basis for the possibility of knowledge and theoretical appropriation. It is this barrier, understood as the unquestioned boundary between subject and object, that totalizes the subject as a self-reflexivity and assures for it the homogenization of nature through knowledge. Hegelian negativity shows itself to be, in Derrida's words, "the reassuring *other* surface of the positive"; in it, death, the breakdown or dissemination of the conscious subject, and the loss of meaning are risked only to the point of a final, possible recuperation.

A similarly restrictive operation is found at work in Hegel's concept of *aufhebung* (a notoriously untranslatable word but usually rendered in English as either transcendence or sublimation). What the term describes is a double movement of both negation and conservation in which each successive step in the mind's theoretical appropriation of the object-field is lifted up, interiorized, and preserved on a higher level. This is clearly not the negativity of general economy (which would be aimless and without meaning) but the action of a subject within restricted economy where nothing is wasted and profit is squeezed out of every negative labor.[10]

In this light, it might be interesting to compare instances of current writing to a "Hegelian project." What is striking in Ron Silliman's *Ketjak*, for instance, is the work's double orientation toward, on the one hand, a textual production through a "random" economy or a free play of signification (the sentences that make up the work functioning as autonomous units that resist the syllogistic integration of traditional discursive prose and thetic discourse), and on the other hand an accumulative, preservational movement committed to the noncontamination of a transcendental "procedure" that seems precisely modeled on the Hegelian *aufhebung* and permits the structure to foreground itself as a first-order attention. For in *Ketjak* certain phrases transcend a particular context and are raised to the order of a new paragraph. Procedurality in this way functions as both the occasion for and the limitation of sign difference. Silliman's adoption of an atemporal "formula" for progressive textual integration comes close to the application of a transcendental rule that functions as an ideal predetermination of sequence settling temporality inside the writing while itself remaining atemporal. This Hegelian aspect applies to most instances of procedural writing: Jackson Mac Low's systematic-chance texts, Dick Higgins's "snowflake" forms, John Cage's mesostics (which can be read as "recoveries" of the paragram from a transphenomenal disposition in writing), and Brion Gysin's permutations.[11] This is not, of course, to condemn the texts, which in many cases represent the most vital and important works of contemporary writing.

General economy proposes a different mode of negativity and transgression in which the struggle for mastery and the transcendental petitioning are abandoned. As we noted, in Hegel's dialectic of lordship, transgression is compelled to enact itself across a permanent barrier that separates the two terms and that remains impervious and inviolable to any appropriation. Transgression consequently occurs as an eruption on one or the other side of the barrier. General economy, however, treats the barrier between terms NOT as a shared boundary but as an actual target for dissolution, the removal of which then allows the abolition of both terms as separate identities. This is the type of transgression that Bataille terms "the sovereign moment": an operation entirely devoid of self-interest and whose direction is toward breakdown and discharge rather than accumulation and integration. Bataille describes sovereignty as "the power to rise indifferent to death, above the laws which ensure the maintenance of life"; it is "the object that deludes us all, which nobody has seized and which nobody can seize for this reason: we cannot possess it, like an object, but we are doomed to seek it. A certain utility always alienates the proposed sovereignty."[12] Breton himself spoke of sovereignty as that point "where life and death, the real and the imaginary, past and future, the communicable and the incommunicable, the high and the low are no longer perceived in contradiction to one another."[13]

A writing based on general economy would strive toward a similar dissolution of categories and boundaries and utterly refuse a line of mastery. Already then, it becomes highly problematic whether or not a *conscious* strategy of sovereignty can ever be possible. Renouncing mastery, it can never find a place within a project of knowledge, and there are doubts as to whether a general economic writing could actually be sustained beyond a fleeting instant, registering its effects as anything more than a momentary rupture. What a writing of this kind would require is a number of losses and an absolute degree of risk taking. It would need to adopt the Hegelian stance of looking negativity in the face but would require going beyond that stance and risking totally the subject-object relationship.[14] Proposed would be a writing that transgresses the prohibition of the semantic operation and risks the loss of meaning. This would not constitute an utter rejection of meaning, for rejection would only resituate meaning (through a kind of negative bracketing) as a separated but still relational term. Rather the loss of meaning would occur within meaning itself in a deployment without use, without aim, and without a will to referential or propositional lordship. A return to the material base of language would be necessary as a method of losing meaning, holding on to graphicism and sonorities at the very point where ideation struggles to effect their withdrawal. An obvious example of this general rematerialization of language is the sound poem, what the Dadaist Hugo Ball called "poetry without words." Sound poetry has a long history through Silesian baroque theories, Dadaism, both Russian and Italian futurism, the Lettriste movement of the 1940s up to its recent manifestations in the work of Bob Cobbing, Jean-Paul Curtay, the Four Horsemen, Bernard Heidsieck, and many others. The sound poem can never be reduced to its textual "equivalent" or notation; it is essentially performative and implicates the subject not as a speaking subject but as a phonic, pneumatic outlay. In contrast to Projective verse that seeks a reincorporation of breath inside the textual economy as part of an extended tradition of representation (namely the representation of the body in language and process), sound poetry is a poetry of complete expenditure in which nothing is recoverable and usable as "meaning." Involved is a decomposition of both an operative subject and the historical constraints of a semantic order. Sound poetry shatters meaning at the point where language commits its move to idealization; it sustains the materiality and material effects of the phonematic structures while avoiding their traditional semantic purpose. As a poetry of purely phonic outlay, the sound poem also puts the subject into process, exploding the unitary contours of consciousness and propelling textual experience into a festive economy.

Another example is this excerpt from a text of Charles Bernstein's. Less grounded in a notion of a performative subject and developing economic implications through its totality of writing effects, it still provides a good example of rematerialization and the accompanying interaction of general and restricted economic tendencies:

> Ig ak abberflappi. mogh & hmog ick pug eh nche ebag ot eb v joram lMbrp nly ti asw evn ditcr ot heh ghtr rties. ey Ancded lla tghn heh ugrf het keyon. hnny iKerw. in VazoOn uv spAz ah's ee 'ook up an ays yr bitder guLpIng sum u pulLs. ig jis see kHe nig MiSSy heh d sogA chHooPp & abhor ih cN gt eGuLfer ee mattripg.[15]

Capitalization here serves no grammatical purpose but is simply a fortuitous registering of eruption at the meeting of the linguistic sign with its unincorporatable materiality. In contestation are both general and restricted economies: a regulating, conservational disposition that limits and organizes the independent letters, pushing them toward the word as a component in the articulated production and accumulation of meaning, and the other disposition that drives the letters into non-semantic material ensembles that yield no profit. Meaning reattaches itself through homonymic agents and associational effects ("in VazoOn uv spAz" suggesting in this way "invasion of space"). Yet the interaction of both dispositions detaches the letter groups from all certainty of meaning. These groups offer themselves as festive expenditures, sacrificial modalities of waste.

The next example is an early poem of Rochelle Owens: *Groshl Monkeys Horses*, which similarly situates a reader in an unavoidable proximity to nonproductive elements with no possibility to master the language through an accumulated comprehension:

Pius 12 (Nahautl) pippin.
Common Bot. Stop talkin!
(Peep) Earliest (Mastic tree)
Wrestled christ chinese
Kunklebone (Mees) Any
Groshl Monkeys Horses
Abt. 25 miles up (full moon)
Zauschneria hanj-
Ing
Forth 70 obs. (Honigcumb)
Suck respect and english
Man huggah-homo-greek
Names and heb. hypop.
Jambey zhak-me-no caucus me-
Yawcus mother MOTHER
HYStrix ANNA BI-BI
BI[16]

There is a nonutilitarian, hedonistic pleasure derivable from the nonproductive consumption of this text. The text has numerous points of indeterminacy (for example, is "Common Bot." a sentence or an abbreviation? Is "Kunklebone" a typographic error? Or further, what would constitute an "error" in a text like this?), all of which call attention to the material relationship of the poem's parts.[17]

As an example of the eruption of a more momentary general economy, I've chosen a short poem by Wordsworth—one of the Lucy poems:

She dwelt among the untrodden ways
    Beside the springs of Dove,
A maid whom there were none to praise,
    And very few to love.

A violet by a mossy stone
    Half-hidden from the eye!

Fair as a star, when only one
   Is shining in the sky.

She lived unknown, and few could know
   When Lucy ceased to be;
But she is in her grave, and oh,
   The difference to me!

Cleanth Brooks, in a reading typical of the New Criticism, explains the poem as structured by an ironic tension that treats the images in the second stanza as equivalent.[18] On close scrutiny of the poem, however, it seems difficult to uphold a unity of tension by a mode of irony. Brooks forces essentially heterogeneous elements to conform to his own presuppositions of what a poem should be. Brooks initiates the question, "Which is Lucy really like—the violet or the star?" and goes on to answer that she is a violet to the world and a star to her lover. Brooks creates the classic double bind; he excludes the third possibility that Lucy is like neither and effaces the fact that the grammatical data in the three stanzas do not support a reading of the images having a common referent. It is certainly permissible to treat the opening shifter "she" as referring to the "maid" of line 3, yet there is a rupture between stanzas one and two that introduces an undecidability. Do we treat the "violet" as a metaphoric device substituting for both the maid and the pronoun of stanza one? Or does it introduce a fresh referent? There is a semantic wandering across the gap of the stanzas, the substitution (if it is a substitution) goes astray and heterogeneity threatens the poem's unity of subject. Line 7 adds a further indeterminacy. Does the stellar simile refer to the violet in the same stanza or to the maid of stanza one? In the final stanza the proper name enters as designator but significantly enters at the precise moment death is announced, entering the poem to mark immediately its own erasure. In a poem predominantly of a restricted economy (the symmetrical balance of line and stanza and use of rhyme scheme all suggest an exchangist economy of signifier and signified), these compound indeterminacies erupt and cause the poem's referential certainties to slide. In the penultimate line, moreover, something quite catastrophic happens to the entire semantic order. The abrupt ending of the line with the gestural cry "oh" injects a sovereign implication that momentarily abolishes both meaning and subject; it is the one point in the poem where the material body inscribes a subject, not as a continuity or a self-consciousness, but as a pure operation of outlay. In the gestural cry, and in a manner similar to laughter, the speaking subject is utterly decommissioned, and language as a semantic, restrictive economy is put in question. Are we in or out of meaning at that point in the poem? There is a risk taking, a sliding away from communication and exchange toward expenditure in what Bataille would call the poem's heterological moment of total expulsion, a suspension of meaning within the scriptive parergonics of meaning, an eruption of silence within sound forcing the text to confess its own precarious status as signification.

The local passage from meaning to meaning is traditionally conceived as an accumulation or integration within a larger meaning and instituted upon the productive basis of a value. In the following example meaning cites itself within a purposeless continuum. The Lucy poem reaches sovereignty as a momentary rupture within the fabric of the meaningful, which, however, in its elusiveness, risks meaninglessness to the full, whereas this text contests discursive difference and articulation (a motion within restricted economy) by grounding signification in a continuum not of presence but of expenditure:

> The night Carson knocked the owl over. I'll go out on a temperature mountain. Cent calls by the way. Vista cardboard. Subgum forks. The Seven Caves. The tribute to the aluminum cylinder. Packed to line up the sights. They buried the openings among the blocks to be carted away. Ball courts. Dogs should have license plates. Front and back. A plastic thermometer. Stalactite plunged in cement. Fossil tubes. Animate gossamer rides on amber beer. Gothic Avenue is dusty. Selected AM radio stations. Cod portions. Vermillion.[19]

Meaning here slides away from a directed purpose into a perpetual overturning of signs that never coalesce into an exchangeable identity. The refusal to integrate and raise to a higher compound level of meaning releases contiguity from the institution of hierarchy. Writing here attains the level of a waste in Barthes's insightful notion of that term as a proof of "the passage of the matter it contains."[20]

In conclusion let me compare general economy with gift economy of the kind enacted in the Haidan potlatch ceremonies or the Kula ring, which Marcel Mauss and Bronislaw Malinowski have detailed[21] and to which I'll appeal in a concluding examination of the following proposition: TO WASTE IS TO LIVE THE EXPERIENCE OF WEALTH.

We can contrast gift economy to barter, a precapitalist exchange that contains striking similarities to the semantic exchange within the dominant conception of translation. Barter rests on the protection of a third, transcendental term, a copula of equivalence that sets up the exchange as an action directed toward equilibrium. Worth (like the notion of a "third" equilibrated meaning between the source and target texts of translation) is inserted as a universal third term against the scale of which the sets of bartered terms float until a point of stasis or equivalence is reached.

In gift exchange, however, the object is exhausted, consumed in the very staging.[22] The status of equivalence is removed along with any structurally necessitated reciprocality. In the potlatch, commodities have an alimentary status and wealth is literally expelled. Consumption is understood as a movement and hence a certain momentum replaces equilibrium as the controlling notion of the exchange. In this way, potlatch can be seen as structureless, or at least as avoiding the closed binary correlation of a giver and receiver in which consumption can only occur across the partition preserved through a condition of purchase and ownership. Potlatch does not demand a presupposition of reciprocity. A receiver is not obliged to return.[23]

Potlatch establishes status and position (i.e., social value and hence a "meaning") not from commodity possession but from the rate and momentum of its disposal. In Kwakiutl communities televisions are thrown into the sea, precious objects broken and their parts distributed in order to catalyze the circulation. The commodity ("meaning") is always kept in movement and gains enrichment as it passes hand to hand. There is no association of wealth with investment and accumulation[24] but the implication of a status that accrues to such people who would actually dispose of wealth. Gift objects are frequently pluralized through a kind of inverse metonymy in which the whole exists in order to generate its parts.[25] The objects are broken and their parts scattered to increase the momentum of the giving. Accumulation is unthinkable in potlatch beyond its provisional power to permit an immediate distribution.

The application of this economic model to writing practice should be obvious, and though falling short of a perfect general economy, potlatch does offer an interesting analog system. The immediate tendency is to stress the homology between the "wealth" of potlatch and writing's "meaning," so that the intense exchange within the textural experience, which would register as semantic loss, would not gain the status of a content (hence a transferable "transmission" to a reader) but would manifest as a loss-exchange among the signs themselves. To envisage such a text would be to envisage a linguistic space in which meanings splinter into moving fields of plurality, establishing differentials able to resist a totalization into recoverable integrations that would lead to a summatable "Meaning." This plurality, moreover, must be irreducible and must demonstrate the intransitive drive toward decentrality, the fact of a limitless loss and the status of writing as a scriptive gesture of infinity within the finitude wherein all spatiotemporal activities must exist. As such it could never rest at a holistic proposal but only stress the infinite play of parts within the significatory activity called writing.[26]

NOTES

This essay was first presented to the Department of Social and Political Theory, York University, Toronto, November 1984, and in revised forms at the Poetry Project, Saint Mark's, New York, January 1985, and New Langton Arts, San Francisco, January 1986.

1. Incest, for example, could only exist within the operation of a restricted language. As Lyotard describes it: "only in words can the mother be conceived as a mistress; in orgasm, she is no longer the mother, no longer anything." Outside of interested meaning, in the system of general economy, libido would not be of the order of a transgression (a crossing of boundaries that simultaneously annuls and preserves the partitionality) but of a liquidation of social definition and categories.

2. The Last Supper, as a problematic moment in diachronic Christology, has been dealt with by Hegel in his early theological writings; it is the issue of the predication of transubstantiation upon an alimentary model. In the conversion of Christ's body and blood into bread and wine (and bear in mind the Eucharist is not a simple metaphoric substitution) there is an intrinsic contamination of two codes. Christ becomes bread and wine, yet the attendant implications of the subsequentiality (digestion, absorption, and elimination) are carefully avoided by the early Fathers, who ignore the repercussions of Communion as a general economic action.

3. Dreams, it would seem, occupy a liminal, indeterminate position between a production and an involuntary expenditure. This indeterminacy is reflected in Freud's own hesitation in affirming the dream as either an absolute communication (and hence capable of being submitted to interpretation) or a conflictual, intrapsychic "spillage." Freud hence draws the distinction between the dream *per se* (which is of the order of an involuntary outlay and eludes intentionality) and the dream *text*, which is open to interpretation. It was Freud's inability to incorporate all elements of the dream text into the productive sphere that led also to his positing of certain *hieroglyphic determinatives* or meaningless elements, whose function is "to establish the meaning of some other ele-

ments" (Sigmund Freud, *Standard Edition*, 13:177). Finally, to take note of Freud's theory of neurosis, it would seem that the latter is located inside a restrictive economy. Freud sees as inevitable the transition from the primary process, which is understood as a direct discharge or expenditure, to the secondary process that postpones this discharge and channels it off into *investment*. This passage from primary to secondary processes, according to Freud, constitutes a necessary condition for the formation of neurosis.

4. The French word *jouissance* is notoriously untranslatable (itself a case of unavoidable loss) but signifies both "bliss" (as a state of pleasure) and "ejaculation" (the precise moment and intensity of the coming).

5. Greimas, for one, speaks of the radical *bi-isotopic* nature of language. For Greimas, the two isotopies are "enunciation" and "statement" (*énoncé*). The latter's subject is determined retroactively, hence, a production of restricted economy, while the subject of enunciation "enacts" itself in real time through the production of linked and temporally deferred utterances. The letter is pure contiguity and presymbolic. Indeed, Lacan has gone so far as to claim that the time of enunciation is a "thing" and, as a thing, exists outside the *structured* time of symbolizing discourse. We might compare Greimas's notion of the posterior statementalization of enunciation with the recently developed notions of digital and analog codes. Through this latter availability, the statement would be comprehensible as a co-optation of a digital (i.e., discontinuous or paratactic) by an analog (or continuous) code. The affiliation (real or imaginary) between these satellitic couplings (digital-analog, paratactic-hypotactic, enunciation-statement, restricted-general) is too large and complex an issue to be dealt with adequately in this endnote.

6. Quoted in Julia Kristeva, *Revolution in Poetic Language*, trans. Margaret Waller (New York: Columbia University Press, 1984), 256. Sections of this discussion of the paragram occur in a slightly altered form in "*The Martyrology* as Paragram," in my *North of Intention: Critical Writings, 1973–1986* (New York: Roof Books, 1986). Both discussions were written in ignorance of Kristeva's own article "Pour une semiologie des paragrammes" (in *Tel Quel*, Spring 1967) to which the reader is encouraged to refer. Both Kristeva's and my investigations seem to have been inspired by a common source in Saussure.

7. Nicholas Abraham, "The Shell and the Kernel," trans. Nicholas Rand, *Diacritics* 9 (1979).

8. One of history's finest paragrammatic moments occurred in August 1610 when Galileo sent Kepler a note containing the cryptogram:

SMAISMRMILMEPOETALEUMIBUNENUGTTAURIAS.

Recognizing it is an anagram, Kepler translated it into five Latin

words—"*salve umbistineum geminatum martia proles*" (Greetings, burning twins, descendants of Mars)—which he understood to mean that Galileo had observed that Mars has two moons. Galileo, however, actually meant the message to read, "*altissimum planetam tergiminum observavi*" (I have discovered that the highest of the planets [Saturn] has two moons). The interest of the paragrammatic mistranslation is that the sense intended is referentially wrong (with his primitive telescope Galileo mistook Saturn's rings for moons), while the interpreted sense is referentially correct. Mars does have two moons, although they were not observed until 1877.
Quoted in Gregory L. Ulmer, *Applied Grammatology* (Baltimore: Johns Hopkins University Press, 1985), 151–52.

Galileo's anagram is fine evidence of the aleatory presence within the combinatory phonetics of Western writing, a presence that always threatens an excess of meaning over intention, thereby guaranteeing a certain semantic loss.

9. For a brief critique of this theory, see my article "And Who Remembers Bobby Sands?" in *North of Intention*.

10. The restrictive goal of Hegelian negativity is evident from this passage in *The Encyclopoedia*: "Our goal [in theoretical activity] is rather to grasp nature, to understand it and to make it our own, so that it won't be for us something strange and beyond" (note to entry 246). Negativity is a strategic continuity of the subject through successive operations that allows the accommodation of all objects as an internalized reserve. The integration of the *aufhebung* is close to Benveniste's notion of linguistic meaning. In chapter ten of his *Problems in General Linguistics*, Benveniste defines the meaning of a linguistic unit as "its capacity to integrate a unit of a higher level" (*Problems in General Linguistics*, trans. M. E. Meek [Coral Gables: University of Miami Press, 1971], 107). Against both Hegel and Benveniste we will cite the following conjecture of Lucretius in *De Rerum Natura*: "if everything is so transformed as to overstep its own limits this means the immediate death of what was before."

11. Chance generated writing is further restrictive in still being tied to a notion of *reward*. Despite the inevitability of loss, an indeterminate profit is involved. Chance, like money, links to a notion of *fortune*.

12. Sovereignty would thus appear to be of an intransitive nature and would hence stand comparison with recent "desire" theories (Lacan, Deleuze, and Guattari) and with proposals for a basis of writing in a nontransitive project. On the latter see especially Roland Barthes, "To Write: An Intransitive Verb?" in *The Structuralist Controversy*, ed. R. Macksey and E. Donato (Baltimore: Johns Hopkins University Press, 1972), 134–56.

13. Once again, however, we trace in Breton a slide back into restricted

economy: the abolition of the terms is seen as a recovery of noncontradiction and the loss thereby rendered profitable.

14. In the strategy of general writing both subject and language get returned to their materiality in permitting meaning to slide. We might say that the subject "forgets" her writing as belonging to a project of meaning, while writing itself annihilates the subject expressing himself through it. The subject's continuity is no longer guaranteed through language (unlike the subject in restricted writing). The moment of meaninglessness, of course, can never occur inside language, but the movement toward it can. The reader likewise would enter the writing as a textual subject to whom reading (in Paul de Man's words) "is dramatized not as an emotive reaction to what language does, but as an emotive reaction to the impossibility of knowing what it might be up to."

15. Charles Bernstein, *Poetic Justice* (Baltimore: Pod Books, 1979), 25.

16. Rochelle Owens in *Yugen* 6 (1960): 25.

17. Samuel Beckett's prose economies require an entirely separate treatment. At this point, however, we might take note of his work *Fizzles* (ca. 1960 but not translated until 1973) whose original French title *Foirades* means "shit" or "diarrhea" and solicits appreciation of the works as expenditures. The constant passage of words in these pieces through metonymic relations and juxtapositions (the techniques of anaphora and parataxis are frequent) certainly suggests an alimentary model for the writing.

18. Cleanth Brooks, "Irony as a Principle of Structure," in *Literary Opinion in America*, ed. M. D. Zabel (New York: Harper and Row, 1962), 735.

19. Clark Coolidge, *Smithsonian Depositions* (New York: Vehicle Editions, 1980), 22.

20. Roland Barthes, *The Grain of the Voice*, trans. Linda Coverdale (New York: Hill and Wang, 1985), 273.

21. See especially Marcel Mauss, *The Gift: Forms and Functions of Exchange in Archaic Societies*, trans. I. Cunnison (New York: Norton, 1967).

22. There are certain gesture signs that suggest a similar exhaustion in their staging. Pointing, the opening of arms, embraces, handshakes—all relate as much to a system of expenditure as to a semiotics of transmission.

23. There are limits to which this analogy can be taken. Potlatch, we must not forget, is an agonistic act designed to elicit a return with interest in the form of further loss. Consequently, a fundamental exchangism is preserved to operate as the raison d'être of the potlatch. As an example of symbolic exchange, it nonetheless illustrates an important transaction that is not based on preservation (beyond the preservation of the exchange itself as continued loss). The exchange, though present, is immediate and instantly subordinated to a termination.

24. The notion of inevitable expenditure and outlay is a commonplace of seventeenth-century baroque eschatology. Among the numerous possible examples, I will cite Jeremy Taylor from his *Rule and Exercises of Holy Dying*, a popular *artes moriendi* from 1651: "while we think a thought we die; and the clock strikes and reckons on our portion of eternity; we from our words with the breath of our nostrils we have the less to live upon for every word we speak."

This is not Charles Olson's concept of breath as a charged energy transfer but the profound coupling of cognition and the subject's ontology with an economy of death.

25. Precapitalist economy furnishes an interesting case of quasi-potlatch. Although exceptions exist, it is in general true to say that surplus value was born only with capitalism. The Middle Ages were characterized by a type of *economic man* whose pattern of wealth was that of a vast accumulation during life, a subsequent renunciation, and a final, indiscriminate dispersal close to death. Philanthropy was born of this condition of a dramatic distribution of wealth that coincided with the moment of death. The French historian Philippe Ariès argues a profound ambivalence in the precapitalist man between a love of wealth as worldly possessions and an ultimate (postponed) belief (the dominant theological belief of the Middle Ages) that all material wealth was unsightly in the eyes of God and must be renounced in order to redeem the soul. Jacques Heers regards this belief, and its consequent effecting of enormous distributions of donations to churches and benevolent institutions, as the major cause of the economic collapse of the fourteenth-century nobility. The spiritual pressure to discharge wealth indiscriminately, together with the preindustrial nature of that wealth (jewels, land, horses, precious objects) made the concept of investment (and thereby the production of surplus value) all but impossible.

There is, too, the interesting example of Adam Smith. In his *Theory of Moral Sentiments* (1759) Smith argues that surplus income is meaningless to the recipient. The wealthy landlord (Smith's argument runs) can hardly consume more than the poorest peasant and accordingly must distribute his surplus wealth to his retinue and servants. This is a forced expenditure (or seen that way) and suggests strongly Smith's recognition of an operating general economy within the "industry of mankind" and the wealth of nations. It should be borne in mind, however, that Smith's argument is part of a complex attempt to justify the proposition that the apparent inequality of human incomes and the restricted control of wealth is in actuality productive of an equal distribution throughout the entire social spectrum (by virtue of this persistently forced expenditure).

26. It would be impossible to conclude without mentioning Saussure who posits (among several binary combinations) the relationship of *langue*

(i.e., the set of linguistic rules, structures, and possibilities that exist apart from the local particularities of usage) and *parole* (the local and particular applications drawn from the sets of *langue*). Saussure's is an important and in many contexts a useful distinction. Subjected, however, to the critique from general economy and gift exchange, it would be halted at one strategic point: where *parole* instantiates *langue* and registers not as an enrichment through continued circulation (leading as it would to a sedimentary theory of language) but as an invested instantiation of a parent term.

13 The Politics of Form and Poetry's Other Subjects: Reading Contemporary American Poetry
Hank Lazer

til other voices wake
us or we drown

—George Oppen

The anxiety to invent an "American" nation and the anxiety to invent a
uniquely "American" literature were historically coincident. As long as we
use "American" as an adjective, we continue to reenforce the illusion that
there is a transcendental core of values and experiences that are essentially "American," and that literary or cultural studies may be properly
shaped by selecting objects and authors according to how well they express this central essence.

—Gregory Jay

It is not possible to write the history of contemporary American poetry,
though it is, of course, worthwhile to attempt to historicize the present. Twenty-five years ago in the first issue of *Boundary 2*, David Antin
claimed that "it is precisely the distinctive feature of the present that,
in spite of any strong sense of its coherence, it is always open on its
forward side."[1] In the 1990s, a writer who attempts both to be in the
present and to formulate the crucial activities in poetry must feel that
open forward side as well as the inevitably partial nature of any individual's attempted formulation. Having admitted the impossibility of the
task, and having acknowledged that a dream of inclusivity would itself
have serious liabilities and hidden partialities, I find few tasks so important as an engaged reading of contemporary American poetry.

The decentralization of literary production in the United States calls
for an active reception in which readers share discoveries and information. Today, there is a great deal of good poetry that is not being read.
To think about contemporary American poetry, with any attempt at
comprehensiveness and seriousness, brings a writer in contact with a
range of controversies. The criticism of contemporary poetry is usually
given over either to aesthetically dominated judgmental reviews (mainly
short blurbs of praise written by peer-poets implicated in the liter-
ary/professional networks they are asked to judge) or to an academically

sanctioned (mis)application of current critical theory to canonically (and professionally) acceptable extended readings of "major" contemporary poets.

In spite of this dismal state of institutionalized criticism of poetry, a number of recent books on contemporary American poetry are adventurous and valuable. Of nine books under consideration in this essay, all are provocative, and eight of the nine extend into that open forward side of contemporary American poetry. Considered collectively, recurring topics and points of controversy emerge. I am surprised to find that debates over the meanings and implications of the "postmodern" in contemporary poetry have not (with the exception of some of Andrew Ross's work) been very productive or interesting. What surfaces instead is an intense struggle over the canon of contemporary American poetry, especially in light of an active rethinking of the nature of the self and the importance of what is called (after Lacanian psychoanalysis) subject position. As nearly all of the books I examine demonstrate, two overlapping areas of thinking emerge as pivotal to a consideration of contemporary American poetry. The first is the dissemination of "the subject," accomplished variously by formal innovation, theoretical argument, and multicultural studies. The second is the politics of poetry as a resistance to appropriation: resistance to the official verse culture, the marketplace, the dominant culture, and hegemonic ideologies.

A broad awareness of the decentralization of poetry production, as well as an established critique of the limited nature of today's professionalized and institutionalized poetry writing, have had a salutary effect on attempts to describe contemporary American poetry. The most fruitful areas of thought are those that begin from a multicultural perspective and those that theorize the relationship of form and politics, where form is considered broadly as an institutional and social practice as well as an aesthetic set of choices.

The book jacket for J. D. McClatchy's _White Paper: On Contemporary American Poetry_ puts forward the claim that his book is "an incisive survey of contemporary American poetry . . . an overview of the current poetry 'scene' . . . [and] a book designed to help us . . . to discriminate the best from the weaker work in a crowded and difficult field."[2] Apparently McClatchy found an easy way to do so: eliminate from consideration most of the challenging work of the day. Eliminate writing by poets of "otherness," especially color or innovation. In _White Paper_, McClatchy presents a regional, class, and aesthetic appreciation masquerading as "the tradition" and "the best."

McClatchy claims: "I bear no ideological grudges. In fact, my brief is against those who would make American poetry over into images of any narrow critical orthodoxy. Ours is a heritage of heresies" (viii). And the ideology of no ideology is one such heresy. I do share, however, one of McClatchy's grudges: opposition to the leveling effect of "the middle-brow expectation brought to poetry over the past thirty years by critics and poets alike" (viii). That particular complaint has been thoroughly developed already by Charles Altieri, Donald Hall, and fifty others. But what of McClatchy's concealed ideology? It rests with an unstated preference for the bourgeois subject and with notions of individual psychological development: "If to help understand them [the poets] I have sometimes turned to modern mythographers like Freud and Jung, that is because the poets themselves have shaped their stories into patterns that psychology had most vividly drawn for them" (ix). That is the funnel through which McClatchy sifts contemporary American poetry to come up with his list of the greatest of the day.

Along the way McClatchy dismisses the terms *academic* and *avant-garde* as bankrupt, failing to realize that his own position is that of the academic par excellence (or, more discriminatingly, the high academic, with the workshop/middlebrow being the low or populist academic). He also fails to grant that there is anything besides an academic poetry, and thus he can fail to locate a significant avant-garde. In his scorn for a "permissive era" of poetry writing, he asks, "what *could* shock or muster these days?" (8). I have three quick responses: Language writing, Antin's talk-poems, and the use of black idiom by poets like June Jordan.

Even so, McClatchy proves capable of questions and assertions that, when thought about from some of the other perspectives I shall introduce in this chapter, can be fruitful. McClatchy argues, "Poetry's work of knowledge and its access to power lie in the poet's instinct, as well as in the reader's capacity, to take *poesis* itself—its repertory of song, choice, play, pattern, logic, trope—and see it as a model of experience, and use it as the means to fathom those same sources of authority and transformation in our lives" (15). The problem with this admirable formula is that the "model of experience" it presumes is highly provincial. It cannot provide an acceptable answer to his inquiry into poetry as knowledge. Again and again, McClatchy returns to a model of the bourgeois subject, in a kind of isolated meditation, mulling over the nature of his individual experience (typically narrated with wit, decorum, and closure). The terrain that McClatchy defends is not that of "great" poetry but that which conforms to an ideology of the self: "More eloquently than any other advocate, Harold Bloom has argued that poetry is precisely that sanction: the defense of the self against *everything*—ideology, history, nature, time, others, even against the self, and especially against 'cultural force'—that might destroy it. If the best poetry today seems more demanding or eccentric than it did when Longfellow, or even Whitman, was writing, so are the conspiracies against the self" (15–16).

Conspiracies, or best thoughts about what that self is (and is not)? Or best thoughts about how else to write, rather than producing a stable self and a personal voice? That McClatchy's is indeed an ideology of the self, and an elevation of that self over and above competing conceptions, becomes most readily apparent in his reading of Robert Lowell's work: "History is, after all, a series of biographies, a series of readings. Lowell's historical quest gives way, finally, to his struggle with the family romance, and his effort is to reconcile history with the self, and thereby gain control over both" (138).

There are serious problems with what McClatchy authenticates as those poems worthy of his reading talent and, by extension, ours too. He is willing to reduce poetry to a matter of voice (which is really only a subcategory of his ideology of the self): "We speak excitedly of a distinctive 'new voice' only when it can be distinguished from all the others. Whole movements in poetry are matters of voice, whether two hundred years ago when 'poetic diction' was the operative term, or right now when the Language poets or the New Formalists are speaking up for themselves" (25). Wrong. Especially about the Language poets, who have each in *many* different ways put the notion of voice itself into question and have written (again, in different ways) poetry that has little to do with "voice" at all.

McClatchy's reading of Elizabeth Bishop's poetry—which satisfies his definition of great poetry as having the quality of "austere grandeur" (68)—reveals the dullness and predictability of his method: "I want now to read through the poem ["The End of March"], and listen for allusions that add to the sense of it. . . . If we can't hear the allusions she is subtly making—and her early readers did not—then we can't estimate the true power of the poems—their thematic ambitions, their autobiographical bearings, the rightful place they should assume in the traditions of American poetry" (56, 57). Theme, the story of the self, and the poet's ranking: these equal the true power of poetry? When filtered through a high modernist and Anglophile reading list of accredited allusions, the result is a dull, smug, arrogant "white paper." A sort of aesthetic and cultural apartheid.

By contrast, what is refreshing about <u>Stephen-Paul Martin's Open Form</u> <u>and the Feminine Imagination</u>, and several other books I shall be discussing, is the effort to break discussions of poetry out of a narrowly defined psychological aestheticism (inherited from New Criticism and absorbed seemingly without a qualm by McClatchy).[3] Martin's way out is via an increased attention to "the extra-literary relevance" (60) of the writers he considers: Gertrude Stein, Hart Crane, Wallace Stevens, Djuna Barnes, Clarence Major, Carla Harryman, Susan Howe, Ron Silliman, and Teresa Cha. Nevertheless, the principal tool of New Criticism—close reading—often remains the dominant methodology for Martin and indeed for most historicized, cultural, political, and theoretical approaches to contemporary American poetry. So too does thematization come in as a ghostly essentialism that reins in more adventurous varieties of criticism. These difficulties are not so much failings of individual critics as they are indicative of a generic difficulty in writing criticism of contemporary poetry.

Despite its unconventional intentions, Martin's book remains bound up in its own dualisms and essentialisms: female/male, open/closed, intuitive/rational, body/mind. Even while advocating a "female" perspective, Martin does so by traditionally "masculine" methods of assertion and argumentation. Also, he is beholden to an evolutionary and developmental model: "I also think that a technologically advanced and politically aggressive (masculine) country like the United States should be aware that it is capable of evolving past its current patriarchal limitations, and that some of its writers—both men and women—have already done so" (56).

Clearly, there is an important pedagogical dimension to Martin's choice of texts. The works he considers force us into different kinds of reading, thinking, and questioning. As such, avant-garde writing ought generally to occupy an important place in all curricula on heuristic and political grounds. As Martin's book demonstrates, reactions to experimental writing matter as engagements with fundamental habits of inclusion and exclusion, as crucial instances of treatment of the "other," and as tests of our tolerance of a broad range of ways to "make sense."

But Martin's claims for the innovativeness of the texts are not matched by new habits of reading and critical writing. The "enemy"—a kind of narrow-minded version of logical, causal thinking—is repeatedly identified. But, as in the Stevens chapter, even when Martin's thematization is profeminine and antipatriarchal, his own criticism remains insistently thematic and thus not so different from the thinking that he criticizes: "We are so trained to conceptualize according to definitions and classifications, fitting them neatly into cause and effect patterns, that anything else seems incomprehensible" (92). Typical of Martin's essentialism is his classification of Stevens's "fat girl" (in "Notes Toward a Supreme Fiction"): "She is that opulent, warm, and fertile essence associated with the Great Mother and the darkness of nonrational expression" (93).

Martin searches for a radical innocence through the deconstruction of masculine dominance. In discussing Major's work, Martin argues that fragmentation "is a way of de-composing the 'ceremony' of masculine domination so that a more authentic form of innocence can emerge" (121–22). Elsewhere, he argues that "the 'difficulty' of poetry is that it will not serve the assumptions of a society based on material prestige" (95). But such a statement is only partially true; as a more rigorously Marxist or materialist approach (by Hartley, Kalaidjian, or Silliman) would have us consider, poetry too, as a mode of production and a social/political activity, has its own particular material conditions that we should scrutinize.

One great strength of Martin's book (and the magazine that he co-edits, *Central Park*) is his ability to link up, intelligently, "post-rational science and post-modern writing" (139). He deserves high praise for fine readings of and introductions to the writing of Harryman, Howe, and Cha. The goal he achieves, for which others could strive, is a multiculturalism within a consideration of innovative writing. Too often, multicultural readings are restricted to "natural" language styles only or to the opposite segregation: experimental writing as the province of whites only. Not so in Martin's provocative book.

In a somewhat less polemical version of cultural criticism, but one that chooses a more formally conservative set of texts for consideration, Walter Kalaidjian in *Languages of Liberation: The Social Text in Contemporary American Poetry* examines the institutional and social setting of recent American poetry by way of Adorno and other cultural critics.[4] Kalaidjian's most important contribution lies in his analysis of the persistent critical methodologies derived from New Criticism:

> Despite the outpouring of rhetoric dubbing postwar verse a "poetry of revolt," its reception was marked by the foundational oppositions of New Critical doctrine: poetry enjoys an aesthetic autonomy from its institutional infrastructures; the "ideal reader" transcends heterogeneous interpretive communities; and the private lyric voice dwells apart from history's social text. . . . [P]oetic autonomy, "disinterested" reading, and voice dominated the center of the New Critical enterprise by marginalizing history, audience, and textuality. (13)

Kalaidjian, like George Hartley in *Textual Politics and the Language Poets*,[5] concludes that "From our vantage point in the 1980s, this theoretical failure can be mapped as the period's political limit: one that actively led readers to invest in ideologies of bourgeois individualism" (14).

Kalaidjian demystifies the role of "poet" by considering this subject position in its institutional and commercial setting. He studies the conglomerate publishing business, mass media, and the networks of prestige and awards tied into the most commercially visible means of publication. He also considers the specific career options and publishing choices made by poets such as Robert Bly, Adrienne Rich, and Gwendolyn Brooks. Such information, as well as Kalaidjian's comments, help desanctify the reading of contemporary poetry and makes material and commercial matters an essential part of reading a poet's work.

In accordance with Ron Silliman's observations, Kalaidjian too observes that "The nexus between academe and poetry writing is vital to the formation of the postwar verse canon" (20). Kalaidjian, to his credit, willingly assesses the harsh consequences of a poet's institutional setting. He admits and analyzes the hypocritical position of most mainstream, canonically accepted academic poets: "Today literature's humanizing rhetoric is often belied by its actual disciplinary formations and institutional limits. This tension continues to be most deeply felt by academics, whose everyday professional lives deny the consoling models of community that humanism traditionally espouses. For better or worse, most of our enduring verse writers are academics whose poetry typically seeks to repress and transcend their institutional lives" (26–27).

Kalaidjian offers critical, intelligent readings of the work of James Wright and W. S. Merwin, but even these fine readings fail to develop adequately the material readings that Kalaidjian advocates. Throughout his own book, Kalaidjian too falls victim, in varying degrees, to New Critical blindnesses. He does not, for example, really consider the material and institutional settings for Wright and Merwin, failing to wonder about Wright's resistance to the workshop format, his revulsion at abstract critical thinking, his interest as a scholar in the work of Dickens and the nineteenth-century novel generally; nor does he consider why Merwin changed publishers for *Finding the Islands*, nor Merwin's ambivalent but lucrative relationship to foundations and academic financial support networks. Kalaidjian's own readings often merely substitute contemporary theoretical language for the isolationist aestheticism of New Criticism.

A more serious failing is his often essentialist and uncritical use of the term *cultural critique*. In an excellent concluding chapter—excellent both for its insights and for attending to the work of an important but neglected poet—he praises Brooks for employing "her poetry . . . as a discursive medium for cultural critique" (173). But throughout his book *cultural critique* remains a term of praise rather than a category for analytical thinking. Could it not be argued that virtually all poetry participates in cultural criticism? As with Martin's difficulty in overcoming a thematic criticism, I see Kalaidjian's essentializing of the term *cultural criticism* as a generic difficulty for criticism of contemporary American poetry.

More important, Kalaidjian's own forms of institutional blindness seriously jeopardize his project. He maintains a narrow version of accepted texts to reflect social and cultural criticism. If, as he claims, one of his chief interests is to study poets' interrogation of "the bourgeois myth of the sovereign subject" (123), how can Kalaidjian deny attention to the work of a number of Language poets? Bob Perelman, Silliman, Charles Bernstein, Barrett Watten, and a host of other poets have spent nearly twenty years investigating this precise area of concern. Especially given Kalaidjian's attention to the Frankfurt School (crucial to the work of Silliman) and to the work of Charles Olson, this omission (inasmuch as Silliman and Bernstein have written important essays on Olson) is all the more puzzling. Kalaidjian's reading of Olson would be deepened by consideration, for example, of Bernstein's critique of Olson's masculinist biases.

Kalaidjian thus dodges writing that would extend and challenge his own analysis of the expressive voice-lyric's failings, the commercial and institutional setting of contemporary American poetry, and the critique of the bourgeois subject. So, too, would his consideration of a feminist poetics be enhanced by attention to work more formally adventurous than that of Rich, whom he sees as practicing what the French call *l'écriture féminine*: "Like Kristeva, Rich invokes the word's somatic body, the libidinal force of the semiotic normally repressed from the symbolic economy of language" (164). While Kalaidjian justly praises Rich's many changes in style, one must also admit that Rich's work remains based on models of thematic coherence, unity, and relatively straightforward transmission of a message. Why not read such cultural criticism, organized thematically, beside the more formally adventurous and innovative work of poets such as Susan Howe, Rachel Blau DuPlessis, and Beverly Dahlen? Overall, Kalaidjian's book, with its basis in cultural criticism, points toward an important (though only partially fulfilled) way of reading contemporary American poetry.

The Politics of Poetic Form: Poetry and Public Policy, a collection of essays edited by Charles Bernstein, extends the critique of the bourgeois subject advocated by Kalaidjian by focusing on the political implications of a poem's formal dynamics.[6] Bernstein declares in the book's preface:

> Poems are imagined primarily to express personal emotions; if political, they are seen as articulating positions already expounded elsewhere. In contrast, poetry can be conceived as an active arena for exploring basic questions about political thought and action. . . . The particular focus of this collection is on the ways that the formal dynamics of a poem shape its ideology; more specifically, how radically innovative poetic styles can have political meanings. (vii)

Instead of McClatchy's white northeastern, Norton British Lit lineup of poets, we are urged to consider the range implied by Jerome Rothenberg's term *ethnopoetics*, which "refers to an attempt to investigate on a transcultural scale the range of possible poetries that had not only been imagined but put into practice by other human beings" (5), a range confirmed and disseminated by Rothenberg's twenty years of making anthologies. Rothenberg concludes that "the multiple poetries revealed by an *ethnopoetics* lead inevitably to the conclusion that *there is no one way*; thus, they contribute to the desire/need already felt, to undermine authority, program, & system, so as not to be done in by them in turn" (9). Rothenberg, from a position outside Kalaidjian's "languages of liberation," describes a language poetics that is "a way of life. An instrument . . . of *liberation*. A private/public healing," stemming from the fact that "I *see* through language" (13).

In contrast to McClatchy's commonsensical notions about the self, we have Bruce Andrews's formulations in "Poetry as Explanation, Poetry as Praxis," which would "define comprehension as something other than consumption."[7] He argues: "If identification is built into the subject-form—so that its positive meanings are already overproduced—then 'subjects speaking their minds' 'authentically' will not be enough. The overall shape of making sense needs to be reframed, restaged, put back into a context of 'pre-sense' —to reveal its constructed character; to reveal by critique, by demythologizing. Otherwise, its apparent immediacy dupes us: the lack of distance is a kind of closure" (31–32).

The act of *poesis* figures into a social resistance for Bernstein in the particular way that poetry reconvenes a public for the choosing of conventions for "acceptable" communication: "Don't get me wrong: I know it's almost a joke to speak of poetry and national affairs. Yet in *The Social Contract*, Jean-Jacques Rousseau writes that since our conventions are provisional, the public may choose to reconvene in order to withdraw authority from those conventions which no longer serve our purposes, and poetry is one of the few areas where this right of reconvening is exercised" (240–41).

But for questions of canon formation and the institutionalization of poetry, Silliman's "Canons and Institutions: New Hope for the Disappeared" is one of the most provocative essays written in quite some time. Silliman asserts that "poetry, particularly in the United States, is an amnesiac discourse."[8] Poets and poetry are read (or not) and discarded at an alarming rate: "The shelf life of a good poet may be something less than the half-life of a styrofoam cup" (150). A chief means of erasure is "the process of public canonization, that which socially converts the broad horizon of writing into the simplified and hierarchic topography of Literature" (152), a disease he refers to elsewhere as "canonic amnesia or Vendler's Syndrome" (169). But Silliman's argument is not a mushy pluralism "in which all poems would be equal for all readers" (152). Instead, he wishes (as do many of the poets identified as Language poets) to make ideology and form apparent and at issue in poetry and thus to make the choices and partiality of what we value in poetry more visible and open to argument. For Silliman, "value . . . is a definable relationship":

> What it is not, however, is a conjunction between tradition and the individual talent. For in and of itself, tradition is nothing: it does not exist. Tradition is a bibliography with implications. It is what one has read and how one links these together. And not just any One, but each and every specific person, that potentially infinite regress of subject positions. Thus one cannot define value without specifying the reader at stake: valuable for whom? to what end? (152–53)

Silliman reminds us that a canon (or a syllabus or a book claiming, as McClatchy's does, to survey contemporary American poetry) involves "socially competing discourses" (154). He argues that "the survival of poets and poetry [is] determined institutionally rather than between texts or aesthetic principles" (157). Syllabus decisions, invitations to poets to read on campus, and decisions about which poetry to review and which poets will be covered in a book or essay are all important choices because, as Silliman notes, the university "provides important mediation and legitimation functions for virtually every other social apparatus that relates publicly to the poem. The university provides the context in which many, and perhaps most, poetry readers are first introduced to the writing of our time; it may even be, as has sometimes been argued, the context in which the majority of all poems in the U.S. are both written and read" (157). As Silliman continues later in his essay, "the academy is a ground, a field for contestation" (165). So we must make sure that it is and that other voices are invited into the field for contestation.

Silliman proposes the tactic of "aesthetic practice raised to an institutional strategy" (169). Such action would involve questioning the institutionalized separation of theory and practice, redrawing (or erasing) boundaries between critical and creative writing, "deconstructing public canonicity and rejoining theory to practice" (167), and "a pluralization of the poetry publishing programs of university presses—a level of the academy that is even more arthritic and senile than MFA programs" (169). To this end, Silliman underscores a chief value of Bernstein's anthology; The Politics of Poetic Form offers sharply drawn perspectives on poetry's American institutionalization from a series of vantage points outside that institutional framework.

George Hartley's Textual Politics and the Language Poets, the first book-length study of Language poetry, does not pretend to be a comprehensive, nonideological survey of what is of value in contemporary American poetry. He examines Language poetry as a critique of bourgeois society. Like many of the contributors to The Politics of Poetic Form, Hartley excels in analyzing the relationship of poetic form and politics. Hartley develops his study out of careful readings of Althusser, Benjamin, Brecht, de Saussure, Jameson, Lukács, Kristeva, and Marx. If there is an abiding weakness to his book, it is his tendency to get bogged down in arguments over fine points of Marxist theory. It is a slight oversimplification to say that the poetry gets lost in the shuffle, because such whining from a reviewer usually presupposes a split between poetry and theory, but the complaint, even from one sympathetic to the poetics of poetry as poetry, is still one that must be lodged against Hartley's book.

Hartley understands that Language poetry, among other things, represents a rebuke of the "voice poem," "the dominant model for poetic production and reception today." For many Language poets "the voice poem depends on a model of communication that needs to be challenged: the notion that the poet (a self-present subject) transmits a particular message ('experience,' 'emotion') to a reader (another self-present subject) through a language which is neutral, transparent, 'natural'" (xii). Language poets propose poetry as "the exploration of the possibilities for meaning-production" (xiii). Hartley argues, "Language poets have developed a poetry that functions not as ornamentation or as self-expression, but as a baring of the frames of bourgeois ideology itself" (41).

Hartley's study, which thinks within the framework of Language poetry, theorizes the political significance of current rethinking of the subject: "Poetry, then, which functions according to the notion of the poet/speaker as an independent subject who, having 'found his voice,' presents a situation seen from a single point of view, fosters the key ideological concept of bourgeois society: the self-sufficient, self-determined individual free to participate in the marketplace" (37). Hartley's analysis of signification and the subject results in an understanding crucial to any conceptualization of an avant-garde. It is not the newness of a method but the oppositional nature—socially, institutionally, politically—of that art that makes of it a vanguard, for it represents "those who challenge their time's hegemonic conceptualization of art" (1). As such, Hartley's reading of Language poetry is correctly "traditional," exploring various Language poets' rereadings of writers such as Stein, Olson, and Williams.

The crux of Hartley's analysis is the claim that meaning, reference, and signification are socially contracted understandings. They are conventions with ideological implications (owing to the inevitable commodification of language products), arrived at by readers and writers through institutionally mediated methods. Reference, meaning, even "excellence" result not from some quality inherent in the poem. Instead, "reference is thus to be seen as the end result of the social process of language production, not as the inherent quality of the words themselves" (34).

Though Hartley does not stumble into the worn path of theme study and tedious middlebrow close readings, he does get led astray by one of the truisms of critical approaches to Language poetry. Hartley tends to stop with the generalization that with Language poetry the reader becomes a collaborator in the production of meaning. We get only scant evidence of what this might mean in practice. Rather than draw this pat conclusion, which really amounts to an assertion of preference for Language writing (and thus might be one more aesthetic judgment), Hartley and other critics of Language poetry (myself included) would do well to begin with the kinds of questions Hartley himself poses elsewhere in his book: "What is the meaning of our particular uses and conceptions of meaning at our particular historical juncture? To whose benefit is the present definition of meaning put?" (70).

Hartley's book overlaps with the work of Marjorie Perloff and Henry Sayre in its reference to the theories of other modernist artists, a set of references that takes us beyond poetry to the visual and plastic arts. Hartley's discussion of conceptual art implies the kind of question to be asked today about poetry: "The Conceptualists therefore turned to less 'material' matter, such as water, inert gas, or ultimately simply ideas, in a process of increasing 'dematerialization' of art. The original conception, the idea, the intention of the artist is the work" (85). Such an observation, and such a context for the consideration of contemporary American poetry, leads us, as Sayre also does, to wonder where in fact the work of art, where the poem, most fundamentally takes place, when is its crucial moment, and where is it found. Such questions lead us back into debates of product versus process, but they also give us new contexts for appreciating a broader range of poetry: from Antin's talk-poems and skywriting poems, to Jenny Holzer's visual displays, to Rothenberg's performance-rituals, to the typographical experimentation of Johanna Drucker and Tina Darragh—all poetry that relies on a more open notion of where and how the poem takes place. As electronic and other digitalized modes of production supplement or replace the book, such rethinking of poesis may well prove crucial to a sustained interest in poetry itself.

Marjorie Perloff's Poetic License: Essays on Modernist and Postmodernist Lyric extends her "ongoing project" of writing "a revisionist history of twentieth-century poetics."[9] Some of the best work in this book consists of readings of specific poets' work: Susan Howe, Lorine Niedecker, Allen Ginsberg, Steve McCaffery, Samuel Beckett, Sylvia Plath, and the legacies of Ezra Pound. Perloff is sometimes mistakenly labeled merely a theoretician of the avant-garde, when in fact her readings are often empirically based. Her most intriguing empirical chapter in Poetic License is "Traduit de l'Américain: French Representations of the 'New American Poetry.'" While several critics have pointed out the competing and mutually exclusive versions of contemporary American poetry by comparing anthologies such as In the American Tree (Silliman 1986) to Helen Vendler's 1985 Harvard anthology or the Morrow anthology (Smith and Bottoms 1985), Perloff seeks out an external point of reference in these anthology/canon struggles. She presents persuasive evidence for a French version of contemporary American poetry that differs considerably from the predominant American erasure of the Pound-Williams-Stein tradition. As Perloff demonstrates, French readings and translations of contemporary American poetry emphasize the work of Stein, Zukofsky, Rothenberg, Jack Spicer, John Cage, Michael Palmer, the Beat poets, and the work of many Language poets. What is at stake in competing versions of contemporary American poetry, as Kalaidjian, Hartley, and others have asserted from an intranational viewpoint, is a refutation of the personal voice poem. Perloff finds the French poets, anthologists, and translators barely interested in our mainstream voice-based poems, having lost interest in poems of "the 'I-as-sensitive-register'" (63) and "late English-Romantic lyrics in which a particular self meditates on the external scene and moralizes the landscape" (61).

A contemporary poetry that interests Perloff begins with the understanding "that Romantic subjectivity is itself a cultural construction whose relevance to modernist poetics is questionable" (80). Perloff demonstrates that the critique of bourgeois subjectivity in poetry is inevitably linked to a rethinking of the possibilities and nature of the lyric. She argues persuasively for the displacement of the lyric, either through radically rewriting it or by discarding it altogether, as a significant development in contemporary (innovative) poetry.

Silliman's argument that American poetry is an amnesiac discourse finds considerable support in Perloff's reading of Merwin's poetry. Merwin's work was and is (see for example Kalaidjian's chapter on Merwin) praised for its adventurous forms. But Perloff points out that Merwin's work seems innovative and shocking only to amnesiac readers: "Merwin's free verse, which may have seemed enormously innovative when read against the background of the formalism of the fifties—the mode, say, of Richard Wilbur or Allen Tate or Howard Nemerov—was nowhere as explosive as the free verse Pound and Williams were writing by 1916, a free-verse model carried on by Louis Zukofsky and George Oppen in the thirties, and by Charles Olson in the late forties and early fifties" (238). Moreover, "it should have struck the critics as slightly odd that a poetry so seemingly explosive—the poetry of 'the wilderness of unopened life'—was routinely published in the New Yorker, Poetry, the Hudson Review, and Harper's—hardly the organs of the avant-garde" (238).

In Poetic License Perloff offers some general formulations concerning the responsibilities of the critic of contemporary poetry. One might assume that her sympathies would lie with an ideologically or theoretically motivated criticism that would lead a critic to claim that "our role as critics is, in the first place, to characterize the dominant discourse and then to read against it that writing it has excluded or marginalized, thus redefining the canon so as to give pride of place to the hitherto repressed" (2). But Perloff rejects such a position, and her critique has important implications for pluralist and multiculturalist perspectives: "Ironically, this [ideologically motivated] stance toward poetry turns out, at least in practice, to be just as essentialist as the first. For in automatically privileging, say, the poetry of women of color over the poetry of white men, we imply that the former are, by definition, more 'sensitive,' more 'authentic,' and, in any case, more 'interesting' than the latter" (2). Perloff proposes that "the impasse of this particular version of a cultural poetics might, I think, be avoided by redefining the term *dominant class* as what Charles Bernstein has called 'official verse culture'" (3). The political implications of style (and a style's relationship to dominant institutional practices of poetry) cut across a vast range of subject positions.

Perloff attacks a pluralism based on message-oriented, ideologically "correct" poetry and sides with McCaffery, who "stresses the need to free poetic language from the co-option by what he calls the 'media model,' the model of 'linguistic transparency' and grammatical rule" (294). At her most exasperated with a poetry of sincerity and clarity, Perloff asks, "if 'poetry' is really no more than . . . straight-but-sensitive 'nuts and bolts' talk broken arbitrarily into line segments so as to remind us that, yes, this is a poem, why read in the first place rather than turning on the TV?" (305). If the new poetry of protest is judged by its message rather than its medium, then "what can it mean to be a critic or literary historian if one does not choose between available alternatives? . . . And how far can we extend the helping hand of 'pluralism' and 'diversity' without making *poetry* so reductive and bland a term that its potential readership merely loses interest?" (35, 36). Perloff's own choice is clear: she sides with a poetry that expresses "the rights of the signifier." (But such an affiliation does not prevent her, in *Poetic License*, from doing sound, thorough writing on Lawrence, Ginsberg, Plath, Paul Blackburn, and others who do not fall readily into the camp of the avant-garde.) She expresses frustration with an academicism that is receptive to poststructuralist criticism but that misapplies that reading to inapplicable strains of contemporary American poetry, "the irony being that the poems of a Charles Bernstein or a Lyn Hejinian, not to speak of Leiris or Cage, are much more consonant with the theories of Derrida and de Man, Lacan and Lyotard, Barthes and Benjamin, than are the canonical texts that are currently being ground through the poststructuralist mill" (23).

Perloff is willing—and here her kindred historian is Sayre—to call into question, fundamentally, where and what a poem is. Her extensive and sympathetic reading of Barthes leads her to claim (over and against Jonathan Culler's reading) "that Barthes's skepticism about 'The Poem' is itself historically determined, that what Barthes is telling us . . . is that perhaps the 'poetic,' in our time, is to be found, not in the conventionally isolated lyric poem, so dear to the Romantics and Symbolists, but in texts not immediately recognizable as poetry" (18).

Though poetry per se plays only a relatively small role in Henry Sayre's *The Object of Performance: The American Avant-Garde Since 1970*, I can think of no better book to juxtapose with an analysis of contemporary American poetry.[10] In contrast to more conservatively genre-bound and claustrophobic studies, Sayre's book illuminates the options and milieus available to poesis. He warns us that "the medium of avant-garde art is itself 'undecidable,' almost by definition interdisciplinary" (xiii). Sayre begins his introduction with an epigraph from Adorno: "Today the only works which really count are those which are no longer works at all." Sayre's book is stimulating precisely because he "reads" works of art that *do* call into question the nature, location, circulation, and presence of the work of art itself. His book is anything but new wine for old bottles. The bottle itself, the liquor store, and the winery are, if not re-invented, subjected to considerable scrutiny and imagination.

One result is that Sayre does some of the most interesting thinking we have on the commodity status of the work of art. From a perspective similar to Hartley's analysis of reification and the resistance to com-modification in the work of the Language poets, Sayre argues that "per-formance and performance-oriented genres could be defined as artistic strategies conceived—like conceptual art itself—in order to defeat, or at least mitigate, the exploitation of their material manifestations" (12–13). In discussing the earthworks of Smithson, Oppenheim, and others, Sayre cites Oppenheim's observation that "one of the principal func-tions of artistic involvement is to stretch the limits of what can be done and to show others that art isn't just making objects to put in galleries" (213). By extension, neither is a poem just for putting in an anthology or in a forty-eight-to-sixty-four-page collection of thematically unified lyrics. Thus Sayre provides us with a sympathetic context for consider-ing writings that question habitual and institutionalized locations of "the poem."

Sayre links his consideration of resistances to the art object as com-modity to his investigation of representations of the self and is at his best in analyzing the implications of the work of certain contemporary photographers. For Garry Winogrand's photographs—in a comment that would be equally astute and helpful in reading much of Perelman's po-etry—Sayre suggests, "It is as if the structural harmonies of his scenes were *poses* beneath which other more complicated and chaotic narra-tions are unfolding" (47). Or, in thinking about Nicholas Nixon's family portraits, Sayre asks us to consider that "what seems staged or dramatic in one age, then, appears natural to the next, and vice versa, but the point, surely, is that this tension between the natural and the staged seems endemic to the portrait genre as a whole" (49). Sayre concludes, in part by way of exploring William Wegman's photographs, that "the self, finally, is a kind of theatre, an ongoing transference of identity, an endless 'acting out' " (57).

Such an observation allows Sayre to offer some interesting insights into the extreme and artificial gestures of self-representation present in punk: "[M]aking oneself up is revealed here as a *signifying process*. That is, it *creates meaning, and it creates it as a function of difference*. . . . [P]unk exposes the signifying process of the cosmetics industry—of glamour and style—by radicalizing and literalizing its conventions. It is possible to say, in fact, that punk is 'excessively' conventional, that it is glamour in excess" (85). Thus from significantly different objects of attention, Sayre makes an essential contribution to current understandings of the self as an artificial, constructed entity. So, too, does he critique the notion of the autonomous artist working in heroic isolation. In an excellent chapter on feminist art of the seventies, Sayre observes that "feminist art offered collaborative activity as not only an alternative to but a specific critique of the traditional modes of isolated, individually motivated artistic production accepted as the norm in Western culture" (101).

Like Perloff's *Poetic License*, Sayre's *Object of Performance* offers a series of challenges to contemporary poetry's norm of the expressive lyric. One of the most significant challenges to such a conception of the poem is the talk-poem of Antin. As distinguished from the oral poetics movement's reversal of the writing/speech hierarchy, "rather than privileging speech or writing, Antin problematizes their interaction" (210). His talk-poems exist both as live presentations and as written texts produced, with revision, from tape recordings of his performances. But what Antin's work and Rothenberg's, and indeed much of the artwork discussed throughout Sayre's book, have in common is an assumption that "art is the act of making, not the thing made" (183). Taken collectively, and considered with some seriousness, the wide range of art examined by Sayre should help to undermine restrictive models for an institutionally sanctioned version of "poetry."

So might *A Gift of Tongues: Critical Challenges in Contemporary American Poetry* and *An Ear to the Ground: An Anthology of Contemporary American Poetry*, both edited by Marie Harris and Kathleen Aguero, help to disturb the institutional practice of poetry.[11] In spite of differences with their approach, I state unequivocally that these books are excellent, informative, and valuable, particularly at a time when teachers, poets, and critics are attempting to imagine and enact multicultural approaches to "American" writing.

In *An Ear to the Ground*, Harris and Aguero aim for a literature of inclusion: "*An Ear to the Ground* . . . affirms the richness and cultural complexity of contemporary poetry in the United States" and "abandons the myopic notion of center (European, male literary tradition) and periphery (all other cultural influences) in favor of the more accurate representation of contemporary U.S. literature" (xix). P. J. Laska, echoing arguments made several years ago by Ron Silliman, argues that a chief feature of contemporary poetry is its radical decentralization: "Those who lament the passing of the old order talk about the seventies as a 'decade of dispersal' and argue, for example, that Robert Lowell is the last of the great American poets because of the scattering of cultural focus and the fracturing of national audience" (A Gift of Tongues, 324). Laska's decentralized art world, resisted by the McClatchys and the Vendlers, verges on a statement of fact, with significant consequences and options.

One such option is the multiculturalism advocated by Harris and Aguero. While no anthology can include "everything" at any given moment, their attempt to be broadly inclusive in a fresh and provocative way is of great worth. Harris and Aguero acknowledge that their "own backgrounds and education have not been without bias" (An Ear to the Ground, xxii). And there are instances of definite bias and confusion, the most serious of which is the nearly total exclusion, in poems and essays, of any representation of avant-garde poetries. The basis for that particular bias can be seen in the conclusion to the preface to A Gift of Tongues: "If it is true that the poet speaks to everyone, it is essential that the listener not hear selectively, responding only to the familiar voice, the expected message. Poets have a gift of tongues. It is our responsibility and delight to hear them when they speak" (x). Perhaps their bias against experimental writing stems from a valuing of voice over text, a privileging of speech over the productions of the page, a bias that leaves no room for Darragh, or Bernstein, or Martin, or Larry Eigner, or Reyes Cárdenas or, at another extreme, the talk-poems of Antin, or the radical (textual) feminism of DuPlessis.

A secondary confusion apparent from the conclusion to the preface to Tongues lies in the assumption that "the poet speaks to everyone." These two books emphatically make out the opposite case. Poets speak (or write) from, within, and often to specific audiences. Our job as readers may be to expand the range of poets (and human beings) to which we respond and attend. Indeed, encounters with poems that do not speak to "us" may well provide "us" with one of poetry's most crucial acts of education. Rather than Frost's transcendental category of education by poetry (meaning education by metaphor), we may begin to have an education by difference, especially differences of culture, context, aesthetic assumptions, audience, and subject position. Rather than an ever expanding canon of ever broadening inclusivity, the more effective strategy may prove to be Silliman's rejection of the process of canonization itself.

While the Harris and Aguero books reveal some of the pitfalls and difficulties of a multicultural approach to contemporary American poetry—particularly some of the essentialisms that haunt the conception of poetry (and subjectivity) from various subject positions—their books solidly contribute to any serious consideration of contemporary American poetry. *Tongues*, which provides an excellent bibliography of publishers, journals, and anthologies, as well as informative notes at the end of each essay, includes fine essays on poetry by women of color, issues of caste and canon, radical poetries of the thirties, feminist poetry, black poetry, multicultural criticism, Native American poetry, Chicano poetry, Asian American poetry, Puerto Rican poetry in the United States, gay poetry, poetry in American prisons, and Appalachian poetry. Several of the most important specific contributions in *Tongues* are Adrian Oktenberg's introduction to the poetry of Meridel Le Sueur, John Crawford's writing on Lorna Dee Cervantes' *Emplumada*, Joseph Bruchac's "Contemporary Native American Poetry," and Carmen Tafolla's important "Chicano Literature: Beyond Beginnings."

Where Perloff objects in *Poetic License* to a reverse prejudice (that values "message" over form) in the evaluation of poetry, Tafolla, by means of numerous examples, provides the most sustained instance I have encountered of writing on "ethnic" poetry noteworthy for its innovations (rather than its imitation of or adherence to a reigning professional version of "good writing"). He cites the work of Alurista (particularly *Spik in Glyph?*) and Cárdenas. I offer an extended paragraph of examples cited by Tafolla to give the reader an idea of the innovations available in contemporary Chicano poetry:

> Regional chauvinists continued to criticize our "Tex-Mex" and to treat it as a "language deficiency" caused by low educational or intellectual levels. And Chicano writers continued to indulge in "language play" (for example, Nephtalí de León's play *Tequila Mockingbird* and Alurista's *Spik in Glyph?*), an inventive and intriguing challenge for linguistic creativity. What had begun with reflections of our own bilingual reality—my own *"me senté allí en la English class"* and Delgado's *"chicotazos* of history"—turned into the formulation of totally new grammatical styles. Lexical creations spring from the discovery of new worlds of thought and literature—the Mayan, Aztec, Native American, and so forth. Formerly we would, in our daily lives, hispanicize English realities: "I missed" would resurrect in Spanish as *"mistié,"* "I flunked" would expand the traditional lexicon with *"flonquié,"* and the "big,

old thing" ending "*azo*" would turn a party in an English sentence into a *porazo* in a Spanish conversation. . . . Acutely aware of the sounds of English, we would accent our Spanish to a mock-Anglicized "free holes" (for *frijoles*) and then play the reverse by accenting our English with the sounds of Spanish: *pino borra* for "peanut butter." Now, reading through Aztec accounts of *teotl, mitotl, couatl, tomatl*, we exclaimed, instead of the commonplace "¡Que loco!" ("Crazy!"), "¡Que locotl!" And the new *mestizaje* of language yielded concentrated high-impact packs, like the three-word label of the moon by Victoria Moreno—"vanilla canela crescent." (208–9)

For such language play, Juan Bruce-Novoa introduces the descriptive term "interlingual." Such examples, as well as Tafolla's claim for a third stage of development in Chicano literature—"a stage of invention and creation" (223) succeeding a statement of protest—makes his introduction to contemporary Chicano writing one of the most exciting essays in the books edited by Harris and Aguero.

There are several essays in *Tongues* I shall explore in greater detail, particularly to illustrate dangers present in today's first approaches to a multicultural contemporary American poetry. Lynda Koolish's "The Bones of This Body Say, Dance: Self-Empowerment in Contemporary Poetry by Women of Color" offers a statement of goals for women writers that is, by now, relatively standard: "The woman writer in this culture— whether Afro-American, Chicana, Asian American, Native American, or white—has written in a language determined by patriarchy as well as racism and thus has a double urgency to redefine that language, to claim a language and form unfettered by those twin forces of the dominant culture" (13). When discussing the dilemmas facing Asian American and Chicana poets, Koolish is sensitive to the dangers of assimilation and standardization: "The paradox here, of course, is that in 'translating oneself into understandable terms' the North American woman of color whose native tongue is not English runs the risk of being increasingly understandable to the Anglo world while becoming increasingly alienated from her own identity" (19). Even so, Koolish praises Audre Lorde for poems of "immediate, unmediated description" and "tremendous impact," poems that catch the reader in visceral experience (6). Koolish exalts certain poems because "poetry makes the unknowable intelligible." She claims that "in Native American poetry . . . access is provided to the mysterious and creative powers of the universe and thus to one's own inner power" (43). Joy Harjo's poems allow the reader "to become one with the earth" (43). From another poem we learn that "memory restores us to ourselves" (46).

What worries me is the mixture of easy aestheticism and an unquestioned faith in humanist platitudes and individual autonomy. Formally, a more subtle threat exists to the "difference" from which Koolish's poets write. The threat of standardization, under the banner of "excellence," derives from a homogenized version of professionalized verse practice: a contemporary academicism of the workshop, a poetry of an "autonomous" individual voice that fails to investigate the rhetorical underpinnings of its stylized and (bourgeois) ideological practice.

Such criticism does not apply only to Koolish's essay. Crawford, in "Toward a New Multicultural Criticism," praises Cervantes' poems because, among other virtues, "she speaks in her own voice" (171). The conclusion to Crawford's essay is especially noteworthy:

> The common element of their [Joy Harjo's, Lorna Dee Cervantes', and Janice Mirikatani's] work, after all, is that it is different from the poetry of the dominant Anglo-American culture which represents the aspirations and interests of the majority of the population of the United States (if we are to count the assimilated white ethnic minorities). All then that we can generalize about is the *difference* of this work, which sees its project in diverse ways as one of rescuing images from the dominant culture, restoring a sense of rightness in a threatened social and personal world, and proposing a means of continuing to exist—and to struggle—in the future. (192)

Not the least of the many problems with such an assessment is that a key portion of this passage—the last sentence—would serve equally well as a blurb for the mainstream poetry of white males such as Gerald Stern, Philip Levine, or any one of a number of other popular poets of personal struggle. The problem is that for Crawford, Koolish, and many other critics there is already in place an uncontested version of "good writing," which I think of as a kind of homogenized academicism. Along with its considerable virtues, *Ear* presents many poems that give ample evidence that the voice poem, of clear simple imagery with heightened emotion and a moment of revelation/closure, is indeed a virus that has migrated from one cultural site to another.

In the latter portions of his essay in *Tongues*, Juan Bruce-Novoa calls attention to what he considers to be the best of recent Chicano poetry (a list considerably at odds with Tafolla's more adventurous readings). The terms of Bruce-Novoa's praise provide one more instance of contemporary poetry's homogenized professionalization. He acclaims the work of Gary Soto (who studied under Levine) and Cervantes for producing "a series of publications that for the most part demanded craft before message" and that "displayed attention to technique" (243). Throughout the last few pages of Bruce-Novoa's essay, this word *craft* pops up again and again. Soto's poems are praised for "craft"—"tight poems based more on image and metaphor than on narrative anecdote" (244)—and for "the quality of his work [that] has set a standard that continues to serve others as a benchmark" (244).

But what version of "craft" and "quality" is being praised? Bruce-Novoa is reasonably clear on this point: a version learned from the academic mainstream, that is, the workshop voice poem, the lyric of personal experience stated in "natural," clear language. Bruce-Novoa's trinity is "craftsmanship, quality, and dedication to a personal vision" (244). Cervantes thus is praised for poems worked on "until each word fits perfectly" and for the display of "brilliant images" (245).

Bruce-Novoa's vision of contemporary Chicano poetry, considerably different from Tafolla's, is that "Chicano poets are less concerned with ideology and more with craft; they explore the personal voice in any register and through any technique" (246). But any version of "craft" is ideological, particularly today's mainstream craft, which makes "the personal voice" the essential product of an accomplished poet. Bruce-Novoa argues that the emergence of craft over message "makes the recent [Chicano] poetry more dynamic, healthy, and interesting" (246). I claim that a poetic culture is "dynamic, healthy, and interesting" when it is oppositional and innovative, not when it is assimilating an already outmoded, conservative poetics of the personal voice. Admittedly, money, power, and prestige may result from such acts of "craft," but at the expense of "difference." The ironically conventional formal character of much that Bruce-Novoa celebrates in Chicano poetry illustrates a serious difficulty in the effort to claim a subject position for a previously marginalized other. That effort may easily fall prey to the lures of appropriation. To state the problem in general terms, the valid need that some poetry work for the construction of communities may be mistakenly conceived as depending on conventions of literary subjectivity borrowed (or appropriated) from the dominant culture, so that a resistance to appropriation may give way to a politics of assimilation. It seems to me that Bruce-Novoa's chief error is to pretend that "craft" is not ideological or institutional in nature. He writes as if "craft" were itself a transcendent, ahistorical accomplishment. The exact opposite is the case, particularly for the version of "craft" he endorses.

The same holds true for Bruchac's conclusions regarding poems written by prisoners. Bruchac states:

> Some continue to view the work of writers in prison as little more than a
> literary curiosity, despite the fact that much of the current poetry from pris-

ons is moving and highly crafted, despite the fact that a large part of the poetic output of American inmates makes no mention of prison and is being published because of its excellence, not its origin. The only fair way to judge the work produced by that varied community of men and women in our nation who have been legally defined as outcasts is to use the same criteria you use to judge all good writing. (294)

But what both *Ear* and *Tongues* and the entire project of multiculturalism teach us is the opposite. In fact, judgment is not the issue, for judgment (as Paul Lauter, Silliman, and others argue) is simply a result of critical method. The issue, says Lauter, is not "'better,' but what we mean by 'better'" (*Tongues*, 66). As Harris and Aguero themselves stipulate in the preface to *Ear*, "we need the opportunity to abandon narrow definitions and limiting assumptions and evaluate the poem from the inside out without comparing one tradition to another or judging against an artificially imposed single standard" (xxii).

The lessons of multiculturalism are varied, but we can begin to assert that subject position and context *do* matter. We cannot, therefore, use the same "commonsense" standards of excellence to evalute poetries written out of radically different traditions. As Perloff, Hartley, and Bernstein demonstrate, definitions of "craft" and "quality" are ideological and are part of cultural and institutional struggles. If poetry is to retain (or return to) a place of importance and excitement, poets must engage in an oppositional practice of form *and* content inseparably. Not just "make it new" for the sake of a commodified novelty, but make it new so that the writing of poetry continues to be radically exploratory, not merely learning how to do what the currently entrenched do.

NOTES

1. David Antin, "Modernism and Postmodernism: Approaching the Present in American Poetry," *Boundary 2* 1.1 (1972): 98–99.

2. J. D. McClatchy, *White Paper: On Contemporary American Poetry* (New York: Columbia University Press, 1989).

3. Stephen-Paul Martin, *Open Form and the Feminine Imagination: The Politics of Reading in Twentieth-Century Innovative Writing* (Washington, D.C.: Maisonneuve Press, 1988).

4. Walter Kalaidjian, *Languages of Liberation: The Social Text in Contemporary American Poetry* (New York: Columbia University Press, 1989).

5. George Hartley, *Textual Politics and the Language Poets* (Bloomington: Indiana University Press, 1989).

6. Charles Bernstein, ed., *The Politics of Poetic Form: Poetry and Public Policy* (New York: Roof Books, 1990).

7. Bruce Andrews, "Poetry as Explanation, Poetry as Praxis," in Bernstein, *Politics of Poetic Form*, 28.

8. Ron Silliman, "Canons and Institutions: New Hope for the Disappeared," in ibid., 150.

9. Marjorie Perloff, *Poetic License: Essays on Modernist and Postmodernist Lyric* (Evanston: Northwestern University Press, 1990), 2.

10. Henry Sayre, *The Object of Performance: The American Avant-Garde Since 1970* (Chicago: University of Chicago Press, 1989).

11. Marie Harris and Kathleen Aguero, eds., *A Gift of Tongues: Critical Challenges in Contemporary American Poetry* (Athens: University of Georgia Press, 1987), and *An Ear to the Ground: An Anthology of Contemporary American Poetry* (Athens: University of Georgia Press, 1989).

14　On Edge
Nathaniel Mackey

I came here with apprehensions about the title "A Symposium of the Whole."[1] This concern probably has to do with living in Santa Cruz, where so many "holistic" enterprises of one sort or another get heavily advertised in various newspapers and on the bulletin boards around town. The prospect of coming all the way here just to get more of that didn't seem all that inviting, so one of the things I immediately did was think about alternate titles. I found I was more drawn to the idea of an edge than to the idea of a whole. This morning, then, I was pleased to hear Nathaniel Tarn speak of Mr. Hyde "trying to get a word in edgewise," because one sense of what I would call "A Symposium of the Edge" is that there the otherwise excluded do exactly that—get a word in edgewise.[2]

With the idea of an edge I mean to offer a possible correction to a too simple reading of Robert Duncan's phrase "symposium of the whole." In the same chapter of The H.D. Book in which the phrase is found, Duncan writes: "Not only the experience of unity but the experience of separation is the mother of man."[3] To bring separation back into the picture is to observe that the edge is a cutting edge, the "mother of my cutting" Jay Wright refers to in The Double Invention of Komo. Edges figure prominently in Wright's book, an extended poem based largely on Bambara ritual motifs: knife's edge, axe's edge, and such assertions as "Each word is my knife's incision" and "What is true is the incision."[4] The old and the new truth of the incision is that one is profoundly and inescapably cut off and cut into by differences. The edge is where differences intersect, where we witness and take part in a traffic of partialities, where half-truths or partial wisdoms converse, contend, interlock.

I would like to underscore this idea of an interface by returning to one of the papers given at the Ethnopoetics Symposium in 1975. The Martinican writer Edouard Glissant had some things to say that merit repeating. Toward the end of his talk, "Free and Forced Poetics," he remarks:

> Finally, my exposé has sufficiently demonstrated that if certain communities, oppressed by the historical weight of dominant ideologies, long to con-

vert their speech into a shout, rediscovering thereby the innocence of
primitive ethnos, our task is rather to transform the shout we once uttered
into a speech which continues it, thus discovering, albeit intellectually, the
expression of a finally liberated poetics.[5]

Glissant is rightly, if I may say so, edgy—wary of "certain communities" whose comfortable hold on "speech" allows them the indulgence
of prioritizing "shout." The danger of such a prioritization becoming a
one-way choice against "speech" leads him to say, somewhat hopefully:
"I believe that ethnopoetics can go both ways." I think it is imperative that it go both ways, an aspect of which would be that the very
enterprise of ethnopoetics confront its First World specificity, its First
World partiality, confront the fact that its valorization of the "shout," as
Glissant makes clear, grows out of a particular history and is not necessarily universal, not, for example, terribly relevant to the historical imperatives facing the community to which Glissant belongs. One of the
things he warns against is overlooking differences: "In opposition to a
universalizing and reductive humanism, we must develop widely a theory of particular opacities."

One way to do this is to sharpen the edge along which the excluded
have their say. In a sense, we have just done so in listening to Glissant,
whose remarks on "speech" and "shout" can be heard as cuttingly or
contrapuntally contending with, say, the endorsement of "shout (tongue)"
at the expense of "discrimination (logos)" in Charles Olson's "Human
Universe," a seminal essay on ethnopoetics' valorization of the oral.[6]
(While Olson makes "speech" synonymous with "shout," it needs to
be noted, Glissant uses it to mean "discourse" or "discrimination.")
Glissant is not alone or atypical. It is instructive to listen to others who,
like him, come from communities we tend to think of as oral. Their
remarks on the orality versus literacy question provide an antidote to
the either/or, too easy infatuation with the oral that ethnopoetics might
lapse into.

Amiri Baraka, for example, in his introduction to Arthur Pfister's
book of poems, *Beer Cans, Bullets, Things & Pieces*, is careful not to dissociate
black people from literacy, as is often done, even as he extols the oral.
We hear from him too that whatever taint may be attached to literacy has
more to do with the alien "weight of dominant ideologies" to which
Glissant alludes than with anything intrinsic to writing:

> We talk about the oral tradition of African People, sometimes positively,
> many times defensively (if we are not wised up), and it's always as a substi-
> tute for the written. What this is is foolfood, because we were the first writ-

ers, as well. . . . Thor is the God of writing, its inventor, an African. It is headstretching to contemplate that the same God translated reduced to manhood and shot up to Greek demigodhood as Hermes . . . to the Romans' Mercury, should end up with the Scandinavians as a God of War. Having made the strange conversion from Inventor of language and poetry and medicine (via residence as a Graeco-Roman pickpocket) to the wodan god of war.[7]

Similarly, in Ishmael Reed's novel, Mumbo Jumbo, we see a repudiation of simpleminded endorsements of orality. Jes Grew, an African-rooted music and dance "epidemic" spreading across the United States, is said to be in search of its text: "Jes Grew was an influence which sought its text. . . . If it could not find its Text then it would be mistaken for entertainment."[8] Or we can go back to the nineteenth century, where Frederick Douglass reminds us that, however much literacy might be the prison house that First World reappraisals of the oral say it is, there is a prison house of orality too, a much more "literal" one in fact. In Douglass's Narrative we hear one of his former owners, a Mr. Auld, say to his wife while forbidding her to teach Douglass to read and write: "Learning would spoil the best nigger in the world. Now if you teach that nigger how to read, there would be no keeping him. It would forever unfit him to be a slave."[9]

We cannot even begin to talk about the whole without observing that ideologies of dominance cut us up and cut us off. I was gratified to hear an admission of this in Nathaniel Tarn's use of the Dr. Jekyll/Mr. Hyde dichotomy. W. E. B. Du Bois in 1903 coined his famous term double-consciousness in discussing an inner division he took black people in this country to be peculiarly afflicted with. What I was gratified to hear in Tarn's talk was validation of a notion I've held for some time that everyone, black and white, has a case of "double-consciousness" and that the black "double-consciousness" Du Bois was talking about is very much an effect of First World "double-consciousness," white duplicity, of the kind of split that divides Dr. Jekyll from Mr. Hyde. Somewhat related to this notion: I notice what might be called a double standard at work in Edmond Jabès's remarks. I find his comments fascinating, but I have to differ with his view that there is something particularly tragic about Aimé Césaire and Léopold Senghor writing in French rather than, presumably, an African language, a language "of their own." If language is the subversive, unsettling force, the engine of displacement he tells us it is, then none of us is at home in it and certainly no one owns it. If language generally, not just a particular language, is catastrophic rather than grounded, then Césaire and Senghor are no more uprooted in French than they would be in Wolof. If, as Maurice Blanchot writes, "to stay within language is always to be already outside," then Césaire and Senghor are no more exiled in French than Jabès or Blanchot.[10]

I once heard David Antin remark that there's no such thing as a native language, no such thing as a native speaker. What I took him to mean by this statement is that language undoes any ostensible group and that we have to part with notions of a sedentary relationship to it, that we have to part with attitudes of "native" simplicity, "native" complacency, "native" gullibility, and so forth. One isn't born speaking one's so-called native language but has to be taught it. To remember this is to keep the weirdness of language in mind. This would seem to be just the point of Blanchot's comment, as well as of much of what Jabès has to say. I would also relate that "antinativist" view to William Burroughs's idea of language as "a virus from outer space," as well as to Jack Spicer's notorious "Martians." To see language as extraterrestrial is to accent its groundlessness. But this too is old news. Most of the "natives" to whom a simplistic relationship to language has been attributed have long testified to language's essential strangeness, its prodigiousness and possible treachery. Among the Yoruba, the linguist and master of languages who serves as messenger between human beings and Olorun, the Owner of the Sky, is none other than Eshu, the orisha of chance, accident, and unpredictability, the trickster. Among the Dogon, it is the fox, the "deluded and deceitful son of God," who acquires the gift of speech by violating his mother, the earth, and is thereafter called upon by diviners to reveal the designs of God (just as Eshu is said to be the best friend of Orunmila, the orisha of divination).

Jerome Rothenberg's maxim in *Technicians of the Sacred* bears repeating: "Primitive means complex."[11] If ethnopoetics is to amount to something other than the First World's assurance of its own complexity (a weary assurance of its own complexity) seeking out refreshing, picture-postcard simplicities elsewhere, it has to keep that in mind. We can learn from the words of Wilson Harris, whose work repudiates simplistic nativity both with regard to language and with regard to place: "In this age and time, one's native land (and the other's) is always *crumbling*: crumbling within a capacity of vision which rediscovers the process to be not foul and destructive but actually the constructive secret of all creation wherever one happens to be."[12] And in the same "Manifesto of the Unborn State of Exile" he remarks of language:

Language is one's medium of consciousness . . . language alone can express (in a way which goes beyond any physical or vocal attempts) the sheer— the ultimate "silent" and "immaterial" complexity of arousal . . . the original grain or grains of language cannot be trapped or proven. It is the sheer mystery—the impossibility of trapping its own grain—on which poetry lives and thrives. And this is the stuff of one's essential understanding of the reality of the original Word, the Weel of Silence. Which is concerned with a genuine sourcelessness, a fluid logic of image. So that any genuine act of possession by one's inner eye is a subtle dispersal of illusory fact, dispossession of one's outer or physical eye.

A *subtle dispersal of illusory fact*. This I would give the name the Dogon give their weaving block, the "creaking of the word." That language creaks testifies to the rickety, telltale base on which its word-weave, its "fabrication," rests.

NOTES

1. This essay was first presented as respondent comments at "A Symposium of the Whole: Towards a Human Poetics" at the Center for the Humanities, University of Southern California, March 1983.

2. See Nathaniel Tarn, "Dr. Jekyll, the Anthropologist Emerges and Marches into the Notebook of Mr. Hyde, the Poet," *Conjunctions* 6 (Spring 1984): 266–81.

3. Robert Duncan, "Rites of Participation," in *A Caterpillar Anthology*, ed. Clayton Eshleman (Garden City, N.Y.: Doubleday, 1971), 39.

4. Jay Wright, *The Double Invention of Komo* (Austin: University of Texas Press, 1980), 29, 6, 48.

5. Edouard Glissant, "Free and Forced Poetics," in *Ethnopoetics: A First International Symposium*, ed. Michael Benamou and Jerome Rothenberg (Boston: Alcheringa/Boston University, 1976), 100.

6. Charles Olson, "Human Universe," in *Human Universe and Other Essays*, ed. Donald Allen (New York: Grove Press, 1967), 3.

7. Amiri Baraka, "Pfister Needs to be Heard!" in Arthur Pfister, *Beer Cans, Bullets, Things & Pieces* (Detroit: Broadside Press, 1972), 4.

8. Ishmael Reed, *Mumbo Jumbo* (Garden City, N.Y.: Doubleday, 1972), 211.

9. Frederick Douglass, *Narrative of the Life of Frederick Douglass, An American Slave* (Cambridge: Harvard University Press, 1960), 59.

10. Maurice Blanchot, *The Gaze of Orpheus and Other Literary Essays* (Rhinebeck, N.Y.: Station Hill Press, 1981), 134.

11. Jerome Rothenberg, "Pre-Face," in *Technicians of the Sacred*, ed. Jerome Rothenberg (Garden City, N.Y.: Doubleday, 1968), xix.

12. Wilson Harris, *The Eye of the Scarecrow* (London: Faber and Faber, 1965), 102.

15 "Unmeaning Jargon"/Uncanonized Beatitude: Bob Kaufman, Poet
Maria Damon

> If reality is taken only as it is given in the immediate impression, if it is regarded as sufficiently certified by the power it exerts on the perceptive, affective, and active life, then a dead man indeed still "is," even though his outward form may have changed, even though his sensory-material existence may have been replaced by a disembodied shadow existence.
>
> —Ernst Cassirer

> . . . the myths themselves are persons.
>
> —Robert Duncan

> These men are metaphors. Whatever they originally were or did as actual persons has long since been dissolved into an image of what [is regarded] to be true spirituality.
>
> —Clifford Geertz

> You must mention Bob's eidetic memory capacity. It was extraordinary. Also his amazing influence on all who met, heard or read him thru the years. They speak of "spheres of influence": Bob's were/are spirals!
>
> —Eileen Kaufman

THE MYTHS

Surrealist poet Bob Kaufman died in January 1986. Prolific and flamboyant during the late fifties and early sixties, and again briefly productive in the seventies, he had drifted into silent obscurity by the time of his death, and he died poverty-stricken and physically debilitated. He has remained, however, a revered cult figure within the somewhat circumscribed San Francisco street poetry orbit. Throughout and despite his silence, this "prince of street poetry" continued to represent Beat values: nonconformism as an all-encompassing "poetic" way of life, antiestablishment anger, scorn for material wealth and comfort, and copious drug use in the search for ecstatic vision.[1]

The vivid legends that coalesced around the "hidden master of the Beats" during his lifetime contributed to this mystique. His hagiography comprises compelling details set forth in tags like: "Grew up in New Orleans, German Orthodox Jewish father and Martiniquan Roman Catholic voodoo mother." (Although Kaufman himself encouraged this version of his genealogy, his brother George says that their paternal grandfather was [part] Jewish, and their schoolteacher mother came from an old, well-known Black New Orleans family, the Vignes. Kaufman's father was a Pullman porter, and many of the poet's siblings have occupied notable positions in electoral politics, charitable organizations, and culture: his youngest sister, for example, married Little Richard's and Sam Cooke's manager Bumps Blackwell; another sister worked in the Reagan administration under George Schultz; and yet another headed the League of Women Voters in her community; when I tried to contact a fourth sister, her husband was being honored by a New Orleans diocese for a distinguished record of community service. Neither voodoo nor Martinique were involved in their early background, and the Kaufmans, all raised as Black American Catholics, could not be said to be Jewish in any meaningful sense—"not in New Orleans," at any rate.) "Joined the merchant marine at thirteen, circled the globe nine times, was introduced to literature by a first mate." (He was, in fact, eighteen when his brother signed him up. What has been less publicly known is his activism in the National Maritime Union. An impassioned grassroots orator banned from shipping out during the McCarthy era because of his union affiliation, he became a communist labor organizer in the South.) "Coined the term 'beatnik.'" (In fact, although Kaufman founded the seminal *Beatitude* magazine, it was *San Francisco Chronicle* columnist Herb Caen who coined the pejorative "beatnik" in writing about Kaufman.) "Took a ten—(or twelve)—year Buddhist vow of silence, from JFK's assassination to the end of the Vietnam war." (The joke among his North Beach friends is that, though he did withdraw from public writing and speaking, he frequently uttered the words: "Got any speed?") "Known in France as the 'Black American Rimbaud.'" "Invented poems extemporaneously; only started writing them down at wife's insistence." "Knew all the jazz greats; Mingus loved him; the quintessential jazz poet." These phrases have worked their way from his immediate circle into dictionaries of literary biography, recent eulogies, brief biographical sketches in anthologies, and editors' prefaces: the legend has become the official story.[2]

One question that warrants further speculation is what purpose the legend has served. There are possible answers for the tenacious longevity of specific pieces of mis/information: the easy visual misreading of 18 for 13, for example, as the poet's age when he became a merchant seaman, as well as the romantic appeal of the unschooled autodidact. (In fact, according to the same interview with George Kaufman, the poet's mother was a schoolteacher who loved literature and whose living room walls were lined with bookshelves she would fill by buying entire libraries at estate sales; although he claims that Bob was the only sibling with literary interests, George Kaufman also mentions that the Kaufman children had extemporaneous limerick contests on the front porch and that the whole family were bibliophiles, passing Proust, James, Flaubert from the older siblings on down.) The power of the half-Black and half-Jewish myth may have arisen, in the war years and afterward, from a sense of solidarity with suffering and the desire to appropriate a doubly marginal status, which might have appealed to a Beat sensibility, as would the idea of a powerful but unorthodox and variegated spiritual heritage. The myth's persistence in contemporary times reflects the utopian dream of a union between two groups whom the media now depict as mutually and violently estranged in American political life.

Moreover, the tenacity of the legend, with all its contradictions, exacerbates the instability of the category of biographical truth and calls dramatic attention to the importance of myth and grandeur in everyday life: as Aimé Césaire has said, "Only myth satisfies man completely; his heart, his reason, his taste for detail and wholeness, his taste for the false and for the true, since myth is all that at once."[3] The power of the Kaufman legend among his surviving North Beach coterie holds together a scene that is struggling to survive the external assaults of gentrification in San Francisco, Reaganomics and its legacy, and changes in national literary taste on the one hand, and on the other, the internal strains of aging, poverty, and the everyday physical and emotional ruin brought about by substance abuse and alcoholism. The myths provide existential nourishment and raisons d'être for a community whose heyday is past and whose material privation—once a defiant gesture of worldly renunciation in the face of national economic prosperity—has become involuntary and inescapable suffering. Tales of Kaufman, its mendicant prophet in all his brilliant decrepitude, make up a large part of the mythology whereby this community constitutes itself as living and eulogizes itself as dying; almost every local poetry reading since his death has featured several elegies that draw direct parallels between the poet's demise and the waning of San Francisco's bohemian culture.[4] These self-consciously larger-than-life stories, an integral part of the street poetry culture in San Francisco, help the remaining "skeleton crew" (to quote Paul Landry, one of the survivors) to withstand increasing hardship. David Henderson's radio tribute to Kaufman, for example, features elaborately metaphysical descriptions of the poet's room in a transient hotel ("we'd sit in silence for hours, and when the wind would move the blue plastic curtain, we'd know we were there"), several anecdotes about "the time Bob pissed on a cop," and many, many interpretations of the poet's years of silence.

In spite of this rich legend telegraphed in dramatic catch phrases, Kaufman's name has remained obscure in mainstream cultural circles. Similarly, although his work is published by the respectable New Directions and a few pieces have been widely anthologized, his corpus is virtually unknown beyond his immediate milieu and has suffered serious critical neglect. Even if his name is familiar to African Americanists, most academics, even specialists in modern poetry, have barely heard of him. The only article on the subject, in twenty years of MLA listings, is Barbara Christian's appropriately titled "What Ever Happened to Bob Kaufman?" (1972). While the personality-cultish, local-legend pieces on Kaufman serve a crucial function, because of, as well as in spite of, their relentless marshaling of dramatic and contradictory facts, it is also important to redress the critical lacuna and to acknowledge Kaufman's contributions to the body of modern American poetry.[5]

Furthermore, Kaufman's case illustrates the role and position of a writer in certain social and historical circumstances: his biographical status as stereotyped Beat legend and overlooked Black poet complements, even as it can obscure, the problematics of a marginal writer's relationship to modernism. His work exemplifies a melange of many of the cultural trends of the American 1950s and 1960s: the "individualism versus groupism" model for understanding social dynamics prevalent in the era of McCarthy and the Beats; the popularizing of European modernist developments such as surrealism and existential philosophy; and the blending of these European influences with African American themes and structures. A quintessential subcultural poet, Kaufman is at once multiply marginal and properly paradigmatic; embodying the mainstream trends and stereotypes of his era, his work is at once high-cultural and streetwise. For example, as Charles Nilon has pointed out, although Kaufman writes in Standard English laden with allusions to Camus, Picasso, and Miro, he also employs street language, Black American verbal structures (rapping, running it down, and signifying), and jazz modalities in his verse.[6] This essay is a twofold attempt: to introduce the reader to Kaufman and his work in general, and through thematic discussion to explore that work as a meeting place of cultural influences. Because, in this particular case, the status of biographical truth is so wonderfully tenuous, my analysis is frankly dependent on the contested and contradictory features of his life as set forth in the legend: his ethnicity, for example, his addictions and commitment to street life, his life as a sailor, his status as a "jazz poet," and the historical periods (extending from the McCarthy/Eisenhower and Kennedy eras into the last decade) across which he wrote and lived. Thus this study primarily documents, and reenacts through that documentation, a crisis in representation in which each possible observation that could be made (that I could make) about Kaufman participates in an implicit or explicit social project—be it canon-building, canon-challenging, subject-forming, or subject-deforming, the academic gentrification of the Beat movement or of street poetry, or the community-building thereof—that goes far beyond (but is always implicit in) the ostensible limits of the "monograph study" or a "special case" plea for inclusion in the pantheon of American letters.

ANONYMITY: THE BLACK BEATNIK

The editor's preface to Kaufman's last book, The Ancient Rain: Poems 1956– 1978, quotes the poet: "I want to be anonymous. I don't know how you get involved with uninvolvement, but I don't want to be involved. My ambition is to be completely forgotten." Although many of the biographical facts to which I have alluded seem to support such a claim, the paradoxes in the words themselves—ambition juxtaposed against anonymity, involvement against uninvolvement—as well as their placement in a published volume, indicate a deliberate antirationalism even as they seem to convey an absolute and unequivocal commitment to a particular stance. As in a Nietzschean aphorism, the tension between the words themselves breaks the sentences apart. This is not surprising, for Kaufman lived out the combinations and conflicts of several different cultural traditions—Euro-American, Judeo-Christian, African American, African Carribean, even African, because his maternal grandmother (or great-grandmother), with whom he was very close, came over on a slave ship.[7] While it is clear that some of these traditions have been violently distorted in the interests of others, and hence have been the locus of much suffering, Kaufman reworks this pain, turning it, as Jean Genet says saints do, to good account.[8] The seeming paradox of Kaufman's claims to anonymity constitutes a rich, if sometimes conflicting, plurality of themes throughout his life and work that radically undermines the hierarchic logic of dominant Euro-American metaphysics and its attendant political and aesthetic organizing principles. His statement, in other words, and his use of surrealist techniques challenge what

Jacques Derrida has criticized as the "logocentrism" of Western poetic and philosophical discourse. His corpus riddled with contradictions and illness, his language rich and heteroglossic (literally: he was fluent in non-English Louisiana patois), he instantiates the Derridean challenge to live—as well as write and speak—by riddles, antilogocentrically.

The concept of anonymity provides a signal opportunity for examining the conventions of naming, which is an integral strategy in Kaufman's work and life. The Beats spurned material goods and fame in favor of "voluntary poverty" and artistic obscurity; this ethos of self-effacement and downward mobility paradoxically appealed to many whose parents had just started to inch out of the working class into middle-class semiprofessional jobs or skilled labor, or who, like Jack Kerouac, were first-generation college kids.[9] Nonetheless, in Kaufman's case, namelessness is not simply or unequivocally a matter of choice. Unnaming, naming, and renaming, as acts of violence, have been crucial in the history of Blacks and Jews in the West. Africans, when imported as merchandise to the New World, were renamed as the property of the men who purchased them as slaves: their new surnames were their masters', often with the genetive marker "s" added to underscore their status as owned things (for example, a slave belonging to Mr. Lee would be Anne Lees). Their new first names were often either infantile, reflecting the theory that slaves were childlike and happy in their servitude, or, especially for men, faintly exotic and regal (names of Roman statesmen, for example), as one might name fine animals. Jews were renamed first in Europe with names that spoke of degradation (Eckstein, for example—curbstone, where dogs urinate) or that alternatively evoked mercenary stereotypes—words for precious metals and jewels. "Kaufman" itself means "merchant," though it could also be a version of "Yakovman." Sometimes these names changed once again in transit through various ports of entry into the United States and still once again in an attempt to hide one's Jewishness—the evolution, for example, of (?) to Diamant to Diamond to Damon, or more dramatically, from (?) to Goldberg to Mont D'Or. The subject who has undergone such a series of transformations is surely, in one sense, anonymous. The "original name," having lost its context, loses its meaning as well—not to mention that its retrieval is virtually impossible and not neccessarily desirable. In this context, the new name testifies to the oppression it seeks to vitiate. Thus untitling, or unnaming, as Kimberly Benston has pointed out, becomes an act of entitlement, as in the case of Malcolm X, who, rather that taking on another designator of oppression as did some former slaves after the Civil War, adopted the anonymous X to convey not only the destruction of his African history but his fraternity with all others similarly violated.[10] By taking himself outside the conventional taxonomy of masters and slaves, he not only commented on it but established an entirely new relationship to it. Another critic speaks of Césaire's poetry as his "most intimate way to conciliate . . . his sense of his own blackness with his yearning for an anonymous and universal presence in the future fraternal world."[11] Positively associating anonymity with a diffuse metaphysical consciousness (consonant with Kaufman's Beat Buddhist leanings) and with social community suggests that in the play between unnaming and renaming, marginal poets create themselves in language.

One's given name is thus simply the top layer of a palimpsest, a series of historical masks that reveal as they conceal. Namelessness implies a multiplicity of names. Because names cannot be removed, one can only add another name to the chain, enriching the linguistic texture of one's sojourn through history. It is the evolution from Malcolm Little to Malik El-Shabazz and Malcolm X, or from Joe Gardner Junior to James Joe Junior Brown to JAMES BROWN that gives the final name its power.[12] Those who are invisible become masters of performance and disguise, and poetry is that mastery. Kaufman plays on versions of his own and others' names chopped up, rearranged, and punned upon. The "Abomunist Manifesto, by Bomkauf" satirically deconstructs what Barbara Christian has referred to as "isms": contrived attempts to regiment thought into systems, "last words" that claim authority as the only words and thus become implicated in such final solutions as the atomic bomb. The manifesto issues behavioral imperatives in descriptive form:

ABOMUNISTS DO NOT FEEL PAIN, NO MATTER HOW MUCH IT HURTS.

***

ABOMUNISTS DO NOT WRITE FOR MONEY; THEY WRITE THE MONEY ITSELF.

***

ABOMUNIST POETS [ARE] CONFIDENT THAT THE NEW LITERARY FORM "FOOTPRINTISM" HAS
FREED THE ARTIST OF OUTMODED RESTRICTIONS, SUCH AS: THE ABILITY TO READ AND
WRITE, OR THE DESIRE TO COMMUNICATE . . . [13]

"Further Notes (taken from 'Abomunimus und Religion')" are attributed to "Tom Man," whose name, a hybrid of Thomas Mann and Tom

Paine (the aesthetic and the political), picks up the crucial syllable the poet left out of "Bomkauf." "Excerpts from the Lexicon Abomunon," we are told, have been compiled by "Bimgo" (Bill Margolis, another founding editor of *Beatitude*). A section of surrealist couplets is captioned "Boms." In the "Abomunist Rational Anthem" language completely disintegrates; Tom Man becomes Shakespeare's Mad Tom, a sane man in disguise to save his life:

Derrat slegelations, flo goof babereo
Sorash sho dubies, wago, wailo, wailo.

Though it is possible to decode this poem to some degree ("derrat" is "tarred" backwards; "slegelations" elides "sludge" and "legislations," indicating Kaufman's assessment of United States justice; "flo," "goof," "dubies," and "wailo" evoke jazz/Beat/drug culture, etc.), the point is not to do so but to experience the disorientation of babble. This type of linguistic play recalls Langston Hughes's "Syllabic Poem," a songlike arrangement of nonsense syllables with which he intended to deflate the pretentiousness typical of poetry readings; he wrote to Countee Cullen, who was to perform it in his absence, that "the poetry of sound . . . marks the beginning of a new era . . . of revolt against the trite and outworn language of the understandable." He suggests that it would lead the literati to "discuss the old question as to whether . . . poets are ever sane. I doubt if we are."[14] Though Hughes calls the whole notion "amusing," another African-diaspora poet foregrounds the militant purposiveness of such nonsense poetry: Césaire explicitly articulates the project of "breaking the oppressor's language" by using it to, and beyond, capacity.[15] This deconstructive syllabification is also reminiscent of scat singing, the improvised nonsense syllables invented and used for sonic pleasure by jazz vocalists, with names like King Pleasure, who influenced Kaufman. Ishmael Reed chose the "Rational Anthem" under another title, "Crootey Songo," as the epigraph for the first volume of the *Yardbird Reader*.[16]

These outbursts of fragmented language joining sorrow, defiance, and (king) pleasure suggest the immediacy of the body and its expulsive processes. In the out-of-print broadside *Does the Secret Mind Whisper?* "clouds of coughed sorrow" echo the opening line of Kaufman's first book: "I have folded my sorrows into the mantle of summer night"; ("I Have Folded My Sorrows," SCL, 3); likewise the weakest personality of the five in the poem "Cincophrenicpoet" "cough[s] poetry in revenge" (SCL, 49). The poet is a "cough-man" whose poetry, as a bodily function, bursts from his innards as if involuntarily, evoking the sharp and rhythmic out-breaths punctuating the work songs of southern chain gangs. The identification of sorrow and poetry as literal "gut reactions" to oppression resonates with W. E. B. Du Bois's discussion of the spiritual "sorrow songs" as the almost instinctive and visceral expression of a tyrannized culture (see especially his transcription of the song, of unknown language, his "grandmother's grandmother" passed down to him, and note its kinship to Hughes's poem); and with Frederick Douglass's impassioned assertion that "[slaves singing] . . . words which to many would seem unmeaning jargon, but which, nevertheless, were full of meaning to themselves . . . breathed the prayer and complaint of souls boiling over with the bitterest anguish. Every tone was a . . . prayer to God for deliverance from chains." Kaufman's unmeaning jargon differs sharply from meaninglessness. His unmeaning—as in unnaming—aims to destroy actively the comfort of meaning, to burst its chains in service of the furious, spasmodic play of jazz energy. His jargon is both the special code of initiated hipsters (the underground cultural counterpart to an elite of educated expertise) and the original "jargon": etymologically, the babble of (yard)birds, gurgling—the bubbling up and over of untamable sound. Julia Kristeva has used Antonin Artaud's term *expectoration* (kauf-ing) to describe this boiling over, a pulsating gush of poetic language as so much bodily excess that " 'creates' [and] . . . reinvents the real" through the physical contortions of expulsion and release. However, the ascetic and fragmented ecstasies of Kaufman's unmeaning jargon partake of a tradition inflected as much by social and physical suffering as by presymbolic *jouissance*. Perhaps James Brown's signature ex tempore ejaculations best epitomize this ambiguous pleasure-pain, especially during the militant "Say It Loud, I'm Black and I'm Proud," which he pierces with "ooee-baby-you're killing me," a cry usually of sexual delight turned in context to social outrage.[17]

Like "Abomunist Manifesto," the long poem "Carl Chessman Interviews the PTA (from his swank gas chamber)" joins social protest and physical fracturing through linguistic play. In the second section of this satiric poem, which opens *Golden Sardine*, Kaufman manipulates Caryl Chessman's name to place him in a heroic pantheon ("Charlie Chaplin," "Caryl Melville," "Carl Darrow," "F. Scott Chessman"), to draw attention to the international dimensions of the case ("Carlos," "carlito," "Carl" as well as "Caryl" Chessman, "Call Chez-Main": appeals for clemency for Chessman came from Brazil, Uruguay, the Vatican, Britain, Denmark, etc.) and to make the name itself physical ("Caul," "Chestman"). Chessman, the victim of one of the most notorious and protracted capital punishment cases in the twentieth-century United States, becomes mythified through the fragmentation and dispersal of his name; and, as in any instance of wrongful death at the hands of the powerful, the analogy to Jesus' crucifixion offers itself, crossing over from the dominant culture to serve as a charged subtext.[18] In "Benediction," the poet announces:

> America, I forgive you . . .
> Nailing Black Jesus to an imported cross
> Every six weeks in Dawson, Georgia. (SCL, 9)

The poet's role itself is Christlike, oral poetry streaming from the sacred bodily wounds that become alternate mouths: he "sings the nail-in-the-foot song, drinking cool beatitudes" ("Afterwards, They Shall Dance," SCL, 6). And Jesus himself was a hip cat who wrote jazz poetry, as the satire on the Dead Sea Scrolls in the "Abomunist Manifesto" implies:

> Had a ball this morning, eighty-sixed some square
> bankers from the Temple, read long poem on revolt. Noticed
> cats taking notes, maybe they are publishers' agents, hope
> so, it would be crazy to publish with one of those big Roman
> firms.[19]

Kaufman's circle has not been slow to associate the Christic attribute of humility, of giving up one's physical integrity and personal claim to sacredness to die in obscurity, with Kaufman's withdrawal and decline; one of the elegies that appeared after his death was A. D. Winans's "Black Jesus of the Fifties." Accordingly, Kaufman's preoccupation with anonymity and silence come, in his life story, to indicate strength and choice even as they continue to evoke their traditional negative association with the silencing of the dispossessed. The vow of silence carries with it the force of the powerful—the users of words—assuming the powerlessness of those whose voices are ignored. Like Gandhi, whose assumption of asceticism enhanced his position of leadership, or more appropriately like Genet, who goes the authorities one better by embracing with enthusiasm the depravity projected on him by the straight bourgeois world, Kaufman, one of the politically marginal and silenced, turns the tables on authority by *choosing*, as an iconic poet-shaman, the silence of religious withdrawal and political disillusionment rather than *submitting* to the silence socially enforced on him as a Black person. The distinction, though, becomes ambiguous. His withdrawal from the world helps to fuel the Kaufman legend among a handful of people; it also assures his ongoing obscurity, contributing to his continued exile from the American canon. The self-mythologizing and powerful aspects of Kaufman's silence are counterweighted by his actual critical neglect, a fate suffered involuntarily by many Black American artists. For example, some years ago a French television camera crew arrived in North Beach with the intention of making a television special on Kaufman. For two weeks the poet managed to elude them completely and they returned to Europe with no footage. This kind of anecdote serves both to explain the poet's own role in maintaining his obscurity (millions of French viewers remained unexposed to him) and to heighten the mystery and mystique of his authenticity (in itself it remains a wonderful anecdote treasured by his North Beach confrères).[20]

THE POETICS OF THE BODY; OR, KNIGHT-ERRANT OF THE LIVING DEAD: THE SHAMAN

If anonymity has to do with presence or absence in history, one's relation to one's body has to do with spatial presence or absence. A noteworthy aspect of Kaufman's career has been his in/visibility as a street person and his experiences with alcohol and drugs, imprisonment, and poverty; the poet's body as well as his literary output bear the traces of the Black American condition. His poetic pantheon prominently features Hart Crane, Coleridge, Rimbaud, Poe, and Lorca, all of whom represent some form of physical destruction or self-destruction in the name of an all-encompassing, implacably demanding poetic vision. But at the same time, Kaufman's commitment to an oral immediacy over graphological meditation indicates that his poetics intimately connects physical being and presence. Moreover, the inclusion of political martyrs such as Crispus Attucks and Caryl Chessman (and, of course, Lorca) in this roster of heroes demonstrates a conviction that physical sacrifice is noble and is necessary to achieve political as well as aesthetic fulfillment—that in fact the two are indivisible. While it seems a contradiction to predicate wholeness on the body's devastation, it is possible to approach this phenomenon in a number of ways that make sense.

The cliché of grandiose and conscious self-immolation enhances an artist's mystique, à la Werther. The idea of the artist as a being made superior through suffering cannot be entirely dismissed in Kaufman's case, though his social status precludes at least the more cynical aspects of this interpretive possibility. Kaufman doesn't have to invent drama to aggrandize or even convey his alienation. Rather than either acquiescing to a failure seemingly predestined by social circumstances or opting full tilt for willfully narcissistic self-destruction, Kaufman makes an aesthetic choice based on exigency. The statement "I would die for Poetry"

("'Michelangelo' the Elder," *GS*, 34) does not swear allegiance to an abstraction; instead, poetry constitutes a way of life as well as a state of mind, both a means and an end coextensive and cofoundational with freedom, transformation, "true" life itself. Death, then, also becomes a means to these ends. According to many who knew him in his North Beach years, Kaufman does not call so much on the relatively modern Western spiritual and literary traditions' notions of mortifying the flesh to feed the spirit, as he does on the older and more inclusive tradition of the poet as shaman, who meditates the spirit world through body as well as through mind and who often undergoes a near fatal illness as part of her or his initiation into shamanism. Kaufman filters this tradition through his Western modernist influences to arrive at his own Beat aesthetic. Furthermore, the verbal aspect of shamanism is oral rather that written; the healing chant derives its power in the ritual speaking or singing of it, as jazz and jazz poetry derive their power—in fact exist—in the improvised moment.[21]

Though the term has specific roots in non-Christian Siberian traditions, *shaman* is an overused word in the poetry world and the current spiritual counterculture, a catchall referent for anyone who has access to nonquotidian states of consciousness; any charismatic who "speaks truth to power" based on an authority other than political fervor; who "heals" with ritual, especially ritual in which words play a crucial role; who assumes priestly powers in unorthodox, guerrilla contexts. Though the word derives from Sanskrit (from a root meaning "to exhaust, fatigue," much as the word itself has become), controversies around irresponsible appropriation of the concept have been publicized primarily by Native Americans, who find their spiritual practices invaded and consumed by spiritually starved white folks.[22] Kaufman clearly is not one of these desperately well-intentioned marauders and, according to some of his supporters, would never have applied the term to himself.[23] Nonetheless, it is one of the tropes that fit him well: he is a figure of exhaustion, excess, and dedication to an unworldly calling. Lynne Wildey, Kaufman's self-described "full-time consort" during his last five years, is one of his cohorts who has attributed shamanistic characteristics to him, describing how he "charged the night with rare magic."[24] Others have mentioned his prophetic acumen. Kush, the unofficial video archivist for the North Beach poetry scene and professor of anthropology at New College, tells of Kaufman announcing to him cryptically that "Nazis will come in pyramids from outer space to take over North Beach"; shortly thereafter, Kush received notice that the building he lived in was to be put on the market by Pyramid Realty, whose agent was a Mr.

Goebbels. Kaufman's utterance, easily dismissible as delusional street-babble, brilliantly connected the bureaucratic gentility of urban gentrification programs to the sci-fi unthinkable horrors of Nazi Germany's gentile-ification pogroms.[25] Others attribute his prophetic abilities to a New Orleans childhood steeped in alternative, diasporic ways of knowing; before he lost the battle to shock treatments, alcohol, speed, and poverty, he had "the touch."[26]

A specifically African American or African Caribbean experience—particularly in the crescent crucible of New Orleans—can put a particular spin on an Orphic or shamanistic creative death. Susan Willis has pointed out the relationship, in the literature of slavery, between forms of mutilation and spiritual as well as physical freedom. Amiri Baraka writes in Blues People, with perhaps some rhetorically affected enthusiasm, of junkies as the ultimate rebels, the nonconformists par excellence. Thus, while acknowledging the self-destructive drive in substance addiction and subsistence living, we can also see its integral role in Kaufman's poetics. Moreover, if we look at the African Caribbean influence on the poet, the African belief that life and death are interchangeable and reversible states, and the Caribbean version of this belief—the zombie myth—physical death becomes another form of life. To die for poetry is to transform oneself for and through poetry—in short, to live for poetry. In this sense, the poet's or political martyr's way of life—death—is simply her or his way, one among many, of achieving freedom. In "The Night that Lorca Comes," Lorca's posthumous advent heralds a Black American movement:

> . . . IT SHALL BE THE TIME WHEN NEGROES LEAVE THE SOUTH
> FOREVER . . .
> CRISPUS ATTUCKS SHALL ARRIVE WITH THE BOSTON
> COMMONS . . .
>
> (AR, 60)

In "Oregon," the poet, transformed into a bird, flies "the Hart Crane trip" (suicide in the Gulf of Mexico) to heaven where the "florid Black [is] found" (AR, 58).[27]

There are different kinds of living dead in Kaufman's poetry: there are those who appear to be dead but live, the lucid minds in impaired bodies who have given their lives to poetry and freedom, and there are those who appear to be alive but are in fact soulless (zombies deadened by exploitation, masters deadened by exploiting). In "The Poet," a work clearly indebted to Langston Hughes's "Wise Men," wherein the speaker wished to have dead and fishlike eyes like all the wise men he has seen, Kaufman sets forth this opposition as well as the simultaneity of life and death, of the womb and the grave, the embryo and the martyr:[28]

FROM A PIT OF BONES
THE HANDS OF CREATION
FORM THE MIND, AND SHAPE
THE BODY IN LESS THAN A SECOND.
     A FISH WITH FROG'S
     EYES,
     CREATION IS PERFECT.
THE POET NAILED TO THE
BONE OF THE WORLD
COMES IN THROUGH A DOOR
TO LIVE UNTIL
HE DIES,
WHATEVER HAPPENS IN BETWEEN,
IN THE NIGHT OF THE LIVING
DEAD, THE POET REMAINS ALIVE,
     A FISH WITH FROG'S
     EYES,
     CREATION IS PERFECT.
THE POET WALKS ON THE EARTH
AND OBSERVES THE SILENT
SPHINX UPON THE NILE.
THE POET KNOWS HE MUST
WRITE THE TRUTH,
EVEN IF HE IS
KILLED FOR IT, FOR THE
SPHINX CANNOT BE DENIED.
WHENEVER A MAN DENIES IT,
A MAN DIES.
THE POET LIVES IN THE
MIDST OF DEATH . . . (AR, 68)[29]

Again Kaufman asserts a connection between truth (or freedom) and mutilation, by associating the poet with the Oedipus who sacrificed his standing in the community and his physical integrity for the truth. The implacable Sphinx plays muse to the poet's Oedipus. Access to "truth," rather than one's biological status, determines whether one is living or dead. Kaufman distinguishes sharply between the soulless living dead and the poet who, though alive, is "born to die" and walks wrapped in a cloak of death:

THE BLOOD OF THE POET
MUST FLOW IN HIS POEM
SO MUCH SO THAT OTHERS
WILL DEMAND AN EXPLANATION.
THE POET ANSWERS THAT THE
POEM IS NOT TO BE
EXPLAINED, IT IS WHAT IT
IS, THE REALITY OF THE POEM
CANNOT BE DENIED,
    A FISH WITH FROG'S
    EYES,
    CREATION IS PERFECT.

. . . .

WHEN THE POET PROTESTS THE
DEATH HE SEES AROUND
HIM,
THE DEAD WANT HIM SILENCED.
YET LORCA SURVIVES IN HIS
POEM, WOVEN INTO THE DEEPS
OF LIFE. THE POET SHOCKS THOSE
AROUND HIM. HE SPEAKS OPENLY
OF WHAT AUTHORITY HAS DEEMED
UNSPEAKABLE, HE BECOMES THE
ENEMY OF AUTHORITY WHILE THE
POET LIVES, AUTHORITY
DIES. HIS POEM IS
FOREVER . . .

The poet's physical sacrifice not only serves as proof that he is alive but incites others to participate in the poetic/communal project by making them ask questions that can't be answered; the poem becomes ritual and public, even though the poet himself is isolated. And Kaufman neatly juxtaposes poetry with authority, the poet who mediates versus the author who dictates. Poetry is an absolute, a state of grace. Note that the poet refers to "Lorca's poem" in the singular: Lorca's poem is his life, which in turn mingles inextricably with the universal "deeps of life."

The mention of Lorca implicates another poet whose influence, though unacknowledged, Kaufman certainly felt. The mystical paradoxes and oxymorons of Lorca's poetic ancestor, Saint John of the Cross, find Beat American expression in Kaufman's dark night of the living/dead soul. Living/dead, engaged/alienated, isolated/public, transcendent/plunged in the most vivid physical and psychic suffering, "less than a second"/"forever": all resonate with the ecstatic suffering of (the also apocryphally Jewish) Saint John, whose rapturous poems were composed under torture. The word *beat* is itself a paradox of joy and suffering: in the 1950s and 1960s, to the people who adopted a Beat life, the term meant beatific, wasted, and, especially in Kaufman's case, steeped in the soulfully erotic tradition of jazz. John of the Cross, along with Lorca, had a tremendous surge of popularity in the 1950s and 1960s. The first year that the poems were published in English separately from the rest of the mystic's work was 1951; interest in him spilled over from the religious domain into the secular, with Pantheon publishing Roy Campbell's translations at the same time as Burns, Oates of London put out E. Allison Peer's translation. By the end of the decade, the Beats and the American literary avant-garde had adopted Saint John as one of them, having found in Saint John's poetry the *ekstasis* they felt to be their trademark. Grove Press in New York, one of the few commercially successful venues for avant-garde writing, published yet another translation of the *Poems* in 1959. New Directions still publishes this translation. Inasmuch as Kaufman lived in New York from 1960 to 1963 and moved in the same circles as these publishers, he could not have escaped Saint John's influence.[30]

In "All Hallows, Jack O'Lantern Weather, North of Time," which invokes the holiday of the living dead, Kaufman presents a negative version of the possibilities of living death. Although extremely dissimilar in style and sensibility, "All Hallows" shows some thematic influence of Eliot's *Waste Land* and the title, taken from the first poem in (another New Orleans writer) Tennessee Williams's *In the Winter of Cities*, resonates sonically with "The Hollow Men." The refrain in Williams's "In Jack-O'Lantern's Weather" echoes the clause that Eliot's "Love Song of J. Alfred Prufrock" forever associated with alienated, depersonalized longing: "I have seen them." (Kaufman committed to memory and rap/recited the works of both Williams and Eliot but especially the latter: the poet broke his vow of silence by reciting Becket's opening speech from *Murder in the Cathedral* and then his own "All Those Ships That Never Sailed.")[31] Kaufman shares Eliot's and Williams's sense of detachment, disembodiment, disorientation; his poem is peopled with "loudly walked bruises, thick string unbeings pouring themselves into each other, filling themselves with each other's emptiness, shouting silences across screaming rooms." Oppressors and oppressed participate in a symbiotic sickness in which emptiness and silence are the exchange currency. But, departing from Eliot's global pessimism and unreconciled alienation, in a move closer to Williams's privileged though closeted erotic gaze on "marvelous" schoolboys, Kaufman asserts that the marginal poet, though he suffers intense loneliness, occupies a privileged position of access:

I KNOW OF A PLACE IN BETWEEN BETWEEN, BEHIND BEHIND, IN
FRONT OF FRONT, BELOW BELOW, ABOVE ABOVE, INSIDE INSIDE,
OUTSIDE OUTSIDE, CLOSE TO CLOSE, FAR FROM FAR, MUCH FARTHER
THAN FAR, MUCH CLOSER THAN CLOSE, ANOTHER SIDE OF AN
OTHER SIDE. . . . IT LIES OUT ON THE FAR SIDE OF MUSIC . . . THAT
DARKING PLANE OF LIGHT ON THE OTHER SIDE OF TIME. . . . IT
BEGINS AT THE BITTER ENDS. (*AR*, 48)

The outsider-poet is both excruciatingly close, intimate with the world, and cast out of it. The consequence of not being allowed to take up space is that one knows the ins and outs of spatiality, and the consequence of being a poet is that one can use that knowledge to advantage.[32]

Space and time, history and geography meet in the poet's body: that is, a Black and Jewish male body takes up space in the United States between 1925 and 1986, survives World War II, the McCarthy era, the sixties and seventies, and most of the Reagan years. The history of this body is marked by its subjection to multiple addictions and brutality at the hands of others. (At thirteen, for example, Kaufman was hung by his thumbs in an icehouse all night by a lynch mob, an event he alludes to in "Unhistorical Events" and "Blue Slanted Into Blueness" [*GS*, 30–31, 35]; in his active Beat days he was arrested thirty-five times in eighteen months; in 1963 he was arrested for walking on the grass in Washington Square Park, given between fifty and one hundred shock treatments, and threatened with a lobotomy. Some of his North Beach friends speculate on a connection between those treatments and his vow of silence.) And like his name, that other conventional index of identity, Kaufman's body and the concepts of space and time themselves appear in his work in characteristic double guise. Like language, they function as arenas of oppression and, to borrow again from Césaire, as "miraculous weapons."[33]

It is not useful, however, to underestimate, glamorize, or pass over in silence the painful aspects of substance addiction and the way the addict experiences his or her body. Kaufman's poetry describes a process in which the subject experiences a separation of mind and body, so that the latter becomes other and foreign. Depersonalization has been noted as a survival technique for, among others, sexual abuse survivors and the concentration camp inmates of World War II; we might want to consider adding to the list social outsiders whose bodies bear the marks of the exclusion. Elaine Scarry has commented on the role of physical pain in undoing a coherent world view and, with it, coherent utterance governed by the will of the speaking subject.[34] To the extent that Kaufman's poetry reflects his experience with the physical pain of police brutality and drug addiction in tandem with the psychic pain of social outsiderhood, its language is made up of fragments, deconstructing back into presymbolic scraps of sound ex-pressed through outbursts of protest and play ("Crootey Songo"); the body is presented alternately as disintegrating, devolving back into nature, separating from the "I" of the poem, or rigidly alien. Like the "unbeings" who pour themselves into each other's emptiness, the poet's body is a hollow space he inhabits or a set of discrete body parts:

> I wish whoever it is inside of me,
> would stop all that moving around
> go to sleep, another sleepless year
> like the last one will drive me sane,
>
> I refuse to have any more retired burglars
> picking the locks on my skull, crawling in
> through my open windows, I'll stay out forever
>
> ("I Wish," GS, 66)

> Sometimes in extravagant moments of shock of unrehearsed
>   curiosity, I crawl outside of myself, sneaking out
>   through the eyes, one blasé, one surprised, until I
>   begin to feel my own strangeness; shyly I give up the
>   ghost and go back in until next time.
>   ("Unanimity Has Been Achieved, Not a Dot Less for
>   Its Accidentalness," AR, 16)

> My body is a torn mattress,
> Dishevelled throbbing place
> For the comings and goings
> loveless transients.
> The whole of me
> Is an unfurnished room
> Filled with dank breath
> Escaping in gasps to nowhere.
>   .   .   .   .
> I have walked on walls each night
> Through strange landscapes in my head.
>   .   .   .   .
> My face is covered with maps of dead nations;
>   .   .   .   .
> I can't go out anymore

I shall sit on my ceiling.
Would you wear my eyes?

("Would You Wear My Eyes?" *SCL*, 40)

These poems demonstrate an acute alienation of body and consciousness; a soul, present or absent, rattles around in and out of a gutted tene-
ment of a body. The reader experiences the poet's objectified body from
the inside and simultaneously sees it, in its various forms of decrepitude, from the outside. The "strange landscapes" and the "maps of dead
nations" on the body's surface point toward the involuntary dissociation
from native landscapes and traditions that underlie African American
history and serve as ties with the past; his history is inscribed in his
body.

Sometimes, however, in the tradition of the waking of the living
dead, despair turns. In "All Those Ships That Never Sailed," the recital
of which broke the ten years of silence, Kaufman sums up his body's
history in terms of political and romantic betrayal and resurrects it, re-
membering it through love:

My body once covered with beauty
Is now a museum of betrayal.
This part remembered because of that one's touch
This part remembered through that one's kiss—
Today I bring it back
And let you live forever. (*AR*, 55)

This poem asserts a universal body; the resurrection of "my" body allows "you" to live forever in the moment that the poet once again joins
words and physical presence. In "Dolorous Echo":

The holey little holes
In my skin,
Millions of little
Secret graves,
Filled with dead
Feelings
That won't stay
Dead.

The hairy little hairs
On my head,
Millions of little
Secret trees,

Filled with dead
Birds,
That won't stay
Dead.

When I die,
I won't stay
Dead. (SCL, 30)

Here the body and its parts are presented as wasted, used up from years
of exploitation, though on hand for resurrection. At the same time,
though, the body is part of nature, a collage of despoliation, dessication,
and rampant fertility:

My hair is littered with drying ragweed.
Bitter raisins drip haphazardly from my nostrils
While schools of glowing minnows swim from my mouth.
The nipples of my breasts are sun-browned cockleburrs;
Long-forgotten Indian tribes fight battles on my chest
Unaware of the sunken ships rotting in my stomach.
My legs are charred remains of burned cypress trees;
My feet are covered with moss from bayous, flowing
      across my floor.

                          (SCL, 40)

My face feels like a living emotional relief map, forever
      wet.
My hair is curling in anticipation of my own wild gardening.
            ("Afterwards They Shall Dance," SCL, 6)

My hair is overrun with crabgrass, parts of my anatomy are
      still unexplored.
             ("Blues for Hal Waters," AR, 28)

Kaufman rewrites the "Song of Songs" *blason* in narcissistic, nightmar-
ish terms. Beside the noticeable influence of Whitman in these pieces,
indicating the landscape as the United States, the ironic use of travel-
section or geography-book cliché suggests his body as a "dark continent." Elsewhere it is "Oregon."

You are with me Oregon,
Day and night, I feel you, Oregon.
I am Negro. I am Oregon.
Oregon is me, the planet

Oregon, the State Oregon, Oregon.
In the night, you come with bicycle wheels,
Oregon you come
With stars of fire. You come green.
Green eyes, hair, arms,
Head, face, legs, feet, toes
Green, nose green, your
Breast green, your cross
Green, your blood green.
Oregon winds blow around
Oregon. I am green, Oregon.
You are mine, Oregon. I am yours,
Oregon. I live in Oregon.
Oregon lives in me,
Oregon, you come and make
Me into a bird and fly me
To secret places day and night.
The secret places in Oregon,
I am standing on the steps
Of the holy church of Crispus
Attucks St. John the Baptist,
The holy brother of Christ,
I am talking to Lorca. We
Decide the Hart Crane trip, home to Oregon
Heaven flight from the Gulf of
Mexico, the bridge is
Crossed, and the florid black found.

("Oregon," *AR*, 58)

Written on the occasion of a trip to Ken Kesey's Oregon farm for the
"First Poetry Hoo-Haw," the poem presents two seemingly contradictory principles. Kaufman presents "Negro-ness" as an arbitrary designation: a "Negro" may be distinguished as well by the color green as any
other—indeed, many different colors are termed "Negro" or Black, because anyone of any African ancestry is referred to as Black in this country. (As Henry Gates has pointed out, "race is the ultimate trope of difference because it is so very arbitrary in its application.")[35] Arbitrarily
yoking "green," "Oregon," and "Negro" draws attention to one aspect
of African American history: one is arbitrarily and cruelly thrust into
a landscape with a preexisting historical meaning and expected to ac-
commodate and conform. But as in so many other instances, Kaufman
simultaneously undermines the arbitrary violence he posits. The poem
samples Lorca's "Somnambule Ballad" with its haunting refrain:

Green how much I want you green.
Green wind. Green branches.

. . . .

Green flesh, hair of green . . .

Lorca's poem is charged both with romance and with hints of a dangerous, possibly fatal political situation, involving the drunken civil guards knocking on the door in the moonlight. (Lorca was himself executed by Franco's troops and his body thrown into an unmarked grave reminiscent of Kaufman's "pit of bones.")

For Lorca, green, like moonlight, may have signified death as well as rebirth and, in the context of the poem, desire. Robert Duncan, another San Franciscan reading Lorca at the same time, discusses the "Romance Sonambule" in a gay context, bearing out this possibility of desire. His Spanish dictionary yields sexual meanings for "verde":

> Verde, we find, means not only "green" with all that sense of freshness and entranced forthrightness . . . but it also means "off-color," "indecent"—the lewd green of hot leaves—even as, in English, getting "fresh" can mean going too far. Is there . . . a magic sense in which the quickening power of being a man, the quickening of a man, and the greening are identical? Is there a greenness to verity, an almost indecent freshness in being aware of what is at issue?[36]

Green, in other words, suggests wildness, potency, and possible insurrection—the rampant fertility of a "living emotional relief map." But Kaufman borrows from this European poet/martyr's work for his own purposes. Here again, Kaufman juggles meanings and countermeanings—he "unmeans." The color symbolism of green resonates multiculturally. Associating Black consciousness with green in a suggestion of fertility and growth, and with landscapes as human ("green eyes, hair"), asserts an identification with nature not based on domination; in the African Caribbean literary tradition, moreover, green often signals magical events or supernatural transitions. Furthermore, Kaufman himself uses green in this way elsewhere, especially in the broadside *Second April* (1959), which interweaves an "autobiographical journey" with "such events as Christ's April crucifixion, death and resurrection by A-bomb, and the author's own birth" (Kaufman was born on April 18). This poem, made up of a series of paragraph "sessions," juxtaposes assertions of "thingness" ("pants, that's a thing . . . mattress, a thing, that's a thing . . . future, that's a thing") against the refrain "look out for green"—the static known of material fixity versus the unbounded energy of life/death and constant change. The poem ends in fiery green apocalypse:

We watch them going on watching us going on going, wrapped in pink
barley leaves, almost, the time is not near, but, nearer we are to time,
and time nearer to ticks. Burning in torch surrender to auto-fantasy, we
illuminate the hidden December, seen, flamelit in the on core of the second April, come for the skeleton of time.

> Kissed at wintertide, alone in a lemming world,
> Green bitches, harlequin men, shadowed babes,
> Dumped on the galvez greens, burned with grass.[37]

Through sheer fracturing of language and imagery, Kaufman abstracts
Negroness, the "florid black," and greenness out of existence, deconstructing their literal significance. Against the abitrariness of racism
Kaufman juxtaposes the arbitrariness of play; if oppression happens in
language it can be undone there. "Oregon," as well as "green," are anagrams for "Negro." Not only is the referent, "blackness," linguistically
and imagistically arbitrary (as well as crucially significant in Kaufman's
case), but the syllables of the signifier are too, and the poet scrambles
the word both to overdetermine and to undermine the notion of Negro-
ness. But as in "North of Time," in which the poet's marginal status
carries with it certain esoteric privileges, the state (condition) of Oregon, of being a Negro, permits certain poetic and political changes. Like
"Poetry," prophetic and all-encompassing, it is a physical, metaphysical,
and absolute state; it belongs to the poet and the poet belongs to it. Kaufman takes the last two lines of "Oregon" almost verbatim from "Los
Negros" in Ben Belitt's translation of Lorca's Poet in New York, in which the
Spanish poet links Black Americans' oppression to their creative vitality,
which he finds the only humanly redeeming aspect of the megalopolis:

> Yes: the bridge must be crossed
> and the florid black found
> if the perfume we bear in our lungs
> is to strike, in its guises of peppery pine,
> on our temples.

Through the meditation of Oregon, the poet can be a Black American
revolutionary martyr like Crispus Attucks, who here associated with
John the Baptist plays the derelict prophet central to Kaufman's aesthetics
(and both of them come to us, like Kaufman, with apocryphal genealogy).[38] The poet can be conversant with Lorca and Crane and can become a nonhuman animal. (L-orca is a dolphin-whale, Hart Crane is a
deer seabird.) As a bird he can fly to heaven the Hart Crane way—jump-

ing overboard in the Gulf of Mexico, as many Africans did, preferring death to slavery. By overturning the Chain of Being, which holds humans higher than animals, he can transcend the limits of human time/space, going to "secret places" (beyond beyond) where the "florid black [is] found." When Crane's bridge is crossed, on the other side of death green gives birth to Black, the flowering of consciousness. On the other side of the United States from northwestern Oregon is southeastern Florida reaching down toward the Caribbean and Africa itself. The movement rejects associations of progress with upward and westward directions, reversing once again the imagery implicit in the dominant world view.[39]

The poem on the right-hand page of the volume facing "Oregon" serves to explicate it: it *embodies* the "florid black," asserting a Black cosmos, but with an all-encompassing sense that tends, by its very absoluteness, toward its own deconstruction:

THE SUN IS A NEGRO.
THE MOTHER OF THE SUN IS A NEGRO
THE DISCIPLES OF THE
SUN ARE NEGRO.
THE SAINTS OF THE
SUN ARE NEGRO.
HEAVEN IS NEGRO.

("Untitled," *AR*, 59)

In "Oregon," Kaufman signals the arbitrariness of referentiality by fragmenting and rearranging letters and syllables; here he effects an incipient return to meaninglessness through hypnotic repetition. Signifying function "unmeans" itself, becoming more sonic than intellectual. However, this unraveling of "meaning" does not simply fall into insubstantial assertion, which sometimes marks surrealist work: images here are not violently forced together or apart. Rather, the poem's antirationalism lies in the intuitive access we are allowed when the repeated words become transformative Words. The imagery, black on black on black, echoes, symmetrically opposes and overturns the hierarchy implicit in the greatest heaven poem of the Western canon, the *Paradiso*, in which Dante similarly deconstructs visual rationality by asserting heaven as white on white—the white pearl on the white forehead. In other words, though both Kaufman's and Dante's poems constitute deconstructive attempts to undermine rationality, they privilege as the central focus of each work the material content they choose to deconstruct: blackness and whiteness respectively; this content is so charged with hierarchic assumptions that hierarchy itself becomes foregrounded within the deconstructive project. Dante implicitly upholds the hierarchy; Kaufman explicitly challenges it. Dante points to the Chain to an abstract God—his anti-rationalism serves a traditional faith that surpasses understanding; Kaufman points toward nature (the sun) and privileges those considered less than human in the Chain's logic.[40] As in "Oregon," though, "Untitled" has its unifying aspect; the pun on sun points toward the coextension of the order of human communal ties with celestial order and reunifies the family shattered by slavery in the image of a holy family extending to saints and disciples. "Creation is perfect" in its Negroness.[41]

NOTES

1. The phrase "prince of street poets" appears in the eulogy "Tribute to a Street Poet," *People's Tribune* 13.6 (March 7, 1986): 7.

2. The biographical details included here were drawn from Raymond Foye's editorial preface to Kaufman's *The Ancient Rain: Poems 1956–1978* (New York: New Directions, 1981), ix–x, and the blurb on the back of that book; *Dictionary of Literary Biography*, vol. 41 (1978), s.v. "Bob Kaufman," by Jon Woodson; ibid., vol. 16, s.v. "Bob Kaufman," by A. D. Winans; and *Contemporary Poets*, s.v. "Bob Kaufman" (New York: St. Martin's Press, 1981). For eulogies, see Steve Abbott's "Hidden Master of the Beats," *Poetry Flash* 155 (February 1986): 1 ff.; George Tsongas, "Local Color: The Passing of a Beat Boulevardier," *Bay Guardian* (February 1986): 5 ff.; "Legendary Beat Poet Bob Kaufman Dies (The 'Black American Rimbaud')," *San Francisco Chronicle*, January 13, 1986, 7; Christopher Hitchens, "American Notes," *Times Literary Supplement*, March 7, 1986, 246; and the "Tribute to a Street Poet" cited in n. 1 above. Alix Geluardi told me the joke among his North Beach friends, February 1986, author's notes; George Kaufman, the poet's older brother, supplied the alternate genealogy in an interview on David Henderson's "Tribute to Bob Kaufman," KPFA radio, April 26, 1986, and in an interview he granted me in January 1991; likewise Marlene Blackwell, October 1990. See also David Henderson's "Bob Kaufman, Poet of North Beach," in *KPFA Folio*, April 1986, 1. The poet's widow, Eileen Kaufman, however, stands by the version of Kaufman's origins made famous in the legend. "Bob Kaufman" in Hayden Carruth's anthology *The Voice That Is Great Within Us* (New York: Bantam, 1970), 538–40, furnishes a typical example of the biographical sketches in anthologies. For some of the wilder pieces of misinformation about Kaufman, see Alan Lomax and Raoul Abdul's *3000 Years of Black Poetry*

(Greenwich, Conn.: Fawcett, 1970), 247, which gives the poet's date and place of birth as "around 1935 in San Francisco"; and Gerald Nicosia's biography of Jack Kerouac, *Memory Babe* (New York: Grove Press, 1983), 525, which characterizes Kaufman as a "Jewish . . . Haitian steeped in Christianity and voodoo."

3. Quoted in A. James Arnold, *Modernism and Negritude: The Poetry and Poetics of Aimé Césaire* (Cambridge: Harvard University Press, 1981), 55.

4. Some of these eulogies are collected in *Would You Wear My Eyes? A Tribute to Bob Kaufman*, ed. Bob Kaufman Collective (San Francisco: Bob Kaufman Collective, 1988).

5. Barbara Christian, "What Ever Happened to Bob Kaufman?" *Black World* 21.12 (September 1972): 20–29.

6. Charles Nilon, "Bob Kaufman, Black Speech, and Charlie Parker," manuscript delivered as a talk at the American Culture Association/Popular Culture Association Conference, Montreal, March 1987.

7. Foye quotes Kaufman in *The Ancient Rain*, ix. Although I don't want to overemphasize the connection, the reference to Nietzsche is not haphazard; Aimé Césaire and Federico Garcia Lorca, both of whose influences permeate Kaufman's work, found aspects of Nietzsche's work deeply inspiring. Nietzsche, like the later surrealists and Negritude poets whom Kaufman emulated, was centrally concerned with antirationalism as a challenge to traditional Western metaphysics. See Clayton Eshleman and Annette Smith's translators' introduction to *The Collected Poetry of Aimé Césaire* (Berkeley and Los Angeles: University of California Press, 1983), 3; Arnold, *Modernism and Negritude*, 54–55; and Garcia Lorca, "The Duende: Theory and Divertissement," in *The Poet in New York*, trans. Ben Belitt (New York: Grove Press, 1955), 155.

The information about Kaufman's grandmother comes from Steve Abbott's "Hidden Master of the Beats." This detail, too, may be apocryphal or partially true. The trope of an older woman—the storyteller—who transmits ancestral wisdom, sometimes along with dominant cultural values, as well as Kaufman's legendary Martiniquan heritage, echoes the life of Césaire, whose paternal grandmother, a "pronouncedly African physical type [who] exercised considerable moral authority and was a kind of spiritual advisor to the people around her," taught Césaire to read and write by age four (see Arnold, *Modernism and Negritude*, 4). In Kaufman's case, the conflated figures of the ex-slave grandmother and the schoolteacher mother work together to provide this double-edged education for the poet. This trope may be what Stephen Henderson refers to as a "mascon" for African American culture: that is, a trope characteristic of that culture. "Mascon" abbreviates "mass concentration," indicating a saturation with cultural significance.

See Henderson, "The Form of Things Unknown," in *Understanding New Black Poetry* (New York: William Morrow, 1972), 3–69.

8. Jean Genet, *The Thief's Journal*, trans. Bernard Frechtman (New York: Grove Press, 1964), 205.

9. On the demography of the Beats, their voluntary poverty, and their active spurning of artistic recognition, see the first chapter of John Arthur Maynard's *Venice West: The Beat Generation in Southern California* (New Brunswick: Rutgers University Press, 1991).

10. Kimberly Benston, "I Yam What I Am: The Topos of (Un)Naming in Afro-American Literature," in *Black Literature and Literary Theory*, ed. Henry Louis Gates, Jr. (New York: Methuen, 1984), 151–74.

11. Emile Snyder, "Aimé Césaire: The Reclaiming of the Land," in *Exile and Tradition*, ed. Rowland Smith (New York: Africana, 1976), 33–34.

12. For a brilliant synopsis on the significance of naming and unnaming in marginal art production, see the first and last paragraphs of James Brown's autobiography. The book takes us from: "I wasn't supposed to be James. And I wasn't supposed to be alive," in incisive summary of the predicament of the Other who isn't supposed to be at all, and yet without whom the socius cannot function, to "there's JAMES BROWN the myth and James Brown the man. The people own JAMES BROWN. . . . the minute I say 'I'm JAMES BROWN' and believe it, then it will be the end of James Brown. I'm James Brown," an equally eloquent representation of the necessity and performative power of Du Bois's "double consciousness." James Brown with Bruce Tucker, *James Brown, the Godfather of Soul* (New York: Thunder's Mouth Press, 1990), 1, 267.

13. Christian, "What Ever Happened," 27. Christian argues that the "Abomunist Manifesto" is a "blueprint for a revolutionary way of life." "Abomunist Manifesto, by Bomkauf," in *Solitudes Crowded with Loneliness* (New York: New Directions, 1965), 75. Henceforth all references to Kaufman's poems will appear in the text with the following code: SCL, *Solitudes Crowded with Loneliness*; GS, *Golden Sardine* (San Francisco: City Lights, 1967); and AR, *Ancient Rain: Poems 1956–1978*.

14. Quoted by Arnold Rampersad in *The Life of Langston Hughes*, vol. 1 (New York: Oxford University Press, 1986), 64.

15. Aimé Césaire and René Dépestre, "Interview with Aimé Césaire," in *Discourse on Colonization*, trans. Joan Pinkham (New York: Monthly Review Press, 1972), 29.

16. Ishael Reed, ed., *Yardbird Reader* (Berkeley: Yardbird Publishing Cooperative, 1972), 1:1.

17. Bob Kaufman, *Does the Secret Mind Whisper?* (San Francisco: City Lights, 1960); for a discussion and examples of work songs, see H. Bruce

Franklin, *Prison Literature in America* (New York: Oxford University Press, 1978), 82–126, and see especially 116–17, 164–65. W. E. B. Du Bois, "Of the Sorrow's Songs," in *The Souls of Black Folk* (New York: Bantam, 1989), 264–76; Frederick Douglass, *Narrative of the Life of Frederick Douglass, An American Slave* (Harmondsworth: Penguin, 1982), 57–58; and Julia Kristeva, *Revolution in Poetic Language*, trans. Margaret Waller (New York: Columbia University Press, 1984), 155. James Brown, "Say it Loud—I'm Black and I'm Proud," in *21 Golden Years*, PolyGram Records, 1977. For more on the jargon and language play of initiated jazz hipsters, see Neil Leonard, "The Jazzman's Verbal Usage," *Black American Literature Forum* 20.1–2 (1986): 151–60.

18. Chessman's case was notable for its role in the death penalty controversy; not only were the crimes of which he was accused not nearly as severe as those of others who got reprieves or lesser sentences but there was evidence of his innocence, as well as substantially questionable conduct on the part of the state of California's judicial system. See Chessman's autobiography, *Cell 2455 Death Row* (New York: Prentice-Hall, 1954), and Milton Machlin and William Reid Woodfield, *Ninth Life* (New York: G. P. Putnam's Sons, 1961).

19. This segment of the "Manifesto" brings to mind, and was probably influenced by, the comedian Lord Buckley's routine "The Naz," with its hip-talking treatment of Jesus: "But I'm gonna put a Cat on you, who was the Sweetest, Grooviest, Strongest, Wailinist, Swinginest, Jumpinest, most far out Cat that ever Stomped on this Sweet Green Sphere, and they called this here cat, THE NAZ, that was the Cat's name. . . . Now the Naz was the kind of a Cat that came on so cool and so wild and so groovy and so WITH IT, that when he laid it down WHAM! It stayed there!" Richard Lord Buckley, "The Naz," in *Hiparama of the Classics* (San Francisco: City Lights, 1960), 14–17.

20. It should be clear that I do not intend the term "self-mythologizing" as derogatory. On the contrary, the inherent sense of drama in the narrative construction of a life like Kaufman's is of ritual necessity. As I have said, dramas like these serve an aesthetic and social function in the literary community.

    Clifford Geertz, in *Islam Observed* (New Haven: Yale University Press, 1968), 28–29 and 87, discusses the power of a public figure's withdrawal and contemplation. More important (from a cultural and communal point of view) than the function they serve in the individual's spiritual development, their periods of withdrawal become the focal point of myths that shape not only spiritual but political aspects of a community. Geertz dramatizes this point through the figure of Sukarno, the charismatic demagogue who first led the Indonesian struggle for freedom from the Dutch and then became Indonesia's first president and who, despite his extremely public and colorful career, had, and mythologized, a period of contemplative isolation that he credits as providing the foundation of his political convictions. Many artists have had periods of silence or have stopped producing "art" altogether, including Genet, Rimbaud, Melville, Miles Davis, Thelonius Monk, and Tillie Olsen, whose *Silences* (New York: Delta, 1978) addresses the "downside"—poverty, overwork, lack of social validation, gender conditioning—of periods of silence.

21. The phrase "makes an aesthetic choice based on exigency" was supplied by Wahneema Lubiano in the course of a discussion about his subject. For details on shamanic illness, see Joan Halifax, *Shamanic Voices* (New York: E. P. Dutton, 1979), 3 ff.

22. For an early taste of the controversy around (mis)appropriation of the term *shaman*, see Gerald Hobson, "The Rise of the White Shaman as a New Version of Cultural Imperialism," *Ybird* 1.1 (1978): 85–95. This issue has become even more pointed in recent years with the popular success of the books of Lynn Andrews, a nonnative who writes ambiguously fictionalized spiritual autobiographies.

23. David Henderson, July 1990, author's notes.

24. Lynne Wildey, letter to the *Berkeley Monthly*, May 1986, 5.

25. Kush, April 1986, author's notes.

26. Henderson, July 1990.

27. Susan Willis's discussion of mutilation and freedom in the literature of slavery appears in "Eruptions of Funk: Historicizing Toni Morrison," in Gates, *Black Literature*, 276–77 and 283n. Baraka on drug addiction: *Blues People* (New York: William Morris, 1963), 201–02. For a fuller analysis of the zombie myth, the coextension of life and death, and its socioeconomic significance in New World–African belief systems, see Maximilien Laroche's "The Myth of Zombi" in Smith, *Exile and Tradition*, 44–61.

28. Langston Hughes, "Wise Men," *Messenger* (June 1927): 11.

29. The simultaneity of grave and womb, in which the poet-shaman, stripped of "personal" identity, finds him- or herself in a transitional, almost larval state that is both prehuman and posthumous, is characteristic of what Victor Turner calls a "liminal" stage. The term comes from the Latin *limen*, or threshold, and refers to stages in rites of passage from youth to adulthood. The youths undergo such an in-between period to shed the known of childhood for the will-be-known of adulthood—they dwell in the unknown for a while, albeit a highly ritualized unknown. More generally, the word *liminal* could be used to characterize anybody or any condition that is "between two worlds," that is, Kaufman himself. I would argue, also, that lyric poetry is a liminal genre, because it mediates the world of polar opposites; better yet,

these opposites dissolve in poetry and certainly in the "Poetic state" in which Kaufman lived. See Turner, "Betwixt and Between," in *The Forest of Symbols* (Ithaca: Cornell University Press, 1967), 93–111.

30. Saint John of the Cross, *Poems*, trans. Roy Campbell (New York: Pantheon, 1951); *Poems*, trans. E. Allison Peers (London: Burns, Oates, 1961). Peers is the major translator of Saint John, whose translations were also published by New York Catholic houses Sheed and Ward and Image Books. Saint John, *Poems*, trans. John Frederick Nims (New York: Grove Press, 1959, and New Directions, 1967). Finally, Saint John was fully integrated into the secular literary mainstream when Penguin Books reprinted the Campbell translations in 1960.

31. Tales of Kaufman's impromptu recitations of Williams, Yeats, Eliot, Hughes, Lorca, and other canonical modernists are plentiful among his surviving North Beach milieu; the phrase "eidetic memory" is another epithet associated with his name. Al Young alerted me to the Tennessee Williams connection through an anecdote of his only meeting with Kaufman; the latter burst into Young's apartment reciting poetry at a furious pace, challenged Young to identify the poet, and then slapped his back pocket emphatically to indicate Williams's then-new volume, announcing in rejoinder to Young's profession of ignorance: "That's my man Williams!" Williams, *In the Winter of Cities; Collected Poems of Tennessee Wiilliams* (New York: New Directions, 1964), 11 ff.: "The marvelous children / cut their pure ice capers / north of time . . . I have seen them earlier than morning across the hall . . . I have seen their pencil-mark distinctions . . . I have seen them / never less than azure-eyed and earnest." In part 2 of the same poem occurs a passage that, according to Alix Geluardi, Kaufman in his declining years would call out from the screen door of his home in Fairfax: "O Mother of Blue Mountain boys / Come to the screen door, calling *Come home! Come home!*"

32. The collapse of time and space implied in a title like "North of Time" and the related phenomenon of synesthesia are two aspects of surrealism integrally connected to Kaufman's predicament. For a European Jewish analysis of synesthesia as an attempt to heal an imaginative consciousness fragmented under industrial capitalism, see Walter Benjamin, "On Some Motifs in Baudelaire," in *Illuminations*, ed. Hannah Arendt, trans. Harry Zohn (New York: Harcourt, Brace, 1968). For discussions of African surrealism and of the Caribbean as natural home of the surreal, see Léopold Sédar Senghor, *Prose and Poetry*, trans. John Reed and Clive Wake (London: Oxford University Press, 1965), 84–85, and André Breton's introduction to the first French edition of Césaire's *Cahier d'un retour au pays natal* (New York: Brentano's, 1947).

33. The issue of shock treatments is complex. Electroshock treatments were a common form of psychotherapy in the fifties and early sixties. Al-

though the term *elective* must be understood as highly qualified, given doctor-patient relations in those years (and particularly male doctor–female patient relations), several well-known poets underwent elective shock treatment (Robert Lowell, for example, and Sylvia Plath, both confessional poets); many others (Sexton, Roethke, Snodgrass, Berryman) were hospitalized for extreme emotional and mental disorders. Kaufman's shock treatments, however, differed significantly in that they were not only not elective in any sense but their administration was explicitly punitive. They were not intended as treatment for diagnosed psychic disorders but, in the context of his color and social class, functioned as consequences of the social and racial transgression of being "uppity" and confrontational.

Along with a positively engaged fascination with psychoanalysis and self-exploration, the era features a body of predominantly antagonistic-antipsychiatric literature concerning mental institutions, including Plath's novel *The Bell Jar* (1966), Kesey's *One Flew Over the Cuckoo's Nest* (1962), and Allen Ginsberg's *Howl* (1955), the last of which became, along with Kaufman's broadsides, the closest thing to a Beat "manifesto."

34. Elaine Scarry, *The Body in Pain: The Making and Unmaking of the World* (London: Oxford University Press, 1985).

35. Henry Louis Gates's analysis of the use of race as an index of difference is developed in his "Editor's Introduction: Writing 'Race' and the Difference It Makes," *"Race," Writing, and Difference* (Chicago: University of Chicago Press, 1986), 5. The Lorca translation offered here is Stephen Spender's and J. L. Gili's, from *The Selected Poems of Federico García Lorca*, ed. Francisco García Lorca and Donald Allen (New York: New Directions, 1955), 64. Alix Geluardi told me about the trip to Kesey's, describing it as a "very green, happy, family time" for Kaufman (author's notes, February 1986).

36. Robert Duncan, *Caesar's Gate* (Berkeley: Sand Dollar, 1972), xxxv. Judy Grahn also mentions the significance of green in gay culture, relating it to pre-Celtic, tribal societies in the British Isles (fairies) who suffered persecution and extinction because of their pagan worship (*Another Mother Tongue: Gay Words, Gay Worlds* [Boston: Beacon Press, 1984], 18). Although Kaufman was not gay, many of his major influences were or may have been (Lorca, Whitman, Rimbaud, Eliot, Crane), and he shares with gay culture the particular shaman-outlaw sensibility under discussion here.

37. Césaire, Edward Brathwaite, and Alejo Carpentier all use green in connection with magical events, transformations, or identification with nature. See especially Carpentier's *The Kingdom of This World*, trans. Harriet de Onis (New York: Alfred Knopf, 1957); and Eshleman and Smith's discussion of Césaire's use of African myths and his "vegetal" identification

in *The Collected Poetry*, ii, and especially "Les pur sang / The Thorough-
breds" ("I grow like a plant / remorseless and unwarped . . . / pure and
confident as a plant"), 90–103; and Brathwaite's *The Arrivants: A New World
Trilogy* (London: Oxford University Press, 1973). The color green comes
up consistently, but the most striking resemblance to Kaufman's use of
it comes in the final lines of "Tom" (16):

> not green alone
> not Africa alone
> not dark alone
> not fear
> alone
> but Cortez
> and Drake
> Magellan
> and that Ferdinand
> the sailor
> who pierced the salt seas to this land.

The quotes describing *Second April*, the title of which is taken from
Edna St. Vincent Millay, come from the blurb on the back of the broadside (San Francisco: City Lights, 1959). The Galvez Greens, George
Kaufman told me, was a park in New Orleans where amateur baseball
players, particularly African Americans who were prohibited from professional participation in the game, would come together to play
(author's notes, January 1991).

38. Saint John's Jewish parents were forced to convert under the terrors of
the Inquisition. According to legend, Crispus Attucks was the first African American—the first American at all—martyred in the American
revolutionary cause at the Boston Massacre, and he has come to be
known as the first African American hero. However, Hiller B. Zobel's evidence argues that Attucks, though he claimed to be a Barbadian by the
name of Michael Johnson, was posthumously declared to be Crispus
Attucks, a Black American, or a Native American member of the Natick
people from Framingham with or without African ancestry. He was
"variously described as a black and an Indian." This ambiguity may
have arisen from Attucks's own use of an alias but also from the use of
epithets referring to Attucks as a "stout molattoe," a "South Sea Islander," or as yelling like an Indian. James Clifford's research on the
Wampanoag Indians reveals that in eighteenth-century Mashpee, Massachusetts, a town that was and continues to be characterized by a large
Native American presence, the local term "South Sea Indian" initially referred to a Native American from south Massachusetts Bay (not from
the Caribbean); furthermore, due to a relatively high rate of Indian/Af-
rican–descent intermarriage and an admixture of Cape Verde islanders,

nonwhite people in Massachusetts were known simply as "colored," and the term "South Sea Islander" or "Indian" could have referred to anyone of any "colored" mixture, including African Americans, of whom fourteen were recorded in the 1776 Mashpee census. The population of that small part of upper Cape Cod shares with that of Louisiana, Kaufman's birthplace, the cultural and ethnic heterogeneity that at once underscores the play of multicultural difference and undermines attempts to essentialize "racial" *categories* of difference. I have come across several informal references to Kaufman's native ancestry. See Hiller B. Zobel, *The Boston Massacre* (New York: Norton, 1970), 191, 214, 350, and James Clifford, "Identity in Mashpee," in *The Predicament of Culture: Twentieth-Century Literature, Ethnography, and Art* (Cambridge: Harvard University Press, 1988), esp. 294–300. During a discussion on the point of Attucks's origins, Father Alberto Huerta, Kaufman's Spanish translator, suggested that both Kaufman and Attucks become, through the indeterminacy of their ancestry, "archetypes of resistance" for people of color in the West.

39. Federico García Lorca, "Los Negros," in *The Poet in New York*, trans. Ben Belitt (New York: Grove Press, 1955), 16–29.

40. Dante Alighieri, *Paradiso*, trans. John Sinclair (New York: Oxford University Press, 1939). The deconstructive significance of the white pearl on the white forehead (iii:10–16) has been pointed out by John Freccero (author's notes, March 1982).

41. The sun has another special significance for Kaufman; the Louis from whom the poet's home state took its colonial name was the "Sun King"; elsewhere Kaufman explicitly acknowledges the connection, punning on the new Louis (Armstrong) to whom the French king's legacy is bequeathed ("Like Father, Like Sun," AR, 35).

Poetics

and

Gender

16   Feminist Poetics and the Meaning of Clarity
Rae Armantrout

In 1978 Charles Bernstein asked me to write an essay responding to the question, "Why don't more women do language-oriented writing?" The first answer that came to mind was that, as an oppressed group, women have a more urgent need to describe the conditions of their lives. This answer, however, seemed rather facile. It implied, for instance, that there was another (that is, a non-language-centered) poetic style in use that could fully and clearly represent the nature of women's oppression. I wasn't convinced of that. The question of how best to represent women's social position remained open, and the answer must depend on what one assumed to be the cause of that position. Moreover, I didn't believe that women had ever shown a marked preference for writing poetry of an easily readable, because conventional, kind. From Dickinson to Stein to Riding-Jackson to the women I discussed in that 1978 essay (Susan Howe, Carla Harryman, and Lyn Hejinian), American women have been radical innovators.

Since 1978 the debate around the role of women and minorities in experimental writing has developed and grown richer, partly because of the influence of French thinkers such as Lacan, Irigaray, and Cixous, and partly because of the recent, varied proliferation of poetry by women. Despite these influences, however, it is still a widely held opinion that formal experimentation is the province (privilege?) of a ruling elite. Ron Silliman summarized this position in *Socialist Review* when he wrote:

> Progressive poets who identify as members of groups that have been the subject of history—many white male heterosexuals, for example—are apt to challenge all that is supposedly "natural" about the formation of their own subjectivity. That their writing today is apt to call into question, if not actually explode, such conventions as narrative, persona, and even reference can hardly be surprising. At the other end of this spectrum are poets who do not identify as members of groups that have been the subject of history, for they have instead been its objects. The narrative of history has led not to their self-actualization, but to their exclusion and domination. These writers and readers—women, people of color, sexual minorities, the entire spectrum of the marginal—have a manifest political need to have their stories

told. That their writing should often appear much more conventional, with the notable difference as to whom is the subject of these conventions, illuminates the relation between form and audience.[1]

I wonder, however, whether the nature of women's oppression can be best expressed in the poem that, as Silliman put it, "looks conventional." The conventional or mainstream poem today is a univocal, more or less plain-spoken, short narrative often culminating in a sort of epiphany. Such a form must convey an impression of closure and wholeness no matter what it says. It is, however, I believe, the core of woman's condition that she is internally divided, divided against herself. This division begins at the level of the symbolic. She is taught that she is Sleeping Beauty, waiting to be awakened (which can be exciting), but she also knows that she is "always already" awake. Lacan says that woman as Subject does not exist because she does not have access to the symbolic order or Law of the Father. He sees the phallus as the symbol of the symbolic order; woman's exclusion from it is then morphologically based. How the phallus myth became such a symbol has, of course, been widely debated. I will only say that the boy who thus invests his sexual organ must already have a prodigious power of symbolic identification. How did he acquire it? It is clear that there are many social forces at work in our culture that encourage the male child to identify himself with some external image of potency. From Father to Sherlock Holmes to Superman—the man is aggrandized into being. As for the girl-child's experience, I always knew that Wonder Woman was an afterthought. But these images, as Simone Weil has said, "are garments. They were ashamed of their nakedness. Lauzun and the office of Captain of Musketeers. He preferred to be a prisoner and Captain of Musketeers rather than go free and not be Captain."[2]

I don't think women's relatively difficult access to the "symbolic order" is inevitable, but, more important, I don't think it is necessarily all bad. Might there not be a moment of potential in that exclusion, a moment of freedom? Perhaps it is not, to quote Silliman again, "white male heterosexuals who are most apt to challenge all that is supposedly natural about the formation of subjectivity." As outsiders, women might, in fact, be well positioned to appreciate the constructedness of the identity that is based on identification and, therefore, to challenge the contemporary poetic convention of the unified Voice.

American feminist critics such as Sandra Gilbert, Susan Gubar, and Alicia Ostriker, however, continue to valorize the poem dominated by a single image or trope and a trustworthy (authoritative) narrational voice. (In her book, *Stealing the Language*, for instance, Ostriker praises Elizabeth Bishop for her "usual tone of trustworthy casualness."[3]) It is easy to see that such a style might be more immediately accessible than others. Is such a poem, then, best equipped to raise feminist issues? Let us use the following poem by Sharon Olds to examine the relation of style and tone to the experience of gender:

The One Girl at the Boys Party

When I take my girl to the swimming party
I set her down among the boys. They tower and
bristle, she stands there smooth and sleek,
her math scores unfolding in the air around her.
They will strip to their suits, her body hard and
indivisible as a prime number,
they'll plunge in the deep end, she'll subtract
her height from ten feet, divide it into
hundreds of gallons of water, the numbers
bouncing in her mind like molecules of chlorine
in the bright blue pool. When they climb out,
her ponytail will hang its pencil lead
down her back, her narrow suit
with hamburgers and french fries printed on it
will glisten in the brilliant air, and they will
see her sweet face, solemn and
sealed, a factor of one, and she will
see their eyes, two each,
their legs, two each, and the curves of their sexes,
one each, and in her head she'll be doing her
wild multiplying as the drops
sprinkle and fall to the power of a thousand from her body.[4]

Here Olds presents us with a version of female identity using her daughter as an example. This is the kind of exemplary narrative often seen in mainstream verse. The apparent narrative impulse, however, and the plain-speaking style that goes with it are almost immediately overwhelmed by a hyperextended and contrived metaphor. In the narrative frame, the daughter is a girl who is good at math; in the metaphor she is sealed, indivisible, a factor of one. Are these adjectives merely a code for virginal? Are we to assume that she is good at math because she is a virgin? Given the fact that the pressure against female achievement increases with adolescence, perhaps so. I don't think the poem really deals with this issue, however. The striking thing about this poem is how oddly phallic the image of the girl becomes. Her ponytail is a lead pencil; her suit is narrow. She is like Dickinson's narrow fellow in the grass. She divides the water with her hard body. Thus Olds makes her entrance into Lacan's proscribed symbolic order, using her daughter as a phallus. Is that what Olds meant to do? If so, are we meant to be troubled by this act of appropriation? Although Olds is not reputed to be a difficult poet, I'm unable to answer these questions. What the poem seems to imply is that people and things are serviceable, interchangeable, ready to be pressed into the service of metaphor. When Olds claims to know what is in her daughter's mind, claims there are "numbers bouncing in her mind like molecules of chlorine," I am repelled as by a presumptuous intrusion. This little girl is only a prop. There is no outside to this metaphoric system, no acknowledged division within it. It is imperialistic.

If women are outsiders in the symbolic order, if they experience psychic division, there is little sign of it in Olds's work. Such a totalizing metaphor as the one in this poem creates an impression of order and clarity by repressing any consciousness of dissent. Only information tailored to the controlling code is admissible; no second thoughts or outside voices are allowed. Whether such a poem is clear depends upon what one means by clarity. Certainly, it is quite readable.

There are, however, many women poets operating apart from this literally dominating methodology. I intend to discuss two of them: Lyn Hejinian and Lorine Niedecker. Though different in many respects, Hejinian and Niedecker both deal with a polyphonic inner experience and an unbounded outer world. Their poems may not be as easily readable as those of Olds, who has her imagistic ducks in a row, but clarity need not be equivalent to readability. How readable is the world? There is another kind of clarity that doesn't have to do with control but with attention, one in which the sensorium of the world can enter as it presents itself. Am I valorizing a long-enforced feminine passivity here? I think not. Writing is never passive. Hejinian's and Niedecker's poetry is subversive. Their poems are dynamic, contrapuntal systems in which conflicting forces and voices (inner and outer) are allowed to work.

In her essay "Strangeness," Hejinian describes her compositional technique as metonymic. She writes:

Metonymy moves attention from thing to thing; its principle is combination rather than selection. Compared to metaphor, which depends on code, metonym preserves context, foregrounds interrelationship. And again in comparison with metaphor, which is based on similarity, and in which meanings are conserved and transferred from one thing to something said to be like it, the metonymic world is unstable. While metonymy maintains the intactness and discreteness of particulars, its paratactic perspective gives it multiple vanishing points.[5]

The restless attention and the preservation of context that Hejinian associates with metonymy are in sharp contrast to Olds's tenacious and all-absorbing metaphor.

I want to discuss the role of metonymy, otherness, and counterpoint in one of Hejinian's works. Her most recent book is *Oxota: A Short Russian Novel*. It is a huge (292-page) book of poems, each poem a numbered chapter, rendering the experience of her travels in the old Soviet Union. But in what sense is it a novel? It certainly does not involve a constructed plot; that would be anathema to Hejinian. It does, however, deal with character and incident. The Russians in this novel seem to act and speak for themselves, often in surprising ways. Hejinian and her characters hear and mis-hear each other across mighty linguistic and cultural gaps. This work is a paradigmatic encounter with otherness and estrangement (and therefore with what it means to be oneself). I will quote chapters 120 and 171 from *Oxota*, with the caution that no excerpt can do justice to Hejinian's work because she always relies on repetition and recontextualization to create a dense weave of meaning. Nonetheless, the following is chapter 120:

One Spring Morning

Divination by clouds must be renounced under a colorless sky
Ostap produced a small cardboard device for divining mood
A staircase
The proportions of temperaments and moods
Zina ran a rag over the table
I turned on the gas for tea
It's a blind day, Zina said
Such a sky produces vast absent-mindedness
Here
Arkadii and then I produced gloom
I too, she said
The device had turned a foreboding greenish black
Papa, it's just a human revelation, said Ostap—such colors
    grow from temperatures and salt
You see?—heliotrope means passion.[6]

The poem poses the problem of knowledge in comic terms. A group of people wonder what moods they are in and what temperaments they have. A device for answering such questions—an emotion meter—is brought in by Ostap. It has replaced the older method of divination by clouds that was plagued by dependence on external conditions. The device proposes a universal standard. The reader can participate in the mixture of interest, light-heartedness, and skepticism produced by this party game. Does the fact that they all "produce gloom" mean that the device is working or that it isn't? The universal standard seems doomed from the start. The reader is allowed to realize that light-heartedness and doubt, gloom and passion, agreement and disagreement—these odd couples—are our permanent companions. Such a comic attempt to ascertain one's own and one's companions' mood is the opposite of Olds's single-minded occupation of her daughter's body and soul.

Like chapter 120, chapter 171, which is untitled, is structured around a counterpoint of oppositions:

> The hunt must accomplish necessity
> Then the hunt goes on
> The hunt goes one
> It widens on the frozen streets
> We're made a mother, our influence sweeps, we can draft our
>   opinions of poverty
> If one doesn't isolate the self, one doesn't experience
>   brevity
> Brevity wasn't Gogol's fear
> Nor Dostoevsky's, though his senses in event occurred from
>   many interruptions
> Such hunger is more memory than disappointment
> Such is our friendship with events
> We have words, and their things must remain in abeyance
> In current
> The shoppers dive—and I follow Zina
> Zina arrives with two chickens   (187)

I will go through the poem almost line by line, discussing its oppositions, metonymic connections, and the situation of its narrator. The rotating polarities of this chapter are forms of contraction and expansion: self and community, event and continuation. In the context of the book, the hunt is the search of Soviet women for life's necessities. What does it mean to "accomplish necessity"? It may mean that necessity itself becomes a goal, like motivation or the equanimity of habit. At any rate, accomplishment implies closure (contraction), but then the hunt goes on. The third line repeats the second, adding an "e" to "on," making it "one." The visual association of "on" and "one" is an example of metonymic adjacency and instability. Its meaning is complex. The addition of the letter becomes part of the ... ope of expansion while the meaning of the word one contracts this ... a single instance. Then the hunt, again, widens, part of a continuum ...

The middle section brings in the ... traditionally female activities of mothering and "sweeping up." These ... do these things may be inspired (by the promises of democracy); ... "their [their] opinions of poverty." These lines seem ironic, moment, ... bitter. "We have words and their things must remain in abeyance ... The things in abeyance might include meat and bread as well as equal ... and power. Still, the women in this work are strong. They ... the fun ...

The last four lines of this chapter exemplify the ... ity of metonymic connections Hejinian described in her essay. The ... is compared to "in abeyance," by semantic as well as syntactic ... ness. Something ... is not gone but in suspension—as if with ... in current." ... "current" with "sleep ... deep" a standard metaphor appears to be ... However, the ... that Zina, the ... to dive, arrives with two chickens ... fish, stops ... in our metaphoric tracks. The switch from metaphorical ... to observational fact is surprising. It's worth noting that in ... story, the hunt (or dive) the Russian women leads. This poem ... is a place where the Other is granted autonomy. Here, as in all her works, Hejinian finds ways (forms) in which opposites and discrepant life experience can be encompassed without being distorted by resolution.

Lorine Niedecker, who died in 1970, was not a contemporary of Hejinian or Olds. She was loosely associated with the Objectivist poets, including George Oppen and Louis Zukofsky, who emphasized in their essays the importance of sincerity, precision, and (thus) clarity. Niedecker is relevant to my argument because her poems (often feminist in their concerns) achieve a brilliant clarity, not because of the predominance of a single image or a subordinating metaphor, but because they follow the labyrinthian twists of thought and circumstance with great agility. Hers are poems of ambivalence, inner division, and second thoughts. Niedecker's poems mix social fact (problem) with epistemological question. Here is an untitled example:

I married

in the world's black night
for warmth
        if not repose.
        At the close—
someone.

I hid with him
from the long range guns.
    We lay leg
      in the cupboard, head
in closet.

A slit of light
at no bird dawn—
    Untaught
    I thought
he drank

too much.
I say   I married
        and lived unburied.
I thought—[7]

This poem, from *The Granite Pail*, is about a problem and a solution that turns into a problem. The original problem is the violence and danger (long-range guns) in America and the world. A kind of agoraphobia sets in and the poet wants to retreat, hide out, marry for security. Agoraphobia turns to claustrophobia soon enough. The lines "We lay leg / in the cupboard, head / in closet" are both grotesque and humorous. The question becomes, are marriage and domesticity really safe for women living in poverty and under patriarchy? "I married / and lived unburied. / I thought—" The reader will notice that "I thought" is repeated; it's an epistemological double take, a double step backward, a potentially infinite regression from solution to problem in which she discovers herself in the wrong more than once. Niedecker's visions seem open to revision. It's as if Olds (whom I imagine writing her poem in her car in a driveway, waiting for her daughter to emerge from the house where the party is being held) put down her pen, went in through the back gate, and caught her daughter in the act with one of those boys. How might that information be added to her poem?

It's interesting that the words that carry the charge of ambivalence and doubt in Niedecker's poem come in rhymed pairs: repose/close, untaught/thought, married/unburied. Rhyme usually conveys not only emphasis but a sense of closure and conviction. Here rhyme is used against the grain to point up paradox and doubt. It's funny, and risky, when weddings are performed by the mere coincidence of sound.

There is something asocial, misanthropic in Niedecker's work and life. She chooses, albeit ambivalently, to distance herself from the sources

of unjust power and inequity. I will read her poem, "My Life By Water,"
beginning with the fifth stanza:

to wild green
 arts and letters
  Rabbits

raided
 my lettuce
  One boat

two—
 pointed toward
 my shore

thru birdstart
 wingdrip
  weed-drift

of the soft
 and serious—
  Water (69)

Here (oddly green) arts and letters are attacked by animals, or animal-
like people. Human contact is minimal: "One boat / two— / pointed
toward / my shore." Is this a source of grief or relief? At any rate, it is
much mediated. Her "self" is difficult to locate or identify, placed, as it
is, in an extremely dynamic natural landscape. To reach her, human beings must make their way through "birdstart / wingdrip / weed-drift."
Here her trochaic, sometimes hyphenated words remind me of the
Pound of the early Cantos. But, unlike Pound, she does not pretend to
speak for Culture. Niedecker (like Dickinson) has done what she could
to place herself outside patriarchy, outside capitalism, outdoors. In this
poem I imagine her as the voice of the lake itself. One almost feels she
is teasing (teasing whom?) when she links soft with serious—a linkage
almost oxymoronic in patriarchal culture. Niedecker's sibilance is soft
and serious, subversive as water.

In the spirit of such subversion, I would like to raise some questions
in the place of conclusion. What is the meaning of clarity? Is something
clear when you understand it or when it looms up, startling you? Is
readability equivalent to clarity? What is the relation of readability to
convention? How might conventions of legibility enforce social codes?
Does so-called experimental writing seek a new view of the self? Would

such a view be liberating? Might experimental writing and feminism be natural allies? I think questions are most useful when left open. I will merely assert that there is more than one model of clarity. One might value a poem that could present the conditions of women's lives, but whose life is a single narrative or an extended metaphor? Metaphorically speaking, such poems are fenced yards. Is this the kind of control we should aspire to? What's on the other side of that fence?

NOTES

1. Ron Silliman, "Poetry and the Politics of the Subject: A Bay Area Sampler," *Socialist Review* 18.3 (1988): 63.

2. Simone Weil, *Gravity and Grace* (London: Ark, 1987), 21.

3. Alicia Ostriker, *Stealing the Language: The Emergence of Women's Poetry in America* (Boston: Beacon Press, 1986), 71.

4. Sharon Olds, *The Dead and the Living* (New York: Knopf, 1983), 79.

5. Lyn Hejinian, "Strangeness," originally published in *Poetics Journal* 8 (1989); reprinted as chapter 8 of this anthology.

6. Hejinian, *Oxota: A Short Russian Novel* (Great Barrington, Mass.: The Figures, 1991), 135.

7. Lorine Niedecker, *The Granite Pail: The Selected Poems of Lorine Niedecker*, ed. Cid Corman (San Francisco: North Point Press, 1985), 93.

17   The Pink Guitar
Rachel Blau DuPlessis

1. The torso, the turban, the turned-away face of Ingres's 1808 painting called *La Baigneuse de Valpinçon* or *The Large Bather* reappear, amid some clutter of bodies, in his later orientalized paintings: the *Harem Interior* (1828) and the *Turkish Bath* (1863).[1] The *Turkish Bath* has, in its great circle, more than twenty female figures, two black, two brown, all nudes, most erotic in conventional gesture, some overtly sexual: playful, lubricious, languid, narcissistic, preening, posturing for the viewer, fiddling with themselves. Whatever all those words mean. That foregrounded back-turned torso, the hidden, inward face of *The Large Bather* were clearly iconic for Ingres, and mysteriously so, for in its interiorized, nonfrontal "purity" it withdraws as much as is exposed in the tarted-up meat-markets of the later works. In his final use of this image, in *The Turkish Bath*, Ingres has given the female something to do. She is playing a hidden instrument, perhaps a mandolin. Her mandolin as hidden as her face.

These well-known images by Ingres, themselves palimpsests of each other, were further overwritten in Man Ray's tampered photo (1924) of Kiki of Montparnasse (a.k.a. a woman artist, Alice Prin).[2] Ray posed his model to evoke the Ingres and drew knowingly upon the progressively more overt orientalizing Ingres proposed for the torso, for Kiki is marked with her turban, her gypsylike earrings, and the exotic silk on which she sits, wide-hipped, a great shadow where her buttocks crack at the base of the spine. Her enfolded arms are hidden, her agency thereby removed. Her solid, curved, lush back has, imposed upon it, brilliantly placed sound holes, black f-openings (f-openings!) which recall the f for function in mathematical symbol, force in physics, forte in music, and the abbreviation both for female and for feminine gender in grammar. She is thereby made sonorous with cultural meanings. Once by Ingres, she becomes, by Man Ray, the *Violin d'Ingres*, the hobbyhorse that plays with the representation of women and sexuality without altering the fundamental relations of power, proprietorship, and possession so succinctly evoked.

Homme-age. I. ngres. These wry and salomesque swirls of veils of other texts. Man. Ray. I am dressed therein. I drape them, they drape over me, they are some of that thru which I see.

Violin d'Ingres. Violin d'anger. Vial in danger.

It "just means hobby in French" it "just means that women are his hobby" "you see, Ingres was really a painter, but he also played the violin" "sort of like our saying 'Sunday painter,' meaning they weren't really serious about"

I am deadly serious.

It is
I pick up this guitar. ↓ ↑ a woman! I say
I am

For when I pick it up, how do I "play" the women whom I have been culturally given?[3]

And find that the languages, the words, the drives, the genres, the keyboards, the frets, the strings, the holes, the sounding boards, the stops, the sonorities have been filled with representations that depend, in their deepest satisfactions, on gender and sexual trajectories that make claims upon me (and could compromise what I do).

My pink guitar has gender in its very grain. Its strings are already vibrating with gender representations. That means unpick everything. But how to unpick everything and still "pick up" an instrument one "picks" or plucks. How to unpick everything, and still make it "formal," "lyric," "coherent," "beautiful," "satisfying," when these are some of the things that must be unpicked. (Kristeva used the phrase "the impossible dialectic."[4]) The writing therefore becomes unpalatable, difficult, opaque, shifty, irresponsible, suspect, and subject to many accusations.

And could I change the instrument (restring, refret, rekey, rehole)

Invent
new sonorities

new probes
new combinations
new instruments

I struggle for a tread. Everything must be reexamined, reseen, rebuilt. From the beginning, and now. And yet I am playing. I am playing. I am playing

with a stringed lever.

2. How much insomnia can any one person stand?

It was an unbreakable drama of silence, to protect his obsessive and incessant speaking. By tag finishings. Polite uninterruptions. No rage. No, or little, spontaneous laughter. No puncture. The seriousness of his obsession and its vulnerability were patent. I had been commissioned with the unspoken responsibility of guardianship. If I had really "had it," I walked away. But that communicated, as it happened, nothing. Or very little. As far as I know. This whole thing was undiscussable, although it occurred for many years. My silence and little spurts of pleasant sound became a canvas, a terrain, a geography he could enter with his words. Irrespective of me. There was no me as me, the only "me" was a necessary, even crucial, occasion ("The Listener"). I certainly was not "attentive," except on the surface of my face. What, then, was "listening"? And what relation had it to really hearing? By which, and thru which repeated events much was damaged, and much was destroyed. And much was learned.

But most cannot be said.

They speak of bi-focal. Or the metaphor of "bi-lingual" for the multiple negotiations into the different cultural practices in which we are constituted. I am bi-silent, tri-silent, am made of dual/duel, trebled/troubled, base/bass, and impacted silences. Which test, temper, distort, and suspect fluencies. This blankness is social (silence is social as speech is social; silence, says Cora Kaplan, silence protects others' speech); it is gendered (or in relation to hierarchies of power).[5]

It is like the ground of the page. The blankness already filled with words thru which one negotiates. The page paradoxically both open and filled.

These rhythms—of start and stop, the praxis of randomness, the choices of motion over, under, through, small tunnelings and explosive rejections are a socially grounded set of structures. These structures or plots of feeling, and the feeling patently evoked (that I want to evoke) correspond to something, some outline of emotions and practices in the social and familial world—the shapes of the social structures in relation to the shapes of the art.[6]

" 'Tell me, given the options, where would your anger have taken you—where has it taken you?' "[7]

3. titles dog food telephone trash bags bath powder (harried mother) decaffeinated coffee dog food network cold medicine toothbrushes hemorrhoids (the rh for redness) toys skin moisturizer women's laxative network local department store tomatoes cookies sauces drain opener coffee stockings toys bacon cough medicine sales batteries (for toys) air freshener credits[8]

To enter from the shifting ground of interstices "between the acts"

I wanted not catharsis but engorgement, not mimesis but uncovering, not mastery by plurality, not a "form" but a method—of montage, of interruption . . .[9]

then ate, walked around, and left my light burning.

4. The man, he said, plays a transformative blue guitar. He bespeaks his difference in a flat, factual, and informative tone. "Things as they are / Are changed upon the blue guitar." The doubling of "are," by its very awkwardness, bolsters the authoritative apothegem. The balance of the situation as Wallace Stevens constructs it: he and them; artist and curious onlookers; a unique one and a group from which he is quite distinct. But still there is a fittedness between them and him, many and one, audience and Man of Imagination. The pleasant singsong aphorisms harness a nursery rhyme or folk melody to the depiction of modernist claims. This makes an endorsement of those claims. However, there is one distinction. The crowd says "A blue guitar." The man says "the blue guitar." The crowd allows for numerous like-colored instruments; the particular artist claims his is the one, perhaps a temporary myth that enables the writing, perhaps a more intellectually aggressive erasure of any other practitioners.

Into this scene gallumphs the female artist, hauling a different-colored "lyre, guitar, or mandolin." You want difference! she says, heehawing into all that elegance and ideological balance. I'll give you difference!

A pink guitar upsets a lot of balances. Including, and first of all, mine.

A rosy writing space, a rose-colored instrument, a new kind of pinko, which I hold and, by my play, try: to hear its sounds, to read its marks.

5. A woman writer is a "marked marker." She is marked by the cultural attributes of Woman, gender, sexuality, the feminine, a whole bolus of contradictory representations that are as much her cultural inscription as ours. She is marked by being variously distinguished—defined, singled out—by her gender. Others may note it even if she does not, or claims not to. She is marked by some unevenly effective traditions of both "unspeaking" and "unspeakable" female self, and by some also uneven set of incentives to cultural production, although she makes many many things. She—any woman—is culturally represented and interpreted (in all forms of representation from pop song to prayer, from B-movies to modern paintings). The works and the workings of these representations, in picture and text, in ideologies and discourses, mark or inflect precise configurations of her personal markings. Her own marks on a page—writing, drawing, composing; her capacity to make those marks, and what she can, or may, mark (or notice) will bear some marks of this matted circumstance of gender. Many possibilities for gender valences of a woman and her artworks are suggested by my remarks. As a "marked marker," a woman writer may not, or need not, be circumscribed or limited by gender, but she will be affected. Marks of these gender narratives can be made legible in feminist readings.[10]

For any woman, and especially for a cultural producer, a vital question is how to imagine herself, and how to imagine women, gender, sexualities, men, and her own interests when the world of images and, indeed, basic structures of thought have been filled to overflowing with representations of her and displacements of "her" by the representations others make. Thus: how to create an adequate work Of and About women (but never exclusively of or about women), while being By a woman, when strata of previous images of women, some quite culturally precious, suffuse and define culture, consciousness, and individual imaginations.

6. "If we *had* a non-patriarchal symbolic order, what would the language be in that situation? What would the non-patriarchal 'word' be?"[11]

7. What is entering this page space, and who is in charge here? What singing cometh, and who's singing what song? And is this "autobiography"? And so on. As very hungry herself, hungry, mostly open and thirsty. Given their thirst they step so lightly, O all right, Holstein, hard not to be sentimental. Once I wrote "giving birth to myself" sincerely. Yet I was never giving birth to myself but to a labor: cultural critique. "Birth" was always an odd metaphor, because what comes out at birth still enters into—already was entered into—nettings of social materials, is not formed in and of itself. Enters and is joined into multiple praxes. It is the newness of the child, the promise of something different, the child as utopian moment. . . . The cows line up, jump, heave their silly weight up. They hunch. Many bones, skin, nouns, many stomachs, and no memory, and the turmoil of regurgitations. Black muck. The stench of the manure pile, the flies against her flank. Soooo Bos. Whose bossy head was second in all the alphabets. In London, 1964, I tore a label (beer: Courage and Barclay) until the word that was thereby isolated in a broken circle is the rip of "RAGE." Make that a collage! The history and relationships, the memories associated with, the meanings, the linkages, the fissures among, the differentials, the fallow, and the shunned, if I were to pick up every item and associate across the bondage of memory (I have covered about twenty inches of space, and, honest enough, have already been singularly selective). . . . Stepping into the same diary twice. So pour the milk back over the cow. This fleisch is milchig. Cows not to convert. Cows not to channel. Cows not to instruct. Only the silky, and o they are milky.

8. Are the facts of my life (like "my best-selling novel." "my face staring from . . . " my rose-colored living room, with "its dramatic ochre entry." my feet tucked up under. "my casual yet my elegant." my half-finished cup of cold coffee.) here? I'd rather eat myself than be consumed. RAVISH myself. "I'm ravished." A slip for "I'm famished." Bad enough, but in front of my uncle?

It is a voice, it is, in fact, voices—and from where? If I said "midrash," it would have some cultural charm, although Hebrew was Greek to me, and Greek was a botch, and it did have something to do with "my father." But by midrash I mean the possibility of continuous chains of interpretation, thinking into

9. the relations of things. It's like when you open a catchall drawer and everything there including your hand, and your gesture, means something, has some history, of its making, and of its being there. A focused catchall. Where the production of meanings is, if not continuous, so interconnected that one has the sense of, the illusion of, the "whole" of life being activated, and raised to realizations and power. Thru language.

The today, the practice of thought   as the practice of writing. A pressure   a vision   a set of interactions   feeling curious   sometimes feeling despised.

the neon bleakness of desire in the mall. The blank page (or screen), the open silent space, and the words well up, as from a conduit. What writes?

"For it is against itself (and against the world as discourse) that the essay struggles. It drifts, it wanders in order to trace a map of its own questionings." [12]

So that my "fig newtons" stand for your "diaper pins" and it looks as if I am getting all of it, in. When the all is not whole (in the globular sense) but not fragmented (in the painful sense), but just slowly in pieces and together, wandering across the page, lunchboxes of violence rejected yet yearned for, night images right at the borders of sense and pleasure, red ribbons invested with symbolic intent, me in contradictory and "uneven development," and the one good Phillips head screwdriver in the house, where is it! It is not women only who live this way, but the sliding up and down the scales of importance, the destruction of scales of importance, the indomitable horizontality of structures, the insistence of nontranscendent heights, and material depths—

ARE

galloping and gulping, elusive, hubristic, subversive

the essay.

"as if hearing an 'other
meaning' always in the
process of weaving itself, of embracing
itself with

words, but also of getting rid of words
in order
not to become fixed, congealed in them"
(L. Irigaray)
"constructivist writing" (C. Bernstein)
"Semiotic/symbolic" writing (J. Kristeva)
multidiscursive, interrogative, polyvocal, heterogeneous,
interactive
recognizing "subjectivity" (S. Griffin)
no more "confines of relevance" (B. Dahlen
citing G. Steiner)
"moments of linguistic transgression"
(M. Jacobus)
associative, critical
"to question the apparatuses" (G. C. Spivak)
"make it impossible for a while to
predict whence,
whither, when, how, why . . . " (L. Irigaray)
a motion captured in motion
"vatic bisexuality" (H. Cixous)
hysterical, site-specific
as interested meditation
"atopical or hypertopical mobility of the
narrative voice" (J. Derrida)
"washed by heteroglot waves from all
sides" (M. Bakhtin)

the site of many centers
a nontransparent textuality
"form as an activity" (L. Hejinian)
contradictory
its multifariousness AS resistance

It is a Way: of talking, of listening; the intense calm of everything connected, everything ruptured, the pleasure of a babble of

10. Touch on any part, on any sight, a sock, a hole, a wall, pictures, a
resistance to museums, yet pictures always on the wall, and defining
eras by those pictures. Wander looking for the odd lots, stop in front of
something smallish, a little unofficial, by someone who did the best he
could. That's all. Or a self-portrait by a woman no one ever hears of. She.

Sincere, intransigent. Or a few squares floating, by an escapee. One or two lines on a page. That's all I need . . .

the entrance into this otherness is fraught discourses come through us and we choose and are chosen by them. But "Otherness" is a dangerous metaphor. Some "I" am very much here, working in a set of spaces and practices. So never writing in the illusion that this play is only textual.[13] This is serious; in many ways its play is a measure of its grief. The material figure of the writer-gendered-female stands, in her political, visceral need

$$\text{for the } \left\{ \begin{array}{l} \text{writing} \\ \text{reading} \end{array} \right. \text{of this} \left\{ \begin{array}{l} \text{reading} \\ \text{writing} \end{array} \right.$$

"Otherness" is a cultural construct like "the feminine," against which and through which I struggle. It is something attractive and confirming that these textual practices are called "feminine," but the argument draws sub rosa on the power of those binary formations that it would reject and overturn. The feminine is where I am colonized. The feminine is the dream of an elsewhere, a someplace uncolonized. The feminine is orange/blush/pink/peach/vibrant red "in" this year. The feminine is a short blue one, or a long plaid one, but never a short plaid one or a long blue one. It is that kind of knowledge.

But to intermingle the utopian "feminine" space (of religious and asocial aura, of "ultimates") with an attracted loathing for the blush/red etc. of feminine with a rooted feminist lust for material social justice in the quirky voice of a person mainly gendered female—well, this is approximately the practice. Have I "undone the binary"? Was it in my power? I did make trinaries, quadrinaries. I have made permanent quandaries.

II. The practice of anguage. The anguish of language. The anger of language. "A 68er," said Meridith Tax: and this is what it means to work.[14] Inchoate in the sixties, coming to focus abruptly in 1968, the idea that culture was a political instrument, that language, hegemony, discourse, form, canon, wrongness, allowable and taboo were always historically formed and were notions constantly debated, reaffirmed, and disallowed. That culture was an arena of struggle.[15] And furthermore, to see from where I was standing meant to see with a specifically formed kind of female eyes. Cross-eyed; cock-eyed. Funny evocations. (It was the female that was the most startling to think about, because it was that around which the most intense contradictions of affirmation and denial occurred.) If one sees inside one's gender, class, race, sexuality, nationality, and these from and engaged with one's time, then culture is a process of rereading and rewriting, a practice. Soon after, by 1969–70, I had seen in a startled and famished (ravished) flash the necessity of the feminist cultural project. No less than the reseeing of every text, every author, every canonical work, every thing written, every world view, every discourse, every image, everything unwritten, from a gender perspective.

This is a major cultural project, intimately linked to the practice of questioning powers of all sorts, to the uses of culture in all arenas, to the nature, or definition of culture. And this is a central project of our generations (of women), this feminist cultural practice.

12. June 1979. Some anger. That is what is framing and saturating this writing. There is an anger and about what? about my life, and how to be female at this moment, the challenge of creating a new self which I am failing. ██ ████████████████████████████ the problem of masculine and feminine ██ ████ paralyzing conflict. Cut off, burned out ████████████ ██ ██ ██ ████ the defenses which are the only thing I nurture.

But how can I insist on anger? ████████████████████████ ████████████████████ Even in these "essays" there must be some decorum! ████████████████████ The reader does not need to be informed of the despair of the writer, a despair compounded by (of) the very difficulty of writing at all, a kind of self-hatred, existing in proportion to the fascination of this writing which I am driven to use while also saying, and hearing others say, it is "too easy" and therefore suspect.

("I have a sense of the writer drunk on her own shrill voice") ("confessional") ("repeatedly questioned the integrity") ("not authentic") ("too experiential") ("healthy self-doubt nonexistent") ("garish") ("untransmuted, not art") ("personal") ("narcissistic")

and therefore suspect.

Don't apologize and too trite and too personal and too busy and too hard and too easy. You get the picture? Being no dope and "reader, it was not to have ended here."[16]

13. Therefore the metaphor of quest. A trek. A climb. A struggle toward— the transfigured. Probably the largest shift in this writing, between the late seventies of its beginning, and the continuations of the mideighties was a muting of the visionary sense of transfiguration. What substituted was something closer in, closer to the ground, examining what I really felt, no matter the contradictions—as in Duchamp. If sincerity led to unresolvable contradiction, the very datum became pivotal. The loss of the quest for (what was essentially personal) "wholeness" was no loss. But what that quest said by using the term remains vital. And what was that? Was it a desire for justice? Was it hope? (Pretend these terms have been properly "deconstructed" yet still, though battered, can be sustained or understood.)

So, quest. (butterfly, spinning sac, threads, cocoons) like an earthworm changing into an airplane. Pupa, chrysalid, butterfly; silkworm weaving the silkword "metamorphosis." Psyche. Haunted by psyche, and hounded by the glories of that telos: Monarch! Swallowtail! Mourning Cloak!

That "psyche" image bound for glory fueled my ambitions and is reflected in certain essays of the 1970s; it also appears in the work of H.D. But there was something about quest narratives that I became uncomfortable practicing. That modified my practice, or drove it underground. The plots and triumphs were too given, and they drew for their appeal on structures of feeling (apotheosis, climax, ending, transcendence) of which I was agnostic, suspicious, and would no longer take for granted. Did quest end? Was there triumph? fulfillment? synthesis? I began to think of these as religious structures, but worse, of the writing that might practice them as "sermon." Sermon, as opposed to essay. They did not narrate the ongoingness and mixed struggles of the writing of rupture and critique: that practice.

My butterflies change. A cabbage white is plain enough: persistent, ubiq-uitous, almost the mosquito of butterflies, and as textual as a little page with its shimmering black spots. Though not to make "textual" the new sentimentality.

And "textual" heras: Arachne, challenging even the goddess with her weaving which depicts the rapes of women by gods. Philomel, muted, mutilated, weaving the depiction of her rape and mutilation; Procne, the reader. Penelope, buying time for personal loyalties and choices with the studied, strategic destruction and remaking of her weaving. Names, identified as constructive agents, figures who make and unmake texts, or, to use an old-fashioned word, works. Who are workers in "writing."

Their strategies of resistant representation.[17] The emphasis to fall on the struggle to make the works. The career of that struggle. But/and the uto-pian project is not ended.

14. 23 November 1981. "I" cannot be displaced I cannot I just got here! feminists the last humanists, yet I have become decentered. I am a walk-ing margin the first decentered creature in the sunny depths harsh crisp color and a triangular shape blurred. Yes. Where there is looking. So hard to compare. But always "I" or I, know.
For when I say "I," I hear voices,
I want to say I (and also some other pronouns),
some me itted,
or she me'd,
yet when I say I
I mean I,
and yet it is only a smallest part of the I that I can use.
And when I say I what might be meant is
"i"
meaning a quarter I or an eighth,
to measure it,
maybe with a little round heart on top to dot it,
to dot the 12-year-old self,
in turquoise ink or a round blank circle of the wide-eyed girl

what I   indeed

So whan I say I
what
I mean is an i
which is it   speaking
it speaks as I speak
(and Creeley knew it and Rimbaud)
squeaked speaked.

At doing the I as she,
the I as me,
a her, a we, a they, a them,
doing the I as he . . . as you
anarchic, wayward, flaw-ridden, maddening
As much no-me as me.

Deployed in playful anguage.

There is no I when I "speak"
but places of gridded and bubbling social voice
a tone   a humming thru a "G" perhaps
or a "B flat"
girl and boy
a sol fa la, a solfeggio moment of the resonant throat
no I no "I" no i
just an mmmmmmm trying to figure justice.

15. I start writing. "January 1982. To honor the plurality, porousness, and
mobility of discourses; to combine personal and analytic; to reveal
thinking as a heart-felt activity; to bring 'subjective' and 'objective' into
dialectical exchange and mutual translation; to name the interests creating interpretation; to reveal the revealer; to fabricate the text as an instance of social and ideological need . . . "

To multiply the tones, the positions, to saturate oneself inside the existing heterogeneity of speaking

To account for the different textures and discourses of like, to include
the angry whine of a child, to bring decorums, pleasures, and taboos
into fructifying mixtures (and a great deal is left out; a whole, different
set of options; they are, in part, censored by the writer).

And "I don't write fiction." ("You're kidding!")

Fighter bombers patrol the borders, cruising along a line drawn in the sky, and it is a low line, 300 meters, they say. Accidents happen. F-16s. Why is it necessary to "train" pilots to fly that low? Below radar, it is said. Is there a prediction that they will be someday flying somewhere, some place so obscure and miserable that it does not have radar, some "them" underneath the rumbling machine? Perhaps they are really showing "us," those in whose name this occurs regularly. The job of these planes is control of their own nation and its neighbors by a banalized terror. The terror is the teasing half-memory, half-visualization, of what is possible from those planes, what is carried inside those planes, and who is, with serious casualness, flying them.

But I am writing. A deliberate intermingled generative. Some voice that thinks, thinking, the process of picking and unpicking, returning to a generative body of work. A voice that accumulates the pressures of its situation and spurts it in allusions to genres: poems, essays, narratives, epigrams, autobiographies, anthologies, handbills, marginalia, glosso-lalia, wire services

writing in the interstices of texts, boring thru the white between the lines, scribbling on the margins
rhythms (of responding   of ceasing   of picking up again)

converging and dispersing sightlines

not finished not caring

16. Her body was more or less her own—she could experience some of its feelings, but as she gridded those feelings or sensations with words, she participated in a cultural knowing in which female bodies have been variously type-cast. Her body was traversed with these ideas, sometimes they were "water off a duck's back," sometimes "they stuck like leeches." Her body, her mind, while they remained private possessions of a named person, were certainly saturated with, brimming with concepts, dunked in the culture, stained with it, the little vascicles, fascicles of "self." All cells are cultural cells.

What body, then, is speaking? Does her body speak? Is it a body of words? Of cultural ideas? A body of language? A body of words inflected with its female body? A body of pulses, impulses, fissured, hopeful and afraid inside of and dyed with a complex of rich and contradictory readings of the female body? A body to whom things have happened AS a female body, rape, for instance, and other tragedies still. Does this statement immediately color things (do you see red; have I willfuly made you see red)? If this language appears defenseless, unguarded, if it mentions certain blood, if it strips itself and waits for impulsive behaviors to strike, waits for the play of association, if it provokes feelings of bemused recognition at quotidiam interruptions

then what? From what is she writing?

Does simply saying "female writer" reduce her to gynecology, when, by the same token, there is no way to take her as anything but a female body speaking words inflected by her being constructed female. In awe. A body speaking words in awe, marginality and resistance.

I would not erase or discount her (or anyone's) experiences $\left\{ \begin{array}{c} \text{in a} \\ \text{as a} \end{array} \right\}$ body.

I would not discount male experiences in a body. How do we know "things" except mediated? Is not the "body" part of this mediation? An African American writer "writes the body" when he speaks of the multiplicity of experiences that follow from his melanin-laden skin.

But one wants, by the same token, no one reduced to body. Isn't isolating "the body" conceptually still an unhelpful gesture from a long-criticized, though apparently inexhaustible, mind/body split that should immediately be declared moot? I am admiring the quality and extent of my own uncertainty. But, yet, do women (do men) write from the body? Does that question remain important? Why was that question posed in that way?

If the effect of this question is to make female writing "natural," downplaying agency and artistic choice, if the question freezes "body" as if there were just one giant Female Body effectively present throughout time and in representation . . . then? If the effect of this question is to free taboos, accept the unacceptable, and promote knowledge that female writing, female emphasis may differ . . . then? If the question allows for the variety and play of that potential difference, but does not penalize if it is "absent" . . . then?

And/But the body is not the body. It is language, it is writing, it is inscription, it is representation, it is hungry, it is sick, it is in political networks of care or rejection, it is mediated, it is not purer, more primal

than what?

One cannot write "the body" for there is no one spot where she can satisfactorily denominate "the body," although it would be folly to go to the other extreme and deny the specificity of her body. One can write bodies, languages of body, languages embodying positions. One can write of bodies crisscrossed, scarred and striated with their matter, their material situations, their embodiments. The body? I think the question occurred that way as a stage on a way to saying "socially and culturally embodied practices."

But then what?

17. Women's shoes.

"Dear Parent: Your daughter's name was referred to us as possibly being an excellent candidate for the 1989 LITTLE MISS PHILADELPHIA GLAMOUR GIRL PAGEANT. . . . Because of her beauty, poise, and appearance I am VERY interested in learning more about her. If you feel she would like to gain some Modeling Experience, Portfolio's, and Talent Scholarships, all you need to do is fill out the enclosed information sheet and submit that along with a recent shapshot of her. . . . There is NO PERFORMING TALENT in this pageant. Judging will reflect Beauty, Photogenticity, and Poise. . . . Our winner's will reign over Philadelphia, Pennsylvania as the 1989 LITTLE MISS PHILADELPHIA GLAMOUR GIRL, and will be making guest appearances at her convenience. We feel this opportunity will open doors for every little girl involved as our judges are all highly respected and well known in their fields of beauty, modeling, and theatrical activities."

Information sheet question: "Does she enjoy having her photograph taken and posing for them?"

Questions: What is "photogenticity"? And who is them?

I am also interested in the possessive's being confused with the plural.

18. I am not writing the personal. The odd and somewhat debased notion of having a voice, or finding a voice, of establishing a consumable personality complete with pix, of engaging in self-revelation, even of engaging in autobiography is precisely the opposite of my deepest feelings about his work. I am not finding a voice, I am losing one.

When I write, I am not writing for myself, or even (grosso modo) as myself. I am writing the voice, a voice, one bricolaging, teasing voice of a working. A raw exhilaration. At ruptures. At relativizing the "universal." At creolizing the "metropole." At writing a feminist-feminine-female bolus of scrapping and loving orts into existence. Writing not as personality, writing as praxis. For writing is a *practice*—a practice in which the author disappears into a process, into a community, into discontinuities, into a desire for discovery.

Pluralist
discontinuous
interplays
of *interference*[18]

not just "language" but "pursuit"[19]

shrill, hysterical, sentimental, washing up then dirtying, obtuse, querulous, unsuccessful, critical, synthetic, ruining

"In other words, in the realm of thought, imprudence is a method."[20]
"Art should expose, not remove contradictions."[21]

I am doing work, and what kind of work is it? for whom am I working? and what am I bringing into being?[22]

19. I am not a writer, as such. I am a marker; maybe that is a way to say it. All the signs that emerge on the page (I put them here, they came here through me) (some were already there, in the weave of the paper, no tabula rasa)

demand my reading. The responsibility for making words is the responsibility for reading. The practice of writing is already a reading, of the writing already written, of the saturated page, smitten with the already-written, in

language, anguage. I am some character in a little folk tale, call me "a-reading-a-writing."

20. A desire to change the authority relations to the text and possibly to language

A practice of interference, or trying to stop a normal, normative, coherent, flowing, and consumable practice.

I am not even writing essays. I am writing, to take seriously this typo, essaus. Essaus. They are hairy and ungainly things, coming a little too late, and earnestly with their little savory stew, and not thinking quickly or slickly. My birthright? A kind of confusion about what happened. About tricks and tests. a rachel goes backward into her generations, writes essaus: Some justice there.

The struggle on the page is not decorative.

I am writing a kind of reverie, a textual practice of feminist leverage, a counter TO culture as it exists, a sincere artifice that raises

21. Say imprecision (I cannot know what I need to know)   say grief (I can barely mourn and yet I am filled with mourning for the lost, for the costs, for the dead of incomplete revolutions)   say repressed arousal (the shards of injustice around us, we stumble on, pierced by)   say longing (for another kind of identity, another kind of nation, other sets of social relations)   say inarticulation   from blinding sun to blinding rain   scotoma, scotamata   dizzy, dizzy, dark areas or gaps in the field of vision, those things that float across the eyes, like fast scudding clouds. Is that what we want? what we can barely see?

Wo and Woe. wie wee que qui ween queen wean. A mental image of myself strumming tunelessly unstopping, at the same time weeping wee and quee. I stop it and resist it. I stop. But I have written some of it.

August 1989
from materials
as early as 1979

1. "Orientalized" with reference to Edward Said, *Orientalism* (New York: Pantheon Books, 1978). The overlayering of representations and ideologies of the "Oriental" onto the "female" produces intense motifs of otherness from a "Western" perspective: "threatening excess," "insinuating danger," "unlimited sensuality," and a degenerate seductiveness. Citations from Said, 56–57, 207. Linda Nochlin discusses aspects of Western ideologies in nineteenth-century "Orientalized" art, including the Orient's function as a "fantasy space" for the ideological projection of absolute erotic possession, in "The Imaginary Orient," *Art in America* 71 (May 1983): 118–31, 186–91.

2. Or perhaps "a.u.a."—also unknown as. Shari Benstock, in *Women of the Left Bank, Paris 1900–1940* (Austin: University of Texas Press, 1986), makes this point in her Janet Flanner chapter, 109. She is used as a marker in a poem about the sexual fulfillments possible—or impossible—at home; see William Carlos Williams, poem 9 of *Spring and All* (1923), in *The Collected Poems of William Carlos Williams* (New York: New Directions, 1986–88).

3. I do not mean by my trope of "pink" to efface the brown that is usually the color of guitars and thus the brown skin that is the marker of other cultural experiences.

4. Julia Kristeva, *About Chinese Women*, trans. Anita Barrows (New York: Urizen Press, 1977), 38.

5. Cora Kaplan, *Sea Changes: Culture and Feminism* (London: Verso, 1986), 79–80.

6. It is useful to think of the psychosexual situations in being female as setting up a specific possibility of a writing practice. Thus Luce Irigaray connects "self-affection" (women's bodies autoerotic in situ) with the practice of openness and plurality in writing, or the rejection of analytic strategies of reversal that repeat hierarchies as generating textual tactics of border crossing, disruption, and rupture. These analyses are in *This Sex Which Is Not One*, trans. Catherine Porter with Carolyn Burke (Ithaca: Cornell University Press, 1985), 68, 78, 122, 222. These motifs of "disruptive excess" (78) will answer all theories that conceptualize the feminine as lack or deficiency (a task also undertaken by Cixous). But it is also clear that the only plausible praxis within hegemony is a writing as critique especially of the deepest mechanisms of meaning. Thus the rupture of language, syntax, sequence, order, structures, and genres in what has been called avant-garde writing is absolutely parallel and interlocked with such feminist practices as are effervescently called forth by Irigaray in a manifesto-like passage in *Speculum of the Other Woman*, trans.

Gillian C. Gill (Ithaca: Cornell University Press, 1985), 142. What then distinguishes a feminist practice of writing from any vangard use is the infusion of these rhetorical practices with urgent and continuous confrontations with the political and representational oppression of wome/an, with an eye to enacting their end. So there is telos after all.

7. Robert Glück, *Jack the Modernist* (New York: Gay Presses of New York, 1985), as cited by Aaron Shurin in a talk called "Narrativity," Painted Bride Arts Center, Philadelphia.

8. Slightly selected and modified list of the commercial sequences, taken from Louise Spence, "Life's Little Problems . . . and Pleasures," *Quarterly Review of Film Studies* (Fall 1984): 307–08. Her appendix cataloged an episode of *The Young and the Restless* in November 1981.

9. Echoes of Walter Benjamin on epic theater and Jane Gallop on Lacan.

10. It is not women's poetry only that is gendered. Men's poetry, what is called "poetry," is saturated with gender, can hardly make a move, make an image, build a poem, make a climax, without a she. Even the most innovative and experimental works cannot move forward, past a certain point in their unrolling, cannot write themselves without a traditional positioning of women. We are just beginning to be able to see male writing as, despite its claims, partial, marked, not gender neutral, not universal. The intellectual implications are terrific. As Elaine Showalter remarks: "The defamiliarization, or problematization, of masculinity is one of the most important tasks facing feminist criticism in the next decade. It is still a tacit assumption in literary studies that gender is significant for one sex only, indeed, that it is a kind of sophisticated, postfeminist code word for women. While *femininity* is now accepted as a construct with relevance to literary analysis, *masculinity* is treated as natural, transparent, and unproblematic. . . . From the perspective of a poststructuralist feminist critique, such blindness and lack of self-reflection is itself a sign of phallocentrism" ("The Other Bostonians: Gender and Literary Study," *Yale Journal of Criticism* 1.2 [Spring 1988]: 182).

11. Peter Wollen and Laura Mulvey, "*Penthesilea, Queen of the Amazons:* Interview," *Screen* 15.3 (Autumn 1974): 128.

12. Laurent Mailhot, "The Writing of the Essay," *Yale French Studies* 65, The Language of Difference, Writing in QUEBEC(ois) (1983): 76.

13. This said with strong reference to Nancy Miller, "Arachnologies: The Woman, the Text, and the Critic," in *Subject to Change: Reading Feminist Writing* (New York: Columbia University Press, 1988). Also in an intersection with Elizabeth Meese's brilliant and emboldening observations on "difference" and "deconstruction" in their uses for feminist theory: "We will need to speak of *** in place of 'woman'—that something the meaning or nonmeaning of which our phallocentric structure will not

allow us to say. And this unimaginable, imaginary something, this understanding of ***, this 'feminism(s)'—the effects of freedom/utopia itself—are not so different from what appears to be deconstruction's utopic project as it asserts its motion toward the unthinkable, unknowable point(s) beyond the system it deconstructs" (*Crossing the Double-Cross: The Practice of Feminist Criticism* [Durham: University of North Carolina Press, 1986], 87).

14. In *In These Times* (Summer 1989).

15. These ideas were focused by the work of Raymond Williams, especially *Marxism and Literature* (Oxford: Oxford University Press, 1977).

16. The final line, from Tillie Olsen's *Yonnondio: From the Thirties* (New York: Delacorte, 1934); the writing was made by me in 1982, reflecting the psychological struggles of the mid- to late-1970s, myself wary and struggling with a writing mode that was being rejected by others, whose voices appear here.

17. Really a triple homage to critics Nancy Miller, Jane Marcus, and Susan Stanford Friedman here: Nancy Miller in her devastating unraveling of Barthes and J. Hillis Miller's denial of agency and authorship in her "Arachnologies," which resists the erasure of "gendered subjectivities" as author; Jane Marcus, who proposes the soral relation of Philomel and Procne as a model for empathetic reading of female texts. In response I have political questions about casting only the Procne figure, of these two, as "the voice which demands justice." See Marcus, "Still Practice, A/ Wrested Alphabet: Toward a Feminist Aesthetic," in *Feminist Issues in Literary Scholarship*, ed. Shari Benstock (Bloomington: Indiana University Press, 1987). And Susan Stanford Friedman, "The Return of the Repressed in Women's Narratives," *Journal of Narrative Technique* 19.1 (Winter 1989): 141–56, proposes "Penelope's web"—a theory about the meaning of drafts and serial texts that offers an approach to the "textual unconscious," to repressed materials, to censorship, and thereby "integrates considerations of the author, the text, and history" (156).

18. "A counter-practice of interference"—counter to the studied holding apart of politics and the humanities/arts. Defined by Edward Said as at least including a breaking of academic field boundaries; an insistence on the political meaning of all acts and choices within the humanities; the denial of the "subjective and powerless" role of literature; a use of representation to "tell other stories than the official sequential or ideological ones produced by institutions of power." The praxis of interference is, as Hal Foster pinpoints, more than a subversive gesture; it is a "practice of resistance." Edward Said, "Opponents, Audiences, Constituencies, and Community," in *The Anti-Aesthetic: Essays on Postmodern Culture*, ed. Hal Foster (Port Townsend, Wash.: Bay Press, 1983), xiv, 155, 157, xv–vi.

19. James Hillman about Clayton Eshleman, "Behind the Iron Grillwork," *Temblor* 6 (1987): 100.

20. Said, citing Gaston Bachelard, using Tristan Tzara, in *Beginnings: Intention and Method* (New York: Basic Books, 1975), 40.

21. Brecht, somewhere.

22. I am echoing Meaghan Morris here, *The Pirate's Fiancée: Feminism, Reading, Postmodernism* (London: Verso, 1988), e.g., 7, 111–12, but I might as well be echoing Charles Bernstein, *Content's Dream: Essays 1975–84* (Los Angeles: Sun & Moon Press, 1986), or Gail Scott, *Spaces Like Stairs: Essays* (Toronto: Women's Press, 1989). Scott: "the job of imagining what I now think of as a 'writing subject' in-the-feminine. Not the 'self' as a (feminist or otherwise) predetermined figure, but a complex tissue of texts, experience, evolving in the very act of writing" (11). Or Kathleen Fraser, *Each Next: Narratives* (Berkeley: The Figures, 1980): "Walking up to a new edge, I discovered in myself an old mute. But I stayed, allowing my curiosity to teethe on the silence. A hope for mutation? A belief in mutability" (54).

These Flames and Generosities of the Heart:
       Emily Dickinson and the Illogic of Sumptuary Values
       Susan Howe

> Spirit cannot be moved by Flesh—It must be moved by spirit—
> It is strange that the most intangible is the heaviest—but Joy and
> Gravitation have their own ways. My ways are not your ways—[1]

An idea of the author Emily Dickinson—her symbolic value and aesthetic function—has been shaped by *The Poems of Emily Dickinson; Including variant readings critically compared with all known manuscripts*, edited by Thomas H. Johnson and first published by the Belknap Press of Harvard University in 1951, later digested into a one-volume edition, to which I do not refer because of Johnson's further acknowledged editorial emendations. For a long time I believed that this editor had given us the poems as they looked. Nearly forty years later, *The Manuscript Books of Emily Dickinson*, edited by R. W. Franklin and again published by the Belknap Press of Harvard University in 1981, and *The Master Letters of Emily Dickinson*, also edited by R. W. Franklin, in 1986, this time published by the Amherst College Press, show me that in a system of restricted exchange, the subject-creator and her art in its potential gesture were domesticated and occluded by an assumptive privileged Imperative.

*   *   *

A CONCRETE COMMUNITY OF EXCHANGE AMONG PEERS

1951: "1860: Alignment of words less regular, letters in a word sometimes diminishing in size toward the end, which gives an uneven effect to the page. *No important changes in form*" [my italics].[2]

1986: "Standard typesetting conventions have also been followed in regard to spacing and punctuation. No attempt has been made to indicate the amount of space between words, or between words and punctuation, or to indicate, for example, the length of a dash, its angle, spatial relation to adjoining words or distance from the line of inscription. Dashes of any length are represented by an en dash, spaced on each side.

Periods, commas, question marks, ending quotation marks, and the like, have no space preceding them, however situated in the manuscripts. Stray marks have been ignored."[3]

*   *   *

FELLOWS

1958: Thomas H. Johnson, Introduction to *The Letters of Emily Dickinson*.

Since Emily Dickinson's full maturity as a dedicated artist occurred during the span of the Civil War, the most convulsive era of the nation's history, one of course turns to the letters of 1861–1865, and the years that follow, for her interpretation of events. But the fact is that she did not live in history and held no view of it past or current.[4]

1986: Ralph W. Franklin, Introduction to *The Master Letters*.

Dickinson did not write letters as a fictional genre, and these were surely part of a much larger correspondence yet unknown to us. In the earliest one, written when both she and the Master were ill, she is responding to his initiative after a considerable silence. The tone, a little distant but respectful and gracious, claims few prerogatives from their experience, nothing more than the license to be concerned about his health. . . . The other two letters, written a few years later, stand in impassioned contrast to this. . . . In both she defends herself, reviewing their history, asserting her fidelity. She asks what he would do if she came "in white." She pleads to see him. . . .

A drop of ink mars the top of the third page [first letter], but it may have come after she had written *an awkward predication* [my italics] further down the same page:

> Each Sabbath on the
> sea, makes me count
> the Sabbaths, till we
> > will the
> meet on shore   — and
> whether the hills will
> look as blue as the
> sailors say—

This would require obstrusive correction, and what was to have been a final draft became an intermediate one.[5]

1951: T. H. Johnson, Introduction to Emily Dickinson's *Collected Poems*, called "Creating the Poems: The Poet and the Muse."

It would thus appear that when Emily Dickinson was about twenty years old her latent talents were invigorated by a gentle, grave young man [Benjamin Franklin Newton] who taught her how to observe the world. . . . Perhaps during the five years after Newton's death she was trying to fashion verses in a *desultory* manner. Her muse had left the land and she must await the coming of another. That event occurred in 1858 or 1859 in the person of the Reverend Charles Wadsworth. . . . A volcanic commotion is becoming apparent in the emotional life of Emily Dickinson. . . . Except to her sister Lavinia, who never saw Wadsworth, she talked to no one about him. That fact alone establishes the place he filled in the structure of her emotion. Whereas Newton as muse had awakened her to a sense of her talents, Wadsworth as muse made her a poet. The Philadelphia pastor, now forty-seven, was at the zenith of his mature influence, fifteen years married and the head of a family, an established man of God whose rectitude was un-questioned. . . . By 1870 . . . [t]he crisis in Emily Dickinson's life was over. Though nothing again would wring from her the anguish and the fulfill-ment of the years 1861–1865, she continued to write *verses* throughout her life [my italics].[6]

1971: *Webster's Third New International Dictionary.*

VERSE: 3 a (1): metrical language: speech or writing distinguished from ordinary language by its distinctive patterning of sounds and esp. by its more pronounced or elaborate rhythm. (2): metrical writing that is distin-guished from poetry esp. by its lower level of intensity and its lack of essen-tial conviction and commitment. [many writers . . . who have not aimed at writing poetry—T. S. Eliot] (3): POETRY [that gives immortal youth to mor-tal maids—W. S. Landor] 4 a (1): a unit of metrical writing larger than a single line: STANZA.

*   *   *

CIRCLES

In 1985 I wrote a letter to Ralph Franklin, the busy director of the Beinecke Rare Book and Manuscript Library at Yale University, to sug-gest that *The Manuscript Books of Emily Dickinson* shows that after the ninth fascicle (about 1860) she began to break her lines with a consistency that the Johnson edition seemed to have ignored. I was interested because Franklin is currently editing the new *Poems of Emily Dickinson: Including vari-ant readings critically compared with all known manuscripts* for Harvard Univer-sity Press. I received a curt letter in response. He told me the notebooks were not artistic structures and were not intended for other readers;

Dickinson had a long history of sending poems to people—individual poems—that were complete, he said. My suggestion about line breaks depended on an "assumption" that one reads in lines; he asked, "what happens if the form lurking in the mind is the *stanza?*" [my italics]

*   *   *

Thomas H. Johnson's *The Poems of Emily Dickinson* did restore the poet's idiosyncratic spelling, punctuation (the famous dashes), and word variants to her poems. At the same time, Johnson created the impression that a definitive textual edition could exist. He called his introduction "Creating the Poems," then gave their creator a male muse-minister. He arranged her "verses" into hymnlike stanzas with little variation in form and no variation of cadence. By choosing a sovereign system for her line endings—his preappointed Plan—he established the constraints of a strained positivity. Copious footnotes, numbers, comparisons, and chronologies mask his authorial role.

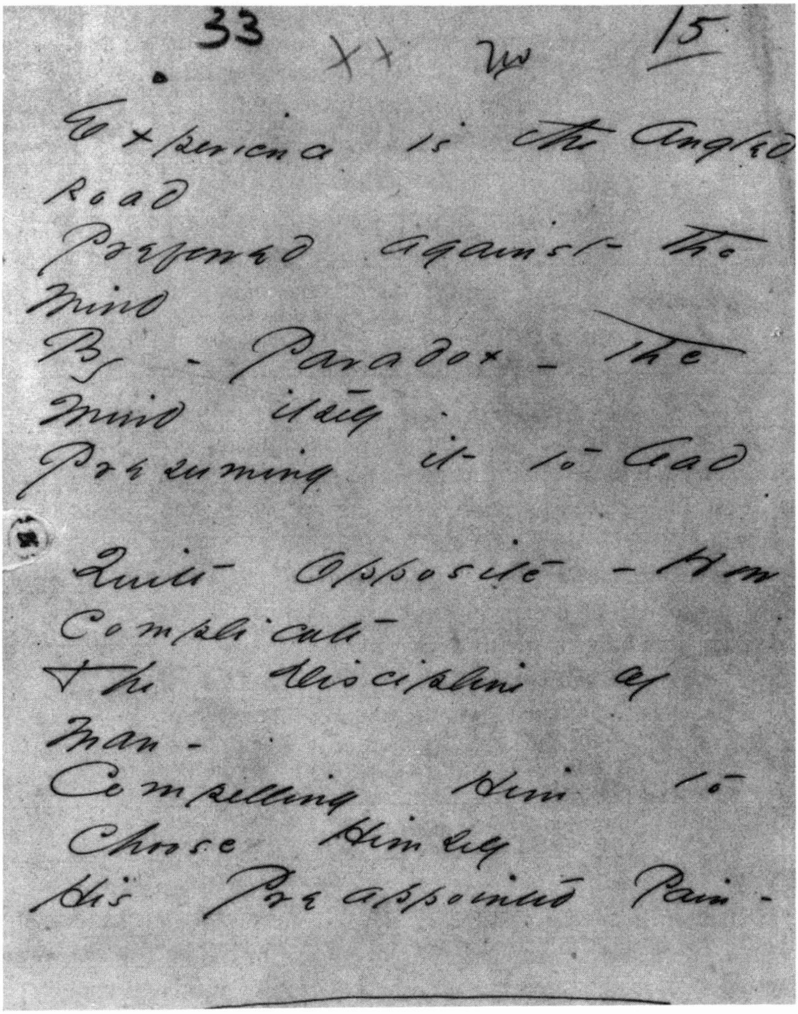
33 XX 2w 15

Experience is the Angled
Road
Preferred against the
Mind
By - Paradox - The
Mind itself -
Presuming it to lead

Quite Opposite - How
Complicate
The Discipline of
Man -
Compelling Him to
Choose Himself
His Preappointed Pain -

Here is a typographical transcription of Dickinson's manuscript version:

Experience is the Angled
Road
Preferred against the
Mind
By - Paradox - The
Mind itself -
Presuming it to lead

        Quite   Opposite   - How
        Complicate
        The   Discipline   of
        Man -
        Compelling   Him   to
        Choose   Himself
        His   Pre appointed   Pain   ⁻

The Manuscript Books of Emily Dickinson complicates T. H. Johnson's criteria for poetic order.
    These lines traced by pencil or in ink on paper were formed by an
innovator.
    This visible handwritten sequence establishes an enunciative clearing
outside intention while obeying intuition's agonistic necessity.
    These lines move freely through a notion of series we may happen to
cross—ambiguous articulated Place.
    At the end of conformity on small sheets of stationery:

        When Winds hold Forests in their Paws _
        ⸝ The Firmaments ⸜ are still –
        ⸝ The Universe--is still ⸝

    Deflagration of what was there to say. No message to decode or finally
decide. The fascicles have a "halo of wilderness." By continually interweaving expectation and categories they checkmate inscription to become what a reader offers them.

        Publication_is   the Auction
        Of   the   Mind   of Man -
        Poverty - be   justifying
        For   so   foul   a   thing

        Possibly -but We -would
        rather
        From   Our   Garret   go
        White -Unto the White Creator_
        Than   invest - Our Snow -

        Thought   belong   to Him who
        gave it   -
        Then -- to   Him Who bear
        Its Corporeal   illustration - Sell
        The   Royal   Air _

In the Parcel ⁻ Be the Merchant
Of the Heavenly Grace ⁻
But reduce no Human Spirit
To Disgrace of Price ⁻

Use value is a blasphemy. Form and content collapse the assumption
of Project and Masterpiece. Free from limitations of genre, Language
finds true knowledge estranged in itself.

Distance ⸜ be Her only
⁺ Motion –
If tis Nay ⸜ or Yes –
Acquiescence ⸜ or Demurral ⁻
Whosoever guess –

⁺ He ⸜must pass the Crystal⁺Angle
That ⁺ obscure Her face ⸗
He ⸜ must have achieved in
person
Equal Paradise ⸜

⁺ too ⁺ Swelling ⁺ fitter for
the feet ⸜ Ever could endow –
⁺ claim ⸜ Signal ⁺⸜ first ⁺⸜ limit
⁺ divide ⁻

*   *   *

1991: *An editor's query.* "You need to give the reader some thoughts about
making use of the words at the end of the 'poem proper' (in this case,
I think, beginning with 'too swelling fitter for'). Are we to attach these
words as alternatives to certain words in the 'poem'?; i.e., *where does 'too'*
go? What am I to do with it?"

This is a good question: Thomas Johnson reads these words as alternatives.

1840: Noah Webster, *An American Dictionary of the English Language.*[7]

TOO, *adv.* [Sax, *to.*]
    1. Over: more than enough; noting excess; as, a thing is *too* long, *too*
short, or *too* wide; *too* high; *too* many; *too* much.

    His will is *too* strong to bend, *too* proud to learn. *Cowley.*

    2. Likewise; also; in addition.

A courtier and a patriot *too*   Pope
        Let those eyes that view
   The daring crime, behold the vengeance *too.*   Pope

3. *Too, too.* repeated, denotes excess emphatically; but this repetition is not in respectable use.

[The original application of *to*, now *too*, seems to have been a word signifying a great quantity; as, speaking of giving *to* much; that is, *to* a great amount. *To* was thus used by old authors.][8]

                    *   *   *

REARRANGEMENT

Much critical and editorial attention has been given to Dickinson's use of capitalization and the dash in her poems and letters, while motivating factors for words and phrases she often added to a "poem proper," sometimes in the margins, sometimes between lines, but most often at the end, have aroused less interest. Since the Johnson edition was published in 1951, it has been a given of Dickinson scholarship that these words represent nothing more than suggested alternatives for specific words in the text the poet had frequently marked with a cross.

Ralph Franklin says that after 1861 these possibilities for alternate readings are a part of the structure of the poems she transcribed and bound together, and his edition of *The Manuscript Books* shows this to have been the case.

After 1861, Dickinson's practice of variation and fragmentation also included line breaks. Unlike Franklin, I believe there is a reason for them.

This space is the poem's space. Letters are sounds we see. Sounds leap to the eye. Word lists, crosses, blanks, and ruptured stanzas are points of contact and displacement. Line breaks and visual contrapuntal stresses represent an athematic compositional intention.

This space is the poet's space. Its demand is her method.

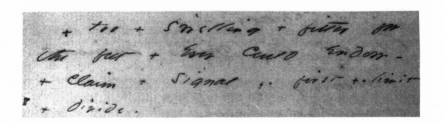

One of Thomas Johnson's contributions to transmission of the hand-written manuscripts into print was to place these words, sometimes short phrases, at the end of a poem, as Dickinson had done. But he couldn't leave it at that. This textual scholar-editor, probably with the best intentions, matched word to counterword, numbered lines as he had reduplicated them, then exchanged his line numbers for her crosses.

3. True] too	17. ask] claim
6. Loaded] Swelling	21. Motion] Signal
13. Fitter feet—of Her]	25. He] first
fitter for the feet	25. Angle] limit
16] Ever could endow—	26. obscure] divide—[9]

Emily Dickinson's writing is a premeditated immersion in immediacy. Codes are confounded and converted. "Authoritative readings" confuse her nonconformity.

In 1998 these manuscripts still represent a Reformation.

*   *   *

SWELLING

NOAH WEBSTER:

SWELL. v.t. To increase in size, bulk, or dimensions of; to cause to rise, dilate, or increase. Rains and dissolving show swell the rivers in spring, and cause floods. Jordan is swelled by the snows of Mount Libanus.[10]

*   *   *

A COVENANT OF WORKS

"The flood of her talent is rising."[11]

The production of meaning will be brought under the control of social authority.

For T. H. Johnson, R. W. Franklin, and their publishing institution, the Belknap Press of Harvard University, the conventions of print require humilities of caution.

Obedience to tradition. Dress up dissonance. Customary usage.

Provoking visual fragmentation will be banished from the body of the "poem proper."

Numbers and word matches will valorize these sensuous visual catastrophes.

Lines will be brought into line without any indication of their actual position.

An editor edits for mistakes. Subdivided in conformity with propriety.

A discreet biographical explanation: unrequited love for a popular minister will consecrate the gesture of this unconverted antinomian who refused to pass her work through proof.

Later the minister will turn into a man called "Master."

R. W. FRANKLIN: "Although there is no evidence the [Master] letters were ever posted (none of the surviving documents would have been in suitable condition), they indicate a long relationship, geographically apart, in which correspondence would have been the primary means of communication."[12]

Poems will be called letters and letters will be called poems.

"The tone, a little distant but respectful and gracious, claims few prerogatives."[13]

" . . . the Hens
     lay finely . . . " (epigraph to letters, part 1, vol. 1)

Now she is her sex for certain editors picking and choosing for a general reader reading.

NOMINALIST and REALIST
"Into [print] will I grind thee, my bride."[14]

Franklin's facsimile edition of *The Manuscript Books of Emily Dickinson* shows some poems with so many lists of words or variants that even Johnson, who was nothing if not methodical, couldn't find numbers for such polyphonic visual complexity.

What if the author went to great care to fit these words onto pages she could have copied over? Left in place, seemingly scattered and random, these words form their own compositional relation.

R. W. EMERSON: "I am very much struck in literature by the appearance that one person wrote all the books; as if the editor of a journal planted his body of reporters in different parts of the field of action, and relieved some by others from time to time; but there is such equality and identity both of judgment and point of view in the nar-

rative that it is plainly the work of one all-seeing, all-hearing gentle-
man. I looked into Pope's Odyssey yesterday: it is as correct and elegant after our canon of to-day as if it were newly written."[15]

Antinomy. A conflict of authority. A contradiction between conclusions
that seem equally logical reasonable correct sealed natural necessary.

*1637: Thomas Dudley at Mrs. Ann Hutchinson's examination by the General Court
at Newton:*
"What is the scripture she brings?"[16]

An improper poem. Not in respectable use. Another way of reading.
Troubled subject-matter is like troubled water.

*   *   *

FIRE MAY BE RAKED UP IN THE ASHES, THOUGH NOT SEEN.

Words are only frames. No comfortable conclusion. Letters are scrawls,
turnabouts, astonishments, strokes, cuts, masks.
    These poems are representations. These manuscripts should be under-
stood as visual productions.
    The physical act of copying is a mysterious sensuous expression.
    Wrapped in the mirror of the word.
    Most often these poems were copied onto sheets of stationery pre-
viously folded by the manufacturer. The author paid attention to the
smallest physical details of the page. Embossed seals in the corner of
recto and verso leaves of paper or part of the fictitious real.

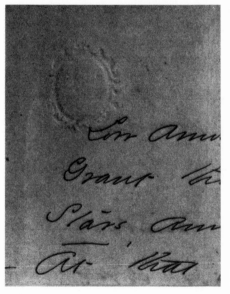

basket of flowers
C. V. Mills, capitol and, CONGRESS
capitol in oval
CONGRESS   above capitol
flower in oval
G & T in eight-sided device
G. & T. in oval
LEE MASS.
PARSONS PAPER CO
queen's head above L (laid)
queen's head above L (wove)
WM above double-headed eagle

Spaces between letters, dashes, apostrophes, commas, crosses form networks of signs and discontinuities.

"Train up a Heart in the way it should go and as quick as it can twill depart from it."[17]

Mystery is the content. Intractable expression. Deaf to rules of composition. What is writing but continuing.

Who knows what needs she has?
The greatest trial is trust.
Fire in the heart overcomes fire without.

*   *   *

Franklin's notes to set 7 tell us: "On her inventory of the manuscripts obtained from her mother [Mabel Loomis Todd], MTB [Millicent Todd Bingham] recorded a small slip laid inside sheet A 86-3/4 bearing only the word 'Augustly!' The paper is wove, cream, and blue-ruled."[18]

*   *   *

DISJUNCT LEAVES

Emily Dickinson almost never titled a poem.
    She titled poems several times.
    She drew an ink slash at the end of a poem.
    Sometimes she didn't.
    She seldom used numbers to show where a word or a poem should go.
    She sometimes used numbers to show where a word or a line should go.
    The poems in packets and sets can be read as linked series.
    The original order of the packets was broken by her friends and first editors so that even R. W. Franklin—the one scholar, apart from the Curator of Manuscripts, allowed unlimited access to the originals at Harvard University's Houghton Library—can be absolutely sure only of a particular series order for poems on a single folded sheet of stationery.
    Maybe the poems in a packet were copied down in random order, and the size of letter paper dictated a series; maybe not.
    When she sent her first group of poems to T. W. Higginson, she sent them separately but together.
    She chose separate poems from the packets to send to friends.
    Sometimes letters are poems with a salutation and signature.
    Sometimes poems are letters with a salutation and signature.

If limits disappear where will we find bearings?

What were her intentions for these crosses and word lists?

If we could perfectly restore each packet to its original order, her original impulse would be impossible to decipher. The manuscript books and sets preserve their insubordination. They can be read as events, signals in a pattern, relays, inventions, or singular hymnlike stanzas.

T. W. Higginson wrote in his preface to *Poems by Emily Dickinson* (1890): "The verses of Emily Dickinson belong emphatically to what Emerson long since called 'The Poetry of the Portfolio,'—something produced absolutely without the thought of publication, and solely by way of the writer's own mind. . . . They are here published as they were written, with very few and superficial changes; although it is fair to say the titles have been assigned, almost invariably, by the editors."[19]

But the poet's manuscript books and sets had already been torn open. Their contents had been sifted, translated, titled, then regrouped under categories called, by her two first editor-"friends": "Life," "Love," "Nature," "Time and Eternity."

*   *   *

WHITE LINES ON A WHITE STONE

On September 12, 1840, Ralph Waldo Emerson wrote to Elizabeth Hoar: "My chapter on 'Circles' begins to prosper, and when it is October I shall write like a Latin Father."[20]

"The one thing which we seek with insatiable desire is to forget ourselves, to be surprised out of our propriety, to lose our sempiternal memory and to do something without knowing how or why; in short to draw a new circle. Nothing great was ever achieved without enthusiasm. The way of life is wonderful; it is by abandonment."[21]

*   *   *

OVERFLOW

1891: Twenty years after the event, T. W. Higginson, with Mabel Loomis Todd, the first editor of Emily Dickinson's poetry, recalled one of his two meetings with the poet.

The impression undoubtedly made on me was that of an excess of tension, and of an abnormal life. Perhaps in time I could have got beyond that somewhat overstrained relation which not my will, but her needs had forced upon us. Certainly I should have been most glad to bring it down to the level of simple truth and every-day comradeship; but it was not altogether easy.[22]

TOO. adv. [Sax. to.]

Over; more than enough; noting excess; as, a thing is too long, too short, too wide, too high, too many, too much.

*   *   *

COMING TO GRIPS WITH THE WORLD

In 1986, Ralph Franklin sent me a copy of *The Master Letters of Emily Dickinson*, published by the Amherst College Press. Along with *The Manuscript Books*, this is the most important contribution to Dickinson scholarship I know of. In this edition, Franklin decided on a correct order for the letters, showed facsimiles, and had them set in type on each facing page, with the line breaks as she made them. I wrote him a letter again suggesting that if he broke the lines here according to the original text, he might consider doing the same for the poems. He thanked me for my "immodest" compliments and said he had broken the letters line-for-physical-line only to make reference to the facsimiles easier; if he were editing a book of the letters, he would use a run-on treatment, as there is no expected genre form for prose. He told me there is such a form for poetry, and he intended to follow it, rather than accidents of physical line breaks on paper.

*   *   *

As a poet, I cannot assert that Dickinson composed in stanzas and was careless about line breaks. In the precinct of Poetry, a word, the space around a word, each letter, every mark, silence, or sound volatizes an inner law of form—moves on a rigorous line.

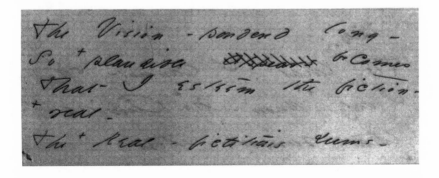

I wonder at Ralph Franklin's conclusion that these facsimiles are not to be considered as artistic structures.

How can this meticulous editor, whose acute attention to his subject matter has yet to be deciphered in the neutralized reading even her fervent admirers give her, now repress the physical immediacy of these spiritual improvisations he has brought to light?

> A   Man   may   ⸍make
> a   Remark -
> In itself ˎa ⸌quiet thing
> That   may   furnish   ⸍ the
> Fuse unto   a   Spark
> In   dormant   nature - lain -
>
> Let   us   ⸍divide ˎwith
> skill -
> Let   us   ⸌discourse -with
> care -
> Powder exists in ⸌Charcoal
> Before   it ⸌exists   in   -
> Fire -
>
> + drop ⸍ tranquil   ⸍ ignition
> ⸍ deport   ⸍ disclose
> ⸍ Elements   - sulphurets
> ⸍ express

Simple reflection should cast light on the inauthentic nostalgia of *A Portrait of the Artist as a Woman*, isolated from historical consciousness, killing time for no reason but arbitrary convenience, as she composes, transcribes, and arranges into notebooks or sets over a thousand visionary works.

During her lifetime this writer refused to collaborate with the institutions of publishing. When she created herself author, editor, and publisher, she situated her production in a field of free transgressive prediscovery.

It is over a hundred years after her death; if I am writing a book and I quote from one of her letters or poems and use either the Johnson or Franklin edition of her texts, I must obtain permission from and pay a fee to

The President and Fellows of Harvard College and the Trustees of Amherst College.

"is this the Hope that opens and shuts, like the Eye of the Wax Doll—
Your Scholar—"

"This is the World that opens and shuts, like the Eye of the Wax
Doll—"[23]

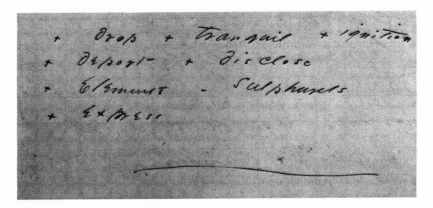

Poetry is never a personal possession. The poem was a vision and gesture before it became sign and coded exchange in a political economy
of value. At the moment these manuscripts are accepted into the property of our culture their philosopher-author escapes the ritual of framing—symmetrical order and arrangement. Are all these works poems?
Are they fragments, meditations, aphorisms, events, letters? After the first
nine fascicles, lines break off interrupting meter. Right-hand margins
perish into edges sometimes tipped by crosses and calligraphic slashes.

This World is not Conclusion -
A ⁺ Species stands beyond ˎ
Invisible ، as Music ˎ
But positive ، as Sound ˗
It beckons ، and it baffles -
Philosophy ⸜ dont know ˎ
And through a Riddle, at the last˷
Sagacity ˎ must go -
To ⁺guess it ، puzzles scholars -
To gain it Men have borne
Contempt of Generations
And Crucifixion، shown ˗
Faith slips ˎand laughs، and rallies˷
Blushes، if any see˷
Plucks at a twig of Evidence˷
And asks a Vane، the way -

Much   Gesture   from   the
Pulpit _
Strong _ Hallelujahs   roll _
Narcotics   cannot   still   the
Tooth
That   nibbles   at   the   soul _

 ⨯ A sequel -   ⨯ prove it _
   ⨯ Sure   + Mouse _ .

Define the bounds of naked Expression. *Use.*

All scandalous breakings out are thoughts at first. Resequenced. Shifted. Excluded. Lost.

"She reverted to pinning slips to sheets to maintain the proper association." [24]

Oneness and scattering.

Marginal notes. Irretrievable indirection—

Uncertainty extends to the heart of replication. Meaning is scattered at the limit of concentration. The other of meaning is indecipherable variation.

In his preface to *The Poems of Emily Dickinson*, called "Creating the Poems," T. H. Johnson referred to her "fear of publication," as many others have done ever since. He called her poems "effusions." During the 1860s, "[h]er creative energies were at flood, and she was being overwhelmed by forces which she could not control." [25]

"Over; more than enough; noting excess; as, a thing is *too* long, *too* short, *too* high, *too* many, *too* much."

Wayward Puritan. Charged with enthusiasm. Enthusiasm is antinomian.

54

The Sea said
"Come" to the Brook—
The Brook said
"Let me grow"—
The Sea said
"Then you will
Be a Sea"—
"I want a Brook—
Come now"—
The Sea said
"Go" to the Sea.
The Sea said
"I am he
You cherished"—
"Learned Waters—
Wisdom is stale—
To me" _____

1. Emily Dickinson, prose fragment #44, in Thomas H. Johnson and Theodora Ward, eds., *The Letters of Emily Dickinson*, 3 vols. (Cambridge: Harvard University Press, 1958).

2. Thomas H. Johnson, ed., *The Poems of Emily Dickinson* (Cambridge: Harvard University Press, 1951), 1:liv.

3. R. W. Franklin, ed., *The Master Letters of Emily Dickinson* (Amherst: Amherst College Press, 1986), 10.

4. Johnson and Ward, *Letters of Emily Dickinson*, 1:xx.

5. Franklin, *Master Letters*, 5, 11.

6. Johnson, *Poems of Emily Dickinson*, xxi–xxiv.

7. Emily Dickinson owned an 1844 reprint of Webster's 1840 edition. The family owned the 1828 two-volume first edition. Webster, a friend of the Dickinson family, was a resident of Amherst, helped to found Amherst College with Samuel Fowler Dickinson, and served on the board of the Amherst Academy with Edward Dickinson.

8. Noah Webster, *An American Dictionary of the English Language* (Springfield, Mass.: George and Charles Merriam, 1852), 1159–60.

9. Johnson, *Poems of Emily Dickinson*, 649.

10. Webster, *American Dictionary*, 1118.

11. Johnson and Ward, *Letters of Emily Dickinson*, 2:332.

12. Franklin, *Master Letters*, 5.

13. Ibid., 5.

14. Ralph Waldo Emerson, *Essays, Second Series* (Boston and New York: Riverside Press, Houghton Mifflin, 1876), 241.

15. Ibid., 232.

16. David Hall, ed., *The Antinomian Controversy, 1636–1638: A Documentary History* (Middletown, Conn.: Wesleyan University Press, 1968), 338.

17. Johnson and Ward, *Letters of Emily Dickinson*, prose fragment 115, 3:928.

18. Ralph W. Franklin, ed., *The Manuscript Books of Emily Dickinson*, 2 vols. (Cambridge: Harvard University Press, 1981), 2:1387.

19. Mabel Loomis Todd and T. W. Higginson, eds., *Poems by Emily Dickinson* (Boston: Roberts Brothers, 1890), iii–v.

20. Ralph Waldo Emerson, *Essays, First Series* (Boston and New York: Houghton Mifflin, Riverside Press, 1865), 433.

21. Ibid., 321.

22. Johnson and Ward, *Letters of Emily Dickinson*, 2:342.

23. Ibid., 553, 554.

24. Franklin, *Manuscript Books*, 2:1413.

25. Johnson, *Poems of Emily Dickinson*, xviii.

My title is the seven last words of Emerson's essay called "Circles":
"'A man,' said Oliver Cromwell, 'never rises so high as when he knows
not whither he is going.' Dreams and drunkenness, the use of opium
and alcohol are the semblance and counterfeit of this oracular genius,
and hence their dangerous attraction for men. For the like reason they
ask the aid of wild passions, as in gaming and war, to ape in some
manner these flames and generosities of the heart."

I have tried to match the poems in type, as nearly as possible, to the
Franklin edition of *The Manuscript Books*. In translating Dickinson's handwriting into type I have not followed standard typesetting conventions. I
have paid attention to space between handwritten words. I have broken
the lines exactly as she broke them. I have tried to match the spacing between words in the lists at the end of poems. I have not been able to
pay attention to spaces between letters. I think that in the later poetry
such spacing is a part of the meaning. Dickinson's frequent use of the
dash was noted in the Johnson edition, but he regularized these marks.
I know that in some books printed during the nineteenth century, variant readings were sometimes supplied at the end of a page, and they
were marked by a sort of cross. *The History of New England from 1630 to
1649*, by John Winthrop, edited by James Savage, and published in Boston in 1826, is a good example of such practice; however, if there were
more than two words, a number was used for the second one, and in
other books the number of crosses increased for each word. Emily Dickinson had enough humor to read these variants as found poems. She
was her own publisher and could do as she liked with her texts. These
were the days of Edward Lear and Lewis Carroll; liberties were taken in
print.

The bottom of a page of the Savage edition of Winthrop's *History*
looked like this:

some other place, which they both consented to, but still the
difficulty remained; for those three, who pretended themselves
||conferred|| ||²step|| ||³we|| ||⁴taking|| ||⁵her||

Reason 2. All punishments ought to be just, and, offences varying so
much in their merit by occasion of circumstances, it would be unjust to inflict punishment upon the least as upon the greatest.
||theft|| ||²presumptuous||

These manuscript books and sets represent the poet's "letter to the

world." The discovery of these packets and sets galvanized her sister
Lavinia into action. If Dickinson sent some of the poems in letters to
friends, she also left these packets in a certain order. It is doubtful, to
say the least, whether her various correspondents would have bothered
to collect and then publish her poem-letters.

I have followed Johnson's choices for capitals, although I feel I could
argue with his choices at times. I have been allowed access only to the
originals of two manuscript books, and as a result I wouldn't dare to. In
a review of *The Poems of Emily Dickinson*, published in the Boston Public Library Quarterly, July 1956, the poet Jack Spicer suggested such marks might
have been meant as signs "of stress and tempo stronger than a comma
and weaker than a period." The new critical edition must reconsider
such questions. In the early fascicles, Dickinson frequently uses exclamation marks. Around fascicles 6–12, as she begins to break her lines in a
new way and to regularly insert variant words into the structure of her
work, nervous and repetitive exclamation marks change to the more abstract and sweeping dash. Sometimes the way she crosses her t's (and
this no printed version could match) seems to influence the length of
the direction of the dash. The crosses she added to her texts when she
included variant word possibilities should also be translated into print.
The most frequent argument in favor of Johnson's changing the line
breaks is the assumption that Dickinson (thrifty Yankee spinster) broke
her lines at the right-hand margin because of the size of the paper she
was using. In other words, she ran out of space and wanted to save paper. Close examination of the Franklin manuscript edition shows that
she could have put more words onto a line had she wished to; in some
cases she did crowd words onto a line. As she went on working,
Dickinson increased the space between words, and eventually the space
between letters. If you follow Johnson's edition, you get the idea that
there was no change in form from the first poem in fascicle 1 to the
last poems in the sets.

In the long run, the best way to read Dickinson is to read the facsimiles, because her calligraphy influences her meaning. However, Franklin's edition is too expensive for most people, and then there is the
added difficulty of reading handwriting. I think her poems need to be
transcribed into type, although increasingly I wonder if this is possible.
If the cost of *The Manuscript Books* is prohibitive, what would an edition
of the *Collected Letters* cost? Can the later letters and poems be separated
into different categories? I am a poet, not a textual scholar. In 1956
Spicer wrote: "The reason for the difficulty of drawing a line between
the poetry and the prose of Emily Dickinson is that she did not wish
such a line to be drawn. If large portions of her correspondence are
considered not as mere letters—and indeed, they seldom communicate
information, or have much to do with the person to whom they were

written—but as experiments in a heightened prose combined with poetry, a new approach to her letters opens up." He based his opinion on careful examination of the letters and poems owned by the Boston Public Library.

For its time the Johnson edition was a necessary contribution to any Dickinson scholarship. It radically changed the reading of her poetry. I can't imagine my life as a poet without it. But as Emerson wrote in "Circles": "The universe is fluid and volatile. Permanence is but a word of degrees. . . . Our culture is the predominance of an idea which draws after it this train of cities and institutions. Let us rise into another idea; they will disappear." A lot has changed in poetry and in academia since 1951. The crucial advance for Dickinson textual scholarship was Ralph Franklin's facsimile edition of *The Manuscript Books*. Now the essentialist practice of traditional Dickinson textual scholarship needs to acknowledge the way these texts continually open inside meaning to be rethought. In a Dickinson poem or letter there is always something other.

Cristanne Miller, in *Emily Dickinson: A Poet's Grammar* (Harvard University Press, 1987), discusses Dickinson's use of Noah Webster's introductory essay to his *American Dictionary*. Paula Bennett, in *Emily Dickinson: Woman Poet* (Harvester Wheatsheaf, Key Women Writing Series, 1990), has kept to Dickinson's lineation and her method of indicating the variants with a cross, as long as she has been able to work from poems in the facsimile edition. Martha Nell Smith discusses the problem of textual meddling with Dickinson's letters to Susan Gilbert Dickinson, in "To Fill a Gap" (*San Jose Studies* 13 [1987]; republished in *Rowing in Eden: Rereading Emily Dickinson* [Austin: University of Texas Press, 1992]). Two other scholars who are showing new directions for Dickinson scholarship are Sharon Cameron, whose recent book has the wonderful title *Choosing Not Choosing: Dickinson's Fascicles* (Chicago: University of Chicago Press, 1992), and Marta Werner, who has worked on a group of late letter-poems (*Scenes of Reading, Surfaces of Writing* [Ann Arbor: University of Michigan Press, 1995]).

Contributors

David Antin, a Professor of Art at the University of California, San Diego, has been an important figure in the postmodern poetic avant-garde. His books include *Tuning* (1984) and *What It Means to be Avant-Garde* (1991).

Rae Armantrout's most recent book of poetry is *Made to Seem* (1994). A West Coast poet with strong ties to Language writing, she teaches at the University of California, San Diego.

Charles Bernstein has been a leading figure in both the poetry and the poetics of the Language movement since the 1970s. Author of two volumes of essays—*Content's Dream* (1986) and *A Poetics* (1992)—as well as numerous books of poetry, Bernstein is David Gray Professor of Poetry and Letters at the State University of New York, Buffalo.

Maria Damon is Associate Professor of English at the University of Minnesota. Her book, *The Dark Side of the Street: Margins in American Vanguard Poetry*, was published by the University of Minnesota Press in 1993.

Michael Davidson is the author of several books of poetry as well as the critical study *The San Francisco Renaissance: Poetics and Community at Mid-century* (1989). An important link between the worlds of West Coast experimental poetry and literary academia, Davidson currently chairs the Literature Department at the University of California, San Diego.

Rachel Blau DuPlessis has been a strong advocate for the feminist wing of the poetic avant-garde. She is the author of the important study of gender and modernism—*The Pink Guitar* (1990)—as well as several books of poetry, including *Tabula Rasa* (1987) and *Drafts* (1991).

Lyn Hejinian has been editor and publisher of Tuumba Press, coeditor of *Poetics Journal*, and translator of the Russian poet Arkadii Dragomoschenko, as well as the author of a number of books of poetry. Her most well known work, *My Life*, is in its fifth printing with Sun & Moon Press.

Susan Howe has been an influential critic and scholar of Emily Dickinson and American literature as well as one of the most celebrated poets of the contemporary avant-garde. Her critical books include *My Emily Dickinson* (1985) and *The Birth-mark: Unsettling the Wilderness in American Literary History* (1993), and her books of poetry include *Singularities* (1990) and *The Nonconformist's Memorial* (1993).

Hank Lazer is Professor of English at the University of Alabama and a widely published poet and critic. His two-part study, *Opposing Poetries*, was published by Northwestern University Press in 1996.

Steve McCaffery has been a major poet and theoretician of the Canadian poetic avant-garde. His publications include *The Black Debt* (1989) and *North of Intention: Critical Writings 1973–1986* (1986).

Nathaniel Mackey is Professor of Literature at the University of California, Santa Cruz, and an important poet, novelist, editor, and critic whose books include *Eroding Witness* (1985), *Bedouin Hornbook* (1986), and the critical collection *Discrepant Engagement: Dissonance, Cross-Culturality, and Experimental Writing* (1993). He is also the editor of the literary magazine *Hambone*, and coeditor of the anthology *Moment's Notice: Jazz in Poetry and Prose* (1993).

Bob Perelman is the editor of *Writing/Talks* (1985), and the author of *The Trouble with Genius: Reading Pound, Joyce, Stein and Zukofsky* (1994) and *The Marginalization of Poetry* (1996). One of the foremost practitioners of Language poetry, Perelman is Associate Professor of English at the University of Pennsylvania.

Marjorie Perloff has been the most prominent commentator on the American poetic avant-garde and is Sadie Pernham Professor of Humanities at Stanford University. Her books include *The Poetics of Indeterminacy: Rimbaud to Cage* (1981) and *Radical Artifice: Writing Poetry in an Age of Media* (1991).

Leslie Scalapino is the founder and editor of O Books and the author of several books of poetry, fiction, essays, and drama. Her most recent books include *Crowd and no evening or light* (1992), *Objects in the Terrifying Sense/Longing from Taking Place* (1993), and *Defoe* (1994).

James Sherry is the author of *Our Nuclear Heritage* (1991) and several other books of poetry. He is also the editor of Roof Books and director of the Segue Foundation in New York City.

Ron Silliman has been a leader of the Language movement—and of the American poetic avant-garde in general—as poet, essayist, and editor. He is editor of the anthology In the American Tree (1986) and author of the book of essays The New Sentence (1987); several sections of his long poetic project The Alphabet have appeared as separate volumes.

John Taggart is the author of several books of poems, including Loop (1991) and Standing Wave (1993), and a book of critical essays, Song of Degrees: Essays on Contemporary Poets and Poetics (1994).

Barrett Watten founded This magazine with Robert Grenier and was publisher of This Press as well as coeditor of Poetics Journal (with Lyn Hejinian). Now an Associate Professor at Wayne State University, Watten is the author of several books of poetry, a collected volume, and the seminal book of essays Total Syntax (1984).

Acknowledgments/Permissions

Permission to reprint copyrighted material has been obtained whenever possible. The editor gratefully acknowledges permission to reprint from the following sources:

The first section of "Artifice of Absorption" (pages 9–30) from *A Poetics* by Charles Bernstein is reprinted by permission of the Harvard University Press, Copyright © 1992 by Charles Bernstein. Emily Dickinson's poem "I would not paint—a picture" is reprinted by permission of the publishers and the Trustees of Amherst College from *The Poems of Emily Dickinson*, Thomas H. Johnson, ed., Cambridge, Mass.: The Belknap Press of Harvard University Press, Copyright © 1951, 1955, 1979, 1983 by the President and Fellows of Harvard College. "Parataxis and Narrative: The New Sentence in Theory and Practice" from *The Marginalization of Poetry: Language Writing and Literary History* by Bob Perelman. Copyright © 1996 by Princeton University Press. Reprinted by permission of Princeton University Press. "Sonnet 15" from *The Sonnets* by Ted Berrigan is reprinted by permission of Alice Notley. Sections from *Oxota: A Short Russian Novel* by Lyn Hejinian are reprinted by permission of the author. "Total Syntax: The Work in the World" from *Total Syntax* (Carbondale: Southern Illinois University Press, 1985) by Barrett Watten is reprinted by permission of the author. Poetic excerpts by Clark Coolidge are reprinted by permission of the author. " 'Skewed by Design': From Act to Speech Act in Language Writing" by Michael Davidson, originally published in *Aerial* 8 (1995), is reprinted by permission of the author. "The Changing Face of Common Intercourse: Talk Poetry, Talk Show, and the Scene of Writing" from *Radical Artifice: Poetry in the Age of Media*, © 1991, is reprinted by permission of the University of Chicago Press. "What It Means To Be Avant-Garde" from *What It Means To Be Avant-Garde* (New York: New Directions, 1993) by David Antin is reprinted by permission of the author. "Pattern—and the 'Simulacral' " by Leslie Scalapino, originally published in *Poetics Journal* 7 (1988), is reprinted by permission of the author. "Strangeness" by Lyn Hejinian, originally published in *Poetics Journal* 8 (1989), is reprinted by permission of the author. "Come Shadow Come and Pick This Shadow Up" from *Songs of Degrees: Essays on Contemporary Poetry and Poetics* (Tuscaloosa: University of Alabama Press, 1994) by John

Taggart is reprinted by permission of the author. Poetic excerpts by Louis Zukofsky are reprinted from "A", © 1978 by Celia Zukofsky and Louis Zukofsky, Bottom: On Shakespeare, © 1963 by Celia Zukofsky and Louis Zukofsky, and All: The Collected Shorter Poems, © 1965, 1966 by Louis Zukofsky. All are reprinted by permission of the Johns Hopkins University Press. "The Boundaries of Poetry" (pages 183–189) from Our Nuclear Heritage (Los Angeles: Sun & Moon Press, 1990) by James Sherry. © 1991 by James Sherry. Reprinted by permission of the publisher. "Political Economy of Poetry" from The New Sentence (New York: Roof, 1989) by Ron Silliman is reprinted by permission of the author. "Writing as General Economy" from North of Intention: Critical Writings 1973–1986 (New York: Roof, 1986) is reprinted by permission of the author. "The Politics of Form and Poetry's Other Subjects" (pages 55–78) from Opposing Poetries by Hank Lazer. Copyright © 1996 by Northwestern University Press. Reprinted by permission of Northwestern University Press. "On Edge" from Discrepant Engagement: Dissonance, Cross-Culturality, and Experimental Writing by Nathaniel Mackey. Copyright © 1993 by Cambridge University Press. Reprinted with the permission of Cambridge University Press. "'Unmeaning Jargon'/Uncanonized Beatitude: Bob Kaufman Poet" (pages 32–58) from The Dark End of the Street: Margins in American Vanguard Poetry by Maria Damon. Copyright © 1993 by the Regents of the University of Minnesota. Reprinted by permission of the University of Minnesota Press and Maria Damon. Excerpts from poems by Bob Kaufman are reprinted from The Ancient Rain: Poems 1956–1978, © 1981 by Bob Kaufman, and Solitudes Crowded with Loneliness, © 1965 by Bob Kaufman, both reprinted by permission of New Directions Publishing Corporation. "Feminist Poetics and the Meaning of Clarity" by Rae Armantrout, originally published in Sagetrieb 11.3 (1992), is reprinted by permission of the author. "The One Night at the Boy's Party" from The Dead and the Living by Sharon Olds. Copyright © 1983 by Sharon Olds. Reprinted by permission of Alfred A. Knopf, Inc. "The Pink Guitar" is reprinted from The Pink Guitar: Writing as Feminist Practice by Rachel Blau DuPlessis (1990) by permission of the publisher, Routledge: New York and London. "These Flames and Generosities of the Heart: Emily Dickinson and the Illogic of Sumptuary Values" by Susan Howe, published in The Birth-mark: Unsettling the Wilderness in American Literary History (Hanover: Wesleyan/University Press of New England, 1993), pages 131–174, reprinted by permission of the publisher. Excerpts from letters and poems by Emily Dickinson are reprinted by permission. The letters are reprinted by permission of the publishers from The Letters of Emily Dickinson edited by Thomas H. Johnson, Cambridge, Mass.: The Belknap Press of Harvard University Press, Copyright © 1958, 1986

Index